The Skills That Matter

CRITICAL PERSPECTIVES ON WORK AND ORGANISATIONS

Series editors:

David Knights, Department of Management, University of Keele
Chris Smith, School of Management, Royal Holloway, University of London
Paul Thompson, Department of Human Resource Management, University
    of Strathclyde
Hugh Willmott, Manchester School of Management, UMIST

Published:

Alan Felstead and Nick Jewson *Global Trends in Flexible Labour*

Craig Prichard, Richard Hull, Mike Chumer and Hugh Willmott
    Managing Knowledge

Andrew Sturdy, Irena Grugulis and Hugh Willmott
    Customer Service

Paul Thompson and Chris Warhurst *Workplaces of the Future*

Critical Perspectives on Work and Organisations Series
Series Standing Order ISBN 0–333–73535–8
(outside North America only)

You can receive future titles in this series as they are published by placing a standing order.
Please contact your bookseller or, in case of difficulty, write to us at the address below with
your name and address, the title of the series and the ISBN quoted above.

Customer Services Department, Macmillan Distribution Ltd
Houndmills, Basingstoke, Hampshire RG21 6XS, England

The Skills That Matter

**Edited by Chris Warhurst, Irena Grugulis
and Ewart Keep**

palgrave
macmillan

First published 2004 by
PALGRAVE MACMILLAN
Houndmills, Basingstoke, Hampshire RG21 6XS and
175 Fifth Avenue, New York, N.Y. 10010
Companies and representatives throughout the world

PALGRAVE MACMILLAN is the global academic imprint of the Palgrave Macmillan division of St. Martin's Press, LLC and of Palgrave Macmillan Ltd. Macmillan® is a registered trademark in the United States, United Kingdom and other countries. Palgrave is a registered trademark in the European Union and other countries.

ISBN 1–4039–0639–4

This book is printed on paper suitable for recycling and made from fully managed and sustained forest sources.

A catalogue record for this book is available from the British Library.

A catalog record for this book is available from the Library of Congress.

10 9 8 7 6 5 4 3 2 1
13 12 11 10 09 08 07 06 05 04

Printed in China

Contents

List of Acronyms

ABS	Australian Bureau of Statistics
ACTU	Australian Council of Trade Unions
AIRC	Australian Industrial Relations Commission
ALP	Australian Labor Party
AMWU	Australian Manufacturing Workers Union (formerly Metal Workers Union)
ANTA	Australian National Training Authority
AQF	Australian Qualifications Framework
ARB	Architects' Registration Board
ARF	Australian Recognition Framework
ASF	Australian Standards Framework
ASI	Architecture and Surveying Institute
AWA	Australian Workplace Agreement
BCA	Business Council of Australia
BIAT	British Institute of Architectural Technologists
BIBB	Bundesinstitut für Berufsbildung
CAI	Confederation of Australian Industry
CBI	Confederation of British Industry
CBT	Competence-Based Training
CIBSE	Chartered Institute of Building Service Engineers
CIOB	Chartered Institute of Building
CITB	Construction Industry Training Board
CIPD	Chartered Institute of Personnel and Development
CSCS	Construction Skills Certification Scheme
DfEE	Department for Education and Employment
DfES	Department for Education and Skills
DIR	Department of Industrial Relations
DTI	Department of Trade and Industry
EDAP	Employee Development and Assistance Programme
ESFC	Employment and Skills Formation Council
EU	European Union
FE	Further Education
FSB	Federation of Small Businesses
GOALS	Gateway to Opportunity, Advancement, and Lasting Success programme
HCT	Human Capital Theory
HDB	Hauptverband der Deutschen Bauindustrie
HE	Higher Education

HEFCE	Higher Education Funding Council for England
ICE	Institution of Civil Engineers, and the Royal Town Planning Institute (RTPI)
IES	Institute of Employment Studies
IiP	Investors in People
ILA	Individual Learning Account
IstructE	Institution of Structural Engineers
ITABS	Industry Training Advisory Bodies
IoD	Institute of Directors
JTPA	Job Training Partnership Act
KMK	Kultusministerkonferenz
LPA	Labour Process Analysis
LPT	Labour Process Theory
LSC	Learning and Skills Council
MAATS	Modern Australian Apprenticeship and Traineeship System
MIA	Metal Industry Award
MOVEET	Ministry of Vocational Education, Employment and Training
NBEET	National Board of Employment Education and Training
NDPB	Non-Departmental Public Body
NFROT	National Framework for the Recognition of Training
NSTF	National Skills Task Force
NTB	National Training Board
NTO	National Training Organisation
NTRA	National Training Reform Agenda
NVQ	National Vocational Qualification
OECD	Organisation for Economic Cooperation and Development
ONS	Office of National Statistics
PIU	Performance and Innovation Unit
PRWORA	Personal Responsibility and Work Opportunity Reconciliation Act
RIBA	Royal Institute of British Architects
RICS	Royal Institute of Chartered Surveyors
RITA	Registered Industry Training Authority
RTO	Registered Training Organisation
SCC	Standards and Curriculum Council
SSC	Sector Skills Council
SSDA	Sector Skills Development Agency
STA	State Training Authority
TAFE	Technical and Further Education
TEC	Training and Enterprise Council
TGL	Training Guarantee Levy

TUC	Trades Union Congress
URCOT	Union Research Centre into Organisation and Technology
VET	Vocational Education and Training
WEP	Work Experience Programme
ZDB	Zentralverband des Deutschen Baugewerbes

Some contributions to this volume refer to qualifications in the UK and Australia as equating to or being Level 1, Level 2 and so on. The basic UK descriptors for these levels are as follows: Level 1 refers to competence associated with general education with the completion of compulsory education and satisfactory school-leaving examination grades; Level 2 refers to a good general education plus a longer period of work-related training or work experience; Level 3 refers to post-compulsory education but not to degree level; and Level 4 normally equates to having a degree or equivalent period of relevant work experience. Some Australian descriptors can be found in Chapter 11.

Notes on the Contributors

PAUL S. ADLER is Professor of Management and Organization at the Marshall School of Business, University of Southern California. He began his education in Australia and moved to France in 1974. Paul received his doctorate in Economics and Management while working as a research economist for the French government. He moved to the US in 1981 and before arriving at USC in 1991, he was affiliated with the Brookings Institution, Columbia University, Harvard Business School and Stanford University's School of Engineering. His research and teaching focus on organization structure in professional, R&D, engineering and manufacturing operations. He is active in the US Academy of Management's Critical Management Studies Interest Group.

SHARON C. BOLTON is Master's Programme Director and teaches Human Resource Management in the Department of Organisation, Work and Technology at Lancaster University. Before embarking on an academic career, she worked as a Senior Administrator in the public and private sectors. She completed her doctorate in 1999 also at Lancaster. Her research interests include the emotional labour process, public sector management, and the nursing labour process. Sharon has published several papers in these areas. She is currently completing a book, to be published by Palgrave, on the management of emotion in organisations.

CHRIS BRIGGS is currently a Research Fellow at the Australian Centre for Industrial Relations Research and Training (ACIRRT) at the University of Sydney. He has previously worked at the Commonwealth Department of Industrial Relations and the Australian Manufacturing Workers Union. His PhD was a history of the Australian peak union body (ACTU) and he has published recently on the ACTU, works councils and decentralised bargaining. Current research interests include lockouts, comparative wage politics and alternative forms of employment.

ALAN BROWN is a part-time Associate Director of the ESRC Teaching and Learning Research Programme with responsibility for work-based learning and continuing professional development. He is also acting as TLRP's European co-ordinator. He is a Principal Research Fellow with the Institute for Employment Research at the University of Warwick. Current research focuses mainly upon changing occupational identities in Europe, continuing vocational training, supporting knowledge sharing and development, and learning in professional communities of practice.

JOHN BUCHANAN is Deputy Director (Research) of the Australian Centre for Industrial Relations Research and Training (ACIRRT) at the University of Sydney. Previously he was director of policy research in the Federal (Australian) Department of Industrial Relations. His major research interests are the demise of the classical wage-earner model of employment, management determinants of labour productivity and the role of the state in nurturing new forms of multi-employer coordination in the labour market.

LINDA CLARKE is Professor of European Industrial Relations at the Westminster Business School, University of Westminster and is responsible for research projects on training, employment and wage relations, skills and gender segregation in Europe, east and west. She has a particular expertise in the construction sector, is on the presidium of the European Institute for Construction Labour Research and is the author of several books including *Building Capitalism* and *EU Enlargement*.

ASAF DARR gained his doctorate from Cornell University in 1997. He is a Senior Lecturer in Organizational Studies in the Faculty of Sociology and Anthropology at the University of Haifa, Israel. His recent publications include 'The Technicization of Sales Work: An Ethnographic Study in the US Electronics Industry' in *Work, Employment & Society* (2002), and 'Gifting Practices and Interorganizational Relations: Constructing Obligation Networks in the Electronics Sector' in *Sociological Forum* (2003).

ALAN FELSTEAD is Professor of Employment Studies at the Centre for Labour Market Studies, University of Leicester. His research is focused on non-standard forms of employment, training and skills formation in Britain and elsewhere. His books include: *In Work, At Home, Global Trends in Flexible Labour*, *The Corporate Paradox* and *The New Entrepreneurs*. He has given labour-market advice to a range of policy-makers, including the Department for Education and Skills, the European Centre for the Development of Vocational Training (CEDEFOP) and a number of Regional Development Agencies.

DUNCAN GALLIE is Official Fellow of Nuffield College and Professor of Sociology, University of Oxford. His research has focused on changes in employment relations and on the social consequences of unemployment. Recent books include: *Restructuring the Employment Relationship* (with Michael White, Mark Tomlinson and Yuan Cheng 1998); *Welfare Regimes and the Experience of Unemployment in Europe* (ed. with Serge Paugam 2000).

FRANCIS GREEN is Professor of Economics at the University of Kent. His research focuses on political economy and on labour economics, with special interests in skills, training, work quality and industrial relations issues. He has published nine books in these areas, and many articles in major economics and interdisciplinary journals and in book collections. He has served on several academic research advisory committees for the Department for Education and Skills, and is currently an editor of the *British Journal of Industrial Relations*.

IRENA GRUGULIS is Professor of Employment Studies at Bradford University School of Management. Her main research interests are in the area of skills and training. She has been funded by both the ESRC and the ERDF and has published in the journals *Work, Employment and Society, British Journal of Industrial Relations, Human Relations* and *Journal of Management Studies*. Recent edited work includes *Customer Service* (Palgrave 2001) and a special edition of *Human Resource Management Journal* (2003).

IAN HAMPSON is a Senior Lecturer in the School of Industrial Relations and Organisational Behaviour at the University of New South Wales, Sydney, Australia, where he lectures in Human Resource Management and Industrial Relations. He holds a PhD in Science and Technology Studies, and History and Politics, from the University of Wollongong. He has published in the following areas: union strategy and the Accord in Australia; technological change and work reorganisation; Australian industrial relations; management education and training policy in Australia.

GEORG HERRMANN is a Research Fellow at the University of Westminster with a particular interest in labour market issues in Europe, especially in the construction sector. He obtained an MA and PhD in Modern History at Munich University, Germany and an MBA at Imperial College, London, and is working with Professor Linda Clarke on productivity, skills, innovation and quality, professional and vocational education and training.

LESLEY HOLLY is a Senior Lecturer in Sociology and Women's Studies at University College Northampton and was formerly a Senior Researcher at the Tavistock Institute of Human Relations. Her research interests include barriers to women's careers in management, the social care workforce and social exclusion in European training initiatives. She has conducted research for the Department of Health, the Joseph Rowntree Foundation, the Cabinet Office and the Low Pay Commission.

EWART KEEP is a Professor in Warwick Business School and Deputy Director of the ESRC Centre on Skills, Knowledge and Organisational Performance (SKOPE). He has written widely on UK training policy, lifelong learning, the learning organisation and youth training, and has acted as an advisor and consultant to the UK Cabinet Office, the Department for Education and Skills, the Department of Trade and Industry, the National Skills Task Force and the Scottish Parliament's Enterprise and Lifelong Learning Committee.

SIMONE KIRPAL is Member of Academic Staff of ITB (Institute of Technology and Education) at University of Bremen, Germany, one of the leading research institutes on vocational education and training in Europe. Areas of interest, research and teaching focus on international comparison of VET systems, work organisation and work identities. Recent publications deal with the issue of the formation of work identities of nurses and other skilled workers in the European labour market.

GORDON LAFER is Assistant Professor at the University of Oregon's Labor Education and Research Center, and is author of *The Job Training Charade*. He served as an economic policy analyst for the New York City Mayor's Office, has written widely on employment and labour policy, and has served as a union organizer with university employees, building and construction trades, and hotel workers, among others.

CAROLINE LLOYD is Warwick Research Fellow with the ESRC's Centre for Skills, Knowledge and Organisational Performance (SKOPE), based at the University of Warwick. Her research interests include the political economy of skill, UK vocational education and training policy, and the UK pharmaceuticals and aerospace industries. She is currently researching the links between product quality and skills in the UK leisure and fitness sector.

ANNE MUNRO is a Reader in the School of Management at Napier University. She has been researching and publishing in the areas of work and trade union organisation and workplace learning in the public sector for over twenty years. Her publications include *Women, Work and Trade Unions* and 'Working together – involving staff: partnership working in the NHS' in *Employee Relations* (2002). She has researched and published on gender, trade union organisation and workplace learning in the public sector.

JONATHAN PAYNE is a Research Fellow for the ESRC's Centre for Skills, Knowledge and Organisational Performance (SKOPE), based at the University of Warwick. His research interests include the social partnership, the political economy of skill, UK vocational education and training policy, and education and training in Norway. He is currently looking at Scandinavian approaches to work reorganisation and job redesign.

HELEN RAINBIRD is Professor of Industrial Relations at University College Northampton and an Associate Fellow at the Industrial Relations Research

Unit at the University of Warwick. She is author of *Training Matters: Union Perspectives on Industrial Restructuring and Training* and editor of *Education and Work in Great Britain, Germany and Italy* (with Annette Jobert, Catherine Marry and Lucie Tanguy), *Apprenticeship Towards a New Paradigm of Learning* (with Pat Ainley) and *Training in the Workplace: Critical Perspectives on Learning at Work* (Macmillan 2000). She has researched and published widely on trade unions, social partnership and workplace learning.

GRAHAM SYMON is a Lecturer in Human Resource Management at the University of Luton. His past research has concerned management and policy in post-compulsory education. His current work is looking at issues in local governance and the voluntary sector. He has published a selection of book chapters and articles in journals such as the *International Journal of Educational Management, Leisure Studies* and *Human Resource Development International.* Also he has presented at a number of conferences including the International Labour Process Conference.

CHRIS WARHURST is Reader in Human Resource Management and Director of the Scottish Centre for Employment Research at the University of Strath-clyde in Glasgow. His teaching, research and publications focus on work, employment and management issues. Current interests include knowledge work and aesthetic labour. He has advised departments and organisations within the Scottish Executive and Scottish Enterprise. Books include *Work-places of the Future* (Macmillan 1998, with P. Thompson), and *Emerging Human Resource Practices* (with C. Mako and J. Gennard). Articles include those published in *Journal of Management Studies, Administrative Science Quarterly, Organization* and *Journal of Work and Education.*

IAN WATSON is a Senior Research Fellow at the Australian Centre for Industrial Relations Research and Training (ACIRRT) at the University of Sydney. His current research interests are in the areas of labour market restructuring, wage inequality and unemployment. In his time at ACIRRT, Ian has worked on a range of projects including: immigrants in the labour market; labour market inequality and the problem of the 'working poor'; the development of a Health of the Labour Market index. He has recently been working on large-scale workplace surveys of earnings, industrial coverage and other industrial relations issues. He was one of the authors of *Australia at Work: Just Managing* and *Fragmented Futures: New Challenges in Working Life.*

ANDY WESTWOOD is Head of Policy Research at the Work Foundation (formerly the Industrial Society). Prior to this position Andy has worked for the Department for Education and Employment, the Employment Policy Institute and in further education. His work mainly covers employment policy, regeneration, urban policy, workforce development and skills issues and has published widely on each subject. Recent publications include *Not Very Qualified: Raising Skills in the UK Workforce, Is New Work Good Work?* and *Are We Being Served? Career Mobility and Skills in the UK Workforce*. Andy is a regular commentator in the national press and on TV and radio.

1
What's Happening to 'Skill'?

Irena Grugulis, Chris Warhurst and Ewart Keep

Introduction

Policy-makers and academics keenly debate the importance of skills as a lever for boosting individual employability, firm productivity and national competitiveness. In these debates it is a 'high skills' model that is favoured, driven by desires for a knowledge economy or at least an informational, net-worked one. As a consequence, in the UK and throughout the Organisation for Economic Cooperation and Development (OECD) countries, a general consensus exists about the importance of 'thinking' and technical skills, the latter related to advanced Information and Communication Technology (ICT). The future is one of Californian-style freewheeling cyber workers with high skills, high incomes and high job satisfaction.

In this approach, active government intervention in shaping the labour market focuses on supply. Emphasis is placed on more young people achieving more and better qualifications (see Chapters 5 and 10). This improved labour supply stimulates demand for more and better jobs from employers (Layard 1997). The underlying assumption, as Keep and Mayhew (1999: 9) point out, is that 'boosting the supply of skilled and educated employees will, of itself, act as a catalyst for economic change and enhanced productivity and competitiveness'.

So far, so simple. The picture becomes more complex, however, with recognition of the difficulties defining, measuring and increasing 'skill'. This complexity is more than a question of semantics. If more skills is the target (and it usually is) then the size and shape of the target, and the distance between it and the current situation matters considerably. So too do the means by which the target is reached. Training someone to become proficient in arc welding or web design may require very different forms of instruction and involve different problems from ensuring that those who present themselves for interview project a persona that is 'passionate, stylish, confident, tasty, clever, successful and well-travelled' (Warhurst and Nickson 2001: 14).

Accordingly, in this chapter, we seek to explore the nature of skill and highlight the way that definitions have changed and are changing, and the consequences for how that skill is (best) formed. For an academic work this is a very practical exercise. The pragmatics that drive policy-makers privilege

1

definitions of skill that can be more readily achieved or measured. Activity within the vocational education and training (VET) system that cannot easily be judged by its ability to generate numerical outcomes (qualifications or parts thereof) is highly problematic.

An example of these problems comes with the fate of the three 'softer' key skills (problem-solving, teamworking, and improving one's own learning and performance). Because the English Qualification and Curriculum Authority (QCA) adjudged that these skills were not amenable to simple and rigorous assessment through written tests, their importance in curriculum reforms in colleges and schools and the work-based route (via Modern Apprenticeships) was downplayed. Indeed, the Department for Education and Skills (DfES) announced that the three wider key skills would henceforth be regarded as non-essential for employability (*Times Educational Supplement* 2001). Paradoxically, survey evidence suggests that teamworking and problem-solving are two of the skills most prized by employers (DfEE 1999). It is these issues that make understanding skill so vital. And, before policy-makers, practitioners and academics intervene further in this area, it would seem appropriate to consider these issues.

Upskilling, Deskilling and Back Again

Once it was much simpler. As both Westwood (Chapter 3) and Buchanan *et al.* (Chapter 11) note, a single, linear trajectory of skill was assumed. By the 1960s there was a growing acceptance that work was getting better, or if it was not, that was of little consequence because there was a 'flight from work' as leisure and consumption gained importance (Dubin 1956; Goldthorpe *et al.* 1968). If work was getting better, so too were the skills used in that work. The reason for these improvements was clear: new technology was eradicating routine and deskilled assembly-line work (e.g. Blauner 1964). This technology required employees to use diagnostic skills and have considerable discretion and initiative in their work to identify and solve problems. Conception was coming back home and skills were being regained.

This 'upskilling' theme was commonplace. Following Aron (1962), Bell (1973, 1974) too embraced technology as that which progresses and transforms society. The old industrial order was passing not just because of the shift from manufacturing to services or because white-collar workers outnumbered blue-collar workers but because power derived from property and position had been usurped by power derived from knowledge, and theoretical knowledge in particular. Entrepreneurs were being displaced by scientists, engineers and technicians. The 'major institutions of the new society' were 'the intellectual' ones (1974: 103). Education was important as it provided 'access to the attainment of technical skill' (1973: 115). Moreover, if jobs did require 'perceptual and conceptual skills', as Trist (1974: 112) says, and the knowledge underpinning these skills had to be continually updated for employability to be maintained, then 'the "learning force" (was) already greater than the workforce' (p. 112).[1]

Braverman (1974) was familiar with this literature and its optimism puzzled him. He believed that it contradicted his and others' perception of the development and organisation of the contemporary capitalist workplace, and that, as a consequence, two incompatible views were emerging about work and skill (pp. 3–4):

> [This literature] emphasised that modern work, as a result of the scientific-technical revolution and 'automation' requires ever higher levels of education, training and the greater exercise of intelligence and mental effort in general. At the same time, a mounting dissatisfaction with the conditions of industrial and office labour appears to contradict this view. For it is also said ... that work has become increasingly subdivided into petty operations that fail to sustain the interest or engage the capacities of humans with current levels of education; that these operations demand ever less skill and training.

If the optimists believed that new technology required, or at least resulted in, upskilling, for Braverman the opposite seemed more evident. He argued that it was deskilling not upskilling that characterised the capitalist workplace, both at that time and throughout the twentieth century. Scientific management rationalised work, deskilled employees and enabled managerial control. Quoting Taylor, he noted that the latter's instruction to management was to 'gather[] together all of the traditional knowledge ... possessed by the workmen ...' and remove 'brain work' from the shopfloor (pp. 112–113). Braverman believed that this deskilling was 'fundamental to all advanced work design' (p. 112).

Initial post-Braverman research confirmed this pessimistic view of the skill trajectory. Zimbalist (1979a) noted that such trajectories could be cyclical. Deskilling in one sector might occur at the same time that new skills were being developed in another. Nevertheless, despite localised increases, over time, work is rationalised and through this, deskilled. Kraft's (1979: 17) study of computer programming was a case in point: 'Programming is still very much an occupation in process ... It is clear, however, that programming has experienced a steady process of fragmentation and routinisation while programmers as a group have experienced a rapid deskilling.' Not surprisingly, with some nuances, the overall conclusion from the contributions to Zimbalist (1979b) was supportive of Braverman's thesis. Subsequent research sought to address some of the conceptual and empirical limitations and omissions to Braverman's work but the acceptance of deskilling remained. Although providing a cogent summary and critique of Braverman's thesis, Thompson (1989: 118), for example, concurs with its main thrust: 'Deskilling remains the major *tendential* presence within the development of the capitalist labour process.'[2] More recent research continues to indicate that deskilling persists as a feature of work in the UK and US, both in services and manufacturing (e.g. Baldry *et al*. 1998; Beirne *et al*. 1998; Milkman 1998; Ritzer 1998). This newer research is interesting because some of it encompasses ICT and knowledge-intensive work – call centres and software development, for example.

This pessimism needs to be tempered. Deskilling is certainly agreed to be a feature of capitalist workplaces in the UK and US (Thompson 1989; Bellamy Foster 1994) perhaps reaching its apotheosis in McDonaldisation (Ritzer 1998). But Thompson (1989: 216) does recognise that different and 'distinctive national and historical traditions' create different 'cultures' that can also affect skill patterns and trajectories. Indeed, research on work in countries other than the UK and US indicates that employers can be less likely to engage in deskilling and more likely to offer employees more and better VET. In Chapter 8, Clarke and Herrmann illustrate this point in their comparison of the skill and skill formation systems of the construction industry in the UK and Germany.

Despite the evidence that many UK and US firms remain wedded to the low road (Milkman 1998; Warhurst 2002) of low skill, low wage, low trust work, or perhaps because of it, policy-makers are once again being seduced by the potential of new technology and the upskilling that many associate with it. Resonating with earlier work from the 1960s and early 1970s, Castells (1999: 40) states that, in what he terms the 'network society' founded on 'information-alism', a highly skilled, creative and increasingly autonomous labour force becomes the fundamental source of productivity and competitiveness, concerned with 'the generation and processing of knowledge and information'. In their examination of ICT-intensive workplaces, Frenkel *et al*. (1999) seem to confirm this development. They conclude that 'work is becoming more complex...reducing the demand for lower-skilled jobs and increasing the demand for jobs with higher-level competencies' (p. 27).

Despite a number of measured critiques, this explanation is so influential that a 'cult of Castells' is evident in the UK and US, according to Crabtree (2002: 50), who suggests that Castells is becoming a 'guru's guru'. Not surprisingly then, this view has become orthodoxy amongst policy-makers throughout the advanced economies. A 'new economy' is said to be emerging dominated by ICT- and knowledge-intensive companies. This 'dematerialising' new economy is replacing the 'old', with wealth created by manipulating intangible inputs, ideas and knowledge, to produce intangible outputs, services and know-how (Leadbeater 2000). A causal effect on work and skills is then assumed. For example, the Scottish Executive (2001: 1) moves without pause from arguing this to be an 'age where knowledge is a key competitive weapon' to stating 'a high skill, high wage economy' to be a subsequent government policy. Similar pronouncements on the importance of knowledge, the new complexity of work and employers' demand for workers with higher order 'thinking skills' emanates from across the governments of the OECD countries (Reich 1993; DTI 1998; Byers 1999; Vickery 1999; DfEE 2000).

Skill Polarisation or Skill Expansion?

Many of the academics involved in the upskilling/deskilling debates have tended to talk past each other and certainly have avoided direct debate. Their work, however, has enabled a consensus of approach to defining 'skill' (see Cockburn 1983; Thompson 1989; Felstead *et al*. 2002; Noon and Blyton 2002). Firstly, there is the skill that resides in the worker. This approach tends to be adopted more by economists concerned with productivity issues and assumes that enhancing workers' human capital, by increasing their skill levels, positively affects firms' productivity (Becker 1964). Secondly, there is the skill that is required of the job. It is this issue that stimulated Braverman. This approach, sociological in orientation, requires an examination of job design, forms of control and the nature of the employment relationship as well as the task at hand (Littler 1982). Thirdly and also sociological in approach, there is the socially constructed skill arising from negotiation between economic actors, collectively or as individuals. This social construction occurs within and outwith the workplace and may advantage members of particular groups (such as professional bodies or craft unions) or a gender (generally male) – a point highlighted in past skill formation in Australia, for example, see Chapter 11.

Because 'skill' is difficult to quantify, proxies are used. That which is accreditable becomes the focus, with the proxy most used being 'qualification' – an especially useful device for policy-makers concerned to encourage and demonstrate upskilling. By encouraging greater participation in education and the accumulation of qualifications, the workforce is assumed to be more skilled. As a consequence, the *possession* of skills (or rather their proxies) rather than their use in work takes precedence in both policy-maker and academic debate and analysis (contrast this with Chapters 10, 12 and 13). To complicate this issue further, the proxies are not always reasonable signifiers for the skills they are intended to represent (Young 2001; Grugulis 2003).

Although the early upskilling and deskilling theses were empirically informed, both lacked the benefit of large-scale representative data, according to Gallie (1991). This deficit was remedied by the UK's ESRC Social Change and Economic Life Initiative (SCELI), which indicated that a pattern of skill polarisation existed in the UK, advantaging those who were already the most skilled (Penn *et al*. 1994). Completed during the 1980s, SCELI concluded that for most occupations in the UK upskilling was occurring. Jobs at the bottom end of the labour market were not being deskilled but this was because, as Rose *et al*. (1994: 8) note, 'some low-skilled jobs cannot be further deskilled simply because they already call for so little skill'. Again this experience had a clear gender dimension, for it was women, predominantly in part-time work, who tended to occupy jobs at this point of the labour market.

Such patterning resonates with more recent research, though this time it is argued that an 'hourglass economy' is emerging in the UK (Nolan 2001) with an expansion of high skill, high wage, high value-added work at the top end of the labour market while, at the same time substantial numbers of low paid, low wage, low value-added work exist at the bottom end. The 2001 Skills Survey indicates that the overall proportion of jobs in the UK economy requiring no qualifications was 27 per cent (see Chapter 9). In other words, there are 6.5 million jobs that require no qualification at all. This imbalance is particularly significant since it arose not because of an increase in the number of unskilled jobs but because of a reduction in the numbers of unqualified people. So increases in workers' skills are not being matched by inflation in demand. Given these developments – high skill top end, low skill bottom end, it is easy to understand why skill polarisation is again suggested; upskilling for the former, deskilling or stagnation for the latter.

Importantly, although jobs have become more complex and most jobs have typically become more skilled, employees' control over their work has not risen over the past 15 years in the UK. In fact, employees' task discretion has declined (see Chapter 9). It seems that employers still want obedient rather than enquiring employees.

These results provide grounds for concern. Instead of the empowered and talented majority anticipated by the 1960s sociologists or the 'knowledge workers' predicted by their more recent descendants, skills are polarised. Moreover, the decline of discretion (see also Grugulis *et al.* 2003; Rainbird and Munro 2003) casts doubts on the extent to which skills as 'knowledgeable practice within elements of control' (Thompson 1989: 92) may be exercised. It may still be possible to retain grounds for optimism. Several of these studies rely on traditional, technical defintions of skill which may have been superseded (Keep and Mayhew 1999; Payne 1999). However, it is difficult to argue that this expansion charts the development of new skills for a new economy; that as technical skills subside, others, more relevant for work and more advantageous to workers, take their place. Many of these 'new' skills are familiar and most are problematic.

The Changing Meaning of Skill

Attitudes and appearances: the new skills?

One of the most fundamental changes that has taken place in the last two decades has been the growing tendency to label what in earlier times would have been seen by most as personal characteristics, attitudes, character traits, or predispositions as skills. Examples include leadership, motivation, positive attitudes towards change and authority, politeness, compromise and respect. It is not that employers in times past have not wanted such qualities. As Reeder (1979: 184) reports, evidence to the 1906 government investigation into Higher Elementary Schools, 'indicated that what employers wanted from these more advanced schools for the children of the working class was a good character, qualities of subservience and general handiness'. It is just that managers then would not have thought of these as skills *per se*, they were attitudes, characteristics or predispositions.

As Oliver and Turton (1982) show, by the early 1980s employers had moved to describing behavioural characteristics such as reliability, stability of work record, and responsibility (what Oliver and Turton call the 'Good Bloke Syndrome') under the banner of skill, and a lack of job candidates possessing such qualities constituted, from an employers' perspective, a skill shortage. Today these qualities, in some cases slightly relabelled, are indeed believed to be skills (usually generic) and are increasingly treated as such by policy-makers (see Chapter 7). This broadening of what the term skill encompasses also has profound implications for the way that work is controlled and the way that people are 'developed' in their roles.

Overall, there is an increasing tendency for organisations to manage the way their employees *feel* and *look* as well as the way they behave so that work is emotional and aesthetic as well as (or instead of) productive (see Chapters 2 and 4; Hochschild 1983; Macdonald and Sirianni 1996; Warhurst and Nickson 2001). This development is particularly true of interactive services, such as retailing, where recruitment and training both focus on the emotions and aesthetics of the labour force deployed to deliver the service (Thompson *et al.* 2001). In the 'style' labour market of fashionable hotels and bars, the appearance, deportment, accents and general stylishness of the bartender, waitress or retail assistant are part of what makes the service being offered trendy and upmarket (Nickson *et al.* 2001). But it is not only in this environment that grooming, dress-sense, deportment, manner, tone and accent of voice and shape and size of body become vital. Workplaces as diverse as call centres, training consultants, investment banks and accountants all recruit, train and promote staff on their emotional and aesthetic 'skills' (McDowell 1997; Trethewey 1999; Anderson-Gough *et al.* 2000; Thompson *et al.* 2001). Many of these characteristics, as Warhurst and Nickson (2001) argue, are open to development and improvement through instruction, and their possession is a new facet of what it can mean to be 'skilled'.

At the same time, this development also provides new routes to deskilling. While people who work with their emotions report higher levels of job satisfaction and take significant pleasure in the emotional aspects of their jobs (Leidner 1993; Wharton 1996; Korczynski 2001), many workers have little discretion about the form such emotional and aesthetic labour should take. Managers can and do seek to control employees' moods, their tones of voice, the way that they feel about customers, their language and body posture, the length of their skirts and their hairstyles, their weight and the size of their bust, hips and thighs, the make-up that they wear, the way that they shave (both faces and legs), their jewellery and shoes and the colour of their hair (Hochschild 1983; Paules 1991; Nickson *et al.* 2001; Thompson *et al.* 2001). This list is not exclusive nor is it uncontested. Employees can and do resist, misbehave and ignore these instructions, as much as they enthuse, cooperate and comply with them (Paules 1991; Ackroyd and Thompson 1999). Nonetheless such detailed demands suggest that it is not only the changing *definition* of skill that is problematic but the site of its control. In emotional and aesthetic labour, employees' feelings and appearance are turned into commodities and reshaped to fit their employers' notions of what is desirable (Putnam and Mumby 1993; Thompson and McHugh 2002). This process may be enjoyed by employees and may equip them with skills that advantage them both in and out of the workplace (Leidner 1993; Nickson *et al.* 2001). But it may also lead to exhaustion, burnout (Hochschild 1983; Kunda 1992), an inability to accept or engage with emotions in the private sphere (Casey 1995) and high levels of turnover (Leidner 1993; Korczynski 2001).

Accrediting generic skills and competences

While employers are primarily interested in skills from the point of view of recruitment, development or control, governmental focus tends to be on accreditation. Here, both the practical limitations of the assessment process and changes in the definition of skill create problems. In the two areas of 'new' skills that are of particular concern, generic skills and competence, rhetorical appeal is coupled with intractable implementation difficulties. Generic skills, it is argued, form a universal foundation for success in the labour market, transcend the individual subjects being studied, and are applicable across a wide range of situations. However, one of the most significant problems is the extreme inexactitude of nomenclature adopted by many of those who seek to label and define different types or forms of generic skill. Generic, key and core skills represent, broadly speaking, the same general category or subdivision of skill, but at different times and in different places the exact list of what constitutes a core/key/generic skill differs as does the degree to which these lists reflect or diverge from the literature on emotional labour. It is also the case that some authorities are willing to include worker attributes and traits (such as motivation, judgement and leadership) within their definition of core/key/generic skills while others maintain that these are not skills but personal attributes (Keep and Mayhew 1999).[3]

Whatever system of categorisation is used, no matter how the items on the shopping list are labelled, the existence of generic skills is now widely accepted as the basis for VET policy. The UK government has chosen six key skills – information technology (IT), numeracy, communication, problemsolving, improving own learning and performance, and teamworking – as the basis on which to proceed and has sought to imbed them in education and training for the young. It should be noted that, while some generic skills are amenable to being treated as being quite 'hard' and technical (for instance, IT and numeracy), others occupy a different end of the spectrum and are quite 'soft' and refer to the exhibition of desired behavioural patterns and mental dispositions (e.g. teamworking).

If the idea of generic skills provides one new conceptual framework for thinking about skill, the second, and the one so far most influential on theory and practice in the UK, was that evolved around the notion of competence (Jessup 1991). It has shaped debates about skills in a range of ways. To begin with, as Payne (1999) demonstrates, it claimed to provide the means to achieve a comprehensive, universalistic mapping system whereby all that the word 'skill' might mean could be neatly and exactly delineated, described and catalogued. Yet, while it is clear that a national and readily understood hierarchy of awards could materially assist participants in the labour market by making credentials comprehensible, it is by no means certain that cataloguing competence in behavioural terms is so efficacious. Regrettably, it is in the latter activity that most progress has been made. Competence-based approaches have also reinforced two seemingly contradictory tendencies in the way skill is perceived. First, they have encouraged the Anglo-Saxon 'practical man' approach, which discounts the value of underpinning theory and knowledge. National vocational qualifications (NVQs), as originally speci-fied, lacked any explicit element of theory, on the grounds that this was embedded in performance. The result has been a tendency towards narrow courses of training and qualifications, and a neglect of general education in contrast to the rest of Europe (Green 1998). Implicit in the competence-based approach is a belief that a competence is a competence – it is wholly generic and can be utilised with equal efficacy and effect, whatever the organisational circumstances or environment. In this perception it is diametrically opposed to Lave and Wenger's (1991) theory of communities of practice or of situated learning. The competence-based approach implicitly denies the importance and specificity of organisational culture and firm-specific skills. The underly-ing belief is that competences are held by the individual, they exist and can be demonstrated more or less independently of context and environment – from prison camp to baked-bean factory.[4]

The main feature that drives this interest in key skills and behaviourally defined competence is a concern with measurable outcomes and targets. Through qualifications, competences and key skills, policy-makers can check the activities of the bodies that report to them and measure increases in 'skills'. But these proxies are problematic. Definitions of key skills are contested, not all are readily susceptible to measurement and they may or may not be transferable. NVQ-style competence is susceptible to measurement (or, at least, is frequently measured) but is based on descriptions of actions that leave little space for a thoughtful use of 'skill' and which may themselves distort the nature of work. If anything, the problem of the gulf between what can be measured and counted and therefore planned and funded, and the broadening definition attached to skill may be getting worse. Unsurprisingly, all the targets set so far relate to the achievement of qualifications or skill standards, and what is easy to count gets counted and what is not gets ignored.

Some Implications of the Changing Meaning of Skill

The implications of these developments are serious. To begin with, as Ainley (1994), Payne (1999) and Nickson *et al*. (2003) point out, some aspects of the current trends in redefining skill have significant and potentially far from benign implications for the reinforcement of advantage in the labour market for those from middle-class backgrounds. Ainley argues that 'at rock bottom, the real personal and transferable "skills" required for preferential employment are those of whiteness, maleness and traditional middle-classness' (p. 80) and Nickson *et al*.'s study of aesthetic labour suggests that many of the particular skills in personal presentation, self-confidence, grooming, deportment and accent that Glaswegian service sector employers are seeking are liable to be linked to the parental social class and educational background of the job applicants.

Moreover, given the generally successful resistance of competences by professional bodies (Raggatt and Williams 1999) and their existence in universities largely as audit mechanisms to be used on staff rather than vehicles for educating students, competence-based qualifications are most likely to be undertaken by people already disadvantaged in the labour market (Grugulis 2003). Since there is reason to believe that the learning and the skills demanded are both different to and much narrower than that supported through 'traditional' or educational qualifications (Young 2001), competence-based awards may act as a ceiling on advancement for these groups, not a springboard to future progress.

In a country where the social class of one's parents remains the prime predictor of educational achievement and where there is some indication that opportunity for upward social mobility is now more restricted (Toynbee 2003), policy-makers should be concerned at any development that might further reinforce the tendency for people from different classes to follow very divergent and distinctive labour-market trajectories. If 'corporeal capital', in the form of deportment, accent and ability to dress appropriately is becoming the determinant of what gets young people a job in some parts of the service sector, the potential for further reinforcement of class divides presents itself (Nickson *et al*. 2003).

At a general level there is a potential for the new conceptualisation of skill and of skill levels in the economy to become trapped in an inflationary spiral.

The problem goes thus. Workers and employers are seeing a gradually widen-ing conception of what skill is, which in turn has the tendency to redefine the degree to which more and more jobs can be seen as being 'skilled'. At the same time, policy-makers are endlessly claiming that skill levels are rising and that the economy needs to invest in far higher levels of skill and qualifi-cation than ever before. Individuals, whether consciously or unconsciously, absorb these messages, and, report themselves as using higher levels of skill, thereby reinforcing policy-makers' belief that economic activity is being transformed into a knowledge economy. Policy-makers then recalculate their projections of future skills' needs and redouble their pronouncements that skill levels are rising and will rise further. There is great potential here for the creation of a self-fulfilling prophecy. Take the example of a sales assistant in a chain store – say Woolworths. Twenty years ago the general consensus would have regarded this job as a low skilled non-manual occupation. Today, the evaluation would be different, stressing the inter-personal and customer-service skills that make the job more skilled than hitherto.

The problem is that it is not clear that the actual content of the job has changed. Sales assistants have always had to interact with the customer and to provide service. It is open to question whether this aspect of the work has fundamentally changed in terms of the quality or complexity of the inter-actions required. Product knowledge in many UK multiple retailers remains close to nil. The use of what might broadly be termed IT has increased some-what but, at the end of the day, operating an electronic till and passing sale items over a barcode scanner does not seem dramatically different in skill content from entering the price into an earlier mechanical/electric till. Indeed, modern electronic tills strip out some intellectual exercise, telling the assistant what change to give; older mechanical and electro-mechanical tills left this calculation to mental arithmetic. As Dench *et al.*'s (1999: xv) study of the use of key skills suggests, the importance of IT skills can be overplayed. They report that:

> Few employers reported any need for elements of the IT (key skills) unit in less skilled occupations, including a range of sales, personal and protective services, operative and other manual jobs...Most employees do not need a detailed understanding of how and why technology operates. They basic-ally have to use an established set of routines and applications.

Does this matter? At one level it might be argued that such a process is either harmless or even benign – jobs previously undervalued due to the social construction of skill are now being revalued upwards. It is certainly true that many of the areas of work that are seen as being upskilled are those under-taken by women and those who have traditionally held relatively low levels of formal qualification. However, before anyone gets too excited about the emancipatory effects of these trends, it is as well to remember that this apparent upskilling of hitherto low-status jobs does not mean that their holders will necessarily be paid more for doing them, or that their overall status will rise in the occupational hierarchy. This is skill as a rhetorical device that carries with it no material benefits. Social skills, though demanded by employers, carry no wage premium (Felstead *et al*. 2002). Relative positions in the hierarchy probably remain unchanged and inflation may even damage the currency of 'skills' itself. Payne's (1999: 42) warnings on this point are apposite:

> We are all skilled now, regardless of the type or quality of the job we do and the level of personal control, autonomy or power we enjoy. This, then, is the most fundamental difference in how skill is officially conceptualised today compared to the past, when to be skilled implied some level of real market power and personal discretion over one's work.

Widening the meanings attached to skill and rising assessments of the skill required to perform jobs also deflects attention from the underlying fact that, compared to their counterparts in most other OECD countries, UK employers' skill requirements, in terms of educational attainment, remain both very narrow (Green 1998) and low.

If redefining skill does not produce labour market advantage for employees, it does shift the responsibility for developing them. The definition by some employers and policy-makers of what might in other times have been seen as attitudes or personal attributes has already been mentioned. One example of this tendency has been the designation of motivation as a skill. What many might regard as a central objective of managerial activity (Legge 1995) – the creation of a motivated workforce – has, to some extent at least, been subcontracted and outsourced to the education system. By changing the meaning of skill to embrace attitudes and behavioural traits or by increasing the emphasis placed upon the possession of such characteristics, employers have been able to shift responsibility for the creation or reinforcement of some of these attitudes and traits away from their role as managers and motivators of their employees and onto the education and training system.

In times gone by, it might well have been argued that if employees did not appear to have the 'right' attitudes towards work this might be taken to reflect failings in job design, work organisation, people management systems, reward structures, and communication and involvement systems. In other words, it might be symptomatic of problems with poor industrial relations or personnel management policies and practice. Instead, great efforts have been made to shift the focus of attention away from the workplace and those who manage it, onto schools, colleges and universities, all of which have failed, it is alleged, to have imbued their students with the appropriate skills. This phenomenon has distinct advantages for management, particularly at a moment when a range of evidence suggests that the high-commitment, high-performance model promised by human resource management, and promoted by the OECD and EU, has failed to materialise (Bach and Sisson 2000).

The bulk of research, from both case studies (West and Patterson 1997; Ackroyd and Procter 1998; Dench *et al*. 1998; Guest 2000) and surveys such as the DTI/ESRC's 1998 Workplace Employee Relations Survey (WERS) (Cully *et al*. 1999), shows that highly routine, relatively low skill jobs, offering very limited opportunities for trust, creativity or discretion remain prevalent in the UK economy. Indeed, WERS suggests that the percentage of UK firms that have well-developed high performance work systems is very small – probably no more than two per cent of the sample.

Despite this evidence, public debate about the current state of workplace employee relations in the UK is, much like the crew of the *Marie Celeste*, noticeable mostly by its absence. In some ways this absence is remarkable. In former times, the results of WERS would have created comment and concern, and formed the point of departure for speculation and debate among policy-makers and practitioners about the quality of managerial strategies and actions, and about the need for change and reform. On the whole, no such debate has been forthcoming. Instead, there are the reports of the National Skills Task Force (2000a,b) pointing to the existence of skills gaps and deficiencies and the need for all to work together to remedy these problems.

Plainly, a range of reasons underlies the absence of workplace issues as a major focus for public debate, of which the relabelling of some problems as skills issues, is but one. Other contributory factors include government reluctance to intervene inside the 'black box' of the firm or be seen to become engaged in conflict with business interests, a fear that such state interventions might be seen as 'old' Labour, a widespread belief in the managerial prerogative to manage and dispose of labour as they see fit, and an apparent faith that the forces of globalisation and competition are enough to ensure the near universal adoption of best practice employment relations sooner or later. This stated, the shifting of the focus of attention onto skills and skill formation as the answer to what might otherwise be seen as industrial relations issues does resonate with the government's predilection for treating education and training as one of the few areas where direct state intervention is now acceptable (Keep 1999a).

Concluding Remarks

The foregoing underlines the extreme complexity of seeking to unpack the simple words 'skill' or 'skills'. Both come with what in bomb disposal terms might be called 'anti-handling' devices. Attempts at deconstruction, particularly within neo-rationalistic and reductionist frameworks of the sort often deployed by those wedded to competences, are liable to come to grief. Skill is a socially constructed phenomenon, and the developments of the last twenty years have, by moving beyond, 'hard' technical skills and manual dexterity, tended to promote the practical importance of precisely those elements of the concept that are least amenable to simple, objective, quantifiable description and analysis. The concept of skill has become bigger, broader and much fuzzier round the edges. More than ever before, skill is a subjective as well as an objective phenomenon.

Leaving to one side the problems inherent in attempts to define 'knowledge workers' (see Thompson *et al.* 2001), the number of such workers using 'thinking skills', such as software engineers, will increase but not to the extent envisaged by policy-makers and mainstream business writers. In fact, they do and will continue to comprise a clear minority of workers. Real job growth will occur in more routine interactive service work. During the 1990s, job growth was most evident in part-time services sector, especially in personal services: hairdressing, waitering, guarding, cooking and cleaning (Warhurst and Nickson 2001).

Whilst a high skill economy is eminently desirable, it is not necessarily a logical management strategy. A low skill, low value-added, simple product/service option is one strategy by which employers can both enter and compete in a market. Rationalising and simplifying – or deskilling – the work process has been a feature of both much of assembly and batch production and is increasingly evident in retail and business services. The incentives for employers to move out of the low skills equilibrium that characterises sections of the economy is by no means evident. Employers perceive a low supply of skilled workers, the costs of training have to be set against other concerns and the threat of competitors poaching the skilled labour. A cycle develops of available workers being utilised in low skill work processes producing low value-added products. This 'low skills equilibrium' is reinforced and itself reinforces related concerns about employability and social exclusion. As Brown and Keep (1999: 85) argue, the demand for low-level skills 'bumps against the demands for universal upskilling for all'. Attempts to promote employability and social inclusion through training are thus weakened. Currently, therefore, there is too little pressure for firms to upskill. Indeed, upskilling would threaten some firms' competitiveness in existing markets. For upskilling to occur would require changes beyond the workplace (Keep 1999b; though see also Chapter 6). So, although skills matter, they are not necessarily the first factor to be considered for the melioration of work, employment and the economy.

Notes

1   Like Bell, Trist also argues that financial-industrial elite is being replaced by a professional-scientific elite. He also suggests that the 'new world of work' also involves interpersonal skills but does not elaborate on this point.
2   Emphasis in the original.
3   For examples of different, and probably mutually irreconcilable typologies and categorisations of generic skills, see NSTF (2000a), CBI (1989) and Whiteways Research (1995).

4 It is worth noting that more recent and sophisticated notions of competence have moved away from this de-contextualised viewpoint, and now argue that competence can be viewed as being held collectively (within a workgroup) and created and sustained by particular work environments (Mills and Tyson 2000; Sandberg 2000).

References

Ackroyd, S. and Procter, S. (1998) 'British Manufacturing Organisation and Workplace Relations – Some Attributes of the New Flexible Firm', *British Journal of Industrial Relations*, 36:2, 163–183.

Ackroyd, S. and Thompson, P. (1999) *Organizational Misbehaviour*, London: Sage.

Ainley, P. (1994) *Degrees of Difference*, London: Lawrence & Wishart.

Anderson-Gough, F., Grey, C. and Robson, K. (2000) 'In the Name of the Client: The Service Ethic in Two Professional Service Firms', *Human Relations*, 53:9, 1151–1174.

Aron, R. (1962) *Dix-huit lecons sur la société industrielle*, Paris: NRF.

Bach, S. and Sisson, K. (2000) 'Personnel Management in Perspective', in S. Bach and K. Sisson (eds), *Personnel Management*, Oxford: Blackwell.

Baldry, C., Bain, P. and Taylor, P. (1998) 'Bright Satanic Offices: Intensification, Control and Team Taylorism', in P. Thompson and C. Warhurst (eds), *Workplaces of the Future*, London: Macmillan.

Becker, G. S. (1964) *Human Capital*, New York: Columbia University Press.

Beirne, M., Ramsay, H. and Pantelli, A. (1998) 'Developments in Computing Work: Control and Contradiction in the Software Labour Process', in P. Thompson and C. Warhurst (eds), *Workplaces of the Future*, London: Macmillan.

Bell, D. (1973) *The Coming of Post-Industrial Society*, New York: Basic Books.

Bell, D. (1974) 'Notes on the Post-industrial Society', in N. Cross, D. Elliott and R. Roy (eds), *Man-Made Futures*, London: Hutchinson.

Bellamy Foster, J. (1994) 'Labor and Monopoly Capital Twenty Years After: An Introduction', *Monthly Review*, 46:6, 1–13.

Blauner, R. (1964) *Alienation and Freedom*, Chicago: Chicago University Press.

Braverman, H. (1974) *Labor and Monopoly Capital*, New York: Monthly Review Press.

Brown, A. and Keep, E. (1999) 'Review of Vocational Education and Training in the United Kingdom', Institute of Employment Research/SKOPE, University of Warwick.

Byers, S. (1999) 'People and Knowledge: Towards an Industrial Policy for the 21st Century', in G. Kelly (ed.), *Is New Labour working?*, London: Fabian Society.

Casey, C. (1995) *Work, Self and Society*, London: Routledge.

Castells, M. (1999) 'Flows, Network and Identities: A Critical Theory of the Informational Society', in M. Castells, R. Flecha, P. Freire, H. A. Giroux, D. Macedo and P. Willis (eds), *Critical Education in the New Information Age*, Lanham: Rowman & Littlefield.

CBI (Confederation of British Industry) (1989) *Towards a Skills Revolution – A Youth Charter*, London: CBI.

Cockburn, C. (1983) *Brothers*, London: Pluto.

Crabtree, J. (2002) 'The Cult of Castells', *Prospect*, February, 50–54.

Cully, M., Woodward, S., O'Reilly, A. and Dix, A. (1999) *Britain at Work*, London: Routledge.

Dench, S., Perryman, S. and Giles, L. (1998) *Employers' Perceptions of Key Skills*, Report 349, Brighton: Institute for Employment Studies.

Dench, S., Perryman, S. and Giles, L. (1999) *Employers' Perceptions of Key Skills*, IES Report 349, Sussex: Institute of Manpower Studies.

DfEE (Department for Education and Employment) (1999) 'Helping Graduates into Employment', *Skills and Enterprise Briefing*, Issue 1/99, London: DfEE.

DfEE (Department for Education and Employment) (2000) *Opportunity for All: Skills for the New Economy*, London: DfEE.

DTI (Department of Trade and Industry) (1998) *Our Competitive Future: Building the Knowledge Driven Economy*, London: DTI.

Dubin, R. (1956) 'Industrial Workers' Worlds: A Study of the Central Life Interests of Industrial Workers', *Social Problems*, 3:2, 131–142.

Felstead, A., Green, F. and Gallie, D. (2002) *Work Skills in Britain 1986–2001*, Nottingham: DfES.

Frenkel, S. J., Korzynski, M., Shire, K. A. and Tam, M. (1999) *On The Front Line*, Ithaca: ILR.

Gallie, D. (1991) 'Patterns of Skill Change: Upskilling, Deskilling or the Polarisation of Skills', *Work, Employment & Society*, 5:3, 319–351.

Goldthorpe, J. H., Lockwood, D., Bechhofer, F. and Platt, J. (1968) *The Affluent Worker*, Cambridge: Cambridge University Press.

Green, A. (1998) 'Core Skills, Key Skills, and General Culture: In Search of the Common Foundation in Vocational Education', *Evaluation and Research in Education*, 12:1, 23–43.

Grugulis, I. (2003) 'The contribution of NVQs to the growth of skills in the UK', *British Journal of Industrial Relations*, 41:3, 457–475.

Grugulis, I., Vincent, S. and Hebson, G. (2003) 'The Rise of the 'Network Organisation' and the Decline of Discretion', *Human Resource Management Journal*, 13:2, 45–59.

Guest, D. (2000) 'Piece by Piece', *People Management*, 6:15, 26–30.

Hochschild, A. R. (1983) *The Managed Heart*, Berkeley: University of California Press.

Jessup, G. (1991) *Outcomes: NVQs and the Emerging Model of Education and Training*, Brighton: Falmer.

Keep, E. (1999a) 'UK's VET Policy and the 'Third Way': Following a High Skills Trajectory or Running up a Dead End Street?', *Journal of Education and Work*, 12:3, 323–346.

Keep, E. (1999b) *Upskilling Scotland*, Edinburgh: Centre for Scottish Public Policy.

Keep, E. and Mayhew, K. (1999) 'The Assessment: Knowledge, Skills, and Competitiveness', *Oxford Review of Economic Policy*, 15:1, 1–15.

Korczynski, M. (2001) 'The Contradictions of Service Work: Call Centre as Customer-Oriented Bureaucracy', in A. Sturdy, I. Grugulis and H. Willmott (eds), *Customer Service*, Basingstoke: Palgrave.

Kraft, P. (1979) 'The Industrialisation of Computer Programming: From Programming to 'Software Production', in A. Zimbalist (ed.), *Case Studies on the Labor Process*, New York: Monthly Review Press.

Kunda, G. (1992) *Engineering Culture*, Philadelphia: Temple University Press.

Lave, J. and Wenger, E. (1991) *Situated Learning – Legitimate Peripheral Learning*, Cambridge: Cambridge University Press.

Layard, R. (1997) *What Labour Can Do*, London: Warner.

Leadbeater, C. (2000) *Living on Thin Air*, London: Viking.

Legge, K. (1995) *Human Resource Management*, London: Macmillan.

Leidner, R. (1993) *Fast Food, Fast Talk*, Berkeley: University of California Press.

Littler, C. (1982) *The Development of the Labour Process in Capitalist Societies*, London: Heinemann.

Macdonald, C. L. and Sirianni, C. (1996) (eds) *Working in the Service Society*, Philadelphia: Temple University Press.

McDowell, L. (1997) *Capital Culture*, Oxford: Blackwell.

Milkman, R. (1998) 'The New American Workplace: High Road or Low Road?', in P. Thompson and C. Warhurst (eds), *Workplaces of the Future*, London: Macmillan.

Mills, T. and Tyson, S. (2000) 'Teams Look to Collective Competence', *Management Focus*, 14, 7.

National Skills Task Force (2000a) *Skills for all: Proposals for a National Skills Agenda*, Sudbury: DfEE.

National Skills Task Force (2000b) *Skills for all: Research Report of the National Skills Task Force*, Sudbury: DfEE.

Nickson, D., Warhurst, C., Witz, A. and Cullen, A.-M. (2001) 'The Importance of Being Aesthetic: Work, Employment and Service Organisation', in A. Sturdy, I. Grugulis and H. Willmott (eds), *Customer Service*, Basingstoke: Palgrave.

Nickson, D., Warhurst, C., Cullen, A.-M. and Watt, A. (2003) 'Bringing in the Excluded? Aesthetic Labour, Skills and Training in the New Economy', *Journal of Education and Work*, 16:2, 185–203.

Nolan, P. (2001) 'Shaping Things to Come', *People Management*, 27 December, 30–31.

Noon, M. and Blyton, P. (2002) *The Realities of Work*, Basingstoke: Palgrave.

Oliver, J. M. and Turton, J. R. (1982) 'Is There a Shortage of Skilled Labour?', *British Journal of Industrial Relations*, 20:2, 195–200.

Paules, G. F. (1991) *Dishing it Out*, Philadelphia: Temple University Press.

Payne, J. (1999) 'All Things to All People. Changing Perceptions of "Skill" Among Britain's Policy Makers since the 1950s and Their Implications', *SKOPE Research Paper No. 1*, University of Warwick.

Penn, R., Rose, M. and Rubery, J. (1994) *Skill and Occupational Change*, Oxford: Oxford University Press.

Putnam, L. and Mumby, D. K. (1993) 'Organisations, Emotions and the Myth of Rationality', in S. Fineman (ed.), *Emotion in Organisations* London: Sage.

Raggatt, P. and Williams, S. (1999) *Government, Markets and Vocational Qualifications*, London: Falmer.

Rainbird, H. and Munro, A. (2003) 'Workplace Learning and the Employment Relationship in the Public Sector', *Human Resource Management Journal*, 13:2, 30–44.

Reeder, D. (1979) 'A Recurring Debate: Education and Industry', in G. Bernbaum (ed.), *Schooling in Decline*, London: Macmillan.

Reich, R. (1993) *The Work of Nations*, London: Simon & Schuster.

Ritzer, G. (1998) *The McDonaldisation Thesis*, London: Sage.

Rose, M., Penn, R. and Rubery, J. (1994) 'Introduction, the SCELI Skill Findings', in R. Penn, M. Rose and J. Rubery (eds), *Skill and Occupational Change*, Oxford: Oxford University Press.

Sandberg, J. (2000) 'Competence – The Basis for Smart Workforce', in R. Gerber and C. Lankshear (eds), *Training for a Smart Workforce*, London: Routledge.

Scottish Executive (2001) *Scotland: A Global Connections Strategy*, Edinburgh: The Stationery Office.

Thompson, P. (1989) *The Nature of Work*, Houndmills: Macmillan.

Thompson, P. and McHugh, D. (2002) *Work Organisations*, Basingstoke: Palgrave.

Thompson, P., Warhurst, C. and Callaghan, G. (2001) 'Ignorant Theory and Knowledgeable Workers: Interrogating the Connections between Knowledge, Skills and Services', *Journal of Management Studies* 38:7, 923–942.

Times Educational Supplement (2001) 20 July.

Toynbee, P. (2003) 'Tax is Out of the Bag', *Guardian*, 25 June, 25.

Trethewey, A. (1999) 'Disciplined Bodies: Women's Embodied Identities at Work', *Organization Studies* 20:3, 423–450.

Trist, E. L. (1974) 'The Structural Presence of Post-industrial Society', in N. Cross, D. Elliott and R. Roy (eds), *Man-Made Futures*, London: Hutchinson.

Vickery, G. (1999) 'Business and industry policies for knowledge-based economies', *OECD Observer*, 215, 10.

Warhurst, C. (2002) 'Towards the "Better Job": Scottish Work and Employment in the "Knowledge Age"', in G. Hassan and C. Warhurst (eds), *Tomorrow's Scotland*, London: Lawrence & Wishart.

Warhurst, C. and Nickson, D. (2001) *Looking Good, Sounding Right*, London: Industrial Society.

West, M. and Patterson, M. (1997) *The Impact of People Management Practices on Business Performance*, London: Institute of Personnel and Development.

Wharton, A. S. (1996) 'Service with a Smile: Understanding the Consequences of Emotional Labour', in C. L. Macdonald and C. Sirianni (eds), *Working in the Service Society*, Philadelphia: Temple University Press.

Whiteways Research (1995) *Skills for Graduates in the 21st Century*, London: Association of Graduate Recruiters.

Young, M. (2001) 'Conceptualising Vocational Knowledge', Paper presented at a joint Network/SKOPE/TLRP international workshop, Sunley Management Centre, University College Northampton 8–10th November.

Zimbalist, A. (1979a) 'Introduction', in A. Zimbalist (ed.), *Case Studies on the Labor Process*, New York: Monthly Review Press.

Zimbalist, A. (ed.) (1979b) *Case Studies on the Labor Process*, New York: Monthly Review Press.

2
Conceptual Confusions: Emotion Work as Skilled Work

Sharon C. Bolton

Introduction

A good deal about organisations has changed, including the way they are supposed to work and, to some extent, this simply reflects social change. The decline in manufacturing, the rise in service industries and the restructuring of the working population that this has entailed have led to a changing emphasis in skill requirements. There is now less demand for the formally skilled male, manual worker and increasing demand for people dealing with customers – typically women – who use more obvious interpersonal skills. The ability to regulate one's own and other's feelings is seen as a core competence for emotion workers in the global drive for competitive advantage through excitement, calm, deference, congeniality and even persuasion (Heskett *et al*. 1997; McEwen and Buckingham 2001). The importance of this type of work is well recognised and often referred to as 'emotional labour', 'emotion work' (Hochschild 1979, 1983; Smith 1992) or, in recent management literature, 'emotional intelligence' (Goleman 1998). The terms 'labour' and 'work' stress that managing one's emotions at work can be hard, demanding and, sometimes, stressful and the term 'intelligence' implies that this type of work requires a certain level of acumen.

Emotion work, of course, is an integral part of everyday social and organisational life, and has always been a vital part of many labour processes. Increasingly, however, the emphasis in the labour market is on creativity, rather than rule-bound behaviour, with communication, teamworking, customer care, individual initiative and self-reliance seen as key skills (DfEE 2000a, 2001; Brown *et al*. 2001). Emotion workers are far from homogenous, with some occupations involved in the production of material goods or requiring complex technical knowledge; while others, such as the front-line service worker, invest the full capacity of their labour power in presenting the desired corporate image and creating customer satisfaction. Occupations involving emotion work can be found in different positions within a skills hierarchy with large differentials in status and material reward between the 'emotional proletariat' who deliver routinised 'niceness' (Macdonald and

Sirianni 1996) and the caring professions who are deemed to be 'angels of mercy' (Salvage 1985).

Yet despite the growing recognition of the importance of emotional 'competencies' (Goleman 1998), and concern over a shortage of 'key' skills in the British labour market (DfEE 2001), employees who successfully carry out emotion work may not be acknowledged as 'skilled' workers at all. Rather, they are said to have certain types of personality, to possess particular character traits or have natural caring qualities (Rafaeli and Sutton 1987; Weatherley and Tansik 1992; Ashforth and Humphrey 1993, 1995; Pitt *et al*. 1995; Morris and Feldman 1996; Mann 1999). Whilst communication skills and interpersonal skills are frequently mentioned as essential qualities in the workforce (DfEE 2000a, 2000b, 2001), such competencies are not easily measured or certified. Instead companies rely on recruiting 'self-monitors' and 'extroverts' who 'will be more inclined to comply with organizational display norms' (Rafaeli and Sutton 1987; Morris and Feldman 1996: 1005). Recognised only as 'personal attributes' (DfEE 2001), emotion work remains a shadowy and ill-defined form of knowledge work.

It is not clear that this distinction between technical skills and innate qualities is helpful, particularly given the growing demand for a new model worker able to employ 'soft', 'generic' or 'key' skills (DfEE 2001). An over concentration on formal education and qualifications neglects the fact that skill acquisition and utilisation is not a technical formality but a social act. Occupations which require large amounts of emotion work, such as the increasing array of front-line service jobs, rely almost wholly on the embodied capacities of the worker. Capacities that though they share many of the common features of skill – discretion, variety and experience – are rarely formally recognised. More fundamentally, the emphasis on emotion work as an individualised innate quality actively contributes to the making and remaking of inequalities based on class and gender thus ensuring that it remains a 'non-skill' (Sayer and Walker 1992).

This chapter seeks to address some of the conceptual confusions around the notion of skill. By highlighting the dynamic nature of skill formation, emotion work can be viewed as a distinctive form of skilled work and employees as multi-skilled emotion managers (Bolton 2000; Callaghan and Thompson 2002). Using Littler's three conceptions of skill, 'namely skill as work routines, skill as socially constructed status and skill as control over process and product' (Littler 1982: 18), it will be argued that even the most routine of jobs involving emotion work require more than spontaneous, natural qualities.

Conceptual Confusions

The debate on skill has always been troubled by conceptual confusions, even over such fundamental issues as the factors which should constitute a classification of skill or how the skill levels of various occupations can be measured. Most often, these are addressed via a behavioural, quantitative approach which focuses on the skills 'owned' by the individual according to objective criteria – length of training, level of wage and task range, for instance.

This linear model is the essence of human capital theory and that predicts that 'expertise' will be the new basis for competitive advantage with wealth creation no longer dependent on the bureaucratic control of resources but upon the exercise of specialist knowledge and competencies. The maxim that a nation's chief economic assets are the skills and insights of its citizens has now assumed a new significance. Writers such as Drucker (1993) assert that productivity is becoming dependent on the application and development of new knowledges and on the contributions of specialist knowledge workers. Drucker's thesis is that knowledge workers are unlike previous generations of workers not only in the high levels of education they have obtained but also in the sense that they own the means of production, that is, knowledge.

However, there are some fundamental failings associated with this approach to skill. Not least the unquestioned equation between investment in education as the route to success in the labour market and a knowledge economy; coupled with a lack of caution about the nature of employment (Thompson *et al*. 2000; Nickson *et al*. 2003). Whilst it remains true that highly educated individuals tend to fare better in the labour market, carrying out more interesting work and attracting higher wages, this path is far from even. And the rhetoric concerning the 'high skills' economy is amazingly adept at avoiding the fact that the largest area of growth is in poorly rewarded front-line service jobs (Brown *et al*. 2001).

This ignorance is largely due to an insensitivity to the heterogeneity of knowledge work. The human capital theorists' conceptualisation of skill can only ever be partial because it only considers mechanical, repetitive and quantifiable certainty (Ainley 1993). In treating skill simply as an appendage to the worker, it does not consider that there may be different forms of knowledge, including that which is inarticulate and pre-rational, embodied in the worker (Thompson *et al*. 2000). This one-dimensional approach neglects the complex process of skill formation and the politics of production in a capitalist economy. As a result large segments of the workforce are neglected, particularly those who make a significant contribution to the knowledge economy or the well-being of society through skilled emotion work. Despite its weaknesses, this school of thought dominates current debates on skill and informs political action at a time when a deeper understanding and broader classification of skill is required.

A Multi-dimensional Approach

Capturing the social process of emotion work requires a multi-dimensional classification of skill. In recognising three dimensions of skill, as task, as a social construction and as control over the labour process, Littler acknowledges the objective notion of skill but counters its weaknesses by expanding the concept to include the social relations of production. The strength of Littler's (1982) understanding of skill is that it does not treat it as a property of an individual but as the 'interaction of the social collectivity' (Collins 1989: 82). As Littler suggests, 'the level of analysis should be, but usually has not been, societal' (Littler 1982: 7). Skills and competencies are not the property of individuals but belong to the collective knowledge developed in society through its division of labour and skill (Ainley 1993).

Though his primary focus of analysis was on manual labour in the factory, Littler's emphasis on the dynamic nature of skill acquisition and utilisation are equally, if not more, pertinent to the 'new' economy. The recognition of the need to account for the control imperative and the 'centrality of job-autonomy' (Littler 1982: 8) in any conception of skill are especially significant when the labour process relies upon capacities embodied in the worker. Littler's analysis highlights the issue of where (and with whom) control of emotion work lies and recognises that emotion work is a matter of negotiation between workers and managers (Thompson *et al*. 2000).

Understanding that skill is about social status also addresses the contradiction in the way that emotion work is seen as a core competence but attracts little material reward unless tied to a recognised technical skill (Green 1999) and why it seems to be the exception to the labour market rule of high demand/shortage of supply equals rewarding work. Essentially skill is not only a label attached to jobs by managers in order to divide and reduce the power of workers or the product of workers' collective resistance (Wood 1982); it is also part of a wider social system, so the structured inequalities of class and gender have a major and durable impact on definitions of skilled work.

The three dimensions of Littler's conception of skill will be explored in more detail, applying the conceptions of skill as 'work routines', as 'control over process and product' and as a 'social construction' (Littler 1982: 18) to an understanding of emotion work as a social process. In this way it can be seen how emotion work is indeed a form of skilled work and deserves to be recognised as such. Such an analysis addresses the complexities of the world of work in recognising the impact of the changing nature of work, patriarchal attitudes to 'women's work' and the contested terrain of the employment relationship.

Emotion Work as a Social Accomplishment

In presenting emotion work as an important skill in the labour market and the emotion worker as a multi-skilled emotion manager, it is necessary to emphasise the link between 'emotion work, feeling rules and social structure' (Hochschild 1979: 276). Contrary to the popular belief that soft skills are natural, emotion is not 'a periodic abdication to biology' (Hochschild 1983: 27), but something which is subject to acts of personal management, according to implicit 'feeling rules'. Emotion work involves attempting to change an emotion or feeling so that it is appropriate for any given situation. In order to be able to asses the situation correctly, and produce the expected feeling, social guidelines are used: 'a set of shared, albeit often latent, rules' (Hochschild 1983: 268) which help fit together the emotion and the situation, for instance, feeling sad at funerals but happy at weddings. The use of the word 'work' to describe the management of emotion stresses that it is something which is actively done to feelings (Hochschild 1979, 1983; James 1989). It also offers a range of potential insights into the employee as social actor, in that the individual may select from sources of conflicting feeling rules and often creatively interpret and manipulate them. For example, social groups in and around work – work groups, professions, peer-groups are all sources of feeling rules, which are to some extent observed.

This ability to manage emotion according to the 'rules' of the situation itself acknowledges the power of the social. Emotion work is a gesture in everyday social exchange; the 'rules' exist to ensure social stability and the well being of those involved (Goffman 1967; Hochschild 1979; Bolton 2000). Goffman describes the exchange of emotion work as the 'interaction order' and insists that it is an area of human activity worthy of independent study (Goffman 1991). What Goffman calls the 'traffic rules of interaction' show how 'public order' is achieved, how it is done; how, indeed, it is possible at all (Kendon 1988).

Participants in a social encounter are highly effective social actors who are able to present themselves according to rules that are often implicit. In other words, social actors can manage to feel or manage not to feel, in order to fit into the accepted 'conventions of feeling' (Hochschild 1979, 1990). A lifetime's social guidance provides actors with the 'traffic rules of social interaction' (Goffman 1959), ensuring a routine compliance with the code of the prevailing 'emotional culture'. This is a necessary attribute if actors are to become 'self-regulating participants in social encounters', enabling them to 'stay in the game on a proper ritual basis' (Goffman 1967: 45–91). The process is so efficacious most encounters pass without note: a stable, taken-for-granted achievement. Nevertheless, though much of the action is routinised this does not mean that it is habitually enacted unconsciously. 'Implicit feeling rules' act as a frame in which action takes place whilst still emphasising that an individual does not passively accept constructed 'meanings' of himself and 'actively participates in sustaining a definition of the situation' (Goffman 1961). In describing the social actor as a 'peg', Goffman usefully summarises how actors are involved in society, a 'double contingency' (Giddens 1984) of interaction:

> In analysing the self, then, we are drawn from its possessor, from the person who will profit or lose most by it, for he and his body merely

provide a peg on which something of collaborative manufacture will be hung for a time. And the means for producing and maintaining selves do not reside inside the peg; in fact these means are often bolted down in social establishments ... The self is a product of all of these arrangements, and in all of its parts bears the marks of this genesis (Goffman 1959: 245).

The attractiveness of this perspective lies in its acknowledgement of 'our all-too-human selves and our socialized selves' (Goffman 1959: 36).

Goffman's (1959) analogy of social action as 'performance' is a useful way of describing how we manage ourselves in social encounters and brings to light the realisation that these performances become extremely polished. Giddens (1984) suggests that such performances are necessary if a sense of trust or 'ontological security' is to be maintained. Actors, not only constantly monitoring their own conduct but also monitoring the conduct of others, sustain the predictability of much of day-to-day social life. Without this, social actors would appear to exist in a cynical world of self-concerned agents, when in fact 'face', and the corresponding sense of self, is a sacred thing and much social interaction is centred around not only saving actors' own 'faces' but also those around them (Goffman 1967; Schwalbe 1993). This continuous monitoring and treatment of fellow interactants with 'ritual care' produces and reproduces a moral order: the aim may be to save face but the effect is to save the situation and the 'ritual structure of the self' (Goffman 1967: 39).

Such is the case even in a complex mass society where there appears to be no commitment to any particular 'rule book' and the self must be fragmented in order to meet the challenge of diverse audiences (Schwalbe 1993). There can be little doubt that the frameworks of social interaction are being redrawn as the result of a general 'informalization of feeling' (Wouters 1989a: 105). Evidence of the breaking down of social barriers in modern society indicates how social actors are now much more familiar with a range of different cultures. They have developed the ability to switch and swap faces according to the demands of many different situations (Goffman 1974; Wouters 1989a,b). However, rather than fragmentation and incoherence, men and women 'have become more strongly integrated into tighter knit networks of interdependencies in which the level of mutually expected self-restraint has risen' (Wouters 1989b: 449). Conditions of late capitalism may have damaged the relations of trust upon which the continued existence of the interaction order depend; nevertheless, we see it, not destroyed but reordered with people ever more sensitive to both process and outcome. 'Informalization' has increased the scope and demand for emotion work in all areas of social life, increasing the diversity of 'rules' of encounter and requiring participants to be truly multi-skilled social actors.

A Material Stage

Most importantly, in order to understand emotion work it is necessary to recognise that the interaction order does not exist in a symbolic realm but requires a material stage for its production. The status of participants in the interaction order will be a defining feature of how face-saving activity is to be distributed with considerations of gender, class, race, occupation and, increasingly, vast material inequalities altering the 'rules of the game' (Goffman 1974; Hochschild 1989; Schwalbe 1993). The social process of emotion work ensures that it plays a large part in the continual creation and re-creation of social inequalities. In fact, it is the structured inequalities of social interaction that provides much of its predictability. Rules of engagement include or exclude social actors on a variety of terms and distribution of 'definitional labour' (Goffman 1959: 21) is far from even, with some, such as women, working much harder at face-saving activity and those who have limited 'embodied dispositions', borne of a limited, class specific, condition of existence, unable to play the game at all (Hochschild 1989; Charlesworth 2000; Witz *et al.* 2003: 41).

Capitalism's appropriation of emotion work distorts the basis of social interaction even further. In consumer capitalism producers' creative capacities are harnessed to serve the needs of capital, so emotion work becomes hard and demanding labour requiring skill and control in the regulation of feeling and the presentation of one's self (Goffman 1967; Hochschild 1983; James 1989; Schwalbe 1993). It is notable, for instance, that the 'rules of conduct', which usually govern general social encounters, ensuring that everyone 'acts appropriately and receives his due' (Goffman 1967: 55), do not apply to the interaction which occurs between service-provider and customer. As Hochschild (1983: 86) states:

> Where the customer is king, unequal exchanges are normal, and from the beginning customer and client assume different rights to feeling and display. The ledger is supposedly evened by a wage

The rules of social encounter change and the emotional exchange becomes unequal – consumers feel within their 'rights' to display dissatisfaction, yet the service-provider is expected to meet aggression with pleasantries, sympathy, or at worst, calm indifference. Emotion work becomes much more than a social process, it becomes a vital part of the labour process and 'social skills' become essential work-based skills.

The Three Dimensions of Skilled Emotion Work

It can be argued that emotion workers have never before required such a high level of skill. Trends in work, growth in interactive service work and the 'reimagining' of the consumer, of both public- and private-sector goods and services, as a 'sovereign customer' (du Gay and Salaman 1992) has meant that emotion workers have had to develop a greater awareness of their social skills and an adaptability in how and when to deploy them (Thompson *et al.* 2000: 128). Littler's (1982) three dimensions of skill allows a reconceptualisation of skill acquisition and utilisation as a dynamic social process. The way an objective understanding of skill as *work routines* is combined with an appreciation of the socially embedded nature of skill as a *process of control* and as a *social-construct* is an especially useful way of offering insight into emotion work as skilled work.

Skill as work routines

Objective measurements of skill often cover two dimensions, that of task variety and discretionary content. If a job can score highly on both of these dimensions then it would be considered skilled. Emotion workers are far from a homogenous group, with many combining emotion work with other forms of mental and manual labour. It is notable, however, how the emotion work elements of a role are not valued in this two-dimensional model. Figure 2.1 displays clearly how the larger the element of emotion work involved, and the lower the task range and associated technical content, the less an occupation is deemed to score highly on either task range or discretionary content.

Of particular interest for an analysis of the notion of task variety as a definer of skilled status, are the 'emotional proletariat' (Macdonald and Sirianni 1996). Those who are engaged in front-line interactive service work which can be variously described as mundane, routine, low-skilled and, most importantly, tightly controlled via scripts and prompts, with predictability and reliability being the desired aim (Leidner 1996; Ritzer 1999; Taylor and Bain 1999). These are the workers who make up the 'have-a-nice-day'

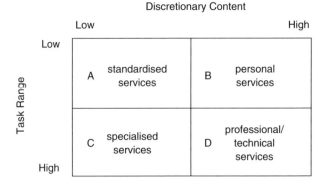

Figure 2.1   Dimensions of emotion work (adapted from Littler 1982: 8)

culture where 'niceness' is routinely delivered: faceless service workers dealing with faceless customers. The emotional proletariat come low in the status hierarchy of knowledge work and, according to objective notions of skill, they would be placed in box A of Figure 2.1.

But their position in box A is a contradiction, particularly given the increasing emphasis on 'quality service'. Whatever the level of technical skill involved, the front-line service worker is frequently the only contact a customer has with an organisation making the quality of interaction a major criterion on which the organisation is judged. Recent studies suggest that the way a product is sold matters more than the nature of the product itself (Korcysnki 2002), that front-line staff build customer loyalty more effectively than marketing or pricing policies (McEwen and Buckingham 2001) and that the British public services are forgiven the lack of resources if public-sector professionals, such as nurses, on the front line of service delivery are seen to be 'friendly' and 'caring' (Hogston 1995; Mahon 1996). This particular segment of the labour force are the focus of much attention but the concentration on an individualised conceptualisation of skill means that the capacity to carry out effective emotion work remains an innate quality not amenable to quantification, classification or compensation.

For many emotion workers, customer orientation programmes and scripted service encounters cannot deal with the unpredictability and variability of the interaction order. If the service encounter does not go according to the organisation's plan, it leaves the service worker little space for manoeuvre. The untoward effects of such controls upon workers' and, perhaps more importantly for the many prescriptive writers, customers' well-being are now well recognised and there are ample studies that recognise the benefits of granting autonomy to front-line service workers (Weatherly and Tansik 1992; Wharton 1996). Nevertheless, due to the lack of recognition of the actual process of the social order of interaction between customer and service provider, there is little trust that any form of order can be maintained without management intervention (Callaghan and Thompson 2002).

Those who work in specialist call centres or in the retail and catering 'style' market may be placed slightly higher in the hierarchy of emotion work and found in box C. Their position relies on the combination of some form of technical or specialist knowledge along with a high component of emotion work and, though their task range may be greater, their autonomy is limited, as discretion is only granted to workers with the 'right attitude' who can be relied on to express 'real feelings' in the interests of creating the right emotional climate and improving customer service (Rafaeli and Sutton 1990; Van Maanen 1991; Ashforth and Humphrey 1993; Morris and Feldman 1996). This is not autonomy but self-rule in line with organisational feeling rules.

Workers who have relatively high levels of discretion in the way they carry out emotion work can be found in boxes B and D. Box B contains workers such as personal carers, nursing auxiliaries, those involved in childcare, security or distribution services. They have few, if any, nationally recognised qualifications and come low in the hierarchy of knowledge work. Due to the lowly status of much of their work and the minimal importance accorded to the satisfaction of the consumers of their services, they are granted almost unlimited discretion in how they present themselves (Hochschild 1983; Lee Treweek 1996). On the other hand, those in box D are allowed considerable autonomy in their emotion work, though a 'professional ethos' will guide and control interaction with consumers of their service. Professional status is based on the acquisition of prestigious and widely recognised qualifications proclaiming specialist knowledge in a particular area. Here we find members of the medical and legal professions, and those who deliver education and social services.

Objective dimensions of skill do have their uses, if only in emphasising the heterogeneity of emotion work and the impossibility of 'boxes' capturing the complexities of emotion work and emotion workers' position in the hierarchy of skill. Personal carers may have almost unlimited discretion in their emotion work and can be found in box B, apparently superior to the 'emotional proletariat' in box A, yet they share the same position in the skills hierarchy. Both doctors and nurses share a place in box D but are positioned very differently in the division of medical labour. In other words, these objective notions of skill neglect the material stage upon which emotion work is performed and take no account of the way skill hierarchies are manipulated via professional or client influence or how deeply they are affected by the structured inequalities of class, race or gender.

It also fails to recognise that, no matter where they are positioned in the hierarchy of emotion work, even the lowest order of emotion workers have some elements of task variety and discretion. This is inevitable since social interaction is unreliable, a risky business that requires adaptability rather than rigidity and routinisation. For instance, employees can use various tactics to restore the ceremonial order when dealing with obnoxious customers. They may employ 'deferential stand-off arrangements' in order to deflect aggression and anger or deliberately upset the hierarchical ordering of a particular interaction; as in the case of a call-centre worker who reverts to a broad regional accent: 'If it is someone from outside the area, I lay the accent on really thick. You can hear them getting embarrassed when they have to say pardon all the time' (Telephone Sales Agent cited in Taylor 1998: 96). Similarly, various forms of humour are often employed to ease anxiety or, via 'playful profanation', remind the consumer of their obligations as an interactant (Goffman 1959, 1967; Emerson 1973). In addition, providing customer service for many front-line workers, not just those who are classed as 'professionals', is actually viewed as 'working with people' or 'helping people' and is framed as a socially relevant activity with all the multiple interpretations and contradictions this brings (Sturdy 1998; Wray-Bliss 2001; Callaghan and Thompson 2002).

Skill as control over process and product

Accepting discretionary content as a dimension of skill clearly links its conception to modes of control in the workplace. As Littler notes, 'it is not possible to define "skill" independently of organizational control and control processes' (Littler 1982: 9). At the time of writing, Littler referred mainly to direct control strategies in the manufacturing sector, whereas the control of the new model worker in the knowledge economy has attracted control strategies of a more normative nature. An essential feature is the bureaucrat-isation of the spirit, rather than externally imposed impression rules (Goffman 1959), leading to an emphasis on the 'transmutation of an emotion system' when acts of emotion management 'fall under the sway of large organisations, social engineering and the profit motive' (Hochschild 1983: 19) and suggesting that presenting a desirable demeanour to customers can be classed as hard and demanding labour that invades the worker's sense of self (Macdonald and Sirianni 1996). In such a scenario, normative control strategies ensure that organisational feeling rules are internalised and front-line service workers become 'perfect company robots' (Wouters 1989a).

An overreliance on the success of normative control strategies, however, repeats the mistakes of the objective measurement of skill. Modes of control may change but the continual negotiation and renegotiation over the trans-formation of emotional labour power into serviceable products – 'the emotional effort bargain' – is a constant (Callaghan and Thompson 2002: 251). The recalcitrant emotion worker can develop many methods, often barely detectable by management, of registering their refusal to be defined by organisational feeling rules. As Goffman (1967: 87) maintains:

> In scrupulously observing the proper form he may find that he is free to insinuate all kinds of disregard by carefully modifying intonation, pro-nunciation, pacing, and so forth.

Some episodes of 'misbehaviour' (Ackroyd and Thomspon, 1999) may be classified as coping mechanisms while others are acts of resistance and defi-ance. Paules' (1996: 266) study of waitresses highlights how they refuse to be denied 'the courtesies of personhood':

> Though constrained to comply with the interactive conventions of master and servant, while clad in a domestic's uniform, the waitress does not internalize an image of service as servitude and self as servant. In times of stress she sees her work as war and herself as soldier. In times of peace she sees her work as a private enterprise and herself as entrepreneur (Paules 1996: 284).

And it is not only the emotional proletariat who defy the ties that bind their interactions; professional status is equally impotent as a reliable emotional straitjacket. There are ample studies that demonstrate how caring professionals flout the prescribed feeling rules in order to display, in varying forms of subtlety, a 'modality of resistance' (Lee-Treweek 1996; Griffiths 1998; Bolton 2003).

Not all acts of defiance will have a detrimental effect upon the encounter between the provider and the consumer of various services. On the contrary, a refusal to abide by a managerially imposed script has the potential to improve the quality of customer relations though it may have negative connotations for the achievement of objective targets (Sutton 1991; Korczynski *et al.* 2000; Wray-Bliss 2001; Callaghan and Thompson 2002). A call-centre worker expresses this tension very well:

> We get a lot of people who are on their own, they're pensioners. They ask for a balance, and then they will want a chat – "what's the weather like?" I'm quite happy to chat to them, but it's always in the back of your mind, got to watch my average handling time. I think you're setting a better example for the bank (Customer Service Representative cited in Callaghan and Thompson 2002: 250).

This call-centre worker, though aware of the material demands made of her, reinterprets encounters with customers depending upon context and motivation. The contradictions inherent in service work become ever more apparent. Whilst resisting managerially imposed display rules, service workers, such as the call-centre worker and the waitress, utilise their emotion work skills and do their job very well. Emotion workers may have little influence on the stage on which they must carry out their work, but they are, nevertheless, an active and controlling force in the labour process (Paules 1996).

Skill as a social-construct

If it can be stated that emotion workers do have discretion and control over their work, thereby fulfilling some of the major criteria for an objective conceptualisation of skill, then why is it only the technical aspects of their labour process that gain recognition in the labour market? The answer is said to lie in the 'invisibility' and the 'tacit' nature of emotion work (Green 1999), which cannot be disputed, but does not address why such a dominant feature of the 'new' economy remains 'invisible'. Once again, this can be attributed to an overly simplistic notion of skill. As Littler notes, 'skill depends not on objective factors, but on custom and tradition plus, collective organization' (Littler 1982: 9). Under this understanding some jobs may have few recognisable skills attached to them but via restricted entry, lengthy training and effective collective organisation, may create and maintain a highly skilled status (Littler 1982; Wood 1982). This is borne out by the position of various emotion workers in Figure 2.1. Those who gain the most recognition have the support of strong professional organisation. The 'emotional proletariat' tend to be poorly represented by trade unions (Taylor and Bain 1999).

Collective organisation is a partial explanation of why emotion work comes low in the hierarchy of skill but a conceptualisation of emotion work as skill must also make an allowance for 'custom and practice' and the 'politics of the workplace and the labour market' (Littler 1982: 11). In considering emotion work as skill and the way that occupations demanding high levels of emotion work are dominated by female labour, it is useful to recognise that the skill attributed to a job has a lot to do with the sex of the person who does it (Cockburn 1985). This is particularly true of jobs requiring emotion work. Since the elements of efficient emotion work are deemed to be rooted in the natural sphere of a woman's abilities they are 'invisible' skills that are not rendered visible when used in the productive sector (Tancred 1995). In other words, emotion work is something that women simply 'do', it is instinctive and intuitive, something that women are born with. Those who make these assumptions draw on the ideology of 'woman', a 'symbolic universe' which defines the attributes of femininity as caring, compassion, sensitivity, nurturing and emotionality (Gherardi 1994). It is little recognised that women's efficiency at emotion work relies on their lived experiences of a gendered division of tasks because the world of 'work' is still defined in terms of men's experiences of productive labour. As Cockburn (1985: 137) eloquently states:

> The sexual division of labour in society is of great antiquity: men and women tend to do different work. Over very long periods of patriarchal time women's particular abilities and work processes have been arbitrarily valued lower than those of men.

The assumption of emotion work being 'women's work' and relying on definitive female qualities reproduces gendered inequalities for both men and women. As gender is a dynamic and continuing process, a distinct social accomplishment that is achieved through the lived experiences of women and men (West and Zimmerman 1987; Davies 1996; New 1998), a sort of gendered closure occurs around jobs involving extensive amounts of emotion work.[1] Men exclude themselves from the 'degradation' of carrying out 'women's work' (Cockburn 1985) but they are also actively excluded by employers due to their perceived lack of particular qualities.

As has been seen in the various forms of emotion work, employers seek various qualities in employees and aim to recruit the 'right' attitude (Callaghan and Thomspon 2002). Possessing the 'right' attitude relies upon a lifetime's guidance in 'the presentation of self' (Goffman 1959) which depends not only on gender position but also social status. Studies show how middle-class mothers offer their children different 'feeling rules' to working-class mothers, thus the middle-class child learns that it is important to know how to manage feelings and 'grows sensitive to feeling and learns to read it well' (Hochschild 1983: 158). So emotion work may be carried out differently, according to social class. However, the management of emotion is a social relationship created in the context of particular social realms and the ultimate presentation of self depends on much more than maternal ties. Charlesworth summarises this well:

> Class is not a simple matter of understanding oneself through a role but a locating of the flesh through inhabiting a particular social realm, constituted by certain objects and certain relations on the basis of one's embodying incorporated forms that lead one to be treated factically, as an object possessed of an essence. These are objective processes that work upon the deepest realms of the intimate lives of persons (Charlesworth 2000: 65).

These processes become inscribed in modes of comportment and inform how emotion work will be performed. Through 'inhabiting the world in a certain way', and with little opportunity to experience the benefits of wider participation in varied social encounters, the 'attitudes' required for employment in many front-line service jobs are never acquired (Nickson *et al.* 2003). Clearly there is a relationship between experiences based on class and gender and a way of being-in-the-world (Charlesworth 2000; West and Zimmerman 1987) resulting in socially recognisable differences which, in turn, dictates the position to be taken on the material stage of the interaction order and the continual reproduction of structured inequalities.

The Future of Emotion Work?

This chapter has argued that emotion work is indeed skilled work which contains recognisable elements of discretionary content, task variety and employee control (Littler 1982). It is the only form of work which involves simultaneous production and consumption, it is the central ingredient of 'quality service' and viewed as a core competence offering competitive advantage to those companies who successfully utilise it. Like other forms of work, there can be little doubt that emotion work in organisations can be demanding, boring, exhausting, tedious, arduous and stressful. Yet because it is intangible, immediately perishable and open to variation, its qualitative features are hard to define rendering emotion work an 'invisible' skill which, though deemed to be a magic ingredient of many occupations, is barely recognised and poorly rewarded (James 1989; Korczynski 2002; Tancred 1995).

These paradoxical themes are rooted in the neglect of the social embeddedness of emotion work. In an economy that values skill on the basis of technical formality, the view of emotion as a natural, taken-for-granted quality leads to many mistaken assumptions. Companies go to great lengths to recruit the right 'attitude' (Callaghan and Thompson 2002) searching for potential employees who possess certain personal characteristics and the ability to 'deal with people'. But ultimately when the customer is 'sovereign', control is inherent in the emotional labour process and management will impose various control strategies, such as performance targets, surveillance and scripted interaction, in order to regulate the 'natural' qualities of service providers and mould their emotion work into a routinised and predictable performance. Service quality is a contradictory combination of the 'hard' and the 'soft' (Pitt *et al.* 1995): efficiency provided in an empathetic and assuring manner (Parasuraman *et al.* 1991).

Though companies desperately seek sincerity from their front-line service workers' interactions with customers, the social process of customer service is essentially violated by the control imperative. The continued emphasis on speedy transactions enhanced with routinised 'niceness' actually constitutes a form of 'mis-involvement' (Goffman 1967: 117). Neither service provider nor customer truly participate in the encounter as, unlike everyday conversation that has a life of its own (Goffman 1967), the service encounter is a fabricated performance with faceless actors. Little wonder then that customer relations in late capitalism have been described as a form of 'abuse' to both producer and consumer (Hopfl 2002).

Utilising insights into the 'interaction order' (Goffman 1959, 1967, 1974), it seems that the ritual of everyday social interaction is something of a feat. It is a social process that relies upon participants monitoring and regulating their own and others' conduct in order to achieve the 'socialized trance' (Goffman 1967: 113) of spontaneous involvement. There is much emotion work involved in achieving the 'order' of interaction. Similarly, the service interaction relies on front-line workers presenting a desirable demeanour and creating an alluring emotional climate. To achieve this they work on their own emotions and seek to manipulate those of the customer, within the feeling and display rules set by the organisation. A successful episode is a fragile accomplishment requiring high levels of skilled emotion work. There is nothing particularly 'natural' about this achievement, yet the illusion remains that certain 'types' of employees are able to carry it off with ease. For instance, the natural qualities of 'people skills' are seen to be the same as feminine qualities and therefore require no other definition than 'women's work', along with the lack of status this implies, and there is a growing shortage of 'soft' skills in the labour market but large swathes of the working population are excluded as training and development is offered in objectively measured skills such as information technology but not in the 'presentation of self' (Thompson *et al.* 2000; Nickson *et al.* 2003).

If emotion work is viewed as a social accomplishment, and customer service accepted as social interaction, front-line service workers could then be conceptualised as multi-skilled emotion managers (Bolton 2000; Callaghan and Thompson 2002) able to judge the type and amount of emotion work required to maintain the order of interaction (Goffman 1967). If the 'customer' is understood as a person rather than a sovereign being, then customer service can be conceptualised as a form of social encounter that is not purely instrumentally motivated and cannot be directly controlled via management intervention (Goffman 1967; Wray-Bliss 2001: 53). Recognising emotion work as a social relationship acted out on a material stage gives the potential for worth to be restored to what is often an unequal exchange and an exclusive production process. It could also mean that the autonomy and higher rewards offered to 'skilled' emotion workers might be extended, with desirable outcomes for all involved.

Note

1   Not, it should be noted, those occupations where a high technical content is combined with emotion work, such as the medical professions. Some occupations may be dominated by women but it is men who account for the majority of senior positions (Porter 1992).

References

Ackroyd, S. and Thompson, P. (1999) *Organizational (Mis)Behaviour*, London: Sage.

Ainley, P. (1993) *Class and Skill: Changing Divisions of Knowledge and Labour*, London: Cassell.

Ashforth, B. and Humphrey, R. (1993) 'Emotional Labor in Service Roles: The Influence of Identity', *Academy of Management Review*, 18, 88–115.

Ashforth, B. and Humphrey, R. (1995) 'Emotion in the Workplace: A Reappraisal', *Human Relations*, 48:2, 97–125.

Bolton, S. (2000) 'Emotion Here, Emotion There, Emotional Organisations Everywhere', *Critical Perspectives on Accounting*, 11, 155–171.

Bolton, S. (2003) 'A Bit of a Laugh: Nurses' Use of Humour as a Mode of Resistance', in M. Dent (ed.), *Dilemmas in the Public Services*, London: Routledge.

Brown, P., Green, A. and Lauder, H. (2001) *High Skills: Globalization, Competitiveness and Skill Formation*, Oxford: Oxford University Press.

Callaghan, G. and Thompson, P. (2002) 'We Recruit Attitude: The Selection and Shaping of Routine Call Centre Labour', *Journal Management Studies*, 39:2, 233–253.

Charlesworth, S. J. (2000) *A Phenomenology of Working Class Experience*, Cambridge: Cambridge University Press.

Cockburn, C. (1985) 'The Nature of Skill: The Case of the Printers', in C. Littler (ed.), *The Experience of Work*, London: Gower.

Collins, H. (1989) *Artificial Experts, Social Knowledge and Intelligent Machines*, Cambridge, MA: MIT Press.

Davies, C. (1996) 'The Sociology of the Professions and the Profession of Gender', *Sociology*, 30:4, 661–678.

DfEE (2000a) *Skills For All: Proposals for a National Skills Agenda*, Final Report of the National Skills Task Force, Sudbury: Prolog.

DfEE (2000b) *Skills For All: Research Report from the National Skills Task Force*, Sudbury: Prolog.

DfEE (2001) *Opportunity and Skills in the Knowledge-Driven Economy*, Nottingham: DfEE Publications.

Drucker, P. (1993) *Post-Capitalist Society*, Oxford: Butterworth-Heinemann.

du Gay, P. and Salaman, G. (1992) 'The Cult(ure) of the Customer', *Journal of Management Studies*, 29, 615–633.

Emerson, J. (1973) 'Negotiating the Serious Import of Humour', in A. Birenbaum and E. Sagarin (eds), *People in Places: The Sociology of the Familiar*, New York: Nelson, 269–280.

Gherardi, S. (1994) 'The Gender We Think, The Gender We Do in Our Everyday Organizational Lives', *Human Relations*, 47:6, 591–610.

Giddens, A. (1984) *The Constitution of Society*, Cambridge: Polity Press.

Goffman, E. (1959) *The Presentation of Self in Everyday Life*, London: Penguin Books.

Goffman, E. (1961) *Encounters*, New York: The Bobbs-Merrill Company Ltd.

Goffman, E. (1967) *Interaction Ritual: Essays in Face-to-Face Behaviour*, Chicago: Aldine Publishing Company.

Goffman, E. (1974) *Frame Analysis*, London: Penguin Books.

Goffman, E. (1991) 'The Interaction Order: American Sociological Association, 1982 Presidential Address', in K. Plummer (ed.), *Symbolic Interactionism: Contemporary Issues*. London: Edward Elgar Ltd.

Goleman, D. (1998) *Working With Emotional Intelligence*, London: Bloomsbury Publishing.

Green, F. (1999) *The Market Value of Generic Skills*, Skills Task Force Research Paper 8, Sudbury: DfEE Publications.

Griffiths, L. (1998) 'Humour as resistance to professional dominance in community mental health teams', *Sociology of Health and Illness*, 20:6, 874–895.

Heskett, J., Sasser, W. and Schlesinger, L. (1997) *The Service Profit Chain*, New York: The Free Press.

Hochschild, A. (1979) 'Emotion Work, Feeling Rules, and Social Structure', *American Journal of Sociology*, 85:3, 551–575.

Hochschild, A. (1983) *The Managed Heart: Commercialization of Human Feeling*, Berkeley: University of California Press.

Hochschild, A. (1989) 'Reply to Cas Wouter's Review Essay on The Managed Heart', *Theory Culture and Society*, 6, 439–445.

Hochschild, A. (1990) 'Ideology and Emotion Management: A Perspective and Path for Future Research', in Kemper, T. (ed.), *Research Agendas in the Sociology of Emotions*, New York: State University of New York Press.

Hogston, R. (1995) 'Quality nursing care: A Qualitative Enquiry', *Journal of Advanced Nursing*, 21, 116–124.

Hopfl, H. (2002) 'Playing the Part: Reflections of Aspects of Mere Performance in the Customer-Client Relationship', *Journal of Management Studies*, 39:2, 255–267.

James, N. (1989) 'Emotional Labour: skill and Work in the Social Regulation of Feeling', *Sociological Review*, 37:1, 15–42.

Kendon, A. (1988) 'Goffman's Approach to Face-to-Face Interaction', in P. Drew and A. Wootton (eds), *Erving Goffman: Exploring the Interaction Order*, Cambridge: Polity Press.

Korczynski, M. (2002) *Human Resource Management in Service Work*, London: Palgrave.

Korczynski, M., Shire, K., Frenkel, S. and Tam, M. (2000) 'Service Work in Consumer Capitalism: Customers, Control and Contradictions', *Work, Employment and Society*, 14:4, 669–687.

Lee Treweek, G. (1996) 'Emotion Work, Order, and Emotional Power in Care Assistant Work', in V. Hanes and J. Gabe (eds), *Health and the Sociology of the Emotions*, London: Blackwell.

Leidner, R. (1996) 'Rethinking Questions of Control: Lessons from McDonald's', in C. Macdonald and C. Sirianni (eds), *Working in the Service Society*, Philadelphia: Temple University Press.

Littler, C. (1982) *The Development of the Labour Process in Capitalist Societies*, London: Heinemann.

Macdonald, C. and Sirianni, C. (eds) (1996) *Working in the Service Society*, Philadelphia: Temple University Press.

Mahon, P. Y. (1996) 'An Analysis of the Concept 'Patient Satisfaction' as it Relates to Contemporary Nursing Care', *Journal of Advanced Nursing*, 24, 1241–1248.

Mann, S. (1999) *Hiding What we Feel, Faking What we Don't*, Boston: Element.

McEwen, B. and Buckingham, G. (2001) 'Make a Marque', *People Management*, 17th May, pp. 40–44.

Morris, J. A. and Feldman, D. (1996) 'The Dimensions, Antecedents and Consequences of Emotional Labor', *Academy of Management Review*, 21:4, 986–1010.

New, C. (1998) 'Realism, Deconstruction and the Feminist Standpoint', *Journal for the Theory of Social Behaviour*, 28:3, 349–372.

Nickson, D., Warhurst, C., Cullen, A. M. and Watt, A. (2003) 'Bringing in the excluded? Aesthetic Labour, Skills and Training in the New Economy', *Journal of Education and Work*, 16:3.

Parasuraman, A., Berrry, L. and Zeithaml, V. (1991) 'Understanding Customer Expectations of Service', *Sloan Management Review*, 32:3, 39–48.

Paules, G. (1996) 'Resisting the Symbolism of Service', in C. Macdonald and C. Sirianni (eds), *Working in the Service Society*, Philadelphia: Temple University Press.

Pitt, L., Foreman, S. and Bromfield, D. (1995) 'Organizational Commitment and Service Delivery: Evidence from an Industrial Setting in the UK', *The International Journal of Human Resource Management*, 6:1, 389.

Porter, S. (1992) 'Women in a Women's Job: The Gendered Experience of Nurses', *Sociology of Health and Illness*, 14:4, 510–527.

Rafaeli, A. and Sutton, R. I. (1987) 'Expression of Emotion as Part of the Work Role', *Academy of Management Review*, 12, 23–37.

Rafaeli, A. and Sutton, R. I. (1990) 'Busy Stores and Demanding Customers: How do they affect the Display of Positive Emotion', *Academy of Management Journal*, 33:3 623–637.

Ritzer, G. (1999) *Enchanting a Disenchanted World*, California: Pine Forge Press.

Salvage, J. (1985) *The Politics of Nursing*, London: Heinemann Nursing.

Sayer, A. and Walker, R. (1992) *The New Social Economy: Reworking the Division of Labour*, Cambridge: Blackwell.

Schwalbe, M. (1993) 'Goffman Against Postmodernism: Emotion and the Reality of the Self', *Symbolic Interaction*, 16:4, 333–350.

Smith, P. (1992) *The Emotional Labour of Nursing*, London: Macmillan.

Sturdy, A. (1998) 'Customer Care in a Consumer Society: Smiling and Sometimes Meaning It?', *Organization*, 5:1, 27–53.

Sutton, R. I. (1991) 'Maintaining Norms about Expressed Emotions: The Case of Bill Collectors', *Administrative Science Quarterly*, 36, 245–268.

Tancred, P. (1995) 'Women's Work: A Challenge to the Sociology of Work', *Gender, Work and Organisation*, 2:1, 11–20.

Taylor, S. (1998) Emotional Labour and the New Workplace', in P. Thompson and C. Warhurst (eds), *Workplaces of the Future*, London: Macmillan.

Taylor, P. and Bain, P. (1999) 'An Assembly Line in the Head: Work and Employee Relations in the Call Centre', *Industrial Relations Journal*, 30:2, 101–117.

Thompson, P., Warhurst, C. and Callaghan, G. (2000) 'Human Capital or Capitalising on Humanity? Knowledge, Skills and Competencies in Interactive Service Work', in H. Pritchard and H. Willmott (eds), *Critical Investigations of Work and Learning*, London: Macmillan.

Van Maanen, J. (1991) 'The Smile Factory: Work at Disneyland', in P. Frost, L. Moore, M. Luis, C. Lundberg and J. Martin (eds), *Reframing Organizational Culture*, California, Sage.

Weatherly, K. and Tansik, D. (1992) 'Tactics used by Customer-contact Workers: Effects of Role Stress, Boundary Spanning and Control', *International Journal of Service Industry Management*, 4:3, 4–17.

West, C. and Zimmerman, D. (1987) 'Doing Gender', *Gender and Society*, 1, 125–151.

Wharton, A. (1996) 'Service with a Smile: Understanding the Consequences of Emotional Labour', in C. MacDonald and C. Sirianni (eds), *Working in the Service Society*, Philadelphia: Temple University Press.

Witz, A., Warhurst, C. and Nickson, D. (2003) 'The Labour of Aesthetics and the Aesthetics of Organization', *Organization*, 10:1, 33–54.

Wood, S. (1982) *'The Degradation of Work? Skill, Deskilling and the Labour Process'*, London: Hutchinson.

Wouters, C. (1989a) 'The Sociology of Emotions and Flight Attendants: Hochschild's Managed Heart', *Theory, Culture and Society*, 6, 95–123.

Wouters, C. (1989b) 'Response to Hochschild's Reply', *Theory, Culture and Society*, 6, 447–450.

Wray-Bliss, E. (2001) 'Representing Customer Service: Telephones and Texts', in A. Sturdy, I. Grugulis and H. Willmott (eds), *Customer Service*, London: Palgrave.

3
Skills that Matter and Shortages that Don't

Andy Westwood

Exactly when and where did we lose track of the meaning of skills? In the past it used to be such a simple issue: having skills, being 'skilful', was good; having none, being 'unskilled', was bad. It was the difference between decent jobs and poor jobs; skills entitled people to better paid, more secure work. Not that skills were solely a feature of the workplace; playing sports, gardening, painting and driving were all things that could be done skilfully; it was possible to be a highly skilled amateur as well as a professional. Now skills are much more confusing. Individuals can be over-skilled as well as under-skilled, skills can be inappropriate or obsolete, workers can be deskilled or upskilled. Of course people can still have 'good' skills, but they can also have other types too: hard and soft skills, basic skills, key skills, transferable skills or poor skills. Debates rage about the definitions of skill, about whether certain skills can ever be taught or assessed. And whatever skills might or might not be, there are now regular claims that skill shortages are very important and dangerous.

This chapter attempts to disentangle some of the problems with both skills and skill shortages. In particular, it looks at the three principle factors that cause the long-standing problems with skills policy in the UK: the changing world of work that has permanently shifted the definitions and applications of skill; the often distorting interests of employers and business organisations; and the practical inabilities and dislocation within and between different government departments.

What are the Skills that Matter?

Most researchers and commentators seem to now accept that the UK has a rather pressing problem with its skills. Over half of all UK businesses are struggling to recruit sufficient skilled workers – the highest proportion ever according to some surveys:

> The share of companies reporting difficulties in recruiting skilled labour rose again to a new peak of 51% in this survey, compared with 20% in the

early 1990s. In terms of recruiting unskilled labour, the share of companies reporting problems rose to 30%, the highest ever level. (Business in Britain Survey: LloydsTSB 2001: 4)

Others too, Bentley (1998: 100) for example, have pointed to this problem:

> Forty per cent of employers recently stated that there was a significant gap between the skills of their recruits and their current business needs, with personal and communication skills among the most deficient. There is growing recognition that effective employees need strong personal qualities as well as good qualifications... Since 1950 the UK has lost five million jobs in the producing industries and gained some eight million in services. We now earn more revenue from Indian restaurants than from coal, steel and shipbuilding combined.

In *Labour Market Trends*, the Office for National Statistics (ONS) distinguishes between the two elements of skill shortages that have hit the UK hardest; skill shortage vacancies where the applicants lack the skills, qualifications or experience required and internal skills gaps where the workforce in a company lack the skills needed to meet current and future business objectives. According to the ONS, the majority of skills deficiencies are in craft and related occupations but also in 'technician' categories now designated 'associate professional and technical occupations'. These skill shortages and others are now impacting on business performance. Sixty per cent of companies are reporting difficulties and problems caused by vacancies and/or difficulties in recruiting the right staff.

According to a recent MORI and Learning Pool (2002) survey, UK workers themselves also diagnose considerable problems with their own and their colleagues' skill levels. It not only finds that one in four British workers lack the skills to do their jobs properly, but also that almost a third of British workers admit to lying about or exaggerating their skills.

The National Skills Task Force (1998: 7), during its relatively short-lived existence, pointed out that over a quarter of firms were reporting significant skill shortages.

> Employers repeatedly express concerns about the employability and key skills of young people entering the labour market for the first time, including graduates. Employers also report a lack of practical skills relating to the application of technical knowledge in the working environment. This is consistent with the relative weakness of apprenticeship and other formal vocational training for young people in the UK compared to other European countries.

Similar findings were reported in Scotland and Wales. The Monetary Policy Committee is also concerned. When deciding UK interest rates, it too, has expressed concerns about the effect of 'bottlenecks' in the labour market on UK competitiveness and underlying inflation.

Why have Skill Needs Changed?

According to the 2002 skills survey carried out by the Institute of Employment Studies and MORI on behalf of the Department for Education and Skills (DfES), the main reported areas of skill deficiency are communication skills – affecting most occupational groups, customer handling – affecting almost half of employers, teamworking – evenly spread across most occupational groups and problem-solving – particularly in personal service occupations (Hillage *et al.* 2002).

These are the specific skills that are most commonly missing from the UK's perpetually low-skilled workforce. The skills problem is, at least in part, caused by fundamental changes in the UK's employment base. There have been several important changes in the labour market over the last thirty years that have each created new demands for, or interpretations of, skill. Firstly and most visibly, there has been a major decline in the number of people in manual employment and manufacturing. The proportion of skilled manual workers in total employment has fallen from 18 to 12 per cent in this period, although there are still 3.2 million such workers in the workforce. Secondly, there has been a rise in the employment of people performing managerial, professional and technical jobs. Over the same period, the share of workers in these occupations has risen from a quarter to a third. Thirdly, there has been a rise in the group of workers classified as 'personal and protective'. These are the jobs that are most evident in new shops, restaurants and in personal service occupations such as childcare. Their share of total employment has risen from around 6 to around 11 per cent. The service sector has brought new characteristics to the labour market far and beyond the skills that its employers might need. Even established employers have become more 'high touch' and service orientated, whether from the public, private or voluntary sectors. As this new service culture has mushroomed, so too has the demand for the kinds of skills and personal attributes that underpin it.

Skilling Me Softly?

Service-orientated skills and attributes are commonly referred to as 'soft skills' – itself suggesting less importance than those skills described as 'hard'. Perceptions of these types of skills, and the jobs and the sectors that utilise them are increasingly outdated throughout the UK. Bars, restaurants and shops look very different today than they did in the 1960s and 1970s. The inherent requirements of these jobs have changed as dramatically as those in manufacturing – with employers developing completely new service strategies, and job functions and descriptions. Pay, conditions and career structures have all become increasingly more sophisticated – at a rate that far exceeds traditional perceptions of such work (Westwood 2002).

Soft skills too are evolving. In some workplaces they make up what Warhurst and Nickson (2001: 1) have described as the demand for 'aesthetic labour':

> Aesthetic labour will feature heavily in future job growth; it also raises significant employment issues, and demands a significant policy response. If employees are required to be able to present themselves to customers in ways that engage those customers' senses – in short, if they have to 'look good' and 'sound right' – this implies major, and to many people, uncomfortable changes in skills and training provision and social inclusion initiatives.

They are referring to the types of jobs that are dominating the rejuvenated service sector throughout the UK: coffee houses, clubs, shops, restaurants and bars, hotels, public and private fitness clubs, and so on. To some extent, it is also applying to wider working and recruitment practices amongst more traditional employers such as financial services, sales and parts of the public sector as well as amongst more long-standing retailers such as Marks and Spencers, Tesco and Asda. Many commentators, policymakers and academics seem to think that these are typically low-skilled jobs. However, it may be that these are simply new or different skills and that, given the perceived shortages described earlier in this chapter, are also the very qualities that can potentially transform the workforce and the UK's overall economic performance (Westwood 2003).

Employers in each of these sectors are likely to value aesthetic skills and select employees by, among other things, their 'aesthetic' ability. Aesthetic labour is about image. Competition in the service economy is now about branding and experience as much as product; employers, therefore, are looking for staff who can embody the image and experience the company is trying to sell; as well as provide great service. Aesthetic skills are likely to be compound, including accent, voice modulation, appearance, presentation and; most importantly, confidence and motivation (Warhurst and Nickson 2001). As such, they are closely related to more recognised social skills: communication, interpersonal abilities, teamworking and so on. In addition, many employers consider factors such as region, gender and ethnicity when determining the aesthetic requirements in their businesses.

However, these are a very long way from the kinds of skills that the UK's education system is used to supplying. It remains more comfortable in the processing and supply of more academic skills and where it has more experience in delivering work-related skills it has typically been in more traditional areas such as manufacturing, healthcare and general administration or 'office' skills. This largely academic comfort zone has meant that attempts to incorporate the teaching and learning of new skills into the system have been met with confusion. It is also the reason that there are rather dubious initiatives such as Modern Apprenticeships and Key Skills, both of which have failed to sufficiently inspire either individuals or organisations. Furthermore, it is also the reason why a profusion of wider organisational initiatives that have struggled for impact; the National Skills Task Force, Learning and Skills Councils, Sector Skills Councils and the University for Industry all face either short or challenging futures.

The UK's Working Problem

The reason for this host of initiatives is at least clear – the real interest comes with the link between skills and productivity. Productivity is firmly on the political agenda and improving it is a key objective of the government. The UK has consistently under-performed its major industrialised counterparts in Europe, North America and the Far East. In 1998, productivity, as measured by output per worker, was 13% higher in Germany than in the UK, 21% higher in France, and 36% higher in the US. The UK has as many graduates as France and Germany, but only half as many with intermediate level qualifications [1] as Germany and two thirds of the number in France. (Westwood 2001)

Compared to France and Germany, the UK clearly under-performs in its numbers of individuals with Level 2 and Level 3 qualifications. The government's diagnosis of the problem is that under-investment and under-participation in workforce development is the primary cause of the UK's relatively poor levels of productivity.

Worse still is the fact that much of the UK's adult population suffers from low levels of basic skills. One in five adults within the workforce are functionally illiterate and as high as one in four are functionally innumerate (DfEE 1998):

Some 7 million adults in England – one in five adults – if given the alphabetical index to the Yellow Pages, cannot locate the page reference for plumbers. This is an example of functional illiteracy. It means that 1 in 5 adults have less literacy than is expected of an 11 year old child ... 1 in 3 adults in this country cannot calculate the area of a room that is 21×14 feet, even with the aid of a calculator; 1 in 4 adults cannot calculate the change they should get out of £2 when they buy a loaf of bread for 68 p and two tins of beans for 45 p each. (DfEE 1998)

So there is a need to improve the level of skills in the workforce if the UK is to improve its comparative productivity performance. This realisation would then seem to suggest a need for a greater emphasis on learning work-based intermediate skills – the very skills that have been identified as lacking amongst the UK's workforce. However, the changes in the labour market and the rise of the service culture have wrong-footed the education system. Whilst it may be clear that intermediate skills are what is needed, the UK still has a system that has failed to adequately incorporate the teaching and learning of these skills into its qualifications or curricula. Think back to the four main areas listed in the DfES skills survey: communication, it could be argued is adequately taught throughout a range of different vehicles, however, the remaining three; problem-solving, teamworking and customer handling are not. In fact, the first two do feature in the recently introduced Key Skills qualification, alongside communication, but are not formally assessed.[2]

There are long-standing concerns in other areas too. Vocational qualifications have long failed to gain 'parity of esteem' with academic alternatives – something that could also be said of service-sector jobs alongside more traditional work (Westwood 2002). This lack of parity is also an institutional issue. The UK's further education colleges that are typically responsible for delivering the majority of its technical and technician level learning have a poor reputation in comparison to either universities or schools (Westwood and Jones 2003). Attempts to repackage and improve either the UK's vocational qualifications or the institutions that are primarily responsible for delivering them have been failing for many years and still show little signs of succeeding.

Thus it is a major problem for the UK. The UK needs to improve the skills of its workforce at the intermediate level, the types of skill most in demand, but as yet there is not the right infrastructure to supply them. Again, this deficiency is partly because of a failure to adequately embrace the teaching of the service-orientated skills that now so thoroughly underpin the UK labour market and partly because although needed by employers, there are questionable financial returns. It is also though, because there is too little demand for taking on any kind of skill from many individuals and organisations. There is a very simple training divide in the UK between those who can access it and those who cannot or will not. Most training is provided for those occupations that already have most education and qualifications – managerial and professional – as Table 3.1 highlights.

Improving skill levels in the necessary areas will be difficult if these levels of disparity or exclusion are allowed to continue. There is more to this problem than just unequal access to training budgets. It is also a problem for those who are happy to avoid the warnings and to stick with work that does not need skill at all.

It has been observed that the UK is stuck in a 'low skills equilibrium' (Keep and Mayhew 1998) and that the incidence of low skill in our workforce has at least in part caused organisations to opt for low-skill business models in resulting product or service specifications. The combination, therefore, of both low-skill and low-employer demand for skill results in a system that may prove difficult to change. Where employers have jobs that suit low-skilled people, an increased supply of more highly skilled individuals might

Table 3.1   **Exclusion from training over last 5 years (%)**

Category	Percentage
Unskilled	71
Partly skilled	68
Skilled manual	51
Skilled non-manual	48
Managerial	26
Professional	20
No qualification	70
CSE or equivalent	51
O Level	38
A Level	38
Degree or above	24

Source: Green (in Burkitt and Robinson ed. 2001).

upset this equilibrium. Similarly, a rise in the number of employers offering jobs needing high skills – the move to a more knowledge-driven economy – and the lack of ability in the UK workforce will lead to more and more skill shortages.

It is a double-edged sword, but at least the government seems clear that they need to advance the cause on both sides of the equation, exhorting both individuals and employers to raise their sights in the skills game. This approach is obviously a sensible way forward although it does not take account of either those organisations that do very well out of running a low-skilled workforce or of those who can still do badly with a high-skilled one (Westwood 2001).

Truth or Dare: Employers and Skills Shortages

> Britain is, in many ways, a competitive country, but when it comes to general educational standards and workplace skills the country is quite simply not world class and we believe that this holds back productivity, economic growth and prosperity. One of the most serious problem business faces is the problem of skills shortages. (Lea 2002: 8)

Although the findings from the DfES Skills Survey are recent, they are far from new. The Institute of Directors (IoD), the Confederation of British Industry (CBI), the Chartered Institute of Personnel and Development (CIPD) and the Federation of Small Businesses (FSB) have all commissioned and published research on skills in the past few years. All conclude that there is a skills gap and that young people leaving education do not possess all the skills that make up employability or 'job readiness'. Both are relatively new phrases that accurately describe this growing shift in attitude from UK

Table 3.2   **Employers reporting skills lacking in 16–24 year olds**

Skill type	Percentage
Technical and practical skills	25
General communication skills	20
Customer handling skills	19
Teamworking skills	17
Computer Literacy	16
Problem-solving skills	15
Management skills	15
Managing own development	14
Numeracy skills	8
Literacy skills	7

Source: Skills Needs in Britain & Northern Ireland (IFF/DfEE 1998).

employers. Tom Shebbeare, the Chief Executive of the educational charity, the Prince's Trust, has recently summed up this situation:

> Employers are expecting people to be job ready; 'dressed' for work – they want people who can read, people who are numerate, they want people who turn up on time, they want people who can work well in a team, people who can communicate well – and they're expecting this to be achieved before they get to the employer…and it's a very difficult thing to do and it will cost more money than we are currently spending on them and it will have to be more intense.[3]

The skills found to be in most demand across the entire workforce closely resemble the attributed shortcomings of those young people most recently out of full-time education. The *Skills Needs in Britain* survey, partly sponsored by the CBI, provides an analysis of perceived skill shortages and subsequently a rationale for intervention in the education system, as Table 3.2 indicates:

Vocational and job-specific skills clearly come out at the top of employers' needs, but wider, more generic skills like those mentioned in the DfES Skills Survey, form the remaining problem areas. This finding is more or less echoed in a recent survey of its members by the IoD. In this work IT comes out on top (29 per cent), followed by Vocational Skills (20 per cent) and Technical Skills (a further 7 per cent). However, basic and generic skills come close behind with 14 per cent, together with management skills (19 per cent) and communication skills (19 per cent).

The interesting elements come with the implied responsibility for types of skill:

> To a crucial extent, it is the owner's or the manager's responsibility to deal with skill shortages, skill gaps and other recruitment difficulties. In the first instance, the owner or manager is much more likely to have the requisite

knowledge to determine what training – if any – his employees need, than anyone else... Additionally, because the performance of the enterprise has direct financial consequences for the owner or manager, he has a powerful incentive to address any deficiencies in skills that the employees in his firm may have. (Wilson: 1999)

In this report, Richard Wilson of the IoD goes on to state that a government's role should therefore be limited and that they could never truly be able to predict future skills needs of employers. The prime responsibility of the government is 'specific and limited' and should concentrate on 'addressing the deficiencies of the British education system':

All school leavers should have a basic mastery of the 3 Rs[4] and the essential generic skills that are needed in the workplace. Individuals who lack these basic skills reduce their chances of employment and, generally speaking, are harder for employers to train than individuals who possess these skills. (p. 12)

The CBI, in its recent publication *Making Employability Work*, is even more explicit in their definitions of employability (see Box 3.1) and in their perception of the relevant responsibilities of education and employers:

The foundation education system needs to develop employability more effectively. The *Skills Needs in Britain* survey reveals that a number of persistent gaps remain in the skills of young people – though specific technical and practical skills are a matter for employers rather than education to tackle. (Wilson 1999: 8)

Box 3.1   Qualities and competences that make up employability

- Values and attitudes compatible with the work – including a desire to learn, to apply that learning, to improve and to take advantage of change.
- Basic Skills (literacy and numeracy).
- Key Skills sufficient for the needs of the work.
- Other generic skills that are becoming increasingly 'key' – such as modern language and customer-service skills.
- Up to date and relevant knowledge and understanding.
- Up to date job-specific skills.
- The ability to manage one's own career.

Source: Based on *Making Employability Work* (CBI 1999: 2).

These organisations have a fair point. However, they should also suggest the types of skill development and training which employers themselves might then assume more responsibility for funding. The CBI suggest that these should be 'specific technical and practical skills'. However, as Tom Shebbeare points out, such a state-led concentration of funding on generic skills at foundation or intermediate levels, would lead to a greater requirement for non-state funds in higher level, more specialist situations. Do the CBI realise how expensive these 'specific technical and practical' skills might prove to be in this reordered context?

Employers' organisations such as the CBI and the IoD are therefore clear about the skills that need to be prioritised by the mainly state education system. However, they make their case in a language that has so often proved alien to both academics and policymakers.

The Classroom and the Workplace

There is a regular semantic dispute between the different meanings and practices of education and training. Once, education happened in the class-room and training in the workplace. Now it applies equally to education and skills. Education is still responsible for the classroom, but also in preparing people for the workplace. Skills are just something that the workplace, and all the interests associated with it, would rather that education took care of. Whilst the difference between education and skills may be an increasingly false dichotomy, it is important to remember that the classroom and the workplace are very different indeed. Yes of course, the curriculum of the UK classroom should be better at providing skills for the workplace – after all everyone who leaves the first will eventually enter the latter. It would be disingenuous to deny the responsibilities for teaching appropriate skills are important.

However, the classroom should not pretend to be a workplace like any other. The majority of the occupants of the classroom – the school-children – are not in a workplace. They need to be taught, coached, mentored, encouraged; they need to recognise the need for their own learning, to have responsibilities and to be developed to the fullest of their potentials – all processes that can be sadly absent from many of the UK's workplaces.

The aim should be to preserve and develop both the difference and the connections between classroom and workplace. Young people in full-time education need to be allowed to develop as fully as possible their skills and aptitudes as well as their specific learning and general social development. This approach, as the CBI and IoD suggest, would serve UK workplaces best.

For there are skill shortages and skill shortages. There are skills in sunrise industries – amongst employers and entrepreneurs who have established organisations at the forefront of the technological frontier where skills, people and teachers are all hard to come by. There are also other skill short-ages that are no less important – in teaching, nursing and policing – workers in sectors that need to be run in distinctly non-market ways. And then there are the skill shortages that are rather more spurious. These are the headlines and hype of very different agendas that merely masquerade as skill shortages: employers who do not want to pay or who do not want to train; the employ-ers who would rather make more money out of perpetuating a low pay and low-skills base.

Amidst the hype of the dot-com boom, it was popularly reported that there were many thousands of unfilled vacancies in the IT sector. A shortage of specific technical skills was holding back a whole fleet of new companies from expansion, profit and sustainability or so the trade press screamed. A few short months later and most of those who had filled similar positions were on the dole.

There are also those who claim that the right people are just not out there anymore. Typically, they might quickly add that they would love to train young people but they would only be poached by some terribly unscrupu-lous employer down the road. But skills do pay their way. Individuals do gain from training and so too do the organisations that employ them. Training significantly boosts productivity, with the overall effect of training on productivity being around twice as high as the wage effect (Dearden *et al*. 2000).

Should Employers be Listened to?

It is, of course, important to listen to employers, but it is just as important to listen to the right ones. It is all too easy for the genuine skills agenda to be distorted. There are skill shortages that do matter and there is the often hysterical bleating and blame that should not. Too often policymakers have attempted to make policy that satisfies both when it should only concentrate on the former. There are many employers who want to complain about skill shortages, about the deficiencies in the education system that fail to ade-quately prepare skill levels. And there has been a shortage of those employers who are prepared to sit on all the task forces and skills councils and tell government what is wrong. Many are quick to criticise the lack of specific skills or the quality of the training available to them, but are loath to do too much about it.

This gap between what employers say, and what they do, has caused significant problems for training policy. We need to move to a situation where Pavlovian responses to official enquiries cease, and where all the actors are willing and able to provide policymakers with an honest view of current and likely future attitudes and intentions. Until this happens, vocational education and training policy is being constructed on sand. (National Skills Task Force 2000: 74)

Just as there is a wide variety of real and fictitious skill shortages, there is also a wide range of different employers in the UK. It is important to make sure that the right ones have been recruited or consulted – formally, informally, temporary or permanent – in the setting up of the numerous skills initiatives that now exist. As the Treasury observed in their *Productivity in the UK* paper:

The most productive plants are five and a half times as productive as the least productive plants...the most productive have productivity levels that are comparable with the best in the world. However, lagging behind the leaders in each sector is a long tail of firms, which are substantially less productive. (HM Treasury 2000: 19)

The best employers are worth listening to and learning from, whereas those further down the chain, probably do not deserve to be heard. In skills terms it will be worth listening to those who have made efforts to advance the learning of individuals and organisations. There is a ready-made government measure that would suit this purpose – Investors in People (IiP). Sadly but perhaps given the UK's skills problem unsurprisingly, it remains the case that a large minority of workplaces have secured IiP accreditation. Only 32 per cent of workplaces with 10 or more employees are IiP accredited (Cully *et al.* 1999). By the end of June 2001 more than 25,000 companies had achieved accreditation and a further 20,000 were committed to working towards the standard. This means that IiP reaches more than nine million employees, representing around 39 per cent of the working population.[5] In this respect, IiP is among the most wide reaching of the government training initiatives currently in operation. However, it must be remembered that employers attempting to achieve IiP accreditation may be merely 'badge collecting' as opposed to introducing major training systems (Hoque *et al.* 2002).

Would it not make sense therefore to insist that any employer purporting to get involved in, or to take up positions driving, the UK's skills policy should at the very least have crossed the government's own threshold? Unfortunately, this does not happen and has to count as an opportunity missed. Furthermore, employers or their representative bodies seem to like IiP, Hoque *et al.* (2002) found, so there should be no accusations of irrelevance if such a condition were brought in.

It should be straightforward enough to sort the wheat from the chaff in terms of employer views, but it is not. Such views are usually made by membership bodies that canvass their members' opinions on these matters. However, therein lies the problem. Business bodies are, by definition, representatives of their membership. As a consequence, the views of both the best and the worst must be reflected in their overall views. The result is necessarily far from a reflection of best practice. So as far as policy responses are concerned – and especially where they concern the labour market – the advice of the CBI, IoD, CIPD and FSB must be handled with appropriate care.

Unfortunately, the government has too often fallen for such collective views hook, line and sinker. It is unfortunate but the government has undoubtedly allowed some businesses that do not deserve their places to sit on and help to run government agencies such as the National Skills Task Force, Learning and Skills Councils and the University for Industry as well as many individual institutions such as further education colleges. Worse still, they may well end up running or influencing the new Sector Skills Councils.

Similarly, in the headlong rush to set up and operationalise the Learning and Skills Council – virtually overnight one of the largest and most significant government bodies in existence – it is clear that appointment panels were happy with any private sector applications at all – even those from the disgraced and disbanded Training and Enterprise Councils (TECs). It is the same problem that did so much to sink Individual Learning Accounts (ILAs). ILAs were a necessary and sound policy idea; a mechanism for switching educational funds away from failing institutions and qualifications, and into the hands of individuals. But it was killed by a fatal combination of poor implementation and the failure to apply any sort of quality requirement on the legions of private training providers who wanted to get their hands on the cash.[6]

The Department for Schools (...and Skills)

The DfES obviously must take some responsibility. It understands the private sector about as much as employers understand it – as their policy implementation record proves. And of course, like any other organisation, there is as much variety in its own performance and skills base as there is in the private sector. Combinations of the two sets of shortcomings have also been a hindrance to curriculum design as well as for major policy-making bodies. Consider, for example, the University for Industry and the Key Skills qualifications – two major initiatives of the Government's first term in office that have failed to deliver against expectations.

The University for Industry (UfI) was New Labour's diagnosis and solution for Britain's low-skills problem. The brainchild of UK Chancellor of the Exchequer Gordon Brown and born in the run-up to the 1997 election as the major workforce development initiative of its time, it has failed to live up to expectations. Very rapidly, the University for Industry's name and mission was challenged – it was not a university and it was not for industry. Credibly, some impressive and essential initiatives have still emerged. The *Learndirect* brand for advice and guidance has been launched and thousands of access points to information and communications technology have been opened across the country. New qualifications and learning programmes have also helped to provide new skills for people with few if any formal qualifications to their names. However, none of these amount to Gordon Brown's initial vision of a resource for boosting productivity through business performance. He was, of course, right to point out the need for such an initiative in 1997 and he would still be right today.

The Key Skills qualification was also launched with high hopes. Launched as the central response to employer criticism of young people's shortcomings in work, the Key Skills qualification has been beset with difficulty. Firstly, the qualification never embraced all six skills – rejecting teamworking, problem-solving and improving own performance, instead concentrating on literacy, numeracy and IT. Secondly, it was introduced during other reforms to advanced level study. Finally, employers continue to support the concept of key skills in a way that the academic community seem unlikely to ever do. The argument over key skills typifies the problems of reforming vocational learning.

Bizarrely, many of the disputes between the separate worlds of the classroom and the workplace took place at the relatively recently unified Department of Education and Employment. Both the Key Skills qualification and the University for Industry were good, and certainly well intentioned, ideas. However, each process of implementation doomed them to failure. As soon as establishment-driven compromises had renamed UfI and halved the number of key skills, the initiatives were finished.

Then came the great divorce between education and employment after the 2001 election. The two partners that used to form the happy marriage at Department for Education and Employment (DfEE) are still rumoured to be on speaking terms – for the sake of the kids. When Education was scratching around for a new partner – to put something after the 'and' – they eventually came up with 'skills'. It seemed so sensible; skills are an appropriate bedfellow for education – are they not? However, with the wrong employer involve-ment and it may prove to be the opposite. Equally, the right type of skills strategy should be an equal partner of the wide-ranging strategies that exist for schools. Sadly this too is far from true. There is no skills strategy. As a senior official recently claimed; 'we haven't really got our heads round skills yet'[7]. But they need to give it some weight. At the Department there are many ministers driving education policy. However, there is only one with skills in their title of responsibility and arguably they are at the most junior level.

In Barbara Ehrenreich's superb investigation into low-wage America, she catches a ride with her boss at a domestic cleaning company, who bemoans how much money he is missing out on because he cannot attract the staff to carry out the volume of work:

> You may remember the time when Ted my boss at the Maids drove me about forty minutes to a house where I was asked to reinforce a short-handed team. In the course of complaining about his hard lot in life, he avowed that he could double his business overnight if only he could find enough reliable workers. (Ehrenreich 2001: 164)

Employers must realise that the labour market is a market like any other. If there are labour or 'skill' shortages then employers must either pay more or train more in order to stay competitive. It is a major irony indeed that employers and business organisations would rather see their workforces subjected to greater levels of government intervention rather than to the effects of market forces. It seems obvious, especially as employers seem to be able to see the value of skills – or at least the problems caused by not having them – impacting on their bottom lines. Even Barbara Ehrenreich's boss at the home cleaning business could work out that extra staff with the right skills would make him much more money. So why do so many employers regularly and deliberately fail to make this connection?

In the same vein comes a complaint that can be regularly heard at dinner parties, on radio programmes and at policy seminars throughout London: 'I cannot get a plumber to come and fix my leaky toilet.' What they also mean is: ' . . . and have you seen how much it costs to get a plumber to come and fix a leaky toilet?' Whilst all of us from time to time bemoan the cost or unavailability of a range of household services – nannies, electricians, plumbers and so on – what we are really upset about are the market forces pushing these services up to new premium prices. Skill shortages in craft sectors drive up wage costs. Plumbers as well as builders and electricians know this market reality, even if their clients – or civil servants – do not. And, of course, there's more than a smattering of snobbery in there for good measure. It is, after all, easy to work out how comparatively little we might be earning per hour while we are waiting for the plumber to arrive.

With all of these demands, it is perhaps understandable that the government is too often confused by skills. But government is also guilty of failing to take full control of the initiatives that will deliver the skills that the economy needs. Using the word in the titles of government agencies and quangos and in the title of the sponsoring department itself is not enough. Sadly, despite the ubiquity of 'skills' in policy-making circles, it remains true that most members of the education establishment would rather let it just go away. Not for them, this lesser type of learning that is irreversibly soiled by the workplace. For this cadre of civil servants and academics, skills are better off left amongst what Alison Wolf (2002: 98) so aptly describes as 'qualifications for other people's children'.

Skills Do Matter

The skills problem is not irretrievable. The Learning Pool (and MORI) (2002) showed that British workers have an appetite for learning and 23 per cent said training was the most important factor when looking for a new job. Almost a third (31 per cent) of these workers also believed that they would do their jobs better with more training and almost all felt that they are good at picking up new skills. A further 44 per cent also said that they trained in order to enjoy their jobs more – worker satisfaction being a potentially useful contributor to boosting performance.

Thus, as far as individuals go, there is useful scope for improvement, and there needs to be. As we have seen, at the level of the firm and the economy as a whole, there is a desperate need for better skill levels and through them, improved performance.

But there is a need to be firmer and more systematic about which employers are engaged in policy making and how these employers are engaged in policy-making. There is a need to be able to spot a skill shortage when one exists. There is also a need to be able to sort the real issues from the hype by listening to, and learning from, the organisations that are worth the attention. Finally, there is a need to address some of the qualities and skill levels within government too and a vital need to develop effective models that bring both worlds together. This must be done in order to deliver the workforce and the skills that the UK so desperately needs. Otherwise, as in so many times in the recent and distant past, the latest attempts to improve the UK position will fail.

Notes

1   Equivalent to NVQ Level II and III.
2   The Key Skills Qualification assesses skills in communication, application of number and information technology but not in the wider skills of teamworking, problem-solving and managing own learning.
3   Tom Shebbeare, Chief Executive, of the Prince's Trust speaking on the UK Radio 4 *Today* programme (12th November 2000).
4   The 3R's are often referred to in the UK as a popular definition of basic literacy and numeracy. They are 'reading, (w)riting and (a)rithmetic (*sic*)'.
5   http://www.investorsinpeople.co.uk/statisticsonthestandard/.
6   Individual Learning Accounts were suspended in 2001 after suspected fraud. The government has announced that the scheme will be reintroduced.
7   In a private meeting with the author.

References

Bentley, T. (1998) *Learning Beyond the Classroom*, London: Demos.
CBI (Confederation of British Industry) (1999) *Making Employability Work*, London: CBI.

Cully, M., Woodland, S., O'Reilly, A. and Dix, G. (1999) *Britain at Work*, London: Routledge.

Dearden, L., Reed, H. and van Reenen, J. (2000) *Who Gains When Workers Train?*, London: Institute for Fiscal Studies.

DfEE (Department for Education and Employment) (1998) *Improving Literacy and Numeracy* – the report of the working group chaired by Sir Claus Moser, Nottingham: DfEE.

DfEE (1998) *Skills Needs in Britain & Northern Ireland*, London IFF/DfEE.

Ehrenreich, B. (2001), *Nickel and Dimed*, New York: Metropolitan.

Green, F. in Burkitt, N. and Robinson, P. (eds) (2001) A Life's Work: Full and Fulfilling Employment?, London: IPPR.

Hillage, J., Regan, J., Dickson, J. and McLoughlin, K. (2002) *Employers Skills Survey*, London: DFES, IES, MORI.

HM Treasury (2000) *Productivity in the UK: The Evidence and the Government's Approach*, London: HM Treasury.

Hoque, K., Taylor, T., Westwood, A. and Bell, E. (2002) *Some of the People Some of the Time: Ten Years of Investors in People*, London: Work Foundation.

Keep, E. and Mayhew, K. (1998) *Was Ratner Right?*, London: Employment Policy Institute.

Lea, R. (2002) *Education and Training: A Business Blueprint for Reform*, London, Institute of Directors.

Learning Pool (and MORI) (2002) *Britain 2002: A Nation Ready to Learn*? London: Knowledge Pool.

LloydsTSB (2001) *Business in Britain*, Bristol: LloydsTSB.

National Skills Task Force (1998) *Towards a National Skills Agenda* – the first report of the National Skills Task Force, Nottingham: DfEE.

National Skills Task Force (2000) *Tackling the Adult Skills Gap*, Sudbury: DfEE.

Warhurst, C. and Nickson, D. (2001) *Looking Good, Sounding Right*, London: Industrial Society.

Westwood, A. (2001) *Not Very Qualified*, London: Industrial Society.

Westwood, A. (2002) *Is New Work Good Work?*, London: Work Foundation.

Westwood, A. (2003) *Are We Being Served?*, London: Work Foundation.

Westwood, A. and Jones, A. (2003) *FEUK: Can Colleges Cope?*, London: Work Foundation.

Wilson, R. (1999) *The Skills and Training Agenda*, London: IoD.

Wolf, A. (2002) *Does Education Matter?* Myths about Education and Economic Growth, Penguin, London.

4

The Interdependence of Social and Technical Skills in the Sale of Emergent Technology

Asaf Darr

Introduction

The shift from manufacturing to service occupations and the expansion of the knowledge sector are two significant yet seemingly contradictory trends in the contemporary world of work. The expansion of the service sector is associated with low skill, low wage and temporary jobs in fast-food restaurants, call centres and retail shops. Knowledge work, on the other hand, is epitomised by highly skilled and highly paid scientists working within R&D, harnessing science to industrial production. The growing prominence of service work and the expansion of the knowledge sector in advanced economies seem to be divergent trends. With the merging of telephone systems and computers, service workers in banking and insurance sales are deskilled. These service workers are controlled by the new technology and must follow ready-made scripts while interacting with customers (Leidner 1993). By contrast, the growing percentage and prominence of knowledge workers such as engineers, scientists and technicians in the workforce suggest that the trend is towards upskilling or reskilling (Barley 1996). Technical sales and sales support are rapidly expanding groups of workers. Within its daily practices, service and knowledge work seem to be merging.

A small but growing body of literature has recently suggested that the sales department in industries leading the current transformation of the socio-economic infrastructure is going through a technicisation process (Darr 2002). For example, in US leading-edge industries, the percentage of engineers holding formal academic degrees in the sales force almost doubled during the 1980s, from 12 to 22 per cent (US Department of Labor 1985, 1988, 1991). Similarly, sales support in the software industry increasingly involves technical experts (Pentland 1997). This is a clear, yet limited, indication that knowledge and service work are intertwined in sales of emergent technologies.

This chapter tells the story of the technical salesperson, whose work transcends most images of sales and knowledge work, questioning the assumed separation of technical and social skills. High levels of technical knowledge and know-how are associated with engineers or scientists working alone behind closed doors in R&D departments and planning offices, isolated from market exigencies. By contrast, workers in sales and services, who interact regularly with clients, are depicted as possessing minimal technical knowledge and know-how but possessing strong social and interactive skills. The technical experts who work in sales, representing a special breed of front-line workers (Frenkel *et al.* 1999), combine social and technical skills in their daily experience of work. Here, for technical skills to be implemented effectively, salespeople must possess and manage social skills.

Drawing on an ethnographic study of sales in a market for emergent technology, this chapter demonstrates that, contrary to many beliefs, as the technical complexity of sales increases, so does their dependence on social and interactive skills. The chapter claims that emergent technology enjoys an 'interpretive flexibility' (Pinch and Bijker 1987). Different social groups, buyers' and sellers' engineers and other technical experts in this case, hold different interpretations of the innovative products being sold, and must negotiate the exact design and use of emergent technology. The sellers' technical experts must develop a technological dialogue (Pacey 1993) with the buyers' engineers, as they adapt their products to their client's needs. To determine the feasibility of customisation work, which is labour intensive, the sales engineers and the client's engineers even engage in shared practice. In this capacity they write code and revise sketches together. This chapter describes the scope of social skills employed by sales engineers searching for prospective clients and extracting local engineering knowledge regarding product application from the client's engineers to customise their products.

Bell (1974: 126–127) claims that different production paradigms are marked by different games that people play. In pre-industrial societies the labour force engaged mainly in '...a game against nature', namely agriculture, mining and so on. In industrial societies, Bell argues, working life is 'a game against fabricated nature', in a society governed by machines. The service-oriented post-industrial society, Bell argues, is marked by '...a game between persons'. This chapter can be viewed as an attempt to flesh out the inner workings of the games between people during the sales of cutting edge technologies. Thus, the chapter contains in-depth descriptions and analyses of interview material, and sales interactions between sellers and buyers of emergent technology, as documented during interviews and observations at trade shows. Before the empirical section, a short discussion of the theoretical distinctions between technical and social skills is offered.

Defining Technical and Social Skills

Governments and economic institutions have long tried to measure and quantify types of skills as well as the complexity of different lines of work. The analytical distinction between technical and social skills underpins some of these attempts. For example, much of the sociological research on skill levels, which is based on the *American Dictionary of Occupational Titles*, combines three main dimensions: complexity in dealing with things, with people and with data, to create an overall measure of job complexity (Attewell 1990: 426). Technical skills are associated mainly with the manipulation of things while social skills are related mostly to dealing with people.

Including definitions of social and technical skills from different academic disciplines, such as economics and sociology, provides better conceptualisation of the growing interdependence of social and technical skills in the sale of emergent technology. Economists typically offer a restrictive definition of technical and social skills, often from the employer's perspective. For example, Green (2000: 253) defines technical skills as '... the ability to turn inputs into outputs' that is '... measured by the productivity of unit labour effort'. By contrast, social skills are defined '... by the propensity to behave in a manner conducive to the firm's objectives. In other words, social skills are constituted as the norm of effort contribution to which an individual assents, and are measured by observed motivation and behaviour' (p. 254).

Most sociologists conceptualise social skills within a broader framework than economists, specifically as part of 'social capital' (Stephenson 2001). Social capital includes the resources that actors can mobilise through their embedded ties with other actors within a network. Social capital is 'created when the relations among persons change in ways that facilitate social action' (Coleman cited in Knoke 1999: 19). Actors' social capital is developed through social interactions and new social ties provide social actors with new learning opportunities. Within the social capital perspective, social skills include interactive skills and strategic planning involved in constructing and manipulating a network of social ties. The aim of social actors, according to this approach, is to move from a peripheral to a more central position, within a network of social ties that constitutes a community of practice (Lave and Wenger 1991). Technical skills and specialised knowledge then become viewed as embedded within a network of social relationships (Uzzi 1997).

In the context of work organisations, there is growing agreement across disciplines that workers' social capital is as important an asset as technical skills to a firm's performance (Fontana 1990; Green 2000). Increasingly, firms are oriented to their clients and must enhance their workers' social skills to provide quality service in addition to exhibiting technical competence in producing high quality goods.

The desire to create a better fit between technical tasks and the social organisation of work has its roots in the socio-technical school. In fact, some of the founders of this school depicted organisations as both technical and social systems (Trist 1981). More recently, some evidence has emerged that social and technical skills are inseparable in contemporary work organisations. For example, Orr (1996) describes how photocopier technicians are part of an occupational community that maintains a collective memory of technical knowledge and know-how by telling stories of past experience when faced with new problems. The stories, which exist only in oral form, are used to devise theories as to the exact nature of the current technical problem. Here, the technicians' ability to solve technical problems hinges on their social capital and interactive skills. The knowledge and know-how is the property of a community of experts, not of individual members. More importantly, those photocopier technicians with a higher level of social capital are better equipped to solve technical problems which they encounter in their daily work since they have better access to these 'war stories'. In the light of the different definitions, the empirical section examines the degree to which social and technical skills are combined in the field of technical sales.

An Outline of the Research Subject

This chapter is based on a larger study that compared the sales process of standard and emergent technology in the US electronics industry (see Darr 2000, 2002). This chapter focuses only on emergent technology. The research involved observation of the work of technical salespeople in real-time computing, whose products assist the transfer, storage and processing of digital signals in real time. Popular applications are industrial robots, medical imaging, testing systems and many internet applications. For example, one company produced electronic filters designed to prepare analogue signals for digitalisation. The filters 'cleaned' the analogue signals of any 'noise', thus ensuring high quality digitalisation. They were used in a variety of applications, one of them being a testing system for noise generated by motorcycle engines, which was part of quality control at a leading US motorcycle plant. This being an emerging technology market, multiple standards exist in the market for real-time computing, and products are often named by the type of standard they adhere to, for example, 'PCI [peripheral component interconnect] products' or 'VME [virtual mode extensions] products', each representing a competing industry standard.

The sales process in the market for real-time computing was typically not mediated but directly between manufacturing firms and buyers. Independent sales representatives did exist but they only initiated sales transactions and played an ancillary rather than a mediating role in the sales process itself. In real-time computing the sales force was mostly composed of engineers, with formal academic training, who were called sales, customer or field application engineers. Other members of the sales department were simply called salespeople. The sales engineers in real-time computing rarely visited more than one client a month. On their sales visits, which lasted a week on average, they met the client's test and design engineers, negotiated the technical features of the client's application, diagnosed and solved technical problems with the products their company delivered, and offered training sessions. Technical salespeople also spent up to a week per month participating in specialised trade shows, where they collected information about prospective clients and new applications for their products.

Salespeople in real-time computing were paid a commission on their sales, which supplemented a basic salary that ranged between $20,000 and $40,000 a year. In general, technical salespeople had slightly higher basic salaries than other salespeople in the electronics industry who sold mass produced and standard 'passive' electronic components such as resistors or capacitors. They also had a better chance of making more commission. The profit margins in real-time computing were 30–70 per cent, compared with 5–20 per cent in the market for passive components. Because technical salespeople in real-time computing received commission on the gross amount of sales they generated, they were motivated simply to sell more products even by reducing the profit margins. By contrast, direct salespeople in the market for passive components received commission on the gross profits of sales they generated. Under these conditions, they were motivated to improve the profit margins rather than simply sell more. Salespeople in real-time computing received an average commission of three per cent on gross sales. One technical salesperson said at one of the trade shows that he was able to double his yearly income with the commission he made.

These salespeople were technical experts and knowledge workers. Like other knowledge workers, the sales engineers in this study earned a living based on neither ownership rights nor selling their muscle power, but instead relied on specialised knowledge and know-how gained, at least in part, through formal academic training. To test the skill levels of technical salespeople in real-time computing, a survey was conducted (N = 33; where N is the total number of salespeople sampled) during observations at a specialised trade show in the field. Of the salespeople sampled, 49 per cent held a formal engineering degree. This percentage is much higher than in more standard fields in the electronics industry (Darr 2002). In addition, 82 per cent of the technical salespeople had very specialised careers in the electronics industry. A questionnaire asked salespeople to specify their jobs since leaving high school. According to their responses, the vast majority of salespeople in real-time computing had launched their careers as design or test engineers, or as engineering technicians in electronics before moving to the sales department. In addition to their formal technical degrees, their previous jobs equipped them with extensive hands-on experience and contextual knowledge that enhanced their technical skills.

Two questions related to skill usage are explored here. Firstly, what types of social skills did the technical salespeople employ in their daily work, and for what purpose? Secondly, in what sense was there a growing inter-dependence of social and technical skills? The empirical section that follows addresses these questions, examining two main junctures of the sales process. First, it presents the social skills technical salespeople employ while searching for prospective clients and securing a sale. Second, it presents the array of social skills associated with extracting local engineering knowledge from the client's engineers as part of the customisation process.

Findings

The skills employed when searching for clients

The search for clients in real-time computing was characterised by a high level of uncertainty regarding the identity of potential clients. This uncertainty was described by a salesperson in real-time computing as follows:

> Our new business, it's based on a very new technology, there are just now beginning to be some commercial products. But we first showed it last November, and what we would do is go out to companies who we had thought would be our customers. We made some guesses, here are who we think we will sell to. We will go meet with them at the show and say, 'Here is what we are offering, we think that it makes sense for your company. Do you think it makes sense also? If you do, can we come and talk to you in more detail, show you what we have, and understand what you want?' And that is often how it started out.

This quote exemplifies how the lack of a common image of product use hindered the salesperson's ability to identify potential clients clearly. To overcome the uncertainty regarding the identity of potential clients, sales-people had to rely on their social skills as they engaged in a specialised search for clients. For example, the so-called 'guesses' regarding prospective clients made by this salesperson and his company were actually educated ones. The trade show at which his company introduced its new product was a special-ised show in real-time computing. In addition, the salesperson approached a small number of firms participating in the show only after he had collected information about their products at a previous show. This example is instruct-ive because it reveals the seller's need to understand the client's application of the product – a process to be resolved through social interaction.

Real-time computing was a nascent industry at the time of the study. Technical experts operating within it often worked in a number of companies in the course of their careers, and they developed specialised social capital. The term 'social capital' denotes here a network of active social ties with other technical experts within the industry. Since they relied on the supply of contextual engineering knowledge from the client to assess the feasibility of customisation, pre-existing social ties and already established trust were important assets. For example, at one of the specialised trade shows, a friendly social interaction between the seller, Bill, and the buyer, Joseph, took place. The two seemed like old acquaintances and mentioned a business lunch they planned for the following day at a Greek restaurant in the city. During lunch they intended to discuss the sale and customisation of a circuit board specifically designed for the quick transfer of large chunks of data over a network. Bill, the seller, had come across Joseph's name while surfing the Internet. Salespeople in real-time computing often surf the Internet in search of specialised bulletin boards in the field. These bulletin boards were used by a virtual community of design and test engineers. Messages typically consisted of calls for help and potential answers. Salespeople were not trying to acquire abstract knowledge of the field, but to learn about new applications in real-time computing. In the process they had to make use of technical knowledge in order to comprehend the questions and to identify those engineers who appeared to be working on potentially interesting applications for their own products. The electronic bulletin boards provided salespeople with what they considered 'qualified leads', but to assess the economic feasibility of adapting their products to the needs of a specific application, they said that they needed to interact directly with the client's engineers.

Bill, a technical salesperson, immediately identified Joseph's name because he used to work with Joseph, who had been a design engineer at a company at which Bill had previously worked. Reading Joseph's message on the electronic bulletin board, Bill noticed that he was asking for advice about video on demand, an application that Bill felt was feasible for a board manufactured by his company. Knowing Joseph personally, Bill described him as a talented and articulate design engineer. He counted on and trusted Joseph to facilitate the transfer of knowledge deeply rooted in engineering practice, which Bill needed to assess the cost of customisation. Thus, the earlier social tie with Joseph (social capital) and the trust existing between the parties was believed to assist the search for prospective applications.

Printed advertisements in the two leading journals in real-time computing were another source of sales leads. Sellers in the market advertised their products in journals that were read mainly by design and test engineers. The sellers' hope was to have their innovative product designed into the clients' prototypes. Typically, a client's engineer replied to the adverts either by sending an e-mail message or calling with a very specific technical question. A sales engineer described the type of problems engineers presented when they called in response to an advert:

> Typically we will receive a request for information from a technical person at a customer site. Much of it is government related. These calls for

information will be typically focused on a specific area or application, and in fact a specific task or challenge within that application. As an example, an engineer would call up with an application where he has to take radar data, move it into a computer system, rinse it through various DSP algorithms, and then display the information and control something like an anti-radar missile or something like that. Typically someone would call up and ask a very focused question: 'Once I get my data in, how do I move it very quickly over a BUS, from point A to point B, so that it will keep up in real-time with data coming in?'

Note that the content of conversation with the client's engineers was distinctly technical. This explains the seller's need to employ well-paid technical experts as what Frenkel *et al.* (1999) refer to as 'front-line workers'. But the technical salespeople also needed to employ social skills in securing the support of the client's engineers in closing a deal.

Requests for information from the client's design and test engineers often included a specific technical problem that needed to be addressed, as well as a description of the client's desired application. In other cases, the client's engineers telephoned to request a demonstration of the product at their plant in order to assess product quality. Some of the client's engineers who approached the sellers were distressed, perhaps because a deadline was looming. The sales engineers used this distress to their advantage and responded to the request for information by telephoning or meeting with the client's engineers. When they could, they offered their assistance but expected something in return. Through their interactions with the client's engineers they tried to enforce a norm of reciprocity. A salesperson in real-time computing described a first meeting with a client's engineer who had sent in a request for information about a circuit board:

In fact, it is sort of a barter system. The engineer would come in and say: 'I need information on your board, I need to know how to solve my problem'. So I would help him here, that is education. I would say, 'Here is a solution that you can use. What I need to know is how do I get your company to buy it? You have to say yes, but who else has to say yes? What is the process? What purchaser would be involved in this? What time frame?' Companies do not realise what important information you can get this way. I was told things by engineers that I would never consider saying to anyone outside my own company.

The sales process in real-time computing started in the engineering department, and then branched out to the purchasing department. From its initial stages it required the sales engineers to enhance their social skills. The example presented above exposes how information was sought regarding the decision-making process in the client's company. The sales engineers were ready to offer free advice to the client's engineers since they viewed this as an excellent investment in securing a sale. The more they gave, the more they could expect in return. The information search is explicitly described here as a social process of barter exchange. Clearly, reciprocity was pursued by the sales engineers to promote their business interests.

Client's engineers often requested a quote for a specific product being advertised, including the cost of the adaptation process. This product typically became part of a system, a client's engineer was working on. It was the responsibility of salespeople to assess the technical difficulties associated with the adaptation process and to come up with a quote. To do so they asked the prospective client to send in blueprints and other documents describing the system of which their product would become a part. This was done before any formal contract was signed. As one sales engineer put it, 'What we needed from these people [the client's design engineers] was information about their product...we needed to know how it works. We needed schematics and we needed to know if the design was changing.' But in most cases, written documents, representing a body of articulated knowledge about the application, did not suffice. The sales engineers had to initiate face-to-face meetings with the client's technical staff.

Salespeople searched for client's agents such as design and test engineers, who had intimate knowledge of the specific client's application. For example, a sales engineer working for a company offering a computerised circuit-board tester described the initial stages of the search for clients:

> The whole thing started with our western regional sales rep Joe Gray doing demos at the customer's site, following the customer's response to our ad...the customer sent out a list of information [about the application]. We sent them a list telling them what we need to evaluate their needs. It is a standard list we come up with. Things like schematics, documentation, a board, a blank board, what their test's goals are, you know, stuff like that. We learned along the years what we need. I also developed a liaison with the engineers, so if I had questions about how their product worked, I could call the engineers directly.

The need to learn about the client's application led the sales engineers to establish informal social ties with a large number of people working on the specific application. Technical experts with a better capacity to socialise with the client's engineers could perform better in customising their products. One salesperson described the variety of people with whom he interacted around a specific client's project:

> Very often we were introduced to the hardware and software team and then to the engineering manager overseeing both. So it was fairly common for us to meet senior engineer software, senior engineer hardware, line engineers for hardware and software. Toward the latter stages it would

be very common to meet with their product engineer, with their Quality
Control managers, Quality Control engineering people.

Thus a variety of actors were directly involved in buying and selling emergent
technology. As the sales process progressed, the sales engineers had to interact
with a variety of the client's employees to try and extract local engineering
knowledge.

Specialised trade shows in real-time computing crystallised an amorphous
field into a concrete form. While no salespeople expected to sell anything
during the trade shows, they did expect the shows to assist them in overcoming
'client uncertainty'. One salesperson described what, in his view, was the
main function of trade shows in real-time computing: 'One thing we have
learned from participating in trade shows', he said, 'is to understand who
our potential customers might be. We do not know any of it at first.'

Trade shows were specialised in that they involved only manufacturers in
real-time computing, and their visitors were design and test engineers working
for buyers in the market. Visitors could attend only at the invitation of sellers,
and this selection process created a specialised body of buyers. Although all
visitors were potential buyers, salespeople still needed to sort out client
applications that were not economically feasible. In fact, the goal of the
information search at trade shows was to identify 'qualified leads', that is,
clients' applications that appeared to be economically feasible.

The first step in obtaining qualified leads was to initiate social interaction
with visitors to the show. When visitors registered at the entrance, they were
handed a tag showing their name and organisation. Interestingly, some of
the visitors, specifically those working for the government or large corporations
such as Xerox and Kodak, preferred wearing their companies' security tags,
bearing their picture, name and the name of the company they worked for.

The salespeople at the show stood before their display tables and looked
at the name tags of customers going by. Jim, a salesperson at a local show,
described the difficulty of attracting the attention of visitors walking by:

> In shows like these, people often just walk by like this [Jim raises his eyes
> to the ceiling and whistles a tune], and you are supposed to say, 'Oh, you
> are from NASA, come on over here'. In a show that I thought was prob-
> ably the worst one, I mean only 75 customers showed compared to 75–100
> vendors, and one guy was walking by, looking up at the ceiling. So I just
> said: 'Department of Energy? What are you doing?' So this guy stopped
> and came by, and asked me if we would be interested to see their request
> for quotes, and I said yes, and the following week he sent me the request,
> and I won the bid for $175,000.

While initiating interaction with clients required some initiative, the rewards
were obviously high. But the vast majority of interactions during the trade
show did not end with a swift and large sale like the one in the example

above. In fact, salespeople were satisfied if they emerged from a specialised trade show with eight or ten qualified leads. To identify those qualified leads, salespeople engaged in intense conversation with prospective clients once they had succeeded in attracting their attention.

Time was a limited resource at the trade shows, and the salespeople wanted to be exposed to as many potential clients as possible. Thus, the prompt termination of a sales interaction with an unqualified lead was crucial to the sellers' success at the trade show. Terminating a social interaction with a visitor required the sales engineers to master their social skills. When salespeople realised that the specific application was not feasible or required too much customisation work, they quickly ended the interaction by sticking their hand out for a quick handshake. To refrain from leaving the visitor feeling insulted, they directed him or her, with a deft gesture, to an open notebook on the display table, where they asked them to write their names and organisational affiliation. They promised the visitors to send them more information about their products by mail and bade them farewell. Then they were free to initiate a new sales interaction.

When a specific application seemed interesting and feasible in economic terms, salespeople invited the prospective client to an on-site demonstration of their product. Product demonstrations proved an efficient way for salespeople to gather contextual knowledge about the clients' application. They used this knowledge to help them assess the economic prospects of the customisation process. The vast majority of exhibit booths included some sort of demonstrations of the products offered for sale. These included, among other things, demonstrations of diagnostics software and digital image editing. A typical demonstration involved sitting the prospective client in front of a computer screen beside a salesperson who guided him or her through the different menus. A second salesperson continued interacting with visitors to the show as they went by the display table.

Test and design engineers who participated in the demonstration typically had a specific technical problem in mind. Frequently asked questions at the start of the demonstration were, 'Could this board add memory power and interact with a VME BUS?' and 'Could this testing system be integrated into a production line and be operated by production workers?' These questions assisted salespeople in presenting features that could address the specific problem. As the salesperson took the potential client through the specific feature, the client often reacted by offering a detailed description of related problems, and allowed the salespeople to offer other features of their product as a possible remedy. By encouraging a potential client's engineers to experiment with the product, salespeople were able to achieve a number of goals. First, they extracted some contextual knowledge about the desired use for their product. Second, they presented their product as a solution to practical problems the client's engineers had encountered. In this way, the salespeople started to integrate their product into a body of contextual knowledge possessed by client's engineers.

At many demonstrations, the sellers or the buyers realised that the product and the desired application were mismatched. But in a few cases salespeople saw potential in a client's application. Following the more 'successful' demonstrations, salespeople asked for the client's business card and wrote on its back the specific application the customer's company sought. They would then put the business card into their shirt pocket. It was only those pocketed business cards, and not the names written in the notebook, which were deemed 'qualified leads' by salespeople. In addition, the number of business cards was a direct measure of the success of a particular show. For example, at the end of a specialised trade show in Houston, Texas, a sales engineer took a stack of business cards out of his pocket and started counting them. 'Eight', he said, 'That's not bad for a low turnout like we had today.'

Sellers in real-time computing were constantly trying to cut the cost of their search for information about the client's application. One skill was to identify visitors to the trade show who had been close to buying from the seller in the past. The seller had already invested in the search for the desired application and could hope to close the deal this time. For example, in one of the specialised trade shows, a company offering a device consisting of a PC and software for the analysis of laboratory tests in the field of electrical engineering had a display booth. Two salespeople were serving visitors. The first was sitting at a PC being used to demonstrate the software. The second salesman was standing in front of the display table, his hands behind his back, carefully looking at the name tags of visitors walking by. It was just before noon and there were many visitors who had gone in to enjoy the free lunch that was about to be served. Suddenly, the salesperson rushed right into a group of visitors standing 15 feet away looking at circuit boards displayed by a different company. The salesperson literally grabbed one visitor by his arm and pulled him towards his booth. 'This is Eric from Houston University', the first salesperson said, introducing the prospective client to the second salesperson sitting at the computer, 'We came to his lab twice and gave him a demo of our last version, but he ended up buying the lab software from Bob (the speaker pointed to the booth of a competing company down the hall), but I still call him a friend. Can I still call you a friend?' The salesperson stared into the eyes of the visitor as he waited for his answer. The potential client, clearly embarrassed by this blunt attempt to make him feel guilty for buying from a competitor, was silent for a while. Then he said: 'We are thinking about buying a new testing software.' The salesperson looked pleased and told his colleague, who was in charge of running the demo. 'Well, Joe, just go ahead and give him the full demo.' He led the client to Joe at the computer and pulled up a chair for him. In this case, the seller did not need to assess the feasibility of customisation. After all, he had a good idea of the desired application from the two sales visits to the client's site a year before. But in this sales interaction the sales engineer employed a different type of social skill, the manipulation of the client's emotions by making him feel guilty – to draw on the discussion of emotional labour by Bolton in Chapter 2.

Skills employed when customising their products

The lack of a shared image of product use required salespeople in real-time computing carefully to assess the feasibility of possible applications for the products they offered for sale. These salespeople were constantly in search of new uses for their innovative products. After all, new applications meant new potential clients. They used specialised trade shows, electronic bulletin boards and their social ties with other engineers working in R&D to identify 'qualified leads'. But at the same time not all applications were economically feasible for the small engineering firms that constituted the majority of manufacturing firms in real-time computing.

The great majority of products in real-time computing had to be customised; that is, adapted to a client's specific application. The customisation process, after a contract was signed, was labour intensive and expensive. The sales engineers often worked on an adaptation process for long periods, often for six months or more. During that time they were prevented from pursuing other possible applications for their products for different clients. In fact, the high cost of customisation was the main constraint on the search for new product applications. To overcome it, salespeople became experts at managing their working ties with the client's engineers.

Salespeople claimed that their companies provided customisation as 'a customer exercise', as one of them carefully put it. What they meant was that sellers in real-time computing tried to transfer the burden of customisation by urging buyers to use their own resources and engineers to adapt the product to their specific needs. Success in this endeavour meant that the sales engineers could save time and money for their firms. Since each customisation process was managed as a 'profit centre', cutting costs and improving profit margins was credited to the sales engineer in charge of the particular project. But in most cases, the strategy of transferring the burden of customisation failed and the sales engineers had to customise their products themselves. The clients often paid a fixed price for the product, which included the customisation process, but the actual work was done by the sales engineers.

Many of the sales engineers worked individually with a number of clients, and were required by management to be responsive to the exigencies of the market. Management held sales engineers responsible for delivering a customised product on time, for ensuring the client's satisfaction and, most importantly, for returning a profit. The sales engineers' professional success hinged on their ability to obtain from the client contextual information through social interactions and the construction of formal and informal ties.

To obtain contextual information about the application, the sales engineers employed a number of search practices, in which social and technical skills were intertwined.

To socialise with the client's engineers once a contract was signed and to construct working ties with them, the sales engineers had to rely on their social skills. They had to present themselves to the client's engineers as members of their occupational community who wished to work together with them. As one sales engineer put it: 'I think people like buying from experts but as engineers they want the experts to be peers, not someone lofty and above them.' In this respect, the social skills involved in technical sales encompassed aesthetic labour (Nickson *et al.* 2001); that is, dressing and talking like an engineer rather than a salesperson or a manager, in order to establish trust with the client's engineers. For example, during trade shows, unlike most salespeople, the sales engineers dressed casually, much like the engineers who visited the show, as if declaring they were members of their professional community, not regular salespersons. The same was the case during sales visits, when sales engineers dressed like design and test engineers, not salespeople. More importantly, their occupational identity was that of a 'real engineer', not a salesperson (see Darr 2000).

The first move of the technical salespeople after a contract was signed, and designed to obtain contextual knowledge about the client's application, was to identify the best 'contacts' in a client's plant and establish informal relations with these engineers. Choosing the right contact was not easy because the problem, as sales engineers often put it, was to find the client's engineer who was actively involved in designing or testing the application. When asked who on the client's side they were searching for, one sales engineer selling a computerised testing device replied, 'I'm looking for the engineer who actually designed the board to be tested.' To identify the right informant, or 'contact', sales engineers consulted their peers and engaged in long telephone conversations with various of the client's engineers. Here again, they also activated their social capital, a pre-existing network of social ties within their occupational community (Van Maanen and Barley 1984).

Establishing new ties with engineers outside the company required time and effort. Since relationships between the engineers were informal and often initiated by salespeople, salespeople had to persuade the client's engineers to answer their questions. In one case, a sales engineer searched for the designer of an application and soon found out that he had left the firm two years before. The sales engineer told a group of sales and R&D engineers over lunch at his company's dining room how he was able to locate the designer even though he had switched companies twice since designing the application. The engineers with better social skills were more successful in soliciting the client's engineers' help. The reason that the design engineer in this example cooperated with the sales engineer was because cooperation among engineers regarding technical problems is a professional norm and serves as a safety net within the profession. This norm of cooperation underpins the success of the many specialised electronic bulletin boards, in which engineers seek help and provide technical assistance to other engineers in cyber space.

Some clients in real-time computing were sometimes reluctant to share information about the desired application. For example, private companies working on innovative products were at times protective of their application. This complicated the work of the sales engineers even further and required them to hone their social skills. A sales engineer described his attempt to gather information in a government agency:

> They have an application where they can't, listen to this, this is really classic, they can't tell me very much about it, because it is a government application. In fact, sometimes I found I knew more about it than the [client's] engineers did, because they are compartmentalised and were only told what they needed to know. And I talked to their colleagues down the hall, and I knew more and more about the application.

As apparent in this example, the activity of the technical salesperson at times resembled detective work and required soliciting the cooperation of various members of the client's technical staff.

The sales engineers treated their social ties with the client's experts as a valuable asset. The maintenance of these ties was perceived as an integral part of the customisation process. A sales engineer at one of the companies, returning from a visit to a client's plant in Mexico, lamented that his contact in the project team in Mexico had told him of his plans to leave his job. The sales engineer felt his sale partner's resignation would hamper his attempts to gather all the information he needed and to complete his customisation process on time and within the budget. The sales engineer also stressed that he would need a 'new contact' in the project team at the client's site as soon as possible.

Conclusion

This chapter has told the story of skilled engineers selling cutting edge technologies, whose highly specialised technical skills are most valuable to employers only when accompanied by a specialised set of social skills. Though an analytical distinction between social and technical skills may be valuable in theory, this distinction makes little sense in practice to sales engineers who have to master both types of skills in order to assess the feasibility of customisation and to extract contextual knowledge and know-how about the client's application. The two skills employed in the sales process in real-time computing are an example of 'bulkanisation' (Barley 1996) in which skill sets are increasingly fused together in work within the advanced economies.

This chapter also depicted the social games that occur during the sale of cutting-edge technologies. Clearly, there is an element of manipulation in the games initiated by technical salespeople, as suggested by Bell (1974). In addition, the empirical section demonstrates that different games between people are initiated at different junctures of the sales process. At the initial stages of the sale, the technical salespeople try to control and manipulate the social interactions with prospective clients. The efficient termination of sales interactions at the trade show without hurting the visitors' feelings is but one example. The technical salespeople also engage in the manipulation of emotions, as when they try to make a visitor feel guilty for not having bought from them at a previous encounter. Finally, basic social norms such as reciprocity are enacted to learn about the political landscape at the client's plant. The sales engineers are part of a barter exchange, where they help the client's engineers solve their technical problems but in return expect to receive information about the decision-making process and about the client's managers who make the purchasing decisions.

After the contract is signed the sales engineers and the client's design and test engineers compose a distinct work unit and jointly engage in co-development. Co-development involves frequent face-to-face interactions, the sharing and replication of experiential knowledge, and the development of shared interpretations of product application. Social and interactive skills are crucial for achieving these tasks. At this stage the social games shift more towards construction of working ties with the client's engineers and the management of the flow of local knowledge and know-how about the exact features of the client's application. The sales engineers have to solicit the cooperation of various members of the client's technical staff. Rather than relying only on universal norms such as reciprocity, the sales engineers activate professional networks to identify the best informants in the client's plant. As in the case of lawyers (Tolbert and Stern 1991) technical salespeople refer to their relationships with buyers as a tangible asset.

Many of the categories scholars use in studying work organisation originate in the manufacturing era. Some of these categories no longer apply to contemporary work organisations. For example, the work of technicians in high-tech settings is neither blue-collar nor white-collar. Instead, technical experts combine in their work intellective and manual skills (Barley 1996). Similarly, the interdependence of social and technical skills seems to be growing in technical sales and sales support. More and more workers, who as with the sales engineers outlined here, must combine and master the two types of skills in their daily work. As a consequence, maintaining the distinction between social and technical skills will fail to address the shifting skill needs in contemporary work organisation.

References

Attewell, P. (1990) 'What is Skill?', *Work and Occupations*, 17:4, 422–448.

Barley, S. R. (1996) 'Technicians in the Workplace: Ethnographic Evidence for Bringing Work into Organisation Studies', *Administrative Science Quarterly*, 41:3, 404–441.

Bell, D. (1974) *The Coming of Post-Industrial Society*, London: Heinemann.

Darr, A. (2000) 'Technical Labour in an Engineering Boutique: Interpretive Frameworks of Sales and R&D Engineers', *Work, Employment and Society*, 14:2, 205–222.

Darr, A. (2002) 'The Technicisation of Sales Work', *Work, Employment and Society*, 16:1, 47–65.

Fontana, D. (1990) *Social Skills at Work*, London: British Psychology Society and Routledge.

Frenkel, S. J., Korczynski, M., Shire, K. A. and Tam, M. (1999) *On the Front Line*, Ithaca: Cornell University Press.

Green, F. (2000) 'The Impact of Company Human Resource Policies on Social Skills: Implications for Training Sponsorship, Quit Rates and Efficiency Wages', *Scottish Journal of Political Economy*, 47:3, 251–272.

Knoke, D. (1999) 'Organizational Networks and Corporate Social Capital', in R. Leenders and S. M. Gabbay (eds), *Corporate Social Capital and Liability*, Boston: Kluwer.

Lave, J. and Wenger, E. (1991) *Situated Learning: Legitimate Peripheral Participation*, Cambridge: Cambridge University Press.

Leidner, R. (1993) *Fast Food Fast Talk*, Berkeley: University of California Press.

Nickson, D., Warhurst, C., Witz, A. and Cullen, A. (2001) 'The Importance of Being Aesthetic: Work, Employment and Service Organisation', in A. Sturdy, I. Grugulis, and H. Willmott (eds), *Customer Service*, New York: Palgrave.

Orr, J. E. (1996) *Talking about Machines*, Ithaca, NY: ILR Press.

Pacey, A. (1993) *The Maze of Ingenuity*, Cambridge, Mass.: MIT Press.

Pentland, B. T. (1997) 'Bleeding Edge Epistemology: Practical Problems Solving in Software Support Hot Lines', in S. R. Barley and J. E. Orr (eds), *Between Craft and Science*, Ithaca: Cornell University Press.

Pinch, Trevor J. and Bijker, W. E. (1987) 'The Social Construction of Facts and Artifacts: Or How the Sociology of Science and the Sociology of Technology might Benefit each other', in W. E. Bijker, E. C. Hughes and T. J. Pinch (eds), *The Social Construction of Technological Systems*. Cambridge, Mass: MIT Press.

Stephenson, S. (2001) 'Street Children in Moscow: Using and Creating Social Capital', *The Sociological Review*, 49:4, 530–547.

Tolbert, P. S. and Stern, R. N. (1991) 'Organizations of Professionals: Governance Structures in Large Law Firms', *Research in the Sociology of Organizations*, 8, 97–117.

Trist, E. L. (1981) 'The Evolution of Sociotechnical Systems as a Conceptual Framework and as an Action Research Program', in A. H. Van de Ven and W. F. Joyce (eds), *Perpectives on Organization Design and Behaviour*, New York: Wiley-Interscience.

US Department of Labor, Bureau of Labor Statistics (1985) *Occupational Employment in Manufacturing Industries*, Washington, DC: US Government Printing Office.

US Department of Labor, Bureau of Labor Statistics (1988) *Occupational Employment in Manufacturing Industries*, Washington, DC: US Government Printing Office.

US Department of Labor, Bureau of Labor Statistics (1991) *Occupational Employment in Manufacturing Industries*, Washington, DC: US Government Printing Office.

Uzzi, B. (1997) 'Social Structure and Competition in Interfirm Networks: The Paradox of Embeddedness', *Administrative Science Quarterly*, 42:1, 35–67.

Van Maanen, J. and Barley, S. R. (1984) 'Occupational Communities: Culture and Control in Organisations', in B. Staw and L. L. Cummings (eds), *Research in Organizational Behavior*, 6, 287–365, Greenwich, Conn: JAI Press.

5

Training Reform in a Weakened State: Australia 1987–2000

Ian Hampson

Introduction

Over the past two decades, Australia has undertaken extensive reform of its training arrangements. This chapter argues that low state autonomy and a lack of cooperation from key business interests have undermined the potential of training reform in Australia. The Australian case may well be unusual internationally in terms of how the trade union movement articulated a series of proposals for training reform and sought to shape national training policy. Training reform was initially driven by reformist elements of the trade union movement via 'corporatist' links to the Australian Labor Party (ALP) Government (1983–1996). These corporatist arrangements have attracted considerable attention and widely varying interpretations. They held together despite strong tensions, created by the damage done to the trade union movement and to state autonomy itself by the economic liberal policies that the ALP pursued (Ewer *et al*. 1991; Hampson 1997).

The training reform proposals sought to increase training expenditure, and put in place national and workplace level mechanisms to ensure transferability of qualifications. Unfortunately, (except in highly unusual circumstances) the Australian state lacks autonomy due to the bicameral and federal structure of government. The Constitution assigns power over training and education to state governments. The most powerful sector of business (finance and mining, comprising the nation's largest firms) opposed the initial training reforms and against this opposition, the union proposals, despite considerable policy sophistication, could not prevail. Thus, the course of training reform in Australia resonates with the pessimistic scenario laid out by Crouch *et al*. (1999). In this scenario, large employers increasingly take responsibility for their own training, effectively withdrawing from national training arrangements. The state abdicates control of skill formation to employers to such an extent that public capacity is lost and national skill formation policy becomes an expression of short-term corporate interests. Employers are enticed through subsidisation to offer employment under the guise of 'training'. 'Training' as skill formation is degraded to 'training' as unemployment amelioration.

The chapter's first section briefly describes the general problems of training policy and the specific problems faced by Australia in the 1980s. The second section sketches the rise and fall of the so-called 'national training reform agenda' (NTRA). The third section describes the increasing marketisation of training under the Liberal–National Coalition Government (1996 to the present) and the fourth section describes the results of reform. Taken together, the chapter chronicles an interventionist training reform agenda, which was dependent on a favourable constellation of state autonomy and/or business cooperation, and which failed because both of the latter were lacking.

The Problem of Training Policy and a Potential Trade Union Role

As Crouch *et al.* (1999) argue, training policy is increasingly dependent on a collective approach, but the core ideas of current policy (economic liberalism) increasingly reject this collectivism. Worse, as Streeck (1989, 1992) has emphasised, effective training is increasingly dependent on the cooperation of employers. But trade union intervention, if appropriately supported by the state and/or corporatist arrangements, could *theoretically* provide much of the collectivism necessary for national training policy to work. Reformist elements of the Australian trade union movement proposed exactly this kind of intervention, but unfortunately just when the forces of economic liberalism and business opposition to 'outmoded interventionism' were strengthening.

Why would employers oppose training reform? First, the oft-quoted 'Beckerian' analysis of market failure applies well to the Australian manufacturing sector. Employers will be reluctant to invest in skill formation because workers may leave, taking the employer's training investment, possibly to a competitor. The most rational course of action from the point of view of the *individual* employer is to recruit skilled labour from an external labour market. However, because each employer seeks to recruit, and not train, the consequence is under-investment in training and an under-supply of skilled workers (Streeck 1989, 1992; Crouch *et al.* 1999). Second, employers that do train are increasingly inclined to ensure training's direct subservience to immediate organisational needs. Modern human resource management stresses the 'strategic training' perspective, in which training and development are key sources of competitive advantages. Training needs analysis and evaluation ensures the minimisation of training activity that is not directly targeted on organisational needs (e.g. Blanchard and Thacker 1998). Training has also become instrumental for the shaping of corporate cultures and identities.

But the cooperation of employers is increasingly necessary for skill formation, especially as a *national* project (Crouch *et al.* 1999). Workplace skills are best learned on the job. 'Advanced' skills must be a broad 'polyvalent' resource, able to be put to as yet unknown future uses; to enable trained employees to deal with unanticipated production contingencies (Streeck 1989: 96–97). The formation of these 'broad, polyvalent' skills may require less 'strategic' training activity and more training 'slack'. Streeck has also argued that a strong trade union presence in the firm, supported by the state or corporatist arrangements, might help with skill formation. Intervention by trade unions could shape employers decision-making to support indigenous skills development (Streeck 1992). Firstly, unions could monitor firms' compliance with externally generated training curricula. Such curricula would stress the formation of the broad and general skills of the 'new' workplace, and would deny firms the 'strategic training' option. Secondly, unions could monitor firms' training expenses and activity, for alignment with training plans agreed in national- or industry- level forums. Thirdly, such monitoring would ensure that trainees received 'proper' training and that their activity was not diverted into cheap labour, with the attendant danger of issuing undeserved or bogus qualifications through compromised assessment systems. Fourthly, payment systems that stress payment for knowledge and skills possessed (and certified) rather than skills employers preferred to use, would encourage production strategies that made greater use of skill (Streeck 1992). Trade union involvement in training reform in the 1980s in Australia echoed the above ideas.

The ALP leadership's rejection of the union reformers' manufacturing industry policy proposals (Ewer *et al*. 1987) directed their gaze to industrial relations and training reform. Transnational corporate penetration of Australia's manufacturing, behind high levels of industry protection prior to the tariff reduction programmes, had discouraged technological dynamism and associated training. But by the mid-1980s, amidst industrial restructuring, certain weaknesses in Australia's skill formation and industrial relations processes were widely recognised, and were politicised by employers. Here, there was some overlap between their aims and those of employers, leaving the way clear for sweeping work reorganisation and training reform.

The reform process converged on the award system which was the central workplace training regulatory mechanism. Awards (the outcomes of determinations of industrial tribunals) defined work boundaries and skill requirements with the force of industrial law. Crucially, some important union structures were also built around skill or occupational categorisations enshrined in industrial awards. Thus many workplaces were afflicted by industrial demarcations that, employers argued, inhibited 'flexibility' (e.g. BCA 1987, 1988, 1989). Work reorganisation therefore implied changes to long-established links between union structures and the regulation and organisation of work. Reformist sectors of the unions also sought to shift union members' loyalties beyond 'craft unionism' to a more politically comprehensive 'political unionism'

(Ewer *et al.* 1991). Training reform was thus highly sensitive within the union movement itself, although broadly supported at the top. The challenge for the union movement was how to control the changes and prevent them simply expressing employers' preferences – with all the dangers for training as emphasised above.

Until reform commenced in the mid-1980s, most training was accomplished through the apprenticeship system, which was vulnerable to the following criticisms. Firstly, it was oriented towards initial training. Mechanisms for further training (or 'lifetime learning') were weak or non-existent. This approach inhibited adjustment to new technologies and promoted technological conservatism. The system emphasised 'serving your time', as opposed to demonstrated competence (Dawkins 1988). Access to trades was limited to young males and lacked gender equity. Training for non-trade workers was limited to 'on-the-job training' via the 'buddy system' (Smith 1983), which was unsupported by public qualification structures, and was often unsystematic, non-comprehensive haphazard and quite possibly dangerous. Secondly, the training system was plagued by under expenditure, arising in part from market failure. Australia's employers have historically been reluctant to contribute to the costs of training, viewing the latter as a cost, as opposed to an investment. This gave rise to chronic and ongoing skills shortages (Dawkins 1988). The availability of skilled labour moved with the economic cycle, as employers cut apprenticeship intakes in times of recession, exacerbating labour shortages in boom times (Ewer *et al.* 1991). Thirdly, there was a yawning gap between schooling and work, with no structured transition between the two. This gap led to charges of irrelevance of training and education by employers, which were often justified, and to new labour market entrants lacking marketable skills (Dawkins 1988). Overseas missions admired training systems, particularly the German, where education, training and the transition to work were much more structured and integrated (DIR/MTFU/MTIA 1988). Fourthly, Australia did not have a unified *national* approach to training, and lacked institutional mechanisms to support the transfer and recognition of skills, especially across state borders (Dawkins 1988; DIR/MTFU/MTIA 1988). This lack of transferability impeded labour mobility by making it difficult for employers to be sure of new recruits' competence. It undermined workers' employment options and their bargaining power. It could also lead to the decay of skills, as displaced workers failed to gain employment. The apprenticeship system was fragmented by federalism. Constitutionally, education, training and the apprenticeship system is the responsibility of individual Australian states (ABS 2000). Thus short of constitutional reform via referendum (an unlikely prospect) any attempt to reform the system towards national integration would require considerable cooperation between state and federal governments of different political persuasions.

The Rise and Fall of the National Training Reform Agenda

In 1987 the trade union reformers and their allies in the bureaucracy issued a crucial document known as *Australia Reconstructed* (ACTU/TDC 1987), which set much of the agenda for training reform. Among other things, this document criticised the misallocation of investment attendant on deregulation (three months prior to the stock market crash) and directed attention towards a number of problems in Australia's skill formation arrangements mentioned above. At the time, the 'industrial' left maintained that industrial efficiency and economic competitiveness were mutually supportive rather than mutually exclusive. Union power, they thought, could be increased through participation in public policies aimed at improving international competitiveness. The trouble was that these policies also struck at the self-interest of major employers.

The union reformers advocated increasing employer expenditure on training through a levy, and making their training activity accountable to unions and public authorities. Employers would be required to pay a proportion of their payroll into a National Employment and Training Fund. They would be able to receive a rebate of 80 per cent of training expenditure once unions and employees agreed that the training satisfied quality requirements (ACTU/TDC 1987). The apprenticeship system would move beyond 'front-end training' towards 'lifelong learning' and away from its 'discriminatory' base in craft unionism. Access to training would be opened beyond the traditional young male constituency (ACTU/TDC 1987; DIR/MTFU/MTIA 1988). Skills-based career ladders, 'objective' recognition of skill and national institutional carriage for qualifications completed the picture. There were thus two strands to the reforms: industrial and political/institutional.

The various industrial reforms converged on a project known as award restructuring (Anon, 1988; DIR/MTFU/MTIA 1988). In many instances, awards prescribed Taylorist work organisation, and cemented distinctions between 'skilled' and 'unskilled' workers, denying career paths to the latter. The union reformers proposed rewriting (restructuring) awards to permit multi-skilling and the development of skill-based career paths. The driving force of these reforms came from within the Australian Metal Workers Union (AMWU) and their principles were laid out in their 'Guidelines for Organisers' (AMWU 1988). These principles were: the career paths would allow progression from the lowest levels to the highest through training and skill acquisition; payment systems would encourage skill acquisition by linking pay grades to skill grades; and the classification system would be based on skill. It would be sufficiently broad and flexible to accommodate changes to technology and management systems. But crucially, award restructuring around skill-based career ladders required a reliable system of skill recognition (assessment) and institutions that would allow cross-industry recognition of skill (AMWU 1988; DIR/MTFU/MTIA 1988; ACTU 1989; Ewer *et al.* 1991).

The solution was competence-based assessment, copied from the British National Vocational Qualifications (NVQ) system. 'Competence' is one of the most vexed terms in the managerial lexicon and prone to slippage. In the hands of the union reformers, the concept was synonymous with 'skill', but integrated with an objective methodology to discern the latter's presence. This chapter is not the place to debate the merits of competence-based training. However, it should be said that at the time the union reformers appeared unaware of the many criticisms made in the educationist literature about competence-based training as an impoverished system of learning and as a suspect system of assessment (e.g. Wolf 1995). The attractiveness of a plausibly objective methodology for the recognition of skill was industrial, not pedagogical.[1] Recognition of prior learning would allow reclassification and pay rises for employees who were till then paid less than they were 'worth'. The potential of competence-based training to reinforce classic Taylorist practices did not dawn on the reformers until much later. The concept of 'competence', plus policies for its implementation in a national framework, was developed by National Training Board (NTB 1991).

It fell to the ALP Government to implement institutional mechanisms to ensure national carriage of qualifications, a task for which it was ill-equipped. The Australian state suffers from weak autonomy for the reasons mentioned earlier – federalism, and constitutional limitations on federal education and training powers. In addition, the government's reforms reflected its economic liberal predilections and its business leanings.

In 1990, Ministers of Vocational Education, Employment and Training (MOVEET) agreed to adopt a national approach to the recognition of competencies and in March 1992 they adopted the centrepiece of the NTRA – the National Framework for the Recognition of Training (NFROT). NFROT's function was to ensure national integration of training outcomes, expressed as competency standards, in an Australian Standards Framework (ASF) – the centrepiece of the NFROT (Allen Consulting Group 1994). The ASF, developed by the NTB, proposed eight levels of competence (NTB 1991) to which was later added the notion of 'key' competencies – generic skills (e.g. literacy, working in teams and working with technology) that any worker should have to some degree (Mayer 1992).

The unions wanted employers to increase their financial contribution to training, while the government, arguing that its contribution was already internationally comparable, sought greater contributions from 'industry', that is employers *and* employees (Dawkins 1988). The implication was a levy on employers and below-award training wages for employees, which unions initially opposed (see ACTU/TDC 1987) but eventually accepted (Carmichael 1992). The government did not support the unions' proposal for a National Employment and Training Fund but instead enacted the *Training Guarantee Levy Administration Act, 1990*. This Act was designed to provide a pool of capital to fund a training market, as recommended by the CEO of Nissan

Australia (Deveson 1990). It required firms over a certain size ($200,000 payroll) to allocate one per cent of their payroll to 'structured' (that is certified and accredited) training that met national standards. If they did not do so, they had to forfeit that amount, or the balance, to the tax office. Training would be assessed by Registered Industry Training Agents (RITAs), composed of representatives of employers and unions, accredited and monitored by the NTB. In the ACTU scheme, employers would have to make a case to retrieve 'their' money and satisfy unions that it had been appropriately spent. In the government's scheme, employers had to satisfy RITAs, on which they had representation, that their training was *bona fide*. The onus of proof was thus favourable to business. The Confederation of Australian Industry (CAI), representing mainly medium-sized manufacturing business, broadly accepted this system (e.g. CAI 1991), but the Business Council of Australia (BCA), representing the largest 'global' sectors of business, opposed it.[2]

In 1992 MOVEET recommended the establishment of the Australian National Training Authority (ANTA) and the government enacted the *Australian National Training Authority Act, 1992*. Part of ANTA's brief was to develop a National Strategic Plan for Vocational Education and Training (VET), which in itself was a tacit acknowledgement that the above institutions were flawed. In 1993 the relevant government minister noted that the NFROT was clearly not working and that the reform process was in danger of stalling (*Weekend Australian* 1993). The reform process was fragmented, sometimes driving in opposite directions. The construction, *ex nihilo*, of a *centralised* institutional backbone for a national training system, against business opposition, required considerable state autonomy and political will, both of which were lacking. But industrial relations *decentralisation* was proceeding apace and award restructuring was being shaped more by business interests than by any national training agenda. These two points are now considered in turn.

First, the constitutional limitations on federal power have already been detailed. They meant that the formation of any national training system required the consent of all state MOVEET, some of them with varying political complexions and views about training reform. Thus the NTB could not be formed under statute, with power to compel firms' compliance with training standards. Instead, it was set up under a 'memorandum of understanding' among the members of MOVEET. Its brief was to assist industry to develop and implement competency standards (NTB 1991). Apart from moral suasion, its main lever was the ability to withhold accreditation from RITAs, which administered employers' tax obligations under the Training Guarantee Levy (TGL) Scheme.

With weak administration of employers' new training expenditure obligations and the logic imposed by the requirement that firms spend their training allocation on 'training' or forfeit it in tax, the stage was set for the abuse of the TGL scheme. The apparent increase in training expenditure evident in statistics is therefore suspect, most likely a result of creative account-ing practices. Nor could the administrative arrangements compel employers' use of national competency standards. In some cases, the competency regime was seen by employers (correctly) as the thin end of the wedge for union interventions with, for example, skills-based payment systems, 'payment for skills acquired' (rather than used) and seeking wage rises through reclass-ification and recognition of prior learning – especially for low paid female workers. In other cases, the competency standards were simply of very poor quality, as was acknowledged by the head of the NTB (Allen Consulting Group 1994).

Second, industrial relations decentralisation was in conflict with the cen-tralisation of the embryonic national training system. The union reformers planned that the new competency standards were to be written into the restructured awards and the award system would regulate workplace training to ensure comparability and transferability of qualifications. On commencing its political incumbency, the ALP built on the already highly centralised nature of the industrial relations system, particularly with respect to wages, with the Accord at the centre.[3] But with the pace and nature of economic change, and pressures from employers and unions to decentralise, it proved impossible to sustain this system. Employers (especially the Business Council) attacked the existing award system as a haven for inefficient 'work practices', and ran a highly successful public campaign against it, pressing for something called 'enterprise bargaining'.

The various Accords from 1988 drove the award restructuring process. The ACTU and the government agreed that wage rises should be contingent on unions accepting major changes to workplace regulation through awards. The Australian Industrial Relations Commission (AIRC) oversaw this process and was the arena for a contest over the *form* that award restructuring should take. The ACTU and the AMWU reformers wanted the Commission to support the nationally oriented skill agenda through award restructuring. However, the BCA was able to convince the Commission that changes to awards should be more wide ranging and should not support a national training system (BCA 1990). Instead, restructured awards should ensure that 'working patterns and arrangements enhance flexibility and meet the com-petitive requirements of the industry' (AIRC 1988: 6, quoted in Ewer *et al.* 1991: 42). Thus a far wider range of matters than training reform would be on the table for negotiation during award restructuring, including changes to working hours, penalty rates, staffing levels, annual leave and sick leave. These inclusions paved the way for a reduction in working conditions.

Another key to a training regime congenial for workers was employers' provision of paid training leave, a statutory requirement in such countries as France, and one sought by the union reformers (DIR/MTFU/MTIA 1988). With poor timing, paid training leave was a matter of contentious negotiations over the terms of the restructured Metal Industry Award on the eve of the

1990 election. The union negotiators wanted the award to specify that training should be undertaken with reference to the NTRA and the NFROT, and contain provisions for paid training leave. This was important not just for the Metal Industry because the restructured award was to be a template for others. These issues spilled into the public arena and the media focused on the issue of the ALP's and ACTU's inability to 'control the unions'. Pressure came from within the labour movement for the union negotiators to drop their demands, as preserving the ALP's political incumbency took precedence over workers' interests in the training provisions in the restructured and exemplary award (Ewer *et al.* 1991; Lloyd 1990). The provisions regarding training leave entitlements and the reference of training standards to the NFROT in the 'restructured' metal industry award were thus considerably weakened.

Adding all this together, it was obvious that the union-oriented training reforms had failed. The statement by Ross Free in 1993 was only public acknowledgement of failures that were widely known throughout the training community. Minister Free thus asked ANTA to recommend ways of improving the NTRA, and to this end ANTA commissioned the Allen Consulting review, which reported in 1994 (Allen Consulting Group 1994). The report was scathing in its assessment of the NTRA, and was essentially a plea to 'deregulate' and marketise it. It argued that the NTRA was not clearly defined (ibid.: 18). Some of its objectives were unclear, and were an inappropriate basis for strategy generation. It was overly bureaucratic, with a 'top-down' approach that business found offensive. Many enterprises felt 'roped in' to the competency standards and felt that they expressed an 'industrial relations agenda'. Thus business felt a 'lack of ownership' of the reforms (pp. 35–37). The training market was not working properly, and was too limited to large firms – smaller firms found it difficult to get access. The ASF and the NFROT were not working, in particular because assessment 'was a major unresolved issue' (p. 35). Crucially, the review questioned the value of the public funding of training and rejected the usual market failure arguments for government intervention and public spending on training, instead suggesting that the biggest impediment to employers spending on training was 'wage inflexibility'.

From this analysis, recommendations followed. These were, in summary, to improve the operation of the training market, and to increase employer 'ownership' and control of the system. Employers and employees should jointly decide on the purchase of recognised, off-the-job training in a training market.

> Australian policy should develop a training market around direct client relationships between training providers on one hand, and enterprises and individuals on the other – and in which skills held by individuals are publicly recognised and portable to the maximum extent possible (p. iii).

Employers should pay only for skills they used, irrespective of employee qualifications. The review affirmed support for the goal of accredited training, portable 'to the maximum extent possible' (p. 37). But the limits were to be set by the needs of the enterprise. Thus the 'strategic training' perspective attained supremacy over public policy goals, although disguised by suitable handwringing and expressions of caution.

> No one is clear about how far a national course can be varied in content to meet the specific needs of an enterprise, while retaining integrity as a course leading to a qualification (p. 25).

'Broad comparability' between higher-level qualifications (above AQF3) would ensure that providers of training have 'the freedom and the will to tailor and customise training responses to enterprise demand yet deliver publicly recognised training at the same time' (p. 39).

All these changes were to take place over a three-year time frame, beginning in 1995. Thus the 'new' national training strategy was born which the Conservatives would shape from 1996, after Labor's electoral defeat. Through 1992–1994, the institutional structures of the NTRA were progressively undermined and a 'new' direction was taken. The BCA took advantage of the institutional flux to reject intervention into its 'strategic training', although it approved of Competence-Based Training (CBT). In July 1993 the BCA argued that large employers themselves could become Registered Training Organisations (RTOs), accredit their own training programmes, and develop an 'enterprise-stream' of training 'within' the NTRA (*Australian Financial Review* 1993). The NTB agreed, on condition that the BCA use its terminology and use generic competencies when applicable. The ACTU objected that the resulting regime would be too deregulatory, leading to reduced quality and transferability of training (Allen Consulting Group 1994). Even so, the proposal was endorsed by ANTA in July 1993, and accepted by the NTB and MOVEET, and indeed by the government in its White Paper on Employment (ANTA 1994; Keating 1994).

Working Nation is the name of the former ALP Government's employment White Paper, released in 1994 as unemployment soared to 11.3 per cent (Keating 1994). The central feature of *Working Nation* is the links forged between training and employment policy. Training and 'job placements' massage downward the politically sensitive unemployment statistics since a person in training is not an unemployed person. But in this process, there is great danger that the trainees/unemployed will be exploited and that the quality of training will be low.[4]

The centrepiece of *Working Nation* was the 'Job Compact', according to which the government undertook to provide the long-term unemployed who were receiving unemployment benefit with a job or training in the private sector for 6–12 months. In return, the unemployed had to accept the 'placement' or lose their benefits for the period of the compact. The long-term unemployed, those who had been unemployed for 18 months or more, were to be assigned to potentially coercive individual case management to become 'job ready'. The major mechanism was to extend an already existing programme known as *Jobstart*, which already provided employers with wage subsidies to take on 'targeted' persons, in particular long-term unemployed. Training wages, justified by the argument that the trainees were being paid full rates for work but less for the training component, shifted training expenditure to trainees. When the two were combined, the effect was to dramatically lower the cost of employing a trainee to as low as $10 per week (Campbell 1994).[5]

In return, employers were obliged to provide 'structured' training. However, the definition of 'training' was flexible – 'formal instruction, both theoretical and practical, and supervised practice' (Campbell 1994: 15). As Campbell points out, the notion of 'supervised practice' could be indistinguishable from paid labour. Moreover, because the greater the amount of training, the less the employer had to pay, there was an incentive to increase the proportion of the latter and to define work as training. And, as described above, because the mechanisms to supervise the training were weak, there is doubt about the value of the training. There were incentives for employers to sack trainees (on some pretence) once they had completed their 'training' to provide a new 'placement' to a new 'trainee' for new subsidies. Thus Campbell expressed concern that the scheme would encourage 'labour market deregulation by the back door', undermining both wages and the quality of training (p. 15).

Marketisation under the Liberal/National Coalition Government

The ALP Government lost power in 1996 and with it went the remnants of the 'corporatist' links to the unions that had, some argued, impeded 'reform'. The Liberal Government was therefore able to pursue the path of training liberalisation further than the ALP could. However, once again the dispersed nature of political power in Australia, in particular the existence of an Upper House of Parliament in which the Liberals lacked a majority, thwarted the new government.

The Liberals sought to drive a wedge between industrial relations and training, and to turn the system over to business. Their first Budget asserted that 'business needs to be in a much stronger position to influence training policy and planning, and individual enterprises need to have more say in how training is delivered' (Kemp 1996: 8). The Liberals sought to dismantle much of the national institutional edifice of training that Labor had built; to implement a 'new' training system known as the Modern Australian Apprenticeship and Traineeship System (MAATS); and to remove training regulation from awards. The context was a breathtaking reform agenda that emerged through 1996.

Key 'corporatist' training institutions such as the National Board of Employment Education and Training (NBEET) and the Employment and Skills Formation Council (ESFC) (both havens for Labor apparatchiks) were simply abolished, though others were kept. The role of the NTB in ensuring compliance of firms' training programmes with national competency standards for taxation purposes was redundant, with the abolition of the TGL in 1996 (having been suspended in 1994 by the Keating Labor Government). It was thus renamed as the Standards and Curriculum Council (SCC) and was subsumed within ANTA. Much funding for ANTA was redirected to MAATS, which was designed as an extension of the 'traineeships' that burgeoned under *Working Nation*, and to overtake the old trades-based apprenticeship system. It aimed to offer 'flexible' mixes of training and schooling, to allow employers to pay trainees less and to provide a 'wage top-up' from the taxpayer when training wages fell too far (Kemp 1996: 3).

This action required a major programme of industrial relations change. Briefly, this programme was comprised of familiar attacks on unions and limitations on the right to strike and organise. For the first time a new stream of individual contracts, known as Australian Workplace Agreements (AWAs), would be part of mainstream industrial relations. The powers of Australia's 'independent umpire', the AIRC, would be further reduced. Labor's 'unfair dismissal' provisions were to be stricken from the Act. Awards were to be 'simplified', and reduced from a primary means of employment regulation, to a 'safety net' (a similar desire had been announced by the then Prime Minister Keating after the 1993 general election). Henceforth they would regulate only 5–6 matters, and training would not be one of them. Training agreements would be regulated by State Training Authorities (STAs), not industrial tribunals, although the training *wage* would be regulated through awards. Income support measures for trainees, where employers' payments did not reach training wage levels, would only be available for trainees employed under individual contracts or non-union collective agreements (known as Certified Agreements) (Kemp 1996). However, the new *Workplace Relations Bill* had to pass the Senate, as explained above, where the Democrat Party in the Senate (with sympathies for small business) agreed to pass a diluted version of the Bill. In this version, awards would regulate '20 allowable matters', of which the first mentioned was 'job classifications and career paths' (*Workplace Relations Act 1996*: s89A). This situation still left it unclear whether training could be regulated through awards and was from time to time contested in the AIRC. However, the drift of reform was clear – awards were becoming unsuited as vehicles to impose national training standards on the workplace.

The training reform agenda was reshaped following the Allen Consulting Group's review in 1994 and a 'new' strategy was put in place to last from 1994–1997. This strategy was in place when the Liberals acquired political incumbency. Then a new strategy was put in place, portentously entitled

A Bridge to the Future, to last from 1998–2003. The key initiatives are 'training packages', strengthening the Australian Recognition Framework (ARF), new apprenticeships and extending the latter into schools. The aim of 'increasing investment' is tempered by its counterpart, 'growth through efficiency' (see ANTA 1998). Training packages include competency standards, teaching resources, assessment guides, guides to how to integrate the achieved competencies into nationally endorsed qualifications and so on in a form that could conceivably be purchased 'off the shelf'. They are nationally endorsed by the SCC, developed by Industry Training Advisory Bodies (ITABS), and in some cases RTOs (training providers), and even some enterprises which have met the appropriate criteria (i.e. have been defined as RTOs). Although the training packages specify which combinations of competency standards make up the qualifications of an industry, the rules are sufficiently flexible to allow enterprises and individuals the greatest possible scope to combine standards towards a qualification. This approach could allow employers to design combinations of competencies directly in accord with their needs (following the 'strategic training' perspective), which could lead to highly idiosyncratic combinations of competencies and defeat the objective of transferability.

The Allen Consulting review pointed out that under Labor, the crucial function of national recognition had been neglected and had essentially failed to work. The review recommended renewed development of what became known as the ARF, which was a direct descendant of the old NFROT, with at least one important difference. The centre of the old NFROT was an eight-level ASF, which represented an ambit claim that professional qualifications, including university qualifications, should be brought within the training framework. The universities successfully resisted this incorporation. In 1997 the Liberals abolished the ASF in the context of the development of a new ARF and Australian Qualifications Framework (AQF). The new AQF is a six-level framework, running from certificates 1–4, with diploma and advanced diploma (but not degree). Thus the dream of Labor reformers of a career path starting on the shop floor and ending with an engineering degree was finally lost.

The Allen Consulting review also insisted that the recognition requirements – that training programmes align with national standards and qualifications – were too onerous for employers. The irreducible tension between national recognition and strategic training was dealt with by having a more relaxed definition of competency standards and more 'flexibility' in their enforcement. This approach was expressed in the post-1998 National Strategy and the national recognition process that was, essentially, a delegation of recognition powers to the RTOs. From the start of 1998, RTOs had to be registered under a state authority and were called upon to self-assess and to self-manage training recognition. This positioning potentially imposed too great a load on the ethics of RTOs to resist competitive pressures that would compromise the assessment process.

Consider: the Liberals' reforms were designed to further the marketisation process begun by Labor. Trainees and employers could choose a mix of work, training and schooling, and a training provider appropriate to their needs. A pool of money was available for the funding of the new apprenticeships, which was to be paid in the form of wage subsidies to employers. Training was further subsidised by low training wages and absolving employers of having to pay wages for time spent in training. The training providers operate in a market, in competitive relations with each other, and tender for training contracts from individual trainees, employers or the government. The training providers, or RTOs, once recognised and accredited, are entrusted with the responsibiltiy to self-assess. They self-manage training recognition and are essentially free from external interference. Here then is a mix of incentives lethal for quality training. Employers have an incentive to take the wage subsidy and define work as training. However, as a condition of receiving the subsidy, they have to provide 'structured', that is nationally accredited training. Whether the training meets this criterion is decided by a RTO, with a structured conflict of interest. The RTO provides the training and assesses whether trainees meet the appropriate criteria. But if it insists on high quality and more expensive training, it risks losing its contract to its competitors. The incentive is for the RTO to pass workers, not properly qualified – in other words, to issue bodgy qualifications.

The Failure of Training in Australia

The outcomes of the training reforms will only be sketched here. Advocates of the system point to the dramatic increase in numbers of 'New Apprentices', in a context of cost containment. But limited financial resources and lax regulation have caused a dramatic failure of quality in the system, as found by a number of inquiries that took place through 1999–2000, including by Australia's Senate.

Under Labor, total training expenditure (as a percentage of gross wages and salaries) rose from 2.2 per cent in 1989 to 2.9 per cent in 1993, before falling to 2.5 per cent in 1996 (URCOT 1999). Since the Liberals took office, there has been a dramatic rise in overall numbers of trainees, or as the new government prefers to refer to them, 'new apprentices'. In 2001 the then Minister for Education and Training claimed a 40 per cent increase in the number of such apprentices in a year (*Australian Financial Review* 2000) and an increase of 60,000 apprentices since the start of the government's scheme in 1996. There has been a 77 per cent increase in the number of 'students' in the VET system between 1991 and 2000 (NCVER 2001: 4), and a 5.6 per cent increase in subject enrolments and 4.6 per cent increase in annual hours since 1999 (p. 11). What is not in doubt is that the system has expanded enormously.

However, the much vaunted increase in training expenditure under Labor was short-lived and almost certainly a result of creative accounting (URCOT 1999). Supporting this view, despite the rise in training expenditure between 1989 and 1993, training hours per employee actually fell, from 5.7 to 5.6, before falling further to 4.9 in 1996 (URCOT 1999: 8–9). Labor suspended the scheme in 1994 and the Liberals killed it off in the 1996 Budget. Furthermore, the dramatic increase in 'new apprentices' is misleading. First, the terminology deliberately obfuscates the distinction between traditional, trades-based apprenticeships and the 'new' traineeships especially in retail and clerical. Failure to observe this distinction disguises the decline in traditional apprenticeships – from 136,664 in 1980 to 123,100 in 1997 (URCOT 1999: 7). Not surprisingly, skill shortages remain in the metals and engineering and other sectors. Second, the bulk of the expansion of training is at lower levels of qualification. Only 21 per cent of student enrolments were at AQF certificate IV level or higher in 2000 (NCVER 2001: 10).

The increase in trainee numbers has not been matched by a corresponding increase in resources injected into the system. In 1998 the Liberals implemented a 'funding' strategy of 'growth through efficiencies'. As a result, $70 million dollars per year of growth funding was removed from the training system (SEWRSBERC 2000: xxiv). Government expenditure on training per course hour fell from $9.34 to $7.73, a decline of 17 per cent in real terms. VET income per course hour fell from $11.24 in 1996 to $11.03 in 1997 to $9.82 in 1999, a fall of 11 per cent in just two years (ABS 2000, in Considine *et al.* 2001: 4, 29–30). It would be surprising if this reduction did not put strain on the quality of training in public institutions.

Quality was also under attack in the workplace and became politicised. Anecdotes of employer abuse of the system compiled to the point that Labor attacked the government in the Senate. Labor claimed that employers were putting new *and existing* employees into training schemes, claiming subsidies and other benefits from the government (in particular, the State Government of Victoria), paying trainee wages while employees were working 'normally' but not supplying training as required by the scheme. In some cases, credentials were issued despite training being substandard or even non-existent. A number of inquiries were held into the state training system and the federal system, which reached broadly similar conclusions (Schofield 1999, 2000; SEWRSBERC 2000).

In sum, the reports found that the 'obvious' conflicts of interests that RTOs, performing the two functions of training and assessing in a competitive market, find themselves naturally gave rise to unethical practices, including issuing faulty qualifications and even types of fraud (SEWRSBERC 2000). The old problems of mutual recognition of courses, qualifications and now RTOs remain. As the Senate report noted, state training authorities have adopted widely differing approaches to the registration of training organisations, auditing and other forms of supervision, and enforcement of adherence to the NTF. There are, therefore, differences in the availability of training packages, differences in nominal hours and therefore funds and training activity allocated to different courses and qualifications. This situation means that it is impossible to assume equivalence, and therefore portability, of qualifications and skills from one jurisdiction to another. Relatedly, the emphasis on meeting the needs of employers is similarly allowing too much enterprise-specific training to be done (at public expense), which, the Senate report argued, should be done by employers themselves (SEWRSBERC 2000).

Conclusion

Australia demonstrates the disarray in training policy that occurs when training reform is undertaken by a weakened state, along economic liberal lines, in the face of determined opposition from powerful employer groups, influenced by notions of 'strategic training'. Here, the tendency is for training policy to reflect short-term employer concerns and political expediency, with deleterious consequences – ultimately, the loss of collective public capacity to shape training, the reduction of the latter to *mere* employment policy, and training's further degradation to subsidised labour for unscrupulous employers and opportunistic trainers. Because there was considerable economic liberal influence on the training policies, and the state was disinclined or powerless to resist, there is considerable continuity between Labor and Liberal approaches to training reform, although the Liberals have taken marketisation and responsiveness to employers' 'needs' to new heights.

Trade union intervention within corporatist arrangements seemed to offer the possibility of a training utopia. However, the union proposals lacked sufficient support from a government too heavily influenced by economic liberal pro-employer interests opposed to the tenor of the proposed reforms. With the collapse of Australia's corporatist experiment, the incoming Liberal National Coalition Government sought to build on Labor's reforms while removing training regulation from the mainstream industrial relations system. In this endeavour it has been partly but not totally successful, as there remain sectors (such as metals) where significant agreement exists between employers and unions over training. Training reforms have increasingly emphasised that training should reflect enterprise needs, with the result that the provision of intra-industry and inter-firm transferable qualifications has been compromised. Perverse incentives and lax centralising mechanisms adversely affect the conduct of training, assessment and the issuing of qualifications at workplace level. The rapid expansion of the training system has been achieved at the expense of the quality of training and in areas where little training is needed to achieve 'competence'. The case of Australian training reform thus conforms to the pessimistic scenario outlined by Crouch *et al*. (1999) in which employers withdraw from national training arrangements and the state relinquishes control of skill formation to those employers. National skill formation policy then becomes an expression of short-term corporate interests and skill formation too closely aligned with subsided employment and policies to address unemployment.

Notes

1 The absence of educationist expertise from central institutions of training has been a perennial issue of concern (e.g. SEWRSBERC 2000).
2 Disunity among business interests is a characteristic of the Australian reforms.
3 Readers unfamiliar with the structures of Australian industrial relations need to note the central role of the Australian Industrial Relations Commission (AIRC). The Constitution gives the Commission a quasi-judicial and independent (although circumscribed by legislation, and declining since the 1980s) role in the arbitration of industrial disputes and the setting of awards. The Commission would hear arguments from employers, unions and government, and make rulings with some independence. Under the centralisation of Australia's 'corporatism' of the 1980s, the Commission could set aggregate wages movements through 'National Wage Cases' at a stroke. The Commission used its central position to oversee the decentralisation of industrial relations (hence 'managed decentralism') and a powerful lever to this end was its ability to make wage rises conditional on certain actions by trade unions, including productivity bargaining and the 'restructuring' of awards. The 'Accords' were agreements between the government and ACTU, which emphasised wage restraint and restrictions on union militancy in return for 'influence' (often minimal) on government policy. The Accords moved from Mk1 in 1983 to Mk8 in 1996, the latter ones enforcing various degrees of decentralisation.
4 See also chapter 7 for discussion about similar developments in the US.
5 In Australian dollars.

References

AIRC (1988) Australian Industrial Relations Commission, *National Wage Case*, August, Print H4000.

Allen Consulting Group (1994) *Successful Reform: Competitive Skills for Australians and Australian Enterprises*, Report to the Australian National Training Authority, Sydney: Allen Consulting Group.

Anon (1988) *The Australian Vehicle Manufacturing Industry: Award Restructuring. Report of the Tripartite Study Mission to Japan, United States of America, Federal Republic of Germany, and Sweden*, Melbourne: Ramsay Ware.

Australian Bureau of Statistics (2000) *2000 Year Book Australia*, Canberra: AGPS.

Australian Council of Trade Unions (1989) *National Wage Case: ACTU Blueprint for Changing Awards and Agreements*, Melbourne: ACTU.

Australian Council of Trade Unions/Trade Development Council Secretariate (1987) *Australia Reconstructed*, Canberra: AGPS.

Australian Financial Review (1993) 'BCA to pursue enterprise-based job qualifications', 17 August, 37.

Australian Financial Review (2000) 'Labor Questions Dr Kemp's figures on apprenticeships, Friday, 28 January, 3.

Australian Metal Workers, Union (1988) *Award Restructuring: Guidelines for Organisers*, Sydney: AMWU.

Australian National Training Authority (1994) *Description of the National Training Reform Agenda*, Brisbane: ANTA.

Australian National Training Authority (1998) *Australian Training*, Brisbane: ANTA.

Blanchard, P. and Thacker, J. (1998) *Effective Training: Systems, Strategies, and Practices*, Englewood Cliffs, New Jersey: Prentice-Hall.

Business Council of Australia (1987) 'Towards an Enterprise Based Industrial Relations System', *Business Council Bulletin*, March, 6–10.

Business Council of Australia (1988) 'Policies for Skill Formation', *Business Council Bulletin*, November/December, 4–11.

Business Council of Australia (1989) *Enterprise Based Bargaining Units: A Better Way of Working*, Melbourne: BCA.

Business Council of Australia (1990) 'Submission to the Training Costs Review Committee', *Business Council Bulletin*, November, 22–33.

Campbell, I. (1994) 'The White Paper: Labour Market Deregulation by the Back Door?', *Just Policy*, No. 1, 13–19.

Carmichael, L. (1992) *The Australian Vocational Certificate Training System, Report of the Employment and Skills Formation Council*, Canberra: National Board of Employment, Education and Training.

Confederation of Australian Industry (1991) *CBT The Australian Vocational Education and Training System*, Sydney: CAI.

Considine, M., Marginson, S., Sheehan, P. and Kumnick, M. (2001) *The Comparative Performance of Australia as a Knowledge Nation: Report of the Chifley Research Centre*, Melbourne: Monash Centre for Research in International Education.

Crouch, C., Finegold, D. and Sako, M. (1999) *Are Skills the Answer? The Political Economy of Skill Creation in Advanced Industrial Economies*, Oxford: Oxford University Press.

Dawkins, J. (1988) *Industry Training in Australia: The Need for Change*, Canberra: AGPS, Department of Employment, Education and Training.

Department of Industrial Relations, Metal Trades Federation of Unions and Metal Trades Industry Association (1988) *Towards a New Metal and Engineering Industry Award*, Sydney: Breakout Printing.

Deveson, I. (1990) *Training Costs of Award Restructuring. Report of the Training Costs Review Committee*, Canberra: AGPS.

Ewer, P., Hampson, I., Lloyd, C., Rainford, J., Rix, S. and Smith, M. (1991) *Politics and the Accord*, Sydney: Pluto.

Ewer, P., Higgins, W. and Stephens, A. (1987) *The Unions and the Future of Australian Manufacturing*, London: Allen and Unwin.

Hampson, I. (1997) *The End of the Experiment: Corporatism Collapses in Australia, Economic and Industrial Democracy*, 18:4, 539–566.

Keating, P. (1994) *Working Nation: Policies and Programs*, Canberra: AGPS.

Kemp, D. (1996) *Training for Real Jobs: the Modern Australian Apprenticeship and Traineeship System*, Department of Education, Employment, Training and Youth Affairs, Canberra.

Lloyd, C. (1990) 'Accord in Discord', *Australian Left Review*, July, 11–13.

Mayer, E. (1992) *Employment-related Key Competencies: A Proposal for Consultation*, Melbourne: Mayer Committee.

NCVER (2001) National Centre for Vocational and Educational Research, *Annual Statistics*, Vol. 7, Australian National Training Authority.

NTB (1991) National Training Board, NTB Network, Canberra: National Training Board, June, 1, 1, 10.

Schofield, K. (1999) *Report: Independent Investigation into the Quality of Training in Queensland's Traineeship System, Prepared for the Vocational, Education, Training and Employment Commission*, Queensland: Department of Employment, Training and Industrial Relations, July.

Schofield, K. (2000) *Delivering Quality: Report of the Independent Review of the Quality of Training in Victoria's Apprenticeship and Traineeship System*, Victoria: Office of Post-Compulsory Education, Training and Employment.

SEWRSBERC (2000) Senate Employment, Workplace Relations, Small Business and Education References Committee, *Aspiring to Excellence: Report of the Inquiry into the Quality of Vocational Education and Training in Australia*, Canberra: Commonwealth of Australia.

Smith, R. (1983) 'Sorting Out Responsibilities for Training the Work Force', *Discussion Paper No. 70*, Department of Economics, Research School of Social Sciences, Australian National University: Canberra.

Streeck, W. (1989) Skills and the Limits of Neo-Liberalism: The Enterprise of the Future as a Place of Learning, *Work, Employment and Society*, 3:1, 90–104.

Streeck, W. (1992) 'Training and the New Industrial Relations: A Strategic Role for Unions?', in M. Regini (ed.), *The Future of Labour Movements*, London: Sage.

Union Research Centre into Organisation and Technology (1999) *Picking up the Pieces: Trade Union Strategies for Vocational Education and Training*, Sydney: URCOT.

Weekend Australian (1993) 'Standards dilemma for National Skills Program', *Weekend Australian*, 3–4 April, 52.

Wolf, A. (1995) *Competence-Based Assessment*, Buckingham: Open University Press.

6

Exploring the Concept of Employer Demand for Skills and Qualifications: Case Studies from the Public Sector

Helen Rainbird, Anne Munro and Lesley Holly

Introduction

The view that the problem of the British education and training system is not simply a question of the problem of supply of qualifications in the labour market has finally been accepted in government circles (Performance and Innovation Unit 2001; HM Treasury 2002). There are ongoing concerns about basic skills and the supply of intermediate level skills, but the recognition of the need to address employer demand for skills has been a significant development. The British economy has been conceptualised as being trapped in a 'low skills equilibrium' (Finegold and Soskice 1988) whereby institutional mechanisms reinforce, rather than counter, low levels of demand for skills. This has been linked to product market strategies and employers' preference for segments of the market where price rather than quality provides a competitive edge. Keep and Mayhew (1999: 12) argue that there are two elements to employer demand. These are: first-order decisions relating to product market and competitive strategy and second-order decisions about work organisation and job design.

The aim of this chapter is to explore the concept of 'employer demand for skills'. We take Keep and Mayhew's distinction between first- and second-order management decisions as a starting point. Because we are concerned primarily with the public sector, we would argue that the concept of product market and competitive strategy can also include the way in which 'quality' is defined in the public services and how this intersects with political decisions concerning the allocation of resources raised through taxation. We recognise that work organisation and job design are central to the ways in which skills are deployed in the workplace, but would add to this the role of training and development in management systems. This would include the use of performance management, quality assurance and tools such as the developmental review for the identification of individual and organisational training needs. Work organisation and job design also need to be examined in relation to recruitment and training strategies so that the skills and qualifications workers bring with them or acquire during their employment are brought into the equation. This includes not only the employer's investment in training and development, but also the extent to which skills and qualifications are used and enhanced through work routines and job mobility in internal labour markets.

Although the concept of employer demand is normally considered in relation to private sector companies in debates on competitiveness, here, we explore it in the public sector. This is a good site to investigate employer demand for skills for all our criteria: business strategy, organisational systems, work organisation and job design. As far as business strategy is concerned, there is a discourse of commitment to the quality of public services, whether it is through the 'Best Value' initiative in local government or to improvements to patient care in the National Health Service. Moreover, the government is effectively the employer in the public sector, so we might expect to see a commitment to 'high skills' exemplified in management processes, in approaches to Human Resource Management (HRM) in general and to training and development in particular. Insofar as the public sector is relatively labour-intensive, it could be argued that the quality of service could be judged by the quality of interactions between the public and front-line workers. We explore the question of employer demand for skills through the analysis of research on low-paid workers in the public sector, which was conducted under the Economic and Social Research Council's 'Future of Work' programme.[1]

The project 'The future of unskilled work: learning and workplace inequality' examined the extent to which changes in manual work and routine clerical jobs have been leading to an increased emphasis on training and development. There were two major elements to the research: case studies of three local authorities and three hospital Trusts, involving more than 330 face-to-face interviews. In two of the case study organisations, a survey of employees' learning experiences was conducted, which produced a similar number of responses. In each case study, interviews were conducted at corporate level; with trade union representatives; with managers and trainers in particular departments; and with workers, their managers and supervisors in individual, often quite small, workplaces which were part of these organisational structures. Officers of the trade union UNISON facilitated access to all six organisations which were chosen because they had established partnership agreements with the union on the provision of learning and development opportunities for low-paid workers (e.g. Communications Skills and Return to Learn). At corporate level all the organisations had a formal commitment to equal opportunities in employment and to the development of employees through the achievement of the Investors in People (IiP) standard. The fieldwork was conducted in 1998–1999 (see Rainbird *et al.* 1999 for a report of the findings).

Product Market Strategies and Employer Demand: The Public Sector Context

The public sector in the UK has undergone a series of reforms over the last twenty years. The period of the Conservative government (1979–1997) has been characterised as involving the increasing centralisation of financial control, the devolution of management authority, the fragmentation of organ- isational structures and support for increasing competition between the public and private sectors (Winchester and Bach 1999). Compulsory competitive ten- dering was first introduced into local government in the 1980s and extended by the 1988 Local Government Act to a wide range of ancillary services. In 1983 the Secretary of State for Social Services issued a circular requiring all health authorities to put hospital cleaning, catering and laundry services out to private tender (Coyle 1985). Although the election of a Labour govern- ment in 1997 has introduced changes to the financing and management of the public sector, Winchester and Bach (1999: 22) argue that very few of the Conservative government's reforms have been reversed. In both local gov- ernment and the NHS, 'quality' is not amenable to a simple definition and, as Kirkpatrick and Martinez Lucio (1996: 6) have pointed out, it has an intensely political nature.

In local government, one of the most significant changes since 1997 has been the introduction of the requirement to seek 'Best Value' in the letting of public sector contracts. This replaced compulsory competitive tendering whereby local authorities were required to put services out to tender and to accept the lowest bid. Compulsory competitive tendering resulted in a signifi- cant reduction in public sector employment and cost reductions were achieved at the expense of the wages and conditions of the workforce. In contrast, 'Best Value' involves placing greater emphasis on service quality as well as cost in the letting of contracts and requires the periodic review of services against performance targets. As Winchester and Bach (1999: 32) point out, this means that public sector managers are frequently confronted by 'difficult, if not incompatible, objectives such as the provision of better-quality services with diminishing real resources'. In other words, quality in this context refers to delivery to specification within budget rather than customisation of ser- vices (cf. Keep and Mayhew 1999: 6).

To what extent does the changing basis of public service contracts affect approaches towards the training and development of employees? Colling (2000: 76–77) argues that subcontracting does not inevitably lead to particular types of employment relationships. Where price competition is the significant driver, contracts are likely to be short term and costs tightly controlled by the buyer. In contrast, where the client organisation works with preferred con-tractors, the contract may provide greater security and a consequence of this may be to reduce the pressures on labour costs. There may be more incen-tives to invest in the training and development of employees in the 'mutual interdependency model'. Nevertheless, the control of quality and the labour process remain an issue for the client. There is evidence that where detailed contract specification is used to standardise the quality of services, it reduces worker discretion and limits training to that needed for narrowly defined job roles (Grugulis *et al.* 2003; Rainbird *et al.* 2003). Where contracts have been retained in-house, public sector managers have been required to control expenditure, monitor performance and introduce private sector manage-ment techniques and this has contributed to work intensification. Wadding-ton and Whitston (1996: 173) argue that labour intensification lies at the heart of workplace relations across all sectors. They report that workload and staffing levels have been a particular source of grievance for trade unionists in the public services.

In the same way, managers in the NHS have attempted to reconcile the political need to improve the quality of service and the economic drive to reduce costs, particularly staffing costs. In the 1980s and early 1990s Conser-vative governments sought efficiencies through the introduction of market relationships. A distinction was established between purchasers (health authorities and general practitioners) and providers (NHS Trusts). This rep-resented a shift from the notion of the public sector as the 'good employer' and established private sector practices as central to efficiency in the public sector (Stuart and Martinez Lucio 2000). The Labour Government, elected in 1997, removed the purchaser/provider divide and encouraged more cooperative employment relations through partnership working and staff involvement. Nevertheless the encouragement of private sector employment practices has remained, with a renewed emphasis on performance targets. The implication for workplace learning and development is that Trust managers feel they have been receiving mixed messages. On the one hand, there are elements of the return to the 'good employer' with opportunities for all staff to develop, learn and progress. On the other, achieving targets often results in narrow, task-specific training and pressure to intensify work.

One Measure of Employer Demand: The Match between the Qualifications held by Workers on the Lowest Salary Grades and those required for the Job[2]

It could be argued that one measure of employer demand for skill would be the qualifications needed to get a particular job. Although this is a poor measure of the ways in which skills and knowledge are mobilised in work routines, it provides a quantitative indicator of the relationship between the formal qualifications held by the workforce and those established as an entry requirement by the employer. The 1997 Skills Survey found that 32 per cent of respondents reported that no qualifications were required on entry to their current jobs although only one-fifth reported having no qualifications at all. On the basis of this evidence, Ashton *et al.* (2002: 63) argue that 'the overall supply of qualifications outstrips demand by a comfortable margin. The imbalance is evident for men, women full-timers and for ethnic minorities but is most striking in the case of women part-timers'.

Our more restricted survey of workers on the lowest pay grades in the public sector also found an imbalance between the qualifications held by employees and those needed for the job.[3] In response to a question about qualifications, one-third of respondents reported having none. Amongst those with qualifications, over 40 per cent had school-leaving qualifications; nearly 8 per cent had advanced school-leaving qualifications (A or A/S level); 5 per cent had degrees; and 6 per cent had other qualifications. In contrast, over 60 per cent of respondents reported that no qualifications were required for their jobs.

Age is a significant factor in the pattern of qualifications. We would expect older workers with few or no qualifications in jobs that require no formal qualification. In contrast, we would expect younger workers who, by and large, have had a longer period of formal education and have higher levels of qualification to be in jobs which also require higher entry requirements. Nearly 60 per cent of the oldest age group (over 60s) had no formal qualifications, followed by 50 per cent of the 41–60 year olds. This fell to 12.5 per cent of 26–40 year olds and just under 8 per cent amongst the under 25s. This compares with 85 per cent of the over 60s who reported that no qualifications were required for their current jobs. This falls to 60 per cent amongst 41–60 year olds, 50 and 47 per cent for the two youngest age groups respectively. These findings challenge some of the central assumptions about the employers' demand for educated labour. What we have found is that both older and younger workers have more formal qualifications than those required by their job, but the divergence between qualifications held and those required by the job is greatest amongst the younger age groups.

How can this imbalance between the supply and employer demand for qualifications be interpreted? It could be argued that employers use qualifications as a sorting mechanism, which is unrelated to actual work tasks and, indeed, to worker productivity. In this respect, they recruit workers with qualifications in excess of their needs simply because they can. Equally, it could be argued that workers with qualifications in excess of those required for their jobs would be dissatisfied with their jobs and might use their initial post as a stepping stone in an internal labour market or might try to influence job design. Alternatively, it might be easier for employers to redesign work processes where the workforce is qualified and, in principle, more adaptable. In this research project, we have found examples of employer-, employee- and union-initiated changes.[4] The quantitative indicators of the mismatch between employees' formal qualifications and those required for their jobs suggest that there is a problem of employer demand in the public sector. We now turn to the analysis of three workplaces, as a means of exploring the qualitative dimension of employer demand in relation to the labour process and the management of labour.

Training and Development: The Limits to Skill Utilisation and Enhancement of Job Design

A restrictive work environment: the NHS Sterilisation and Disinfection Unit (SDU)

In some work environments, there are limits to skill development and work in the SDU is an example of a low-paid, monotonous and distinctly unglamorous unit where trays of instruments for theatre and community services are received, sorted and sterilised. The main work areas include: the sterile and linen stores; the wash up area, where used equipment and instruments from theatre are washed; the wrap areas, where trays of instruments are checked for working order and assembled ready for sterilisation; and the autoclave, where trays are sterilised by steam at high pressure. In recent years there has been a major effort to improve the operation of the department as a response to more stringent hygiene standards. Attempts had been made to standardise quality through the attainment of the ISO9002 quality standard. As a result of this, the SDU was able to expand its activities to service other Trusts as well as the hospital. Although the different work areas had been physically separated off, there had been attempts to expand the range of tasks performed by each worker through job rotation.

Despite these developments, there are limitations to the extent to which job roles can be expanded to increase the levels of skill utilised. Instruments for community services may involve preparing hundreds of packs of basic instruments, a highly repetitive task needing little knowledge. In contrast, other packs require greater know-how. Trays may vary from one or two complex instruments to those with hundreds of similar looking instruments, each of which must be examined and checked for working order, a labour-intensive activity. The instrumentation changes frequently, so staff have to keep learning as the packs alter and the procedures for each process are detailed in the staff duty book. One member of the staff described her initial reaction to the number of different instruments as 'mind boggling'. So the work requires a high degree of familiarisation with the instruments, but little skill and no formal qualifications.

When the profile of the staff is examined, it is clear that many have formal qualifications that are in excess of those needed for the job. The staff group is equally divided between men and women, and between part-time and full-time working. Work is organised on a rota over seven days a week; from 8.00 a.m. to 9.00 p.m., Monday to Friday, and 8.00 a.m. to 4.30 p.m. at the weekend. The manager has made considerable efforts to accommodate the hours sought by staff and this flexibility is one of the key attractions in relation to the recruitment of younger women with children. Staff ages vary from 17 to 60, although there are identifiable groups: younger men with few qualifications; women in their 20s and 30s with considerable experience and training but needing part-time hours; and older women who had been made redundant from more skilled work. Amongst the nine women interviewed was a qualified chef, a supervisor from British Telecom (BT), someone who had worked on the counter at the Post Office, a qualified hairdresser and three nursing auxiliaries. Two of the nursing auxiliaries had previously worked in the Trust and when their nursing posts had been made redundant had been offered redeployment into the SDU. Amongst the six men interviewed was a retired history teacher and a milkman

What became apparent, particularly in the case of the women staff, was that they had a wide range of skills that were not used at all in their present jobs. The younger women had taken the jobs for the flexibility of hours and the older women because it was all they could get. There was an impression that no one in the Trust saw any value in enabling the SDU staff to progress into other areas of work. There were no specific training programmes for them. All training was on-the-job and there had been a move to formalise the process through staff records. One supervisor estimated that it might take nine months to learn all the areas in the department because of the sheer number of different instruments. Yet, once learnt, many staff found the work boring and repetitive. Most spoke positively about the changes to the organisation of the department and felt that it was better to work in well-organised boring work rather than poorly organised boring work. Yet the reality of life in the SDU was that there was no opportunity for career progression, except into supervision. As one male member of staff commented, 'I've hit a brick wall, there's nowhere to go.' Two male employees expressed a desire to move into care assistant roles, though getting relevant experience was a problem. An attempt at work redesign had aimed to make jobs slightly more interesting, yet there were no obvious ways of designing them to develop skills that might facilitate progression within the Trust or to provide skills for wider employability. For most staff, working in the SDU was part of a downward skills spiral and the longer they stayed there, the more difficult it became to move into or return to more skilled work.

Generic working and work intensification: the Housing Department

Generic working involves the redesign of work and this could potentially involve the development of a wider range of skills. We have argued elsewhere that the way in which workers experience and perceive generic working is highly dependent on context. Similar developments can be experienced positively or negatively according to who initiated the development and who benefits from it (Rainbird *et al.* 1999). The Housing Department was responsible for the maintenance of housing stock and sheltered accommodation for the elderly. The context was one of reorganisation and the halving of capital budgets. Staff numbers had been cut from 200 to 140. Through privatisation the most desirable properties had been sold. Some new housing had been built by housing associations, but the department remained responsible for the large number of council houses in the area. There were seven area offices, each with a divisional manager, some of which were responsible for over ten thousand council houses. The direct labour organisation, responsible for repairs and maintenance, had been absorbed into the department in a reduced form. This was the context in which flexibility and generic working had been introduced.

Neighbourhood managers in each office dealt with the day-to-day management of the houses and were responsible for 350 houses each. The term 'manager' was misleading since they were essentially front-line staff who dealt with everything, including repairs, rents, allocations, transfers and debt recovery. There was one person in each office who assessed repairs for the whole district and a jobbing handyman who carried out tasks such as minor repairs, cleaning and graffiti removal. Most offices had three staff on the help desk answering the telephone, handling queries at the counter and dealing with housing benefit. Where there used to be a range of assessors, rent collectors and homelessness officers, there were generic workers who were expected to cover everything. This included understanding the legislation and rent-recovery processes that might include court appearances and required a major training effort. As a neighbourhood manager explained, '(y)ou have to deal with all the administration. You've got to inspect housing stock, make sure they are fit to let. If they are not you have got to get them measured and the work issued to a contractor. Then you have got to let them'.

Issues of quality within the Housing Department were complex. The housing stock itself was in a state of disrepair. Some of the estates were rundown and had bad reputations locally, so there was a high turnover of tenancies. There were drug problems amongst tenants and staff highlighted the financial issues that arose. 'A lot keep moving on, running away from debts. The more you push for financial recovery to reduce the debt the more likely the tenant will move on, so you get high turnover.' This made rent collection difficult and undermined the achievement of the business objectives of the department. Some of the estates were due for demolition. One neighbourhood manager wryly commented, '(w)e are about to demolish this estate. Until we do that, people from the area are doing their best to do it themselves'.

The neighbourhood managers' work involved some difficult interactions with clients, including rent collection, sorting out disputes between neighbours and court appearances. Many found the work demanding and stressful. Repairs were often uppermost in residents' concerns but diminishing resources often meant waiting. Their frustrations could erupt in the form of abusive behaviour directed at front-line staff. Apart from their other attributes and skills, staff had to be adept in dealing with irate tenants.

Training had been essential to developing staff skills for generic working. This had taken the form of in-house courses to address areas of work such as arrears and recovery and court procedures. There were also plans to develop customer care training. A considerable amount of tuition was one-to-one. This system could have worked well if there had been sufficient time to do it properly, but many staff found it stressful because it took place at the end of the day or in periods when work was slack. The training concentrated on the job in hand and there was little development for the future or for career progression. Most staff could not even aspire to promotion. Staffing was pared down to an absolute minimum: sickness could not be covered since staff did not know each other's jobs. Both generic working and the training that was supposed to provide employees with the skills they needed were experienced negatively because there was insufficient time to do them properly (cf. Rose 2000).

Staff cuts and generic working were the solutions to financial problems in the department but have resulted in work intensification for the front-line staff. Some workers had adopted minimalist approaches to work as the only way to survive the workload. One technical officer explained, 'I am on my own in what was a three man department. So you spread yourself very thin. You never finish your work. I used to look at other things and check work carefully. I don't have time to worry about standards.' Many front-line staff mentioned health problems and stress as continual features of their lives. Unsurprisingly, the commitment of many staff to the organisation was low. As this was an area of high unemployment, there was not always an alternative to their current jobs, and work intensification relied, in part, on this situation. The Deputy Director was particularly unsympathetic to these problems. He claimed '(w)e changed the culture of a lot of our staff. They are generic officers not assessors, rent collectors and homelessness officers. Now the deal is you have 300 properties and that is your patch. Handle it. Some people find it difficult to cope. It is always difficult to look at yourself and say what do I lack?'

The concepts of quality service and clients as customers are inherently problematic in relation to social housing. Fitzgeorge-Butler and Williams (1996) point out that service users are not in a powerful position. They have little choice and little redress against unfair decisions nor can they easily go elsewhere for these services. Although the service had not been privatised, management objectives of attaining efficiency and reducing costs had been uppermost. Private sector management solutions have been grafted onto a local government department in an area of high unemployment and have resulted in stressful working conditions as staff struggle to learn new specialisms. As Foster and Hoggett (1999) found in their study of the Benefits Agency, the language of quality and utilising resources enabled the Benefits Agency to dispense with a range of specialists but the broad knowledge base required rendered the innovation of the 'one-stop shop' almost unworkable. The changes in this local authority Housing Department have not been unworkable but have taken a toll on staff. Generic working may have contributed to maintaining the service, but it is difficult to apply the notion of quality to such an under-resourced area. Although training was provided so that employees could develop their skills, it was done in a way that increased their stress and legit-imised unrealistic workloads.

A restricted work environment but with training and development opportunities: the local government cook-freeze centre

The relationship between articulated knowledge embodied in formal qualifi-cations and what is actually needed for the job is another way of assessing employer demand for skills and qualifications. In this example, we explore a small, relatively stable workforce working on a production line in the cook-freeze centre. This is a factory employing 14 staff, who are part of a much larger organisation (the functional department in which they are located and the City Council itself). This is the central production unit for the 'meals on wheels' service and the customer is the Social Services Department. Each week 15,000 meals and 11,000 sweets are produced and these are sent out to nine satellite kitchens. The work is monotonous – the manager referred to it as 'repetitive, boring and low skilled'. He reported that 'with this type of work we can't retain people with City and Guilds certificates, because they want to go on and do more interesting work. We can't retain them and we can't offer more interesting work'.

The main work involved is food production and packaging, and knowledge of food hygiene regulations is a formal requirement. In addition, two staff drive forklift trucks, two are qualified as first aiders and there is a driver who delivers the prepared meals to nine satellite kitchens where they are 'regen-erated'. Machinery has been introduced to automate the putting of food into containers and the packaging process. Despite this, much of the work contin-ues to involve repetitive actions such as putting carrots and peas into containers for an hour, or using an ice cream scoop for an hour. Both can contribute to repetitive strain injury. Job rotation is used less as a means of making work more interesting because there is little scope for this, but to reduce the risk of repetitive strain injury. Even though work tasks are extremely limited, workers become proficient at their jobs and the work group has an interest in the way in which this proficiency is deployed. The manager reported that some of the women are 'experts at putting 80 grammes of meat into the containers'. The factory operates on a 'task and finish' basis and the workforce can go home once the work is completed, so they all have an interest in having someone at the beginning of the conveyor belt who is fast.

Despite the limited nature of the work, some of the staff mentioned their pride in doing a job that, even if not well-paid, was socially useful and had given them a sense of responsibility and progression. For example, the production supervisor explained, 'I like the welfare side, fulfilling a need for deprived people. I didn't want a career on the glam side ... you need a commitment to the public sector to work here.' The packaging supervisor explained that she had come into the job, initially as a catering assistant, from the school meals service. She felt that the latter had been a 'dead-end job' and she had wanted to expand and to better herself. Her present job had not really involved learning new skills since there were set things that they had to do. There had been some changes in the job with the introduction of new machinery and a new labelling system. Her current job involved taking more responsibility for fault-finding, but most of what she knew had been learned on the job as she went along. She felt that this was a good mechanism for learning because 'the faults are real, in a classroom they're put there and you don't react in the same way'. She acknowledged that she could speak to the supervisor or another member of staff if there was anything that she was unsure about. In this woman's case, it was not primarily the process of learning to do her job well which had given her a sense of achievement, but rather learning opportunities outside the workplace, linked to the job. She admitted that she was not self-confident but she had recently attended a four day First Aid course, which she felt had 'brought her out of herself'. In this she had had the support of her colleagues (particularly her manager and his deputy) and family and was now contemplating a course in advanced food hygiene and supervision. These external courses had also contributed to her awareness of the possibilities of external job mobility.

Becoming a manager or supervisor is another form of developing skills, but this does not always take the form of knowledge of the immediate labour process. The production supervisor explained how she had come to be recruited to the job. She had all the formal qualifications that were required and relevant experience in both cookery and supervisory skills from a previous job. Like her colleague, she felt that she could ask others if there were things she needed to know. She could point to a range of mechanisms for learning about the work: from shadowing the manager, attending meetings and receiving training on new equipment from the suppliers. Part of her status derived from her recognition of the value of her own problem-solving skills and the fact that the workforce knew their own jobs extremely well. She pointed out, 'It took two years to realise that there wasn't anything I couldn't solve, if I tried, like knowing where the manuals are kept ... with the quality system, which is always kept up to date, I always knew the answer was in the building. My job is solving problems. All the staff are long term and know their jobs – I will talk myself out of a job if I keep saying it.' Although her job was primarily concerned with the day-to-day running of the shop floor, she saw herself as having a role in building the self-confidence of the staff. She did this by providing reassurance in relation to off-the-job training programmes and encouraging them to take an interest in the use of computers 'not just for work but for home, the new age'. She felt that she received many opportunities for her own training and development and felt privileged and valued in her work.

Some workers had been attending formal education courses in their own time. One example of this was a catering assistant who had done a course in Afro-Caribbean cookery. Although they had planned to use this knowledge at the cook-freeze centre, the cost of providing the meals was too expensive, so he was not applying this knowledge. Nevertheless, he was also attending a course leading to an NVQ in cookery and another in intermediate food hygiene. He was taking these courses on his own initiative, paying the fees and receiving encouragement from work, insofar as if he needed to take time off he could. Since it was difficult to apply the skills in his current workplace, he saw this as helping his CV and potentially leading to an external promotion. In the same way, a part-time general assistant was taking a computer course on one of her free afternoons and the deputy manager had said she could practice on the computer at work. The benefits of this were not directly related to her current job, but she saw it as a mechanism for helping her daughter with school work, as a means of achieving something for herself.

Despite the monotonous nature of the work, there are extremely low levels of labour turnover and in this sense the workers have a commitment to their workplace. The workforce is drawn from the immediate area: all live within an eight-mile radius of the factory, they work Monday to Friday and there is no evening work involved. They are predominantly women and they are seen by the manager as doing a good job. He contrasted the regular workers with agency staff (taken on to cover sickness and holiday absence) whose standard of work was 'abysmal'. A number of the staff could point to examples of courses they had taken, often unrelated to their immediate work tasks, which had contributed to their self-confidence and personal fulfillment. It is difficult to point to a direct relation between these and the work environment, but management's support and knowledge of these activities may have contributed to the employees' commitment to remaining in otherwise monotonous jobs as well as providing employees with skills which were of value outside the immediate workplace.

Employer Demand for Skills and Qualifications: Discussion

The three workplaces illustrate different dimensions of the concept of employer demand for skills and qualifications and its relationship to work organisation and job design. In the Sterilisation and Disinfection Unit, there was a demand for familiarisation with the range of instruments, but no demand for skill. It was not just that the job was extremely limited, but there were limits to what could be done to make it more skill-intensive. The introduction of the ISO9002 quality standard, and attempts to expand the range of tasks through job rotation, had had relatively little impact. Nevertheless, it was not just that job design was limited, but the SDU was also extremely isolated from the rest of the Trust and there was no route out. For some of the younger women, flexible hours were an attraction and suited their commitments outside work. For them, there was a possibility of doing something different in the future, but the majority stayed because they could not go anywhere else. This was particularly the case for the older women, who had been deskilled and moved from a job where they had had a progression ladder into a dead end. Not only were the staff more qualified than their jobs required, but it is also extremely difficult to see how the job design could be changed further. In some cases, there are absolute limits to the way in which job design can be modified.

The situation in the Housing Department was somewhat different and, superficially, the development of generic working, underpinned by different types of training activities, would appear to be capable of generating a higher level of skill utilisation. In front-line services and, indeed, in much of the public sector, the major cost is people and it is the time they have available for providing the service which is central to its quality. In this instance, managers had resolved the tension between cost pressures and providing a quality service by making major cuts in staffing. So whilst in theory these developments could have contributed to the development of the workforce, in practice, cuts in staffing, job redesign and training all contributed to work intensification and undermined employees' ability to provide anything other than a minimalist service. Training had been used by managers to implement the new service delivery strategy, but it was experienced by staff as an additional pressure because they were expected to do so much. It contributed to undermining their sense of worth and pride in their work, legitimised new and inadequately resourced patterns of working, and contributed to stress levels. To some extent, dealing with dissatisfied and disempowered clients in relation to tasks such as rent recovery will always be difficult and requires a high level of interpersonal skills. Perhaps more importantly, it should be stressed that their skills were not being mobilised to provide a quality service, but to hold an under-resourced service together at enormous personal cost. In this instance, our original distinction between the demand and the supply of skills is rather simplistic. There are also fundamental issues about resources.

In the cook-freeze centre there was a limited demand for skills on the production line and this was evident in the inability of the staff to use the catering skills and qualifications they had acquired at college because the Social Services budget for the 'meals on wheels' service was limited. The resources were not available to enable the staff to shift from working with pre-prepared foods to using fresh ingredients and doing the cooking themselves. Although the ultimate clients might have appreciated a more varied diet and food from their own cultural backgrounds, it was the corporate client, the Social Services Department, which controlled resources. Despite the restrictions of monotonous work and the absence of internal job progression, the workforce was very stable. Some workers felt they had developed as a result of learning opportunities provided through the workplace (first-aid training) or external to it (food hygiene, computing). Even though learning opportunities relating to the job were restricted, formal learning accessed through the employment relationship contributed to transformation, not to work routines and practice, but to individual self-confidence and potential. The cook-freeze centre managers recognised that the workforce knew their jobs and perceived their own role as facilitating learning opportunities for the workforce even if they do not directly relate to the current organisation of work. These latter aspects can be attributed to the 'softer' aspects of human resource management that emphasise communication, motivation and leadership, as opposed to managing labour as an economic factor of production (cf. Storey 1989: 8) and to the way in which the psychological contract has been established in this workplace. As in the Housing Department, lack of resources restricted the demand for skills in the organisation of production and job design, but this had not restricted the staff's access to broader development opportunities. In stark contrast to the culture of blame in the Housing Department, the managers were making an effort to facilitate the learning and self-confidence of employees. This was reflected in a culture where they felt they could learn from others and ask for help if they needed it.

This leads us to a discussion of the conditions necessary to transform the demand for skills. Two points are very clear: *an increased supply of qualifications and management systems which address current business needs have little impact on their own* on employees' access to training and development and their utilisation in the workplace. Earlier we examined the extent to which employees had more qualifications than those required for entry to their jobs. Although there was evidence from our research findings that some employees had developed strategies for expanding their jobs and acquiring new skills, this was not always possible (Rainbird *et al.* 1999). Therefore, the idea that increasing the levels of formal qualification of the workforce automatically has an impact on job design is incorrect. It depends on context and the scope that workers have individually and collectively to negotiate with managers and implement change. Equally, management systems such as ISO9000, the IiP award and tools like the development review process have the capacity to affect the way in which training is incorporated into management decision-making, but their starting point is the organisation's business strategy. If this is to deliver an under-funded service within budget, this will restrict resources to the needs of the job as it is currently constructed. Although some workers learn creative ways of subverting this process, many of those interviewed in our fieldwork expressed their frustrations and disillusionment with it (Munro and Rainbird 2002). These systems may be effective in identifying the need for training for the immediate job, but will do little to alter the organisation of work.

In contrast, it is clear that *training and development can have a significant impact on the workplace and workers' skills, but this can be experienced as positive or negative*. In the Housing Department, work reorganisation drove training interventions, but organisational resources were not available to allow the work to be done properly. In the labour-intensive public services, the time workers need to interact with clients is central to any concept of quality. No amount of training can make up for inadequate resources allocated to staff time. In the Housing Department, significantly increased resources (for the housing itself and for managing the service) would make a difference to the service delivered and to the quality of the work environment. Conversely, it is likely that if increased resources were available for the 'meals on wheels' service, the cook-freeze centre could produce a wider range of meals, drawing to a greater extent on the catering skills that the staff already have and could develop. In other words, the resources available for providing a service are central to the demand and utilisation of skills, on the one hand, and to the quality of service, on the other.

Nevertheless, it is also the case that in many workplaces *there are real limits to the way in which job design can be altered to increase skill utilisation, but this does not mean that there is no role for training, development and forms of informal learning in the workplace*. In the SDU, it is difficult to see how the work could be redesigned and increased resources would probably have little impact on this service department. The majority of workers felt they had been deskilled and that they were in dead-end jobs. Despite being part of a larger organisation, where there were potentially a range of jobs they could move into, the isolation of the unit meant that there were no job progression routes. In addition, because of difficulties in recruiting staff, managers were not keen to help staff to acquire skills that would help them leave. This contrasts with the situation in the cook-freeze centre. Despite the limitations of the organisation of production, managers' encouragement of learning contributed to workers' sense of worth, pride in the social usefulness of their work and commitment to the organisation even if they could not apply the skills they learned in their jobs. This involved some commitment of resources, but also support for learning activities outside the workplace (e.g. time off for exams, access to the computer at work). It provided staff with skills and, in some cases, qualifications that opened up opportunities in the wider labour market. Learning was not restricted to participation in formal training events and they could point to a number of ways in which their learning had been facilitated in the work environment. Despite the restricted nature of job design, the approach adopted by the management contributed to the quality of the work environment.

Paradoxically, in promoting skill development capable of promoting workers' external employability, the management had achieved low levels of labour turnover and savings in recruitment costs. The contribution of training and development to the quality of the work environment is a dimension that was absent in the Housing Department and the SDU and is also missing in the debate on the systemic problem of employer demand for skills and qualifications.

Conclusion

We started this chapter by welcoming the government's recognition of the significance of employer demand for skills and qualifications. We have explored this in relation to the dimensions identified by Keep and Mayhew (1999) of product market and competitive strategy, on the one hand, and work organisation and job design, on the other. In the public sector the concept of 'quality' in public services is highly politicised and managers struggle to reconcile the provision of better quality services with containing expenditure. We have argued that resourcing issues are significant to the quality of service provision, to managers' investment in skills and qualifications, and their deployment in the workplace. Management systems designed to deliver under-funded services will ensure that service delivery needs are met within budget, but are unlikely to transform the demand for skills. Nevertheless, the relationship between business strategy, work organisation and the demand for skills is not mechanistic. In the same way the recruitment of well-qualified workers does not automatically affect job design, nor does investment in training necessarily lead to improvements in service provision, as the case study of the Housing Department demonstrates.

We have argued that significant resource allocations to the public sector could have an impact on the quality of service provision and the demand for skills, but this is most unlikely. In the absence of such a transformation, it is clear that many jobs will continue to require few formal qualifications, with limited scope for job enlargement and greater use of skills. A better starting point for addressing the question of employer demand for skills might therefore be to recognise this rather than adopting Human Resource managers' rhetoric of 'all our staff are skilled'. The recognition that many employees are isolated in monotonous and unfulfilling jobs makes it possible to identify the scope that training interventions have for contributing to the quality of the work environment and to job mobility in internal labour markets. Apart from developing an appreciation of the context of workplace change, it is this qualitative dimension of employer demand for skills that we would like to see included in the analysis.

Notes

1 This research project, 'The future of unskilled work: learning and workplace inequality' (ESRC ref. L212 25 2017), focused on workers on the lowest salary grades in local government and the National Health Service. The research team was made up of Helen Rainbird, Lesley Holly, Ruchira Leisten and Anne Munro.
2 The concept of skill is contested and widely debated. The focus of this section is on formal qualification, which is only one of a number of measures which can be used to measure skill. See Ashton *et al.* (2002) for a discussion of methodological issues concerning the measurement of skill.
3 For details of the methodology and findings from the Employees' Learning Experiences Survey see Rainbird *et al.* (1999: 17–27).
4 We have discussed the general directions of job change in another paper (see Munro and Rainbird 2002).

References

Ashton, D., Davies, B., Felstead, A. and Green, F. (2002) *Work Skills in Britain*, SKOPE, Universities of Oxford and Warwick.
Colling, T. (2000) 'Personnel Management in the Extended Organisation', in S. Bach and K. Sisson (eds), *Personnel Management*, Oxford: Blackwell.
Coyle, A. (1985) 'Going Private: The Implications of Privatisation for Women's Work', *Feminist Review*, 21, November, 5–23.
Finegold, D. and Soskice, D. (1988) 'The Failure of Training in Britain: Analysis and Prescription', *Oxford Review of Economic Policy*, 4:3, 21–53.
Fitzgeorge-Butler, A. and Williams, P. (1996) 'Quality and Social Housing: Irreconcilable Partners', in I. Kirkpatrick and M. Martinez Lucio (eds), *The Politics of Quality in the Public Sector*, London: Routledge.
Foster, D. and Hoggett, P. (1999) 'Change in the Benefits Agency: Empowering the Exhausted Worker?', *Work Employment and Society*, 13:1, 19–39.
Grugulis, I., Vincent, S. and Hebson, G. (2003) 'The Future of Professional Work? The Rise of the "Network Form" and the Decline of Discretion', *Human Resource Management Journal*, 13:2, 30–44.
HM Treasury (2002) *Developing Workforce Skills, Piloting a New Approach*, London: HM Treasury.
Keep, E. and Mayhew, K. (1999) 'The Assessment: Knowledge, Skills and Competitiveness', *Oxford Review of Economic Policy*, 15:1, 1–15.
Kirkpatrick, I. and Martinez Lucio, M. (eds) (1996) *The Politics of Quality in the Public Sector*, London: Routledge.
Munro, A. and Rainbird, H. (2002) 'Job Change and Workplace Learning in The Public Sector: The Significance of New Technology for Unskilled Work', *New Technology, Work and Employment*, 17:3, 224–235.
Performance and Innovation Unit (2001) *In Demand: Adult Skills in the 21st Century*, London: Performance and Innovation Unit, The Cabinet Office.
Rainbird, H., Munro, A., Holly, L. and Leisten, R. (1999) 'The Future of Work in the Public Sector: Learning and Workplace Inequality', *ESRC Future of Work Programme Discussion Paper No. 2*, University of Leeds.
Rainbird, H., Munro, A. and Senker, P. (2003) 'Running Faster to Stay in the Same Place? The Intended and Unintended Consequences of Government Policy for

Workplace Learning', paper presented to the ESRC TLRP Network/SKOPE meeting, University of Warwick.

Rose, M. (2000) 'The Skill Discrepancy Problematic: Three Challenges to Upskilling', paper presented to the Future of Work Programme workshop, Manchester School of Management, UMIST.

Storey, J. (ed.) (1989) *New Perspectives on Human Resource Management*, London: Routledge and Kegan Paul.

Stuart, M. and Martinez Lucio, M. (2000) 'Renewing the Model Employer. Changing Employment Relations and 'Partnership' in the Health and Private Sectors', *Journal of Management in Medicine*, 6:2, 115–143.

Waddington, J. and Whitston, C. (1996) 'Empowerment versus Intensification: Union Perspectives of Change at the Workplace', in P. Ackers, C. Smith and P. Smith (eds), *The New Workplace and Trade Unionism*, London: Routledge.

Winchester, D. and Bach, S. (1999) 'Britain: The Transformation of Public Service Employment Relations', in S. Bach, L. Bordogna, G. della Rocca and D. Winchester (eds), *Public Service Employment Relations in Europe*, London: Routledge.

7
What is 'Skill'? Training for Discipline in the Low-Wage Labour Market[1]

Gordon Lafer

For the past twenty years, one of the most popular prescriptions of economic policy-makers in the United States has been for workers to improve the skills and education that they bring to the labour market. As manufacturing employees compete with low-wage workers abroad, as the nation's older cities confront high poverty rates, and as families across the country contend with lay-offs and downsizing, politicians of both major parties have increasingly focused on job training as the path to renewed prosperity.

Over the past thirty years, most Americans witnessed a variety of immediate causes which seemed to account for falling real wages: mass lay-offs and relocation of jobs abroad; the replacement of regular jobs with temporary or part-time staff; the use of striker replacements and the demand for trade unions to give up benefits won previously; continued discrimination against women and minorities; the deregulation of industries; and the lack of constraints on cannibalistic mergers and acquisitions. Throughout this period, however, government officials have sought to convince the public that our eyes have deceived us. In fact, they argued, these seemingly obvious causes of decline were actually either incidental to or symptomatic of a deeper malaise, namely the failure of workers to provide themselves with adequate skills.

These officials insist that the current economy is characterised by a 'skills mismatch', in which workers are unemployed because they lack the right skills and firms are understaffed because they cannot find skilled employees. Job training is the win-win solution that simultaneously solves both problems. Thus, skills mismatch advocates argue that by equipping unemployed workers to meet the frustrated demand of private employers, training can solve the problems of poverty and unemployment. On this basis, job training has come to be prescribed for a wide range of working Americans. Whatever the problem, job training is the solution.

Unfortunately, the actual track record of US training programmes is dismal. The primary policy of the past two decades, the Job Training Partnership Act

(JTPA), has failed utterly to significantly improve the employment and earnings of its participants. The programme's central evaluation, a massive study mandated by the Department of Labour, tracked 20,000 people over a four-year period. For the majority, the programme had no statistically significant effects whatsoever. The largest earnings gains were realised by adult women. Yet even this most successful group achieved extremely modest improvements. The control group of women who were excluded from JTPA earned wages equivalent to 46.9 per cent of the poverty line for a family of three; yet the programme's participants earned 54 per cent (Bloom *et al.* 1993).

The history of job training evaluations indicates that JTPA's results are well within the normal range of training impacts. Over the past forty years, there have been many hundreds of job training programme evaluations, and there are commonalities that emerge. Almost all varieties of education and training services have resulted in small or insignificant earnings gains. Indeed, there is not a single study that suggests that job training has enabled impoverished Americans to earn their way out of poverty.

Why has Training Failed?

The primary source of job training's failure does not lie in programme design. Rather that there are simply not enough decently paying jobs for the number of people who need them; and where there are jobs, skills and education have only a weak effect on wages. For the United States as a whole during the 1980s and 1990s, the number of people in need of work exceeded the total number of job openings by an average of five to one (Lafer 2002). In 1996 (the year in which President Clinton implemented sweeping welfare reform), the country would have needed 14.4 million jobs in order for the entire low-income population to work its way out of poverty. However, there were at most 2.4 million job openings available to meet this need; of these, only one million were in full-time, non-managerial positions. Thus, demand for decently paying jobs outstripped supply in this year by a ratio of fourteen to one. One of the central assumptions of training policy, then, turns out to be mistaken. The data show incontrovertibly that there simply are not enough decently paying jobs and that training programmes cannot address more than a small fraction of the poverty problem.

In addition, it appears that, contrary to much government assertion, there is no meaningful definition of 'skill' that, if acquired, would guarantee a decent living for working-class citizens. While both scholars and policy-makers have insisted that skills are the key to workers' advancement, the question of exactly which skills are most important has proved elusive. Over the past twenty years, the skills-mismatch thesis has shifted from a focus on technical skills, to an emphasis on basic English and maths, to résumé writing and interviewing, and finally to the attitudinal 'skills' of punctuality, loyalty and discipline.

Demand for technical skills – imagination and reality

When job training first became the dominant labour market policy of the US government, it was almost universally conceived as an effort to equip laid-off workers with specific technical skills. In the Congressional hearings leading up to the adoption of the JTPA in 1982, computer programmers, systems analysts, word processors, data processors, medical and laboratory technicians, machinists, and electricians were identified as among the 'new and expanding sectors of the economy' in which 'demand exceeds supply' (US Senate 1982). As one supporter of JTPA explained:

> Employers are looking for engineers, technologists, computer analysts, and medical workers, while unskilled and semi-skilled workers are increasingly unable to find work. In our country today, good jobs are going begging while millions are out of work because of a mismatch between the skills of the work force and the requirements of the work place. (Kososki 1982: 102)

The shortage of highly skilled technicians has remained a recurring theme of employment policy. Employers report that scientific and technical positions are the hardest to fill (Johnson and Linden 1992). However, technical professions are a small percentage of the overall workforce. The combined total of jobs for mathematicians, computer scientists, computer programmers, numerical control tool programmers, science technicians, electrical and electronic technicians, health technicians and health assessment and treating occupations amounted to only 4.1 per cent of the total workforce in 1984. After twenty years of unprecedented growth, this share is projected to grow to only 6.4 per cent by the year 2006 (Bureau of Labor Statistics 1996). Faced with this evidence, training programmes gradually shifted away from occupation-specific skills towards an emphasis on basic education.

This shift reflected the conviction of many economists, who projected a near-explosion in demand for more general skills, as even non-technical employees were called on to perform increasingly sophisticated work. The Reagan administration's landmark *Workforce 2000* report, for instance, noted that the majority of new jobs had been created in clerical, retail and service occupations, but insisted that:

> even for these jobs...workers will be expected to read and understand directions, add and subtract, and be able to speak and think clearly...jobs that are currently in the middle of the skill distribution will be the least-skilled occupations of the future, and there will be very few net new jobs for the unskilled. (Johnston and Packer 1987: 99)

In this view, the growing income inequality that marked the past few decades (and the deterioration in wages for the majority of non-supervisory workers) is explained by the shift from low skill manufacturing jobs to higher skill service and technology jobs. The new jobs require new skills, with those who have not mastered them left behind, and those who can supply them rewarded handsomely.

The economic data, however, shows that, for the two-thirds of American workers in jobs that do not require a college degree, the link between education and earnings is weak. There is no question that, on average, workers with more education earn higher salaries. As shown in Table 7.1, for both men and women, workers at every level of education earn significantly higher wages than those at the level below them. Thus, it is intuitive for individuals to believe that a college education will attract higher wages.

However, it is equally clear that many factors beyond education affect wages. As shown in Table 7.1, for instance, the effects of gender are sometimes more powerful than those of education. Thus female high school graduates earn less than male dropouts, and women with post-graduate degrees earn less than men with first degrees alone. Indeed, while the data in Table 7.1 is dramatic, the distribution of wages according to other criteria (gender, race, age, industry, or degree of unionisation) are equally dramatic. Since these factors cut across levels of education, the wage earned is determined by the interaction of these factors.

A series of studies have been conducted that consistently show a lesser role for education in setting wages. The most important of these studies found that from 1967 to 1993, education and experience explained only one-third of the variation in men's wages and less than 20 per cent of the variation in women's wages (Karoly 1992, 1996). Karoly's findings are dramatic: 66 per cent of men's and 80 per cent of women's annual earnings were determined by criteria other than education.Thus, while education is a significant factor in determining how much one earns, it accounts for only about one-third of the story.

It might seem that Karoly's findings have definitively lain to rest the mismatch thesis. Nevertheless, economists have continued to explore the possibility

Table 7.1   Annual earnings of workers 18 years and over in 1999

Education	Men	Women
High school dropout	$18,855	$12,145
High school graduate	$30,414	$18,092
Some college	$33,614	$20,241
College graduate	$57,706	$32,546
Advanced degree	$84,051	$46,307

Source: US Bureau of the Census (2000).

that the demand for skills has increased in ways not captured by this analysis. Some economists maintain that demand for skill has increased *within* existing occupations and have suggested that the growing importance of maths skills might be the cause of growing inequality and the solution for low-wage workers. However, the relationship between maths scores and non-supervisory earnings is ambiguous at best. Educational analysts Levy and Murnane (1994: 366), whose work has gone furthest to identify the link between maths ability and wages, conclude that '[even] helping all students to achieve mastery of basic maths skills would contribute only modestly to restoring the earnings of high school graduates'.

'Unobserved skill': the final formulation of the mismatch thesis

As discussed above, two-thirds of the increase in income inequality since 1970 has occurred among people with the same levels of education and experience. No known measure of human capital can explain more than a small share of the distribution of wages. Thus, for skill to be the prime determinant of wages, there must be some critical dimension of skill that has eluded detection in the studies done to date. Based on this assumption, a number of economists have taken to asserting a growing demand for 'unobserved skills'. Levy and Murnane (1994: 367) speculate that the unobserved phenomenon might reflect 'increasing demand for interactive skills, defined as skill in mentoring, negotiating, instructing, supervising, and persuading'.

Other economists have advanced similar and increasingly fanciful notions of personal behaviour and character traits that might determine wages. Moss and Tilly (1996: 252–267), for instance, suggest that what entry-level workers really need are 'soft skills', which they divide between 'interaction', or the ability to deal with customers and to display 'friendliness, teamwork, ability to fit in, and appropriate affect, grooming, and attire'; and 'motivation', defined as 'enthusiasm, positive work attitude, commitment, dependability, and willingness to learn'. The National Centre for the Educational Quality of the Workforce focuses on the importance of 'behavioural skills' such as 'showing up on time, following instructions, and taking pride in a job's outcome' (Capelli 1995: 3). Finally, management guru Daniel Goleman insists that the critical trait is 'emotional intelligence', defined as a combination of 'self-confidence, empathy, the need to get results, constant improvement, influence, and teamwork' (Salopek 1998: 29). Even while traditionally defined, 'observable' skills show no signs of a mismatch, some theorists assert that there is indeed a mismatch if we account for these more important, if less visible, criteria. However, the definition of these unobserved soft skills is expressed so vaguely as to require a definition of the definition.

In summary, while skills unrelated to formal education undoubtedly play a role in the determination of employment and earnings, there is no reason to believe that they constitute the driving force behind the income trends of the past two decades, or that they point to a path of upward mobility for the majority of American workers.

Ultimately, no matter how defined or measured, the data fails to support skills mismatch theses. Furthermore, the mismatch argument appears to be driven more by ideological conviction than by empirical evidence. The debate reveals a pattern in which the mismatch thesis is repeatedly disproved, only to reappear, Hydra-like, in the guise of alternative claims. Thus, early articulations held that there had been a significant decline in educational attainment. When this turned out to be false, the argument shifted to the suggestion that even if workers' education had not declined, the demand for workers with formal education had skyrocketed. When this claim, too, was found to be unsubstantiated, many theorists turned to yet more untestable assertions: that while there was no educational mismatch in the present, a future mismatch was inevitable – or, yet more hypothetically, a future mismatch *should* occur *if* employers retool for 'high performance' production. Similarly, the argument regarding exactly which skills workers are lacking has metastasised from claims about formal education to measures of basic maths and reading competencies, and finally to vague assertions focusing on punctuality, discipline and 'higher order thinking skills'. In each case, mismatch advocates have responded to contradictory evidence not by questioning the logic of their assumptions but by reformulating the argument in terms that are less and less susceptible to empirical verification. This pattern reflects the political and ideological tenacity of the argument's proponents. Measured against more scientifically rigorous standards, the mismatch thesis cannot be substantiated, no matter how cleverly the terms of debate are juggled.

Employer surveys

The bottom line in the demand for skills is the evidence from direct surveys of private employers. Unfortunately, while many employers complain of a shortage of skilled workers, there is little evidence that a more highly trained workforce would generate either more jobs or higher wages. When asked exactly which skills it is that their workers lack, an extremely small number of firms mention the type of technological competencies imagined by mismatch theorists. A larger number, but still a distinct minority, emphasise basic English and maths skills. By far the most common complaint of employers focuses not on any traditionally defined skill at all, but rather on workers' discipline, punctuality, loyalty and 'work ethic'.

In 1990, the Commission on the Skills of the American Workforce (1990: 27) surveyed a wide range of businesses. For the bottom third of the labour market, comprising 40 million jobs, the Commission found no increase in skill requirements at all: 'a pleasant personality behind the service counter, physical stamina on the construction site or a steady hand on the wheel tend to be the important requirements.

As the Commission (Commission on the Skills of the American Workforce 1990: 3) reported:

> While businesses everywhere complained about the quality of their applicants, few talked about the kinds of skills acquired in school. The primary concern of more than 80 per cent of employers was finding workers with a good work ethic and appropriate social behaviour: 'reliable,' 'a good attitude,' 'a pleasant appearance,' 'a good personality.' ... Employers do not complain about an inability to do algebra or write essays.

Likewise, a survey of New York City employers, spanning a wide range of industries, found that 'the most important hiring criteria across all occupational categories have to do with personal characteristics such as work attitude, work habits, punctuality and overall personality' (New York City Department of Employment 1994: 45). Asked to rank the importance of 23 qualifications on a scale from 0 to 100, employers ranked the 'work habits' of job applicants as almost twice as important as whether or not they had completed high school. Indeed, grooming, drug screening and applicant's realistic expectation of wages were all deemed more important than any measure of education. Employers surveyed by the Michigan state legislature and the Rochester, New York Board of Education reported similar sentiments (see Table 7.2). The single most comprehensive survey of employer needs was carried out by the US Census Bureau, in conjunction with the National Centre on the Educational Quality of the Workforce (1995). Asking employers to rank the most important criteria for hiring new employees, they found 'applicant's

Table 7.2 Most important and least important skills for future employees reported by Michigan and Rochester, NY Employers

Michigan	*Rochester*
Most important 'skills'	
No substance abuse	No substance abuse
Honesty, integrity	Follow directions
Follow directions	Read instructions
Respect others	Follow safety rules
Punctuality, attendance	Respect others
Least important 'skills'	
Mathematics	Natural sciences
Social sciences	Calculus
Natural sciences	Computers
Computer programming	Art
Foreign languages	Foreign languages

Source: Sandia Laboratories 1993: 295.

attitude' to be the single most important criteria, followed by a series of measures designed to gauge general work habits rather than academic skills.

However, it is unclear that punctuality and discipline can be termed a 'skill': they may constitute acquired habits, but they are also in large part commitments which one chooses to offer or withhold on the basis of the wages and conditions provided. To the extent that employers are simply paying too little to get the work commitment they desire, this is a mismatch of a different sort. And the project of solving this dilemma by 'training' people to work hard at low wages seems an inappropriate agenda for federal employment policy. Moreover, the fact that millions of Americans work full-time and year-round and yet remain below the poverty line indicates that even demonstrating a satisfactory work ethic does not guarantee a living wage. Taken together with the evidence from economic studies of wage determinants, then, employer surveys suggest that even a well-designed training policy cannot hope to have more than a marginal impact on poverty; and that an anti-poverty strategy focusing on job training is fundamentally misguided.

Soft Skills

The workplace attitudes demanded by employers constitute what Levy and Murnane term 'the new Basic Skills'. The National Centre for the Educational Quality of the Workforce similarly insists that employers do not want people who simply follow orders, but rather are looking for the skills of 'conscientiousness', 'dependability' and, above all, 'motivation, the driving force behind the need to achieve' (Capelli 1995: 3–4).

But how different, really, are these traits from what employers have always wanted? When we look behind the labels applied by academics to the words of employers themselves, the new basic skills seem in fact to be closely related to the *old* 'skills' of deference and discipline. The fact that companies look for enthusiasm and commitment in addition to discipline does not herald a fundamentally new economy in which workers are called on to be independently creative and collaborative. Rather, it is a sign that employers have become even more ambitious to the extent to which they seek to mould the will and personality of employees. From the workers' point of view, however, the fact that they are now asked to be enthusiastic about assembling products, stocking shelves, or typing letters may not represent an increase in freedom, but a decrease – with the employer now seeking to control not only their physical labour but also the thoughts in their heads.

Conscripts and convicts: models for soft skills?

Ultimately, the most commonly voiced business concerns seem to point back to the oldest of employer mantras: employees are just not working hard enough. In this sense, it is revealing to note how often both employers and mismatch theorists point to the military as an example of effective training. One survey reported that employers were optimistic that urban teenagers could ultimately make suitable employees because they 'saw evidence in successful military service that the potential worker was both disciplined and trainable' (Zemsky 1994: 10). The National Centre for the Educational Quality of the Workforce suggested a legislative proposal aimed at developing a youth national service programme that would enable a teenager to 'demonstrate his or her capacity for work': 'What we have in mind is to make national service more like military service, in that successful completion of a volunteer assignment would be viewed by the employer community as evidence that the volunteer...is ready for work' (Zemsky 1994: 11).

If the skills in demand are those learned in boot camp, this suggests that the new 'skills' are in fact indistinguishable from simple discipline. Similarly, the bottom-line hiring criteria of private employers is revealed in the growing number of companies that have turned to prison labour as the ultimate in disciplined workforces. The former head of Wisconsin's corrections system praised prison industries for enabling inmates to develop those work habits that training advocates identify as critical: 'learning discipline, how to follow directions [and] how to work with others' (Elbow 1995: Oct.). 'The productivity and quality of this workforce is as good as, if not better than, any that I've ever worked with', stated the manager of one prison-based IBM supplier. Indeed, IBM gave its prison supplier a quality award for delivering defect-free cable (Sexton 1995: 7). If private employers find the motivation and work ethic they need in prison, it suggests that the interactive skills, teamwork and emotional intelligence they seek are not a matter of *skill*, but rather of *will*. Anyone, it seems, can be a good team member, if they are only desperate enough for the job or institutionally deprived of the means to resist.

The extent to which the work ethic is a matter of will rather than skill is further evident in the power of good wages to produce effects that training programmes seem incapable of providing. It is striking that in entry-level occupations where wages are just slightly higher than normal, the apparently intractable behavioural problems of 'low-skill' workers seem to disappear. Moss and Tilly, for instance, surveyed two distribution warehouses in the same neighbourhood in Los Angeles, both employing large numbers of current and past gang members. In the first, managers 'complain sarcastically about employees' laziness, their propensity for theft...and even the poor personal hygiene of the workforce', and the company struggles with a 25 per cent turnover rate. The second warehouse drew on the same labour force, but paid entry level workers several dollars an hour more than their competitor. At this company, managers had few complaints about the workers, and the turnover rate was just two per cent (Moss and Tilly 1996: 268). This finding reflects what most of us take to be common sense: traits such as discipline, loyalty and punctuality are not 'skills' that one either possesses or lacks; they are measures of commitment that one chooses to give or withhold based on the conditions of work offered.

What is 'skill'?

The notion of 'skill' is one of the most elusive and hard to define concepts. In the academic focus on unobserved skills and in employers' demand for work habits, the mismatch debate has converged on attitude and discipline as the central definition of skill for non-supervisory workers. But this formulation makes nonsense of the very category it seeks to explain. If discipline is a skill, any possibility for a class of unskilled occupations is defined away. In this case, 'skill' means nothing more than 'whatever employers want'.

In some ways, it does not matter whether or not punctuality or discipline is regarded as a skill. From a policy perspective, the only reason to be interested in skills is the extent to which they enable otherwise impoverished citizens to make a decent living. At the start of the 1980s, job training focused on traditionally defined skills for the same reason that generations of parents urged their children to learn a trade. The skill of tool and dye making, computer programming, or nursing was something that would enable one to earn a decent living. Clearly, whatever punctuality is, it is not a skill in the policy-relevant sense. It may or may not be a prerequisite for getting an entry level job, but in itself it offers no grounds for upward mobility and no hope for living-wage employment. That the original idea of a skill as a *trade* has been replaced by 'behavioural skills' reflects the fact that there are not enough job openings in well-paid technical occupations to accommodate the full population that training policy aims to serve. It also indicates that the search to identify the right skill set that might enable low-income workers to reach the middle class is at a dead end.

Attitude Adjustment: Welfare-to-Work Training

Despite the lack of evidence suggesting that workplace attitude skills can guarantee a living wage, these attitudes have increasingly become the focus of government training curricula. This evolutionary process reached its apogee in the welfare-to-work programmes enacted in the wake of the 1996 Personal Responsibility and Work Opportunity Reconciliation Act (PRWORA). For the most part, such programmes, following a model that in the US has been termed *Work First*, have abandoned all pretence in training participants in any identifiable skill whatsoever. Instead, the programmes assume that participants will benefit (in unspecified and unmeasured ways) from simply being required to show up on time and perform whatever menial tasks they are assigned. As one conservative scholar and editor of the *Manhattan Institute's City Journal* suggests: 'We need to provide the means for [poor people] to gain the skills of employability...And those skills don't have to do with rocket science; they have to do with being able to take orders and be polite to customers' (Magnet 2001).

To the extent that officials rejected education and training strategies based on these programmes' history of failure, their actions reflect a correct perception. Several decades of welfare training programmes have proven universally incapable of providing participants with a way out of poverty. However, the root of this failure lies in the shortage of decently paying jobs. To conclude instead that welfare recipients must simply be subjected to harsher discipline and forced into the low wage part of the labour market is not to solve the problem posed by the failure of earlier programmes. It is, rather, to give up entirely on this problem, and to reformulate the goal of welfare training as encouraging public assistance recipients to dutifully accept their lot at the bottom of the economy.

For families on public assistance, federal and state regulations require that able-bodied recipients be engaged in some form of work activity. Across the country, states have established two broad categories of such activity: unpaid work experience, or 'workfare'; and short-term job search assistance or 'job readiness' training. The supporters of workfare insist that it is a 'training' programme. However, there is little recognisable training in any traditional understanding of the word. Across the country, tens of thousands of Americans have been set to work at menial jobs that can be learned in hours. Furthermore, since many workfare programmes screen participants not for the skills they need but for those they already possess, thousands of impoverished workers are performing jobs that they have already done for years, except that they now do the work without pay. In both cases, there are no new skills being imparted, and there is generally no path that leads from workfare assignments to decently paid jobs.

New York City has the largest workfare programme in the country, with over 40,000 workers sweeping streets, cleaning parks and filing records in dozens of public agencies. City officials acknowledge that their records show no more than 10 per cent of workfare workers secure regular jobs. Instead, the city's Work Experience Programme has been used to eliminate tens of thousands of regular civil service jobs. The Giuliani administration cut 20,000 city positions at the same time as expanding the workfare programme (Greenhouse 1998). In the Parks Department, virtually, the entire regular workforce has been replaced with workfare, with the inevitable corollary that there are few regular Parks jobs to which workfare participants might aspire to graduate (Gonzalez 1997). In 1997 the city's Parks Department gave full-time jobs to only 10 out of its 7000 workfare workers (Albanese 1997). One Parks Department worker, quoted in Freeman (1997: 7), describes the problem:

We were told that we would be on the WEP assignment for three months. It's supposed to be a training programme. When you first hear this you say, 'Hey, maybe there's some hope after all.' It's a lie. You never get any training. The extent of your training is basically being given a broom and a dustpan. You can't go into the private sector submitting an application to be a computer technician when your training actually has been cutting branches and leaves and picking up dog faeces... You're in the WEP programme and you're being trained to use Park equipment. But you are not going to get that job. The government says it is downsizing. So why are they going to hire you when they just got rid of somebody?

Beyond promoting workfare as a training ground for entry-level employment, each of the states also runs welfare-to-work training programmes aimed at enabling recipients' transition to private sector jobs. However, these are training programmes only in name since they offer very little instruction in either occupational skills or remedial education. The PRWORA legislation explicitly bans states from counting basic education, maths, literacy or English as a Second Language training as 'work activities' for the purpose of satisfying federal workfare requirements. Individual states have established similar policies. New York Mayor Giuliani, for example, forced thousands of city residents to drop out of college in order to work off their grants raking leaves or alphabetising files; in 1996 alone, 8000 New York City welfare recipients were forced to leave the City University system in order to perform workfare assignments (Bader 1997).

Rather than focus on English, maths or occupational skills, welfare training is increasingly defined by a combination of harsh discipline and hokey motivational seminars. In the early 1990s, the federal government designated 'low self-esteem' as one of the barriers to employment keeping welfare recipients from securing gainful employment, thus enshrining in federal policy guidelines the conviction that it is the *attitudes* of poor Americans which are substantially to blame for their poverty (US General Accounting Office 1994: 10). In keeping with this assumption, state programmes have placed self-help rhetoric at the heart of their welfare-to-work efforts. The very names of the programmes indicate the centrality of motivational discourse to welfare reform strategies. A partial review of state welfare-to-work initiatives lists programmes titled GAIN, GOALS, REACH, REACH UP, JET, MOST, PATHS, KANWORK, Project First Step, Project Independence, and in two different states, Project Success (McDonnell and Zellman 1993). Somewhat less misleading is Illinois' Project Chance; nevertheless, it is still far from an honest welfare programme, which would have to be named Project Not Very Likely.

The primary training service provided in these programmes is job search assistance, described by the Manpower Demonstration Research Corporation as 'sessions designed to build self-confidence and job-seeking skills' (Gueron 1990: 89). But what is the real content of this training? One participant-observer provides a partial answer to this question in the following account of Wisconsin's Gateway to Opportunity, Advancement, and Lasting Success programme (GOALS), one of the motivational seminars that have become mandatory under welfare reform regulations:

> During the first week of GOALS, about a dozen women and two men sit around a conference table at the Dane County job centre. The instructor, who introduces herself as Kelly, shows flashcards. One flashcard says, 'You'll never amount to anything.'
> 'Has anybody ever heard this in your life?' she asks.
> No response.
> 'Good! Because it's not true!'
> She holds up another flashcard: 'You can do anything you set your mind to.'
> 'How about this one? How often do we hear this?'
> No one says anything.
> This is day three of the two-week GOALS session. The topic: communication. From Kelly's point of view, things aren't going so well. 'People aren't talking a lot,' she says.
> Several participants are clearly trying, though. Kelly holds up a flashcard that says 'I'm so proud of you.' 'How do we feel when someone says this to us?' she asks.
> 'Good?' one participant offers.
> 'Yeah!' says Kelly. She hands out pieces of paper and asks everyone to write down the names of two people who have had a positive influence in their lives.
> 'It's the person who believes in you,' she says.
> She writes 'belives' in magic marker on a flip chart, then crosses it out and writes 'beleives.'
> 'Don't tell her,' the woman in front of me whispers.
> 'What?' Kelly asks. 'Don't tell me what?'
> 'You still spelled [sic] "believes" wrong,' someone says.
> Kelly stares at the flip chart.
> 'It's I before E except after C,' another participant explains.
> 'That's okay,' the woman in front of me says. 'That's a hard one.'
> After a short break, Kelly lists some more rules for good communication. 'Here are two of the hardest things to say in the English language,' she says, and writes 'Thank you' and 'I'm sorry' on the flip chart...
> I interview some participants after class. 'I don't want to knock the programme or anything – maybe someone is getting their self-esteem raised,' says one participant.... 'But...they've given me an ultimatum: "You either go to this class or it's your check."' (Conniff 1994: 18–21)

Across the country, Americans who are unfortunate enough to need public assistance are being forced to undergo training programmes such as that mandated by GOALS: programmes which have virtually no content apart from 'can do' hype. The goofiness of self-esteem training is backed by the ever-present threat of sanctions and the spectre of time limits. The nation's largest welfare-to-work programme, Los Angeles' Jobs-First GAIN, exemplifies this two-pronged approach. Fully 70 per cent of recipients are threatened with grant reductions in a typical year, and 23 per cent have had their grants cut as punishment for non-participation in work-training activities (Freedman *et al.* 2000: 5–10).

As elsewhere, the content of GAIN's motivation seminars varies between cloyingly Pollyannaish and eerily Orwellian. In the six-hour orientation meetings, 'the message [is]...upbeat, stressing how work can lift self-esteem and that a low-paying first job can lead to a better one in the future' (Freedman *et al.* 2000: 6). In one sense, the rhetorical hype serves to legitimate very low standards of programme success. The programme promises neither improved skills nor a living wage; expectations of the actual jobs that recipients are to be placed into are kept low, and justified on the unlikely assumption of upward mobility. Indeed, the GAIN 'message' rings with brutal cheerfulness, relentlessly hawking the idea that work is its own reward (LA County GAIN web page 1999):

> By working, you demonstrate the self-growth and independence which provide the positive role model that your children need to become successful, productive adults. Participants are encouraged to work full or part-time even if they want to pursue education or training. A job is an education too.

But the programme provides stick as well as carrot. A flyer from the Los Angeles GAIN office captures the sense of impending doom that awaits those who resist this smiley-faced vision of the low-wage labour market (Freedman *et al.* 2000: 5): 'Everyone will be expected to work...Work experience is the best training. Remember: "WORK IS IN, WELFARE IS OUT".'[2]

The motto of GAIN is 'A job, Another Job, A Career', suggesting that any job is a first step up the ladder towards a middle class standard of living. The reality is that with few exceptions, most welfare recipients are unable to find decently paying jobs and are condemned to cycle through a continuing litany of low wage, no benefit jobs. As a Milwaukee welfare administrator explains, 'people are placed in low income and temporary jobs that they work a few days here and there for a few hours. There's no chance for stability at a job with a liveable wage that will allow them to lead a wholesome life' (Freedman *et al.* 2000: 3). In this context, the hype surrounding job club activities becomes obnoxious. As one recipient recalls (quoted in Edin and Lein 1997: 74):

> It was disgusting. Here were these women getting jobs at a fast food restaurant for minimum wage, and people were clapping and cheering. And then they would find out that they couldn't make it on that amount,

so they would just come right back on welfare a month or so later. And that was the best they seemed to do. They didn't offer any real good jobs to anyone.

The political content of welfare training programmes: training for discipline

If job readiness training is not preparing participants for living-wage jobs, then what is its function? In programme after programme, it appears that welfare-to-work training serves largely as a disciplinary mechanism, aimed at disabusing participants of the notion that they can refuse, resist, or even complain about, the type of jobs being offered.

Considering that these jobs are often unstable, with low wages, no benefits and little prospect for upward mobility, the call for discipline and diligence becomes offensive. These are the worst jobs in the labour market: the lowest paying, the dirtiest and the least secure, often with the most petty and personal supervision. For healthy adults, it may be appropriate to view such jobs with distaste and resentment. In a study commissioned by the US Department of Labour, the American Society for Training and Development declared 'self-esteem' one of the 'basic skills' required by employers. However, one early study found that those with the highest self-esteem were *least* likely to accept the sort of jobs being offered to graduates of government training programmes (O'Leary 1972).

Indeed, if there is a chance of improving working conditions in low-wage industries, it may lie partly in the ability of low-wage workers to participate in collective rebellion against employers who prosper on such standards. The goal of welfare-to-work training, however, is not to encourage *this* sort of self-esteem, but its opposite. The US General Accounting Office (1999: 24) stresses the importance of training welfare recipients in 'soft skills', including 'eliminating inappropriate responses to authority'. Similarly, a programme lauded by the *Wall Street Journal* (Project STRIVE) aims explicitly at curbing 'the self-defeating postures of passivity, racial blaming or the strut of "attitude"' (Hymowitz 1997: 15). Instructors explain that harsh, tough-love treatment is needed for participants such as,

> Gloria [who] . . . leans back with her arms crossed over her chest – just the kind of subtle gesture of defiance bound to irritate a supervisor on the job. Other participants will be challenged to recognise their own resistance to authority, displayed in their bored facial expressions, smirks, slouching and unconscious clucks of disgust.

Thus, the mission of training programmes has been fundamentally transformed. No longer are they to provide the skills or education that might enable participants to gain greater leverage in the labour market. Instead they are intended to lower the sights and aspirations of participants, producing a disciplined class of low-wage workers.

In both the public and private sectors, the rhetoric of 'self-esteem' and taking charge of one's life serves to mask the reality that 'world of work' programmes primarily train workers to be submissive: to follow orders, to accept the superiority of the boss's judgment, to effect personalities which are pleasing to those in power, and above all not to challenge the prerogatives of management. The skills-as-discipline curricula of training programmes are a predictable result of a business-dominated employment system facing a job-shortage economy. Thus, training has become not only irrelevant but increasingly reactionary, as a growing share of training resources are devoted to channelling economic discontent in directions which are benign to employers. To the extent that this project is successful, training becomes something worse than a misplaced hope; it becomes an ideological tool for preventing a political solution to the very problems of poverty that JTPA purports to address.

Conclusion: What Attitude Should Low-Wage Workers Embrace?

The most productive direction employment policy can take is to abandon the search for supply-side solutions and concentrate instead on the demand side of the labour market – improving the wages and conditions of available jobs. It may be thought that this is an impossible task. However, recent history shows that while there is no easy path to expanding the supply of decently paying jobs, there are clear and promising ones for moving in that direction.

Trade unionisation, in particular, is the elephant in the corner of employment policy debates, the looming option that most analysts choose to ignore. While the data linking education with earnings shows inconclusive results, the relationship between unionisation and wages is unambiguous. Across the economy as a whole, the salaries of union members are significantly higher than their non-union counterparts in almost every major occupational and industrial category. Union wages were 28.4 per cent higher than those for unorganised workers in the year 2000. Since union members are also far more likely than others to win employer-provided pension and medical benefits, the union premium is almost twice as large when accounting for total compensation (Bureau of Labor Statistics 2001: 181). Even confining the comparison to union and non-union workers with the same occupation, industry, work schedule, geographic region and company size, unionisation raises wages by 21 per cent and total compensation by 28 per cent.

The union differential is even more dramatic in the service occupations that are projected to provide the bulk of new jobs for non-college workers. The discrepancy between union and non-union wages for service occupations as a whole averaged 69.4 per cent, with weekly earnings of $554 and $327 respectively. For cashiers, clerical workers and janitors (exactly the type of entry-level service jobs that graduates of training programmes might aspire to) the impact of unionisation is the equivalent of between 41 and 66 per cent of the poverty threshold. For non-union high school dropouts, the advantage of organising one's workplace is, on average, worth twice as much as going back to finish school. Unions have pursued a direction that is not generally contemplated in employment policy discussions: solving the problem of low wage employment not by changing anything about the employees, but by changing the quality of jobs available. Nor is unionisation the only such strategy; minimum wage increases, living wage ordinances, and progressive economic development policies all promise similar impacts (see Figure 7.1). What all these strategies have in common, however, is a willingness to face employer opposition in order to improve wages.

Both in its ideological function and increasingly in the actual curricula of training programmes, the ideology of job training at its heart is an argument about power. On the simplest level, the promotion of training as an alternative to public jobs, plant closure laws and unionisation rests on the assertion that the interests of working people and the poor are best served by cooperating with, rather than challenging, the profit-maximising strategies of private corporations.

A progressive policy agenda is economically realistic. However, it is not politically realistic at the current time. The administration of George W. Bush

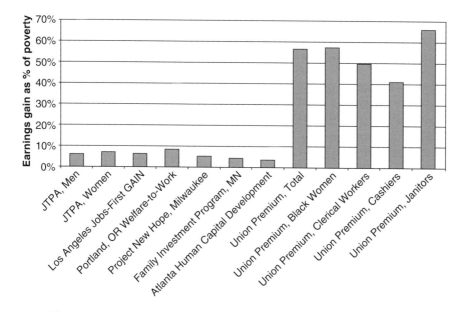

Figure 7.1 Impact on wages of training programmes and unionisation

is unlikely to support any of the above proposals. More to the point, most of these policies are unlikely to be passed even if a Democrat retakes the White House. Democrats as well as Republicans operate within the realities of budget restrictions and political dependence on corporate contributions. Even if some members of a Democratic government might personally prefer a more progressive approach to poverty, the current balance of forces makes it impossible for elected officials to pursue policies that alienate their business constituency. Thus, if there is a hope of moving in a more progressive direction, it lies not in winning the hearts and minds of those in power, but in changing the political constraints under which they operate. In this case, the most important skill for working people to acquire is not the discipline demanded by employers, but the solidarity required for collective mobilisation.

Notes

1   This chapter is adapted from Lafer (2002).
2   Capitalisation in the original.

References

Albanese, S. (1997) 'How I'd Make Workfare Work', *New York Daily News*, 9 July.
Bader, E. (1997) 'Unfair Workfare', *Dollars and Sense*, 213, 31.
Bloom, H., Orr, L., Cave, G., Bell, S. Dolittle, F. and Lin, W. (1993) *The National JTPA Study: Title II-A Impacts on Earnings and Employment at 18 months*, Washington, DC: US Department of Labor.
Bureau of Labor Statistics (1996) *Occupational and Projections Data 1986 Edition*, Washington, DC: US Department of Labor.
Bureau of Labor Statistics (2001) *Union Members in 2000*, Washington, DC: Department of Labor.
Capelli, P. (1995) 'Challenge: To acknowledge the role of work-related behavioral skills and attitudes as both a cause of and remedy for the skills gap', National Center for the Educational Quality of the Workforce, University of Pennsylvania, Philadelphia.
Commission on the Skills of the American Workforce (1990) *America's Choice*, Rochester, NY: National Center for Education and the Economy.
Conniff, R. (1994) 'Big Bad Welfare: Welfare Reform Politics and Children', *The Progressive*, 58:8, 18–21.
Edin, K. and Lein, L. (1997) *Making Ends Meet*, New York: Russell Sage.
Elbow, S. (1995) 'Doing Time, 9 to 5', *Isthmus*, 6.
Freedman, S., Knab, J. T., Gennetian, L. and Navarro, D. (2000) *The Los Angeles Jobs-First GAIN Evaluation*, New York: Manpower Demonstration Research Corporation.
Freeman, K. (1997) *Welfare Reform As We Know It*, Washington, DC: Jobs With Justice.
Gonzalez, J. (1997) 'Read These Ballots and WEP', *New York Daily News*, 21 October.
Greenhouse, S. (1998) 'Many Participants in Workfare Take the Place of City Workers', *New York Times*, 13 April.
Gueron, J. (1990) 'Work and Welfare: Lessons on Employment Programs', *Journal of Economic Perspectives*, 4:1, 79–98.

Hymowitz, K. (1997) 'Job Training That Works', *Wall Street Journal*, 13 February, 15.

Johnson, A. and Linder, F. (1992) *Availability of a Quality Work Force*, New York: The Conference Board.

Johnston, W. and Packer, A. (1987) *Workforce 2000*, Indianapolis: Hudson Institute.

Karoly, L. (1992) *The Trend in Inequality Among Families, Individuals, and Workers in the United States*, Santa Monica: Rand Corporation.

Karoly, L. (1996) 'Anatomy of the US Income Distribution: Two Decades of Change', *Oxford Review of Economic Policy*, 12:1, 77–96.

Kososki, C. (1982) Testimony cited in United States Congress, *Employment and Training Policy, 1982, Part 1*.

LA County GAIN (1999) www.dpss.co.la.ca.us/gain.

Lafer, G. (2002) *The Job Training Charade*, Ithaca: Cornell University Press.

Levy, F. and Murnane, R. (1994) 'Skills, Demography and the Economy: Is There a Mismatch?', in L. Solomon and A. Levenson (eds), *Labor Markets, Employment Policy, and Job Creation*, Boulder, Colorado: Westview.

Magnet, M. (2001) *Talk of the Nation: Welfare Reform in the US*, National Public Radio, 7 May.

McDonnell, L. and Zellman, G. (1993) *Education and Training for Work in the Fifty States*, Santa Monica: Rand Corporation.

Moss, P. and Tilly, C. (1996) '"Soft" Skills and Race: An Investigation of Black Men's Employment Problems', *Work and Occupations*, 23:3, 252–276.

National Center on the Educational Quality of the Workforce (1995) *First Findings from the EQW National Employer Survey*, University of Pennsylvania, Philadelphia.

New York City Department of Employment (1994) *New York City Employer Survey: Summary Report*, New York.

O'Leary, V. (1972) 'The Hawthorne Effect in Reverse: Trainer Orientation for the Hard-Core Unemployed Women', *Journal of Applied Psychology*, 56:6, 491–494.

Salopek, J. (1998) 'Train Your Brain', *Training and Development*, 52:10, 29.

Sexton, G. (1995) *Work in American Prisons: Joint Ventures with the Private Sector*, National Institute of Justice, US Department of Justice, Washington, DC.

US Bureau of the Census (2000) *Educational Attainment in the United States: March 2000 Update*, Release date 19 December, www.census.gov.

US General Accounting Office (1994) *Welfare To Work*, Washington, DC.

US General Accounting Office (1996) *Welfare Reform: States' Experiences in Providing Employment Assistance to TANF Clients*, Washington, DC: US General Accounting Office.

US Senate (1982) *Senate Report 97–469: Report Accompanying S-2036, the Training for Jobs Act*. Washington, DC.

Zemsky, R. (1994) *What Employers Want*, National Center for the Educational Quality of the Workforce, University of Pennsylvania, Philadelphia.

8

The Institutionalisation of Skill in Britain and Germany: Examples from the Construction Sector

Linda Clarke and Georg Herrmann

Introduction

Skill formation is central to the structuring of labour markets; indeed, the French 'societal effect' school posited education and training systems as key to differences in labour organisation (Maurice *et al.* 1986; Rubery and Grimshaw 1998). Marsden has qualified the role accorded to labour market institutions in his distinction between production and training approaches, the latter depending on transferable and general skills, which require most institutional intervention in the labour market (Marsden 1999). He suggests that institutions and hierarchies differ qualitatively with respect to the type of skill and labour market.

The suggestion of different institutional arrangements associated with different skill formations is apparent from this research into the construction sector.[1] The research has been constantly confronted not only by distinct differences in the concept, nature, structure and constellation of skills in different European countries, but by seemingly uncrossable institutional divides, in particular between professionals and operatives. This chapter seeks to explain the deep-rooted nature of the different institutional arrangements governing the construction of professional and operative skills in Britain and their forms of accountability. At the same time, it shows the ways in which these institutional arrangements act as barriers to change and draw out the implications for the concept of skill and for skill formation.

The concern is the role of the state in the structure of learning. The reproduction of skills takes place through a dynamic relationship between the state, its vocational education organisations and industry, comprised in most European countries of the social partners (trade unions and employers' institutions). To take the example of Germany, qualitative differences with Britain in this relationship are to be observed, with implications both conceptually, in terms of the way skills are defined and understood, and in practice, in terms of divisions and levels of skills. The British system is based on the principle of governance through quangos, whilst the German principle is of tripartite consultation and social partnership. The British state, through the two arms of its Cabinet government – the Privy Council and Parliament, has delegated (in some instances, privatised) important responsibilities for training and education to quangos and chartered institutions. In the higher education (HE) sector the professional institutions play a pre-eminent role and in vocational education the employer-led Sector Skills Councils (SSCs) (formerly National Training Organisations or NTOs) and further education (FE) colleges, account-able to the Department for Education and Skills through the Learning and Skills Council (LSC). The German state, in contrast, has organised vocational education through institutionalised cooperation with the social partners. The comparison of institutional arrangements in Britain with those in Germany is presented here in order to illustrate just how distinct the British system is in a European context, to identify where these differences lie and to explain how particular skill divisions are embedded and maintained. The first part of the chapter examines the British system and the second part outlines the German system.

Governance through Quangos

There are in the UK over 800 public bodies, called quangos (quasi-autonomous non-governmental organisations), executing and administering a wide range of government business. A quango is officially defined as '. . . a public body which has a role in the processes of national Government, but is not a govern-ment department or part of one, and which accordingly operates to a greater or lesser extent at arm's length from Ministers.' More simply a quango means a national or regional public body operating independently of Ministers but for which Ministers are ultimately responsible. Such bodies are formally classified as Non-Departmental Public Bodies (NDPBs). Governance through quangos is claimed by its proponents to be both flexible and eco-nomically efficient because it brings in the expertise of the private sector and the public consequently benefits. The democratic accountability of quangos is, however, a critical issue, given their significant powers and control of well over £20 billion of public spending (Cabinet Office 2003).

Quangos play a pivotal role in the field of vocational education. Vocational education itself is under Ministerial control, though responsibility is delegated to the new national and 47 local LSCs – government quangos that were set up in 2002 as a merger of the Training and Enterprise Councils (TECs) and the Further Education Funding Council (see Chart 8.1). The LSCs have the statutory task of administering the £6 billion budget for education and train-ing in response to employment needs. They support the 15 new Sector Skills

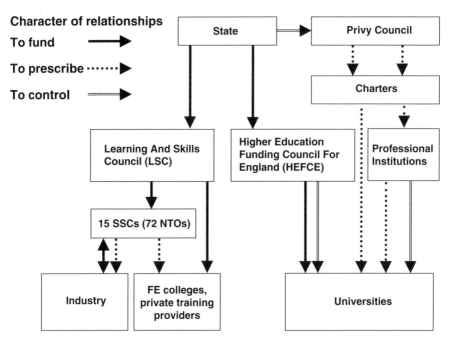

Character of relationships

To fund ⟶

To prescribe ⋯⋯▶

To control ⟹

Chart 8.1   **The structure of learning in the UK**

Councils (SSC), which operate under a government licence that is reviewed every five years, and have the task of making sure that the skills needs of the sectors are met and of organising the provision of training and education together with the industry, FE colleges and private training organisations (DfES 2001).

The SSCs represent a merger of the 72 NTOs that covered 90 per cent of the UK workforce. The government's intention is that they be set up as private companies, limited by guarantee, and run by 'employers for employers', with the responsibility to identify and tackle skills, productivity and employ-ability issues (SSDA 2002a). The aim is to secure employer participation, ownership and leadership in these new vocational training organisations and to turn them into the UK's voice of employers. In this way the reproduction of skills has been referred to business interests and to market forces – to the private sector (Keep 2002). Neo-liberal ideas have thus returned to dominate the education and training agenda, based – as in the 1950s – on the notions of demand-led skill supply and market needs.

A pivotal role in the new arrangement is given to the Sector Skills Devel-opment Agency (SSDA), a body that 'will develop, monitor, support and regulate the Sector Council network' (SSDA 2002b). The composition of this organisation reflects the dominant mix of private business interests. Of the ten board members of the SSDA appointed in 2002, only one, with a formal mandate as a trade union representative and a council member of a HE institution, represents the interests of a wider section of society. Seven board members represent private companies and include, for instance, the CEO of a recruitment agency. The state is present in an observer's role through a Permanent Secretary of the Department for Education and Skills. The educational representatives on the board number four, three of whom have been governors of HE institutions. No organised business interests are included, such as a representative from the Confederation of British Industry (CBI). It is symptomatic of the individualistic British approach to the fundamental issues of training and education that the new bodies do not encompass wider interest representation and, apart from a token presence of one trade union official, lack social partner organisations and hence social dialogue in the continental European tradition.

At sector level it is possible to observe how the UK system operates in practice and to discern its implications for vertical and horizontal skill divisions. In this respect, the construction industry is an ideal sector given its size, that it employs approximately seven per cent of the workforce, the range of skills deployed – professional, intermediate or technical, and operative – and its long tradition of vocational education and training (VET) as one of the main apprentice industries, even from the fourteenth century.

In terms of vocational education, the Construction Industry Training Board (CITB), one of the two remaining statutory industry training organisations, is, as with the SSDA, similarly dominated by private business interests. Originally it was set up in 1964 as a tripartite body, but in the 1980s contractors were given the majority on the board, although there are still two trade union members and a change in board structure to include clients has been considered. Two-thirds of its funding is through an industry levy of 0.5 per cent of the payroll of main contractors and 1.5 per cent of labour-only subcontractors, which in 2002 amounted to £95 million, with the bulk of the remaining income stemming from the state (CITB 2002a). The levy may even be passed down by the labour-only subcontractor to its self-employed workforce, who will have this amount subtracted from their pay so that it is in effect paid by those employed, although their interests are scarcely represented on the Board. One-third of its overall levy income comes from members of the Major Contractors' Group of the Construction Confederation and the smaller firms complain that the interests of large contractors dominate. As well as being the new SSC, the CITB operates as the lead body for setting occupational standards, as the National Vocational Qualifications (NVQs) awarding body for the industry, the accreditor of assessors, manager and policy developer for industry training, and manager of the Construction Skills Certification Scheme (CSCS). In terms of the training of construction operatives, pivotal roles are played by both the CITB and the LSC, who are accountable to the Department for Education and Skills but to all intents and purposes operate as autonomous organisations dominated by members of individual private companies.

A key aspect of the CITB's responsibility is the recognition of skills for the purpose of qualification. For instance, new qualifications have been developed for tunnelling and public utilities and for multi-skilled maintenance operatives. A critical role in the recognition of new qualifications is played by the numerous specialist and trade organisations in the industry, such as the six federations in the Construction Confederation, the six Specialist Engineering Contractors' associations and the 23 associations under the National Specialist Contractors Council. In effect, specialist employer organisations such as the Mastic Asphalt Council lobby the CITB for a qualification in the area and the CITB, as lead body, responds by developing an NVQ for mastic asphalters. The result of this demand-led process is that, excluding building services and related occupations, there are now over 50 different NVQs available in construction, representing an excessive fragmentation of operative skills (Clarke and Wall 1998).

National Vocational Qualifications are intended to assess skills or competences in the workplace rather than going together with a recognised programme of training. Thus, although they have been devised for so many specialist areas, this does not mean that they are awarded or that training takes place. Indeed it is ironic that training continues to be concentrated in the main traditional trades even though these employ a decreasing proportion of the workforce; 86 per cent of trainees are to be found in the wood trades, bricklaying, plastering, roofing, painting and decorating, electrical work and plumbing although these trades employ less than 60 per cent of the workforce (CITB 2002b). There are few, if any, trainees to be found as plant operators or in civil engineering, though general operatives, plant operators and other civil engineering operatives constitute nearly 30 per cent of the workforce.

In responding only to current needs rather than having been devised as part of a comprehensive vocational education scheme for the industry of the future, it is inevitable that training is concentrated in traditional areas. This concentration is compounded by the fact that the majority of trainees (62 per cent) working towards NVQs in the main building trades are doing so in FE colleges and whilst unemployed (CITB 2002c). The alternative training route is through employer-based Modern Apprenticeships, a route that has been increasingly constrained by the employers' reluctance or inability to take on apprentices due, amongst other factors, to high levels of self-employment and subcontracting. One problem with the college-based training route is, however, the weak institutional link between industry and FE colleges, as shown in Chart 8.1, making it difficult for trainees to obtain working experience, thus deterring completion and subsequent successful employment. The overall result, in addition to skill fragmentation, is low levels of training relative to other leading European countries, with trainees representing less than six per cent of the workforce (CITB 2002b).

Construction therefore illustrates the main characteristics and problems in the institutional structure of the British vocational education system. Through the delegation by government to quangos, it has become an employer-based system, with many new skills being recognised for qualification because of employer demand, on the basis of existing practice, with training organised on a voluntaristic basis, assumed to respond to demand and geared to outcomes. The result is a highly fragmented skills structure, a reliance in practice and in training on existing and traditional skills, a serious gulf between industry and training provision, and low levels of training. In effect it is a system built on the often firm-specific skills of the work process, that is on the ability to fulfil particular tasks, rather than on the general trans-ferable skills acquired through a recognised vocational education scheme that brings together industrial and educational interests (Clarke and Wall 2000).

Granting Skill Monopolies

The system of professional education in Britain is similar to vocational edu-cation in that the state has not directly taken on the regulatory role, though it does exert control through the funding body, the Higher Education Funding Council for England (HEFCE) (as Chart 8.1 indicates) that '...promotes and funds high-quality, cost-effective teaching and research in universities and colleges in England' (HEFCE 2003). The HEFCE has now widened this control to include monitoring and assessing the quality of teaching. How-ever, it is the professional institutions that historically have had the role of determining what their members learn, as they did under the system of tutel-age. This was the dominant system – akin to apprenticeship – for training professionals such as architects and surveyors until the interwar period whereby the trainee was trained or 'articled' with a practice and paid by the practice under an agreed contract. The controlling role of the professional institutions continued as the system was replaced by a system of academic learning. The professions and the universities are in turn regulated whether through royal charters or statutes, by the Privy Council, which is largely composed of present and former Cabinet ministers and acts as a link between Cabinet government and the monarchy by exercising the prerogative of the Crown.

Before the Companies Act came into force in 1900, chartered status used to be the only way of incorporating and registering a body. In the context of HE, charters are the chief means by which a professional organisation can exert control over the content of learning. Royal Charters define the objectives, particular skill area and working structure of the respective institution in order to safeguard the public interest. A professional body applying for a charter must be able to prove that it is a *unique* profession, that it has no significant overlap with other bodies and that it serves the public interest (Privy Council

Office 2003). There are about 400 institutions, charities and companies incorporated with a Royal Charter, a number that increased significantly throughout the twentieth century. Though the Privy Council claims that new charters are rarely issued, in the last few years several were granted: in 2002 to the Institution of Occupational Safety and Health, in 2001 to the Institute of Waste Management and the Institution of Incorporated Engineers, and in 2000 to the Institute of Personnel and Development. It is, therefore, still a highly relevant and powerful instrument of government via the Privy Council that sidelines Parliament.

Charters are in effect privileges granted in perpetuity and can only be revoked in the case of a severe breach of the charter. Professional institutions are – as with the old guilds – accorded the right to control entry into the profession via the categories of membership laid down in the bye-laws and to control the content of education via the regular four-yearly validation of HE courses. In effect this means that the practitioners of today determine the skill needs of tomorrow and that the universities themselves play a restrictive role in education and training because of their concerns about accreditation and the importance of membership of a professional institution to future practice (Nisbet 1989; Gann and Salter 1999). Ministerial, and thus public accountability, is weak and remote and effective monitoring of 'public interest' is difficult. The system creates constitutional barriers blocking the dynamic development of innovation and skills because professional institutions are incorporated on their ability to demonstrate that they can claim an exclusive area of knowledge and these areas remain fixed; new areas of skill and knowledge become issues of conflict and rivalry between institutions.

The eminent role of charters in the regulation of education and training is evident from the charter of the Engineering Council, granted in 1981. Article 5, for instance, stipulates: 'The objects of the corporation shall be to advance education in, and to promote the science and practice of engineering (including relevant technology) for the public benefit and thereby to promote industry and commerce in Our Kingdom' (Engineering Council 2003).

Notable in the charter are the references to public benefit and the limiting of the institution's role to education and training. This educational remit is generally clearly expressed, for instance, in the charter of the Chartered Institute of Personnel and Development (CIPD), granted in 2000:

> In furtherance of the objects of the Institute but not otherwise the Institute shall have the following powers: To establish programmes of education and training and continuing professional development with recognised standards of achievement to support the systematic development and accreditation of members...To establish, promote and monitor standards of competence, good practice, conduct and ethics and to issue codes of professional conduct and statements of good practice. (CIPD 2003)

Pinpointing and defining exactly a professional body of knowledge is, however, difficult and inevitably becomes very general, as evidenced again by the CIPD charter: 'The objects for which the Institute is established are the promotion of the art and science of management and development of people for the public benefit.' Such generalities are similar in the case of the Supplemental charter granted in 1971 to the original charter of 1837 of the Royal Institute of British Architects (RIBA): 'the objects of the Royal Institute are the advancement of Architecture and the promotion of the acquirement of the knowledge of the Arts and Sciences connected therewith' (RIBA 2003).

Professional institutions have thus acquired a monopoly status in controlling the content and development of curricula in HE and hence, in effect, in their particular skill area. This situation gives rise to competition between the professional institutions that further hinders the development of the system, the content of learning (including joint learning), the recognition of overlapping areas of knowledge, teamwork and the greater integration of professional skills. Construction provides a good example of these problems, as the exclusive privileges granted through the charters have created deep divisions and fragmentation in built environment professions. There are altogether seven main chartered bodies – the RIBA, the Institution of Civil Engineers (ICE), the Institution of Structural Engineers (IstructE), the Royal Institute of Chartered Surveyors (RICS), the Chartered Institute of Building (CIOB), the Chartered Institute of Building Service Engineers (CIBSE) and the Royal Town Planning Institute (RTPI) – and a myriad of other professional organisations. The competition between them was evident, for instance, in attempts by the CIOB to change its name to the Chartered Institute of Constructors. Decisions related to any change in charter are based on ministerial responsibility, so in this case the Department of the Environment, Transport and the Regions and the Department of Trade and Industry (DTI) consulted with the affected professional institutions and subsequently refused the name change.

One key issue is determining the core skill areas for professional education according to priorities set and interests pursued, and to adjust these to changing situations. The professional institutions prescribe 75 per cent of the content of accredited courses as core knowledge, leaving little room for general educational or specialist content. The system of course accreditation, is however, now being altered, affecting the role of the educational institutions in the determination of course content. The RICS has, for example, changed to a new audit system whereby instead of measuring curricula and course material (i.e. input), value-added and output standards such as entry and admission procedures and student achievement in coursework and examinations, the assessment and quality of graduate output and effective quality control and quality assurance procedures are measured. Architectural education is similarly being validated against the outcome, not the process. A change in the nature and content of architectural education has also been discussed by the RIBA and the Burton and Stansfield Smith reports have been published with proposals to restructure the whole system of courses, to widen the training to include management skills, and to distinguish between the interior designer, project manager and conservationist (RIBA 2000). The outcome of this process is still open and clashes have occurred with other professional bodies in the field of project management, targeted and claimed by both the RICS and the CIOB. Such demarcation disputes are inevitable, given the fixed skill monopolies of the institutions through the skill profiles of the different professional occupations that are, in practice, constantly changing and developing.

A further issue concerns the role of the state and its ability to challenge the professional institutions. In the field of architecture the role of the professional institution has come under public scrutiny and a situation untypical for the professions exists whereby, after almost 100 years of self-regulation, the state introduced in 1931 the statutory body Architects' Registration Council of the UK (ARCUK), alongside the professional institution, the RIBA, to protect the title of 'architect'. Until the Architects Act of 1997, ARCUK was firmly under the control of the RIBA (Warne 1993; Lean and Morgan 2000). The name of the statutory regulator has since changed to Architects' Registration Board (ARB), and its board is composed of 15 members, of whom eight are not architects but represent consumer interests. Its remit has significantly widened to include, most importantly, professional education and it has been given statutory responsibility for prescribing the standards of architectural education and professional competence required for entry into the register of architects. The professional institution, the RIBA, and the regulator, ARB, used to carry out joint visits to schools of architecture every five years, validating and accrediting their courses, with ARB nominating half of the 46 members of the validation panel from which each visiting board of six members is selected. These joint validation panels were, however, open to conflict, as ARB members of the panel are paid for their work and RIBA members were expected to continue to undertake this work on a voluntary basis. In 2002 the ARB and the RIBA jointly agreed on criteria for qualification prescriptions and ARB is reviewing the validation procedure with the intention of replacing the time-consuming validation visits to schools of architecture with an application process for the prescription of qualifications to ARB (ARB 2003).

The inclusion of professional education within the state-regulated system of VET is another contentious issue. The NTOs – six covering the construction industry – set-up in 1998 by the Department for Education and Employment (DfEE) to replace the multitude of Industry Training Organisations, Lead Bodies and Occupational Standard Councils, extended in theory across all professions in the industry. However, no separate NTO was set up for the professions, although the CITB was given responsibility for Training Organisation for Professionals in Construction, TOPIC, with a view to including professionals under the NVQ system. With the establishment of SSCs, TOPIC no longer exists in its own right but has been reabsorbed into the Construction

Industry Council, which originally set it up 'to support the provision of high quality training and development for professionals in construction' (TOPIC 2001).

There have been other attempts to bridge the divisions between the professional institutions and to overcome significant overlaps in skill areas. The Construction Industry Council itself, founded in 1988 by the CIBSE, the CIOB, the IstructE, the RIBA and the RICS, and later joined by the ICE, was a response to requests from the government for a unified forum for construction professionals to discuss the possibility of a common curriculum for construction professionals. Recommendations for such a curriculum were published in 'Crossing Boundaries' in 1992 and were partly included in the Latham report proposing major changes to the structure of the industry (Andrews and Derbyshire 1993; Latham 1994). They included:

- setting up multi-disciplinary undergraduate and postgraduate degrees and promoting greater commonality in professional education with particular emphasis on design, technology and basic design-management skills;
- rationalising the duplication, overlap and repetition in entrance and examination requirements;
- making Continuing Professional Development obligatory;
- agreeing on common criteria for accreditation, possibly leading to a single body to oversee accreditation of all professional courses in the built environment similar to the Engineering Council; and
- extending reciprocal membership arrangements.

There has been some progress towards fulfilling some of these recommendations. Cooperation has been established between the CIOB, the Architecture and Surveying Institute (ASI) and the British Institute of Architectural Technologists (BIAT), but not between the larger leading institutions. Universities such as Westminster have successfully introduced some core modules at first level, as well as some at the next level in their undergraduate courses in the Construction Department, and, with costs savings, is considering extending this approach across the whole Department of the Built Environment. In spite of these reforms, however, the fundamental structural divisions between institutions remain intact, as does their separate system of accountability to the Privy Council and their divorce from the vocational training system.

This structure of learning has far-reaching implications for the construction process itself, also well illustrated in the case of architecture. Substantial and vociferous criticism has been made of the RIBA, including the complaint that architectural education does not provide graduate architects with the skills and knowledge relevant for the construction industry of today and focuses too heavily on design, which is only one component in the whole construction process. The RIBA commissioned a strategic study of the profession in 1992 that identified a fundamental misperception emanating from the architectural profession and the 'habit of exclusion' (RIBA 1992):

> A certain rigidity leading to the exclusion of whatever is unusual, novel, non-central lies very deep in the British architectural psyche. Taking a long historical perspective, British architects have consistently tended to exclude from their concern of 'normality' whatever activity doesn't seem to fit – aspects of surveying management skills, cost estimating, landscaping, town planning, building science, the competences of building technicians, interior design. The list is very long. Meanwhile antipathy and mistrust between architects and constructors have grown. The habit of such puritanical exclusivity seems to be peculiar to architects. (Warne 1993: 38)

This exclusiveness ascribed to architectural skills is in large part attributable to the charter, which grants a monopoly or privilege to exercise and control the particular skill area of 'design' to an autonomous institution.

As with vocational education for operatives, the professional level is characterised therefore by a fragmentation of skills and an apparently fixed structure whose reproduction is geared to existing practice through the control of the professional institutions and of education. The system of privilege over skill areas granted by the charters acts as a serious barrier to development and has meant increasing overlaps in educational courses.

Not only are professional skill divisions thereby fixed but education for the professions and the trades is irrevocably and constitutionally divided, as illustrated in Chart 8.1: there are no institutional links bridging this divide. Professional education is regulated by the professional institutions through their charters granted by the Privy Council and they in turn accredit university courses in their particular skill area. Vocational education for the trades is regulated by the quango, the LSC, which funds the training provision, whether by private training providers, FE colleges or industry itself. This structure and practice presents an obstacle to permeability and career progression, enforcing a class divide between professionals and operatives and hindering the development of intermediate skill areas.

Comparison with Germany: Tripartite Governance and Social Partnership

Education in Germany, including vocational education and cultural affairs in general, is under regional ministerial control; the sixteen *Länder* have preserved their autonomy and at federal level the Standing Conference of the Ministers of Education and Cultural Affairs (*Kultusministerkonferenz* or KMK) represents the common interest. This institution has the task of ensuring comparability of certificates and qualifications, of safeguarding quality standards in schools, vocational training and HE, and of promoting cooperation among educational, scientific and cultural institutions (KMK 2003). The federal government sets the legal framework for HE by establishing principles such as 'freedom to teach, to research and to learn' within the limits of the basic law, *Grundgesetz*. The federal government has recently opened up the higher educational sector to private universities, necessitating adaptation of the regulatory framework. Quality standards have traditionally been set by the HE institutes themselves, while constitutional, financial and administrative issues are dealt with in cooperation with the regional state and the standing conference of education ministers on the advice of the specialist advisory institution on science policy, the *Wissenschaftsrat*. In response to European legislation a new method of accreditation of quality standards is to be carried out by the science council (Wissenschaftsrat 2000).

The German vocational system is based on the 'dual' system whereby the firm and the vocational schools are jointly recognised as places of learning and vocational training is the responsibility of both the private and public sectors. The KMK represents the federal state and lays down the guidelines and principles for education and training in all occupations within the dual system (*Rahmenlehrpläne*). The educational content of learning in the vocational schools is broadly defined, with, for instance, general skills regarded as technical, social and personal competences.

> Personal competence encompasses personal qualities such as independence, critical thinking, self-confidence, reliability, a sense of responsibility and duty...social competence refers to the willingness and ability to form and engage in social relations, the development of social responsibility and solidarity. (KMK 1999)

The training regulations have been revised by the social partners – the industrial trade unions and employers' associations – to specify the occupations in the sector, the length and stages of training, the actual content, examination and qualification. This revision was carried out together with the Federal Institute of Vocational Training, *Bundesinstitut für Berufsbildung (BIBB)*.

The integration of the social partners is at the core of the system of skill formation, operating at various levels and safeguarded through the laws on vocational education, *Berufsbildungsgesetz 1999*, and on the promotion of vocational education, *Berufsbildungsförderungsgesetz 1994* (see Chart 8.2). It is illustrated by the BIBB, whose tasks are clearly laid down: to prepare changes to legislation; to publish the annual report on vocational education; to participate in vocational statistics, scientific pilot projects and international cooperation; to support the planning, maintenance and further development of training facilities; and to maintain and publish the list of 345 legally recognised vocational occupations. The institute receives its instructions from the Federal Minister for Education and two tripartite committees – general (main)

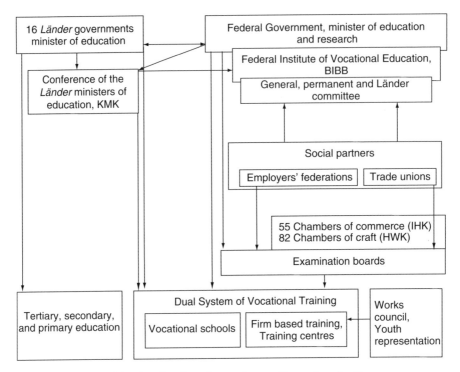

Chart 8.2   The institutional structure of learning in Germany

Hauptausschuss and permanent *Ständiger Ausschuss*. The former consists of 16 members each from the employers' and employees' organisations, the Federal state and *Länder*, and the latter of eight members from the main committee made up of two representatives from each of the four groups. The permanent committee carries out business in between the sessions of the large committee and if expert committees are set up, for instance, to develop particular occupational profiles, the law requires that these are also set up on a tripartite basis.

The social partner basis of the organisation is replicated at regional level. The tripartite regional committee for vocational education, *Länderausschusse*, is a subcommittee of the general committee, *Hauptausschuss*, and comprises 16 representatives of the *Länder* and three representatives each of the employers' and employees' organisations and the federal government, in total 25 members. The committees act as advisors to the regional ministries, whose main responsibility is to link general and vocational education since general education is under the control of the regional or *Länder* government and vocational education under the Federal government. The 16 *Länder* also have their own tripartite vocational training committees, which participate in formulating curricula, *Lehrpläne*, whilst the Federal government passes educational codes, *Ausbildungsordnungen*. Tripartite representation, the social partners and representatives of the vocational schools, is given at the local level in the examination boards, *Prüfungsausschüsse*, which examine trainees on the completion of their training. These examination boards are set up by the local Chambers of Trade and Commerce and fulfil an important function in the representation of business interests. Vocational education is based on the 345 occupational profiles and defines the content of vocational education, length of training, standards and the skill level required. The vocational schools, *Berufsschulen*, are part of the 'dual system' training and hence come under federal and *Länder* authority and within the area of social-partner influence (Streeck and Hilbert 1991). Chart 8.2 illustrates the cooperation between state and social partners in the structure of vocational learning.

For construction, as for the whole economy, the system of vocational training in Germany – and to some extent general education – is based on this principle of tripartite representation, with social-partner involvement at all levels built into the different institutions involved. The model depends on a high degree of business representation through the statutory system of chambers and interest representation of German employers in one of the two federations – *Hauptverband der Deutschen Bauindustrie* or HDB (Association of the German Construction Industry) for industry firms and *Zentralverband des Deutschen Baugewerbes* or ZDB (Central Association of the German Building Industry) for craft firms – and *Industriegewerkschaft Bauen-Agrar-Umwelt* for employees in the construction union. The three organisations play a central role in social-partner cooperation in the construction sector.

The local chambers, claiming to represent all business interests and set-up according to geographic area, are key to this cooperation in vocational training. They are legally constituted through Federal Chamber law, *Bundeskammergesetz*, and form the system of corporate self-governance in conjunction with carrying out public tasks. Membership of a chamber is compulsory for all firms, either in one of 82 local craft chambers, *Handswerkskammer*, or in one of 55 chambers of industry and commerce, *Industrie- und Handelskammer*, with firms defined as belonging to the craft or industry federation according to the activities carried out. Funding is provided from obligatory membership subscriptions and chambers, as well as providing a wide range of services, lobby for members' interests at all administrative and political levels. The state has transferred important tasks to the chambers, including administering the vocational training system, setting up the examinations boards and holding all examinations, as well as selecting, appointing and monitoring the system of 'sworn in' experts, and setting up conciliation boards for conflicts between members and clients.

Unlike in Britain, where access to most trades is unregulated, the regulation of craft in Germany through the chambers is strict, with firms belonging to a craft area according to the 94 craft profiles of the German craft code, the *Handwerksordnung*. Access to the trades and the terms and conditions for trading are controlled through the system of master craftsmanship (*Meister*), which is at the core of the craft regulatory system. The Master certificate is the precondition for establishing a business and for entry into the craft roll. As well as giving entitlement to train, craft licences issued by the chambers are in effect permissions to trade. Proponents of this system of regulation claim that it has the advantages of quality assurance for craft activities (consumer protection), the prevention of destructive competition (safeguarding existing standards) and the setting of incentives and means of qualifying for apprenticeship training. It has been forcefully argued that the system of chambers as highly organised business interests is a necessary and constituent part of the German vocational training system (Soskice 1994). Extending this argument, they can be seen to provide part of the backbone of the successful German social partnership model, with vocational training as one of its core elements.

In 2003 the reform programme of the Social Democratic Party-led government, *Agenda 2010*, includes a revision of the craft code, in place since the 1950s. This code restricted free trade for the public benefit, as the federal constitutional court maintained in 1961, but is now seen to contravene European legislation stipulating freedom to trade. The new revision involves drastic changes, with abolition of the master certificate as the entry requirement for 65 craft occupations, though it will be retained for the remaining 29 occupations, which present a danger to the life or health of the public.

At federal state level, bipartite and tripartite cooperation is therefore exercised through the various committees of the institute for vocational education (BIBB) and at regional level is organised and set up through the chambers. The third level where institutionalised cooperation can be observed is the firm. The system of democratic workplace representation was first introduced through the Works Constitution Act in 1952. In 1998 the German government produced a detailed assessment of the social, political and economic significance of the works council system, leading to a further strengthening of the system through legislation in 2001, including, for instance: more works councillors in firms with more than 200 employees, release from work to carry out works council tasks; simplified election procedures; the introduction of proportional representation of women; and strengthening the work of the trainees' committee. In general, information, consultation and co-determination rights were confirmed and in some instances strengthened. This system of co-determination and the recent revision will greatly increase unions' influence on the workplace, as a large majority of works councillors are union members who rely to a great extent on the training facilities and expertise of the unions to carry out their roles.

German Professional Chambers

In terms of HE, the structures that support professionalisation are very different from those in Britain, particularly with respect to the role of the state in initiating, sanctioning and administering established and new professions (Lean and Morgan 2000). UK professions have developed as the result of voluntary associations, whereas in Germany the state plays an active role in their establishment, structuring, administration and training. One of the key differences lies in the role of civil servants and the integration of the university system with the state apparatus.

Professionals in Germany are self-organised in chambers established at federal and regional level and regulated through laws or ordinances, a compromise between the state and self-regulation. Membership of the chambers is obligatory for certain professionals, such as lawyers, accountants, doctors and pharmacists, and for the two construction industry professions – architects and engineers. The Chamber of Building in Berlin, *Baukammer Berlin*, for instance, specifies who by law is required to become a member (*Architekten- und Baukammergesetz 1994*): all consulting engineers, all engineers who can submit planning applications, and publicly appointed and sworn surveying engineers (*Baukammer Berlin* 2003). In 2000 the federal engineering chamber, *Bundesingenieurkammer*, had 16,622 members and almost twice as many more took up voluntary membership, whilst the federation of professionals, *Berufsverband der freien Berufe*, included amongst its membership 45,200 engineers and 53,378 architects in private practice (*Bundesverband der Freien Berufe* 2003).

Academic qualification and state examination are the entry requirement to the chambers, with engineers additionally requiring three years and architects two years of professional practice; in contrast to the UK there is no other entry examination. The titles 'architect' and 'engineer' are protected and can only be used by members of the chambers. Members of a profession are also bound by the rules of conduct incorporated in the legislation to serve the public benefit. Chambers are accountable to the minister and have a supervisory role regarding the professional duties of members, setting up mediation boards for disputes between professionals and clients and disciplinary procedures for professional misconduct. Professionals are obliged to follow the rules of professional conduct, for instance, through occupational ordinances such as *Musterberufsordnung* for engineers, which embodies the ethical codes of professional practice that prescribe duties, such as the requirement for professional indemnity insurance, representation of the client's interest, continuous professional development and maintenance of independent status. Legislation regulates fees, and competition between professional practices is not permitted, likewise advertising, although some form of publicity is allowed as public information.

One fundamental difference between professional institutions in the UK and the German chambers is the very limited role of the latter in the education and training of their members. The federal chamber of engineers in Germany, for example, the umbrella organisation of all building engineering chambers representing the interests of engineers at federal, European Union (EU) and international level, has amongst its six committees none dealing with education and training (*Bundesingenieurkammer* 2003). This is also the case for the federal chamber of architects whose remit in education and training only includes continuing professional development. The objectives of these federal chambers are: to further construction, to participate in building legislation, to comment on building and planning matters, to provide expert advice for public authorities and courts, to preserve their professional interests and supervise the fulfilling of members' duties, to keep the list of architects and examine the entitlement of their members to the title, to participate in the regulation of the tendering procedure and to endeavour to mediate in disputes between members of chambers and clients (*Bundesarchitektenkammer* 2003). In terms of numbers, the system appears successful. Germany, together with Denmark, has one of the highest proportions of architects in Europe: 106,592 in 2000, compared with 6000 in Denmark, 30,600 in the UK and 7500 in the Netherlands, that is one for every 777 inhabitants compared with one in 1869 for the UK. There are many reasons for the large disparity between the numbers of architects in Germany and elsewhere, including the different nature of the occupation, its wide scope and broad job specification, and the high level of employment in the public sector.

Conclusion

The professional institutions in Britain have a vested interest in preserving and maintaining their monopoly even in the face of clear changes to the process and growing overlaps, but they also have little incentive to cooperate closely with other institutions – let alone merge. The exclusiveness that this gives rise to is enforced by the strong link with practice built into the structure of learning. This link applies equally to professionals and operatives with, on the one hand, professional organisations controlling courses in universities and, on the other, the new SSCs as business-led and owned companies overseeing vocational training. Those who lay down guidelines, validate, accredit and fund are the professionals and businesses themselves which holds the danger of too close an adherence to practical prescriptive application that can blind the development of courses to future developments and fail to impart to students transferable skills that rely more on a strong educational than a vocational element (Winch and Clarke 2002). These problems are inevitable given that the employers' interest in vocational education is to fulfil the immediate task in hand, hence concern with its outputs and with the short term. Employees, on the other hand, seek to acquire skills to enhance, equip and fulfil their potential over a working life and are thus more concerned with the inputs and with the long term.

Basing the system of education and training on the immediate needs of employers or current practices in industry makes for serious difficulties in changing the process, given that it is built around existing skill sets. Not only are skill divisions and even outmoded practices constantly perpetuated and reproduced, but there is no clear means to enhance skill potential or to plan for skill needs at industry level. This situation contrasts sharply with continental countries such as Germany, where vocational education is itself critical for promoting innovation and change in the process through imparting skills planned at industry level that are not just transferable but also often in advance of practice.

There are qualitatively distinct differences in institutional structures regulating VET in Britain and Germany. In the first place, the constitutional divide in Britain between Privy Council responsibility for professional education, delegated to the professional institutions, and state responsibility for vocational or operative training and education does not exist in Germany. In Britain this organisation makes for what is in effect a class divide and lack of permeability between professionals and operatives and for a skill structure with strong feudal characteristics that is relatively impervious to change. It remains a system built on delegating or granting privileges to private or employer interests over the control of vocational education and its contents. In contrast, in Germany, social partnership between employers, trade unions and the state is the key to regulation, with representatives of the social partners involved at all levels and in all aspects, whether in the training itself, in determination of its content or in the examinations.

Perhaps most striking of all is the very different concept of labour and nature of skills in the two countries that accompany such different structures. German skills are socially constructed, collectively negotiated and recognised not only through the work process but through different levels of education and attachment to different institutions and means of regulation. In Britain they remain individual attributes required to fulfil particular outputs, whose fragmentation is enforced through the autonomous and unaccountable institutions that control or govern their formation.

Note

1 The research has been supported by the Engineering and Physical Sciences Research Council: 'Standardisation and skills: a transnational study of skills, education and training for prefabrication in housing' (1999–2001) and 'From Process to Product: comparing quality in social house-building in Europe' (2001–2002), and to be published as *Innovation and Skills* by Blackwell in 2004.

References

Andrews, J. and Derbyshire, A. (1993) *Crossing Boundaries*, Construction Industry Board, London.

Architects' Registration Board (2003) *Education*, www.arb.org.uk/frame.html.

Baukammer Berlin (2003) *Mitgliedschaft, Pflichtmitglied*, www.kmk.org/beruf/rlpl/rlpbau.pdf.

Bundesarchitektenkammer (2003) *Aufgaben und Struktur*, http://www.bundesarchitektenkammer.de.

Bundesingenieurkammer (2003) *Fachgremien*, www.bundesingenieurkammer.de/152.htm.

Bundesverband der Freien Berufe (2003) *Statistik – Zahlenmäßige Struktur der Selbstständigen in Freien Berufen*, www.freie-berufe.de.

Cabinet Office (2003) *Public Bodies 2002*, www.publicappointments.gov.uk/publications/publicbodies.pdf.

Chartered Institute of Personnel and Development (2003) *Royal Charter*, www.cipd.co.uk/download/anonymous/charterandbyelaws.pdf.

CITB (2002a) *Business Plan 2002–2006*, Bircham Newton: Construction Industry Training Board.

CITB (2002b) *Survey of Employment by Occupation in the Construction Industry 2001*, Bircham Newton: Construction Industry Training Board.

CITB (2002c) *Skills Foresight Report February 2002*, Bircham Newton: Construction Industry Training Board.

Clarke, L. and Wall, C. (1998) *A Blueprint for Change: Construction Skills Training in Britain*, Bristol: Policy Press.

Clarke, L. and Wall, C. (2000) 'Craft versus Industry: The Division of Labour in European Housing Construction', *Construction Management and Economics*, 18, 685–698.

DfES (2001) *Meeting the Sector Skills and Productivity Challenge*, Nottingham: Department for Education and Skills.

Engineering Council (2003) *Royal Charter*, www.engc.org.uk.

Gann, D. and Salter, A. (1999) *Interdisciplinary Skills for Built Environment Professionals*, London: Ove Arup Foundation.

Higher Education Foundation Council for England (2003) *mission statement*, www.hefce.ac.uk.

Keep, E. (2002) *The Changing Meaning of Skill and the Shifting Balance of Responsibility for Vocational Education and Training – Are Employers calling the Shots?*, paper presented at the Conference on Training, Employability and Employment, Monash University Centre London.

Kultusministerkonferenz (1999) *Rahmenlehrpläne für die Berufsausbildung in der Bauwirtschaft*, http://www.kmk.org/beruf/rlpl/rlpbau.pdf.

Kultusministerkonferenz (2003) *Aufgaben*, http://www.kmk.org/aufg-org/home.htm. gesch.

Latham, M. (1994) *Constructing the Team, Final Report of the joint governmental/industry review of procurement and contractual arrangements in the UK construction industry*, London: The Stationery Office.

Lean, M. and Morgan, J. (2000) 'The Professionalization of Everyone? A Comparative Study of the Development of the Professions in the United Kingdom and Germany', *European Sociological Review*, 16:1, 9–26.

Marsden, D. (1999) *A Theory of Employment Systems*, Oxford: Oxford University Press.

Maurice, M., Sellier, F. and Silvestre, J. J. (1986) *The Social Foundations of Industrial Power*, Cambridge, Mass.: MIT Press.

Nisbet, J. (1989) *Called to Account, Quantity Surveying, 1936–1986*, London, Stoke Publications.

Privy Council Office (2003) *Chartered Bodies*, www.privycouncil.gov.uk/output/Page44.asp

RIBA (1992, 1993, 1995) *The Strategic Study of the Profession*, phase 1: *Strategic Overview*, phase 2: *Clients and Architects*, phase 3 and 4: *The Way Forward*, London: Royal Institute of British Architects.

RIBA (2000) *Architects and the Changing Construction Industry*, London: Royal Institute of British Architects.

RIBA (2003) *Royal Charter*, http://members.riba.org/byelaws/charter.pdf.

Rubery, J. and Grimshaw, D. (1998) 'Training, Skills and The Changing Production and Employment System', paper presented to the *Work, Employment and Society Conference*, University of Cambridge.

Sector Skills Development Agency (2002a) *Speech by Adult Skills Minister John Healey*, www.ssda.org.uk/cgi-bin/go.pl/news/index.html.

Sector Skills Development Agency (2002b), *Sector Skills Council Development Guide*, www.ssda.org.uk/pdfs/sscdguide.pdf.

Soskice, D. (1994) 'Reconciling Markets and Institutions: The German Apprenticeship System', in L. M. Lynch (ed.), *Training and the Private Sector; International Comparisons*, Chicago: Chicago University Press.

Streeck, W. and Hilbert, J. (1991) 'Organised Interests and Vocational Training in the West German Construction Industry', in G. Syben and H. Rainbird (eds), *Restructuring a Traditional Industry: Construction Employment and Skills in Europe*, Oxford: Berg.

Training Organisation for Professionals in Construction (2001) *mission statement*, www.cic.org.uk/topic/topic.htm.

Warne, E. J. D. (1993) *Review of the Architects (Registration) Acts 1931–1969*, London: Royal Institute of British Architects.

Winch, C. and Clarke, L. (2002) '"Front-loaded" Vocational Education versus Lifelong Learning', *Oxford Review of Education*, 29:2, 239–252.

Wissenschaftsrat (2000) *Empfehlungen zur Akkreditierung privater Hochschulen*, www.wissenschaftsrat.de/texte/4419-00.pdf.

9

Job Complexity and Task Discretion: Tracking the Direction of Skills at Work in Britain

Alan Felstead, Duncan Gallie and Francis Green

Introduction

Concern over Britain's relative economic performance compared to other industrialised countries has been the subject of debate over many years. One common explanation centres on Britain's comparatively low-skill levels. There is now widespread recognition by policy-makers that the long-term rate of productivity growth in Britain lags too far behind that of many other advanced industrial economies and that '[N]arrowing this gap is key to delivering higher living standards, better public services and greater opportunity for all' (HM Treasury 2002b: 17). Whatever the measure, a sizeable productivity gap is apparent. Measured in terms of output per worker, estimates suggest that US productivity is around 38 per cent higher than it is in Britain, with France and Germany 18 and 9 per cent higher respectively. Similarly, unfavourable productivity comparisons provide the backdrop to, and motivation for, a range of recent policy initiatives, consultations and reviews. These include the establishment of employer-led Sector Skills Councils (SSC) (DfES 2001), a consultation exercise on post-compulsory education and training provision (LSC 2002), several reviews of the state of skills in Britain (DfES 2000; Campbell *et al.* 2001) and a strategic overview of workforce development (PIU 2001).

The government's solution rests on the impact that improvements in skills are expected to have on productivity. Research examining the causes of international differences in productivity suggests that differing skill levels play a crucial, if complex, role. For example, estimates suggest that between half and all of the productivity gap with Germany can be explained by skills differences alone (O'Mahony 1999). The idea is that skilled workers learn to adapt faster and more easily to new circumstances. Thus, they increase the ability of the organisation to update its practices and products at the rate

148

demanded by rapidly changing product markets, hence making the economy more flexible and more productive.

Based on this premise, a number of specific policy initiatives, including target setting, the development of innovative delivery mechanisms and providing tax credits for employers (HM Treasury 2002a,b) have been launched to drive up skills and narrow the productivity gap. In the main, these have been directed at raising the numbers of adult workers with intermediate level qualifications and reducing the numbers of those experiencing literacy and numeracy difficulties. Both are areas where Britain compares poorly internationally. Tackling them also has the additional benefit of increasing social inclusion by breaking the low skills/low pay trap many individuals find themselves in and by spreading access to training and development opportunities more widely.

Despite this flurry of activity, empirical evidence on skill trends is limited by comparison to that available on productivity. Tracking movements in skills are hampered by the narrowness of focus (e.g. recording qualification levels), the inconsistent way in which data are collected (by different sector bodies, training organisations or regional institutions, see Blake *et al.* 2000) and/or the infrequency with which national wide-ranging skills surveys are carried out. Nevertheless, the latter provide the most detailed insight into skills movements and offer the most comprehensive barometer by which to measure progress. The aim of this chapter is to provide an overview of some of the findings to emerge from the most recent of these – the 2001 Skills Survey (see Felstead *et al.* 2002 for more detail). The 2001 results are compared with those gathered from similar surveys carried out in 1986, 1992 and 1997. The chapter is structured as follows. The next section outlines the two main aspects of 'skill' captured by the questions posed to respondents, and the four data sets on which the chapter's substantive empirical contribution is based. Trends in these two skill dimensions are then examined: the complexity of jobs as measured by broad and generic skills are considered first, while the scope to exercise choice and judgement in carrying out tasks is the focus of the chapter's penultimate section. The chapter ends by drawing out some implications for policy-makers and the conduct of future skills research.

Skill Measures and Data Sources

Despite the enormous interest in how skills in Britain have changed over time, how they are distributed, and how these trends and patterns compare with competing nations, there is surprisingly little agreement on what 'skills' actually refer to. In practice, different authors often refer to different aspects of skill and are influenced by the theoretical standpoint from which their interest in the phenomenon stems. This variety is evident from the empirical evidence on skills patterns, trends and future trajectories compiled by the

National Skills Task Force (DfES 2000) and recently updated by Campbell *et al.* (2001). As designers of the 2001 (and 1997) Skills Survey, our aim was to collect data of relevance to the measurement of skills that would reflect these multiple concerns.

However, despite different emphases and nuances, most studies of skill focus on either the complexity of jobs or the discretion jobholders exercise in carrying out the tasks involved (Spenner 1990; DfES 2000). Complexity varies according to the nature of the job such as the abilities and techniques required, the intricacies of the steps involved, and the knowledge of equipment, products and processes needed for competent performance. The data on which this chapter is based measures the complexity of jobs in two ways. First, the abilities and capacities of those in employment are measured by questions that focus on the attributes respondents report they require for the job. These broad skill measures include: the qualifications required to get the job; the length of training required for that type of work; and the time taken to learn to do the job well. Secondly, the generic skills demanded of those in work are also examined. These are measured by asking jobholders to rate the importance of particular activities to their work.

However, some authors argue that skill levels vary according to the extent to which jobholders can exercise discretion and judgement at work (e.g. Braverman 1974; Zuboff 1988). While all jobs are carried out within prescribed rules – whether set by law, occupational standards or custom and practice – an element of choice/judgement remains. The greater this choice/judgement is, the higher the skill of the job in the overall skill hierarchy. The surveys on which this chapter draws asked respondents about the amount of choice they had in carrying out their job as well as a series of questions about the personal influence they had over how hard they worked, what tasks they did, how tasks were to be completed and what standards they had to achieve.

The 2001 Skills Survey replicated many aspects of the 1997 Skills Survey, including the research team involved, the market research company and the methods of sample selection. In particular, many of the same questions were used. Comparability between the 2001 and 1997 surveys was thereby maximised. Several questions asked in 2001 were also used in a nationally representative survey of the workforce in 1992 – Employment in Britain (EIB) – and in a survey of six contrasting localities in Britain in 1986 – the Social Change and Economic Life Initiative (SCELI). This chapter examines how the complexity of jobs and discretion levels have changed over time by comparing, where possible, the responses given to identical questions asked of respondents to each of these surveys. All four of these are nationally representative sample surveys of individuals in employment aged 20–60 years. Each comprises a large number of respondents: the 1986 SCELI contains information from 4047 respondents, the 1992 EIB comprises 3855 individuals, the 1997 Skills Survey is based on 2467 interviewees and the

2001 Skills Survey contains data on 4470 individuals (Gallie 1994; Gallie *et al.* 1998; Ashton *et al.* 1999; Felstead *et al.* 2002).

The Complexity of Jobs

In relation to the complexity of jobs, respondents to all four surveys were asked identical questions on the qualifications that would now be required to get their job, the length of time needed to train for that type of work and the time taken to do the job well. These are referred to as broad skills measures.

Table 9.1 outlines the distribution of skills according to these broad measures at each of the four data points – 1986, 1992, 1997 and 2001. Overall, this evidence suggests that the trend over these fifteen years is a general increase in the levels of skill required of those in work. At the beginning of the period, 20 per cent of jobs required level 4 or above qualifications for entry, but by 2001 this had risen to 29 per cent. The most rapid increase was in the demand for degrees, up from 10 per cent in 1986 to 17 per cent in 2001. The same pattern is repeated at the other end of the scale, where there was around a 12 percentage point drop in the proportion of jobs requiring no qualifications for entry over the fifteen-year period. The Required Qualification Index (a summary measure, see Table 9.1) also reflected these trends, rising from 1.71 in 1986 to 2.10 in 2001.

Trends in training time over the period also suggest that skills demand in Britain have increased. Comparing the results in 1986 with those in 2001 shows that training times have lengthened – greater proportions of the employed workforce reported that training periods for the type of work they were now doing lasted over two years, while smaller proportions reported that their training lasted less than three months. The Training Time Index rose from 2.01 in 1986 to 2.27 in 2001.

Similarly, the length of time needed to do jobs well rose considerably throughout the 1986–2001 period. Lengthy learning times accounted for more of the jobs in 2001 than in 1986 and shorter learning times for less. This pattern was reflected in a consistent rise in the Learning Time Index over the period – rising from 3.30 in 1986 to 3.57 in 2001.

By examining the changes in broad skills in each of the sub-periods – 1986–1992, 1992–1997 and 1997–2001 – it is possible to investigate when significant skills changes took place and whether upskilling continued strongly in recent years. The first row of Table 9.2 summarises the findings. None of the three measures have risen significantly within all of the sub-periods. The Required Qualification Index rose significantly in 1986–1992 and 1997–2001 but changed little in 1992–1997. The Learning Time Index rose in all three sub-periods, but only rose significantly in the years 1992–1997. The pattern of change in the Training Time Index is different again, displaying significant

Table 9.1   Trends in broad skills 1986–2001

Broad skills[a]	Sample percentages/scores			
	1986	1992	1997	2001
Highest qualification required[b]				
Level 4 or above	20.2	25.5	24.3	29.2
Degree	9.7	13.2	14.1	17.3
Non-degree	10.5	12.3	10.2	11.9
Level 3	15.2	16.6	13.8	16.3
Level 2	18.5	19.0	21.2	15.9
Level 1	7.7	5.0	9.2	12.1
No qualifications	38.4	34.0	31.5	26.5
Required qualification index[b]	1.71	1.95	1.90	2.10
Training time[c]				
>2 years	22.4	21.9	28.9	23.6
<3 months	66.0	62.6	57.0	61.1
Training index	2.01	2.21	2.53	2.27
Learning time (employees only)[d]				
>2 years	24.3	21.6	24.3	25.6
<1 month	27.1	22.3	21.4	20.2
Learning index	3.30	3.36	3.48	3.57
Sample base: all in employment, aged 20–60	4047.0	3855.0	2467.0	4470.0

[a] The data reported here and throughout have been weighted by a factor that takes into account the slight over-representation of women in all of the samples and according to the number of eligible respondents at each address visited. All calculations exclude missing values.

[b] Respondents in all four surveys were asked: 'If they were applying today, what qualifications, if any, would someone need to *get* the type of job you have now?' A range of options was given. From this the highest qualification level, ranked by NVQ equivalents, was derived. The Required Qualification Index was calculated from the responses: none = 0; level 1 (equivalent to fewer than 5 General Certificate of Secondary Education grades A*-C) = 1; level 2 (equivalent to 5 or more General Certificate of Secondary Education grades A*-C) = 2; level 3 (equivalent to 2 or more A levels) = 3; and level 4 or above (first degree and above) = 4.

[c] Respondents to all four surveys were asked: 'Since completing full-time education, have you ever had, or are you currently undertaking, training for the type of work that you currently do?' Respondents answering 'yes' were then asked: 'How long, in total, did (or will) that training last?' A range of options was given. The Training Time Index was calculated from the responses: none = 0; less than 1 month = 1; 1–3 months = 2; 3–6 months = 3; 6–12 months = 4; 1–2 years = 5; and over 2 years = 6.

[d] Respondents to all four surveys were asked: 'How long did it take for you after you first started doing this type of job to learn to do it well?' This question was asked only of employees in 1986 and so the 1992, 1997 and 2001 figures have been restricted accordingly. The learning time index was calculated from the responses: less than 1 month = 1; less than 3 months = 2; 3–6 months = 3; 6–12 months = 4; 1–2 years = 5; and over 2 years = 6.

Table 9.2 Trends in broad skills by gender and full-time/part-time status 1986–2001

	Required qualification index[a]			Training time index			Learning time index		
	1986–1992	1992–1997	1997–2001	1986–1992	1992–1997	1997–2001	1986–1992	1992–1997	1997–2001
All	+0.23*	−0.04	+0.19*	+0.20*	+0.32*	−0.26*	+0.06	+0.12*	+0.09
Male	+0.16*	−0.10	+0.19*	+0.02	+0.25*	−0.41*	−0.06	+0.08	+0.06
Female	+0.37*	+0.02	+0.20*	+0.49*	+0.40*	−0.10	+0.29*	+0.16*	+0.11
Female full-time	+0.39*	−0.04	+0.17*	+0.50*	+0.37*	−0.25*	+0.19*	+0.20*	+0.01
Female part-time	+0.28*	+0.08	+0.22*	+0.39*	+0.44*	+0.09	+0.36*	+0.07	+0.21*

[a] The figures refer to indices changes between 1986–1992, 1992–1997 and 1997–2001. A positive (negative) figure indicates a rise (fall) between the two sample points. Any differences between the figures in Tables 9.1 and 9.2 are due to rounding.
* a statistically significant index change (p < 0.10).

increases in 1986–1992 and 1992–1997, but significantly falling back almost to 1992 levels by 2001.

Table 9.2 also shows how the distribution of broad skills has changed over time according to the gender and status of the jobholder. The skill level of women's jobs has risen faster than men's, thereby serving to narrow the gap between the skills of men's and women's jobs. This change applies on each measure and in every sub-period studied. An example underlying the change in the indices is the decline in 1986–2001 in the proportion of jobs requiring no qualifications: from 48 to 29 per cent for women and from 31 to 24 per cent for men. Thus, the gender gap narrowed from 17 to just 5 percentage points.

Female part-timers have, on the whole, been the main beneficiaries of the narrowing of the gender gap. It is notable, for example, that while the Training Time Index implies a fall in skills in recent years (1997–2001), female part-timers appear to have bucked the trend with a significant increase. Similarly, while female full-timers had only a small, insignificant, increase in the Learning Time Index, for part-timers the increase was substantial and statistically significant.[1]

A common way of measuring skill movements is to examine changes in the stock of qualifications held by the workforce. Data sets such as the Labour Force Survey (LFS) and their equivalents in other countries make this type of analysis possible on a regular and consistent basis. Measuring skills in this way is at the heart of the government's National Training Targets, initially launched in 1991 albeit under a different name, for which the Learning and Skills Council (LSC) is now responsible. However, such an approach focuses exclusively on the supply of skills as proxied by qualifications. The original contribution of the 2001 and 1997 Skills Surveys and, in part, SCELI and EIB, is their focus on the measurement of skills actually used in the workplace. Although it is possible to track accurately the qualifications held by those actually in employment (using the LFS, see NACETT 2000), the mismatch between the qualifications held by jobholders and the qualifications they require has, until now, been largely unknown. However, the analysis that follows includes a tracking of the extent of this discrepancy.

First, this discrepancy is presented in aggregate terms. That is to say, the difference between the number of jobs requiring qualifications of various levels and the number of economically active individuals holding qualifications at each of these levels. In other words, the aggregate is the demand for and supply of qualifications (which are, of course, only proxies for skills). These figures are derived in the following way. The estimates of *demand* for qualifications are based on the 1986, 1992, 1997 and 2001 survey evidence on the highest qualification required to get the job respondents occupied at the time of interview. Using the appropriate spring quarter of the LFS, these proportions are grossed up to the number of 20–60 year olds recorded to be in work in Britain. It should be remembered that these demand estimates are based on the jobholder's perceptions of required qualifications rather than the views of their employer. However, evidence from elsewhere suggests that line managers' perceptions of the qualification requirements of jobs are, on average, not substantially different from the perceptions of their subordinates (Green and James 2001). Estimates of the *supply* of qualifications, on the other hand, are based exclusively on the relevant spring quarter of the LFS. All 20–60 year olds who were economically active in Britain at the time of interview are included in these calculations. Table 9.3 gives a breakdown of the supply of individuals qualified at each level, whether in or actively seeking work. These data have been categorised according to the same qualification protocols as the demand data derived from each of the four surveys.[2]

A comparison of the columns in Table 9.3 shows where in the qualification hierarchy demand and supply are broadly equal and where there are deficiencies or excesses in demand. At the bottom of the qualification hierarchy such a comparison reveals that the phenomenon of a large excess of jobs over people requiring/having no qualifications only emerged in the 1990s. This excess arose not because the number of jobs requiring no qualifications rose (they, in fact, fell, see Table 9.1) but because the number of people holding no qualifications fell at a substantially faster rate. At the end of the decade, there is an indication of a small fall in the total of the excess, largely resulting from the fact that the 1997–2001 period saw a fall of over one million in jobs needing no qualifications. However, there were still 6.5 million jobs for which no qualifications at all were required compared to 2.9 million economically active people who matched this qualification profile.

The balance of supply and demand for level 3 qualifications has fluctuated considerably. In 1986, the supply of level 3 qualifications appears to have been substantially greater than the number of jobs requiring them. By 1992, this excess had largely disappeared, following a rise in demand at this level, and a fall in supply as more people moved up the qualification ladder and less qualified older workers retired. However, an excess supply at level 3 reappeared in the 1990s, as more people moved up to this level from below. In 2001 there were approximately 6.4 million people qualified to level 3 but only 4 million jobs demanding this level of qualifications were on entry. Deficiencies in demand for qualifications were somewhat less at levels 2 and 1 where in 2001 the gap between requirements and supply was 1.4 and 0.6 million respectively.

At level 4 or above, there has been an approximate balance of supply and demand for most of the period. The exception is 1997 saw a small excess supply emerging but this had shrunk by 2001. The broad aggregate balance in 2001 meant that around 7.1 million jobs required level 4 or above qualifications for entry, while there were 7.4 million individuals in Britain in possession of this level of qualification. For degrees, the figures diverge a little more with 4.2 million graduate jobs compared to 4.8 million graduates. This stable balance over time has arisen from supply and demand at this level growing together at broadly similar rates and doing so from a similar starting points.

Table 9.3   Qualifications demand and supply 1986–2001

	1986		1992		1997		2001	
	D ('000s)	S ('000s)	D ('000s)	S ('000s)	D ('000s)	S ('000s)	D ('000s)	S ('000s)
Level 4 or above	4176	3820	5666	4988	5671	6324	7122	7359
Degree	2005	2319	2933	2979	3291	3877	4220	4774
Non-degree	2171	1501	2733	2009	2381	2447	2903	2585
Level 3	3143	4905	3688	4124	3221	6209	3976	6379
Level 2	3825	4080	4222	7276	4948	5255	3878	5302
Level 1	1592	2198	1111	2269	2147	3754	2951	3549
No qualifications	7939	7748	7554	5831	7352	3274	6464	2881

Notes: D indicates the number of jobs with highest qualifications requirements at each level; S indicates the number of people holding highest qualifications at each level. Estimates were obtained as follows:

D: For each year, using the appropriate LFS, an estimate was derived of the total number of individuals aged 20–60 years who were in paid work in Britain. This figure was multiplied by the percentage of survey respondents who reported that access to their jobs required highest qualifications at one of the levels shown. These percentages are reported in Table 9.1. The demand figures are thus estimates of the number of jobs in Britain that demand qualifications at various levels. The analysis is restricted to individuals' main job; secondary jobs are not included.

S: The supply figures, giving the total number of individuals who possess qualifications at each level, are also derived from the LFS. They are constituted from all economically active people, including the unemployed, using the *employee* and *looking* variables for the 1986 LFS, and including those recorded as International Labour Organisation unemployed using the INECACA derived variable for 1992 onwards. For comparability with the demand figures, the analysis is restricted to those aged 20–60 years living in Britain. Despite the greater detail provided by the LFS on qualifications held (such as the ability to differentiate those with one or two A levels, hence allocating individuals precisely across the Level 2/3 divide), for comparability we used the simpler qualification protocols used in deriving the qualification bands for Table 9.1 (see Felstead *et al.* 2002; Tables 3.1, 4.1 and 4.5).

However, the labour markets at the different qualification levels should not be thought of as completely segmented from each other. It is quite common for people to take jobs which demand a lower level of qualification than the one they possess, and also possible (though less common) for people to be in jobs which now demand higher qualifications than the ones they possess. This is the second way in which mismatches between jobs and qualifications can arise.

Imbalances in the aggregate supplies of workers and numbers of jobs at each qualification level (reported above) are an important factor underlying mismatches at the individual level in which workers may have too high or too low qualification levels for their jobs. To obtain, therefore, a fuller picture of the utilisation of qualifications in the economy, the match between each individuals' qualifications and their job's requirements, and how this match has changed over time is analysed. Each respondent's qualification levels are compared with the qualification levels someone would need to get that job. From this we can calculate whether the respondent is 'over-qualified' in rela-tion to their current job – they have a higher level of qualification than is required – or whether they are 'under-qualified', their qualifications fall short of those now required.

It should be noted that the term 'over-qualified' does not mean that a person has received too much education. First, the qualifications may yet be necessary for a job that the person will do in the future. Some 'over-qualified' people may be currently constrained by their domestic circumstances from taking a job that would use their qualifications better, but would still hope to use the qualification in the future. Second, there are, in any case, many wider benefits of education that are not just to do with their jobs. The cultural and social benefits of education, both to the person being educated and to others in society, are hard or impossible to quantify, but should not be ignored. Third, qualifications can vary substantially in the skills that they stand for, even within the same level and type of qualification. Equally, if people are 'under-qualified', this does not imply that they are under-skilled for the job. Rather it is likely that they have increased their skills in other ways as job demands have changed. Any new person undertaking the job might now need to have a qualification. Moreover, some older workers may have professional or vocational qualifications that have since been formalised as higher academic qualifications. Nevertheless, the changing prevalence in the workforce of people who are 'over-qualified' or 'under-qualified' for their jobs can be regarded as a useful indicator of how well the job system is being matched with the qualifications system.

Previous research has shown that the prevalence of over-qualified workers in Britain, while increasing in the 1970s and early 1980s, remained fairly stable up until 1997 (Green *et al.* 2002). Table 9.4 brings this analysis up to date and also analyses the recent trend in the prevalence of under-qualified workers. This shows that during the 1986–2001 period, between one in six and one in

Table 9.4   Trends in the proportions 'over-qualified' and 'under-qualified' for their jobs, 1986–2001

	1986	1992	1997	2001
Percentage 'under-qualified'[a]	20.5	16.5	19.8	17.6
Percentage 'over-qualified'[b]	30.0	31.2	33.0	37.0
Percentage 'over-qualified' among those holding qualifications at levels:				
Level 4 or above	27.9	25.3	25.8	28.0
Degree	30.2	29.7	31.6	33.9
Non-degree	32.1	28.4	29.8	33.9
Level 3	47.7	41.5	52.0	48.1
Level 2	42.4	42.7	40.8	50.0
Level 1	54.3	48.9	42.5	43.2

[a] An 'under-qualified' individual has a highest qualification at a lower level than that currently required to get the job he/she now holds.
[b] An 'over-qualified' individual has a qualification at a higher level than that currently required to get the job he/she now holds.

five workers were 'under-qualified' in the sense outlined above. There is no detectable trend over this period. Nevertheless, systematic cross-sectional variation is evident. For example, the prevalence of 'under-qualified' workers is greater amongst older workers. Only about 10 per cent of 2001 workers in their 20s were under-qualified, compared with 23 per cent for those in their 50s.

In contrast, the prevalence of over-qualified workers has been increasing since 1986. The increase up until 1997 was only small, and was not statistically significant. However, the change was more rapid over the 1997–2001 period. Over this four-year period, the proportion rose from 33 to 37 per cent. It is also notable that in 2001 around half of those qualified to levels 2 and 3 were in jobs not requiring these qualifications for entry compared to around a quarter (28 per cent) with level 4 or above qualifications and 34 per cent of graduates. Being over-qualified, therefore, appears to be concentrated among those holding levels 2 and 3 qualifications. This finding is consistent with the aggregate imbalances reported above (for more detail see Green and McIntosh 2002).

Considerable attention has been paid in recent years to the proposition that several identifiable generic skills have risen in importance in the modern workplace. This putative growing importance has led to attempts to improve the acquisition of certain generic skills in the education system. As Westwood (in Chapter 3) also notes, there has been a policy focus on 'key skills', namely: 'communication skills', the 'application of number', 'information technology skills', 'problem-solving skills', 'working with others', and 'improving one's own learning and performance'. The government has inserted key skills into both the school and the university curriculum.

There have been few attempts so far, however, to investigate the extent of usage of these 'key skills' and other generic skills across the British economy. Generic skills are not easily quantified, and are frequently defined in slightly different ways by different researchers. Recently, however, two approaches have proved to be informative. The Organisation for Economic Co-operation and Development (OECD) developed the International Adult Literacy Survey (IALS) in which Britain participated in 1995. This survey measured the frequency of usage of literacy and numeracy skills in the workplace, and also tested respondents on their levels of these skills. Two notable findings are: first, quite high proportions of British workers were seriously deficient in their literacy and numeracy skills (OECD and Statistics Canada 1997; Carey *et al.* 1997); second, no matter what skills they held, the skills they had to use at work were robust and strong determinants of the pay they received (Green 1999). One drawback with the IALS method is that such surveys are expensive to administer and conducted infrequently. A second drawback is that they do not cover a very wide range of generic skills. These problems were addressed initially through work on the first Skills Survey in 1997. Using the job analysis approach, measures of a wide range of generic skills were obtained. Through questions asking respondents to recall earlier jobs, some idea of the trend in generic skills was also obtained (Ashton *et al.* 1999).

The 2001 Skills Survey subsequently repeated these questions (and asked some others focused on, e.g. managerial skills, see Felstead *et al.* 2002: 38–40, 53–54). The questions were formulated and selected to cover the wide range of activities involved in a variety of jobs. Respondents to both the 2001 and the 1997 Skills Surveys were asked a series of questions about particular activities their job might involve. This section of the questionnaire was prefaced by the following: 'You will be asked about different activities which may or may not be part of your job. At this stage we are only interested in finding out what types of activities your job involves and how important these are.' Respondents were then asked: 'in your job, how important is (a particular job activity)'. Examples of the activities included 'caring for others', 'dealing with people', 'using a computer', 'analysing complex problems' and 'planning the activities of others'. The questionnaire covered 36 activities designed to span the tasks carried out in a wide range of jobs. The response scale ranged from 'essential' to 'not at all important', with 'very important', 'fairly important' and 'not very important' in between. It is also worth pointing out that those respondents who reported their job involved 'using a computer, PC or other types of computerised equipment' were asked to indicate their level of computer usage. The response options were 'straightforward', 'moderate', 'complex' and 'advanced'. Each option was accompanied by a set of examples.

The analysis which follows adopts the following approach: scores are awarded to each respondent according to how important each activity is in their job – the higher the score, the more important the skill. Scores of 5, 4, 3,

2 and 1 respectively are allocated according to an individual's response so that those responding 'not at all important' score 1 whereas those reporting the activity to be 'essential' score 5. The figures reported here refer to the average scores and hence summarise the entire distribution of responses to each activity question.

By subtracting the average scores for 1997 from those recorded for 2001 for each particular skill, we can track how job demands have changed over time, albeit over only a four-year period. The results of these calculations are shown in the middle column of Table 9.5, while the right-hand column indicates whether the change between 1997 and 2001 is statistically significant. To gain an idea of how substantial the implied changes are, note that changes of around 0.1 on an index which ranges from 1 to 5 are relatively modest. To give an example, as a proportion of the average skill level, the 0.1 rise in the average index for 'reading long documents...' is approximately four per cent of the 1997 level. A change in any index of 0.1 is roughly equivalent to, for example, a three per cent rise in the proportion saying that this skill is 'very important' in their jobs, matched by a three percentage point fall in the proportion for whom the skill is 'not very important'. The analysis presented in Table 9.5 shows that according to 26 out of 35 particular skills measures, job demands have risen significantly. Furthermore, there are no activities that show statistically significant falls in skill levels. Notably, the uses of physical strength and stamina exhibit no change.

The largest change is in the index for the importance of using computers at work. There is a rapid ongoing increase in computer usage. Somewhat smaller rises are recorded for 'listening carefully to colleagues', 'counselling, advising or caring for customers or clients', 'skill or accuracy in using hands or fingers', 'specialist knowledge or understanding', 'knowledge of how your organisation works', 'thinking of solutions of problems or faults', 'writing short and writing long documents', and 'medium or advanced number skills'. Other skill rises are more modest, showing a high degree of stability in the nature of British jobs. It is not surprising to find relatively small changes when looking at a period of just four years. Nevertheless, the consistency of the direction of change is suggestive of a steady ongoing transformation of jobs. This remarkable finding provides formal confirmation of the continuing rise in the skills levels used in British workplaces, although broad skill trends suggest that the increase has slowed down over the last four years (cf. Table 9.1). A similar finding was obtained with the 1997 survey alone, but there the source of information was ultimately the respondents' recall of the jobs that they had done five years earlier. Here, the finding is on a firmer footing in that it derives from comparing two high quality, randomly drawn, representative sample surveys conducted with very similar methodologies and carried out by the same team. Nevertheless, only regular monitoring will confirm if these changes are sustainable and are not the product of swings in the economic cycle.

Table 9.5 Differences between detailed skills in 2001 and detailed skills in 1997

Detailed Skills	Average for 2001 minus Average for 1997	Significant Change?
Paying close attention to detail	−0.02	None
Dealing with people	+0.01	None
Instructing, training or teaching people	+0.12	Rise **
Making speeches or presentations	+0.13	Rise **
Persuading or influencing others	+0.07	Rise **
Selling a product or service	−0.05	None
Counselling, advising or caring for customers or clients	+0.16	Rise **
Working with a team of people	+0.07	Rise **
Listening carefully to colleagues	+0.15	Rise **
Physical strength	−0.03	None
Physical stamina	−0.01	None
Skill or accuracy in using hands or fingers	+0.19	Rise **
How to use or operate tools/equipment/machinery	+0.02	None
Knowledge of particular products or services	+0.09	Rise **
Specialist knowledge or understanding	+0.18	Rise **
Knowledge of how your organisation works	+0.22	Rise **
Using a computer, PC, or other types of computerised equipment	+0.38	Rise **
Spotting problems or faults	+0.05	Rise *
Working out the causes of problems or faults	+0.11	Rise **
Thinking of solutions of problems or faults	+0.15	Rise **
Analysing complex problems in depth	+0.08	Rise **
Checking things to ensure that there are no errors	+0.08	Rise **
Noticing when there is a mistake	+0.10	Rise **
Planning your own activities	+0.13	Rise **
Planning the activities of others	+0.08	Rise **
Organising your own time	+0.10	Rise **
Thinking ahead	+0.11	Rise **
Reading written information such as forms, notices or signs	+0.07	Rise **
Reading short documents such as short reports, letters or memos	+0.12	Rise **
Reading long documents such as long reports, manuals, articles or books	+0.11	Rise **
Writing written information such as forms, notices or signs	+0.14	Rise **
Writing short documents such as short reports, letters or memos	+0.18	Rise **
Writing long documents such as long reports, manuals, articles or books	+0.20	Rise **
Adding, subtracting or dividing numbers	+0.07	None
Calculations using decimals, percentages or fractions	+0.15	Rise **
Calculations using more advanced mathematical or statistical procedures	+0.15	Rise **

Notes: In each case, the statistical significance of the difference between the means of the skill level for 2001 and 1997 is assessed. The level of significance is ** = 5 per cent, and * = 10 per cent. This means that, where ** is indicated, we can reject the hypothesis of no change, but risk being wrong only 5 per cent of the time; for * we could be wrong 10 per cent of the time.

Discretion at Work

Inevitably, the next question is whether the growing complexity of jobs is also accompanied by higher levels of task discretion – that is to say, greater control over the detailed execution of the job.[3] This discretion is thought to reflect the need to motivate employees who are carrying out more complex work and the greater difficulties entailed in externally monitoring such work. Discretion affords the potential productive advantages of flexibility but requires the exercise of judgement and hence skill. The alleged connection between task discretion and skill has been assumed or proposed in a number of long-standing social scientific traditions (e.g. Blauner 1964; Braverman 1974; Zuboff 1988). In recent years the connection has been given renewed emphasis by the idea, common among management commentators, that many ordinary workers may be (and should be) becoming more 'empowered' as their skills and responsibilities are increasingly broadened (see Hales 2000 for a review).

Previously, this chapter has presented evidence to suggest that the complexity of jobs in Britain has risen over the last decade. This section examines the proposed connection this complexity has with autonomy at work and considers whether there has been a corresponding increase in the extent of task discretion as one might expect.

Three out of the four surveys used here included an identical question that asked respondents: 'How much choice do you have over the way in which you do your job?' This allows comparisons to be made between the answers given to the 1986, 1997 and 2001 surveys. In addition, four more detailed questions were asked to assess how much personal influence people thought they had over specific aspects of their work: how hard they worked, deciding what tasks they were to do, how the task was done, and the quality standards to which they worked.[4] However, these questions were not asked in 1986. Comparisons of levels of discretion exercised at work based on these questions are therefore limited to 1992, 1997 and 2001.

The first indicator was designed to provide a general picture of job autonomy, covering the range of different possible dimensions. Taking their overall judgements about the choice they could exercise in their work, it is clear that the majority of employees felt they had some opportunities for initiative on the job. However, only a minority of employees (39 per cent) in 2001 thought they had a 'great deal' of choice over the way they did their job. A further 44 per cent reported that they had 'some' choice. The extent of choice was, as expected, related positively to other broad measures of job skills. For example, in those jobs that required a qualification of at least level 3, some 45 per cent reported a 'great deal' of choice, whereas jobs requiring less or no qualifications afforded only 33 per cent a 'great deal' of choice. The choice variable was also positively related to both the Learning Time and Training Time indices discussed above.

The more detailed questions enable us to assess the influence that employees had overspecific aspects of their work task. Answers show that, in 2001, influence was felt to be highest with respect to work effort and quality standards, where half of all employees thought they had a great deal of influence, and lowest with respect to decisions about which tasks were to be done and how to do the task, where this was the case for only 30 and 43 per cent respectively. All these other indicators of task discretion are also positively correlated with the broad measures of skill. This finding again confirms the view that skill and task discretion are related as expected.

Despite the fact that discretion is positively correlated with skill, comparison of the pattern for 2001 with earlier years points not to a rise but to a considerable decline in employee task discretion over time. Between 1986 and 2001, there was a decline of 14 percentage points in the proportion feeling that they had a 'great deal' of choice in the way they did their job (see Table 9.6). Between 1992 and 2001 there was also a marked decline in employees' perception of their influence over each of the specific aspects of the work task. To provide an overall picture from these items, a summary index is constructed by giving a score ranging from 0 (no influence at all) to 3 (a great deal of influence) and then taking the average of the summed scores.[5] As can be seen from the last row of Table 9.6, the index score for task discretion declined from 2.43 in 1992 to 2.25 in 1997 and continued to fall reaching 2.18 in 2001.

The decline in control was sharpest with respect to work effort (20 percentage points) and quality standards (19 percentage points). For the first three aspects of task control – over work effort, decisions about which tasks to do and how to do them – the decline was continuous between the three surveys, although control over work effort declined particularly sharply between 1997 and 2001. With respect to control over work quality, the change occurred primarily between 1992 and 1997.

This decline in task discretion is evident for both men and women. The overall measure of 'choice over how the job is done' indicates that women felt they had a lower level of control than men in each of the years (Table 9.7). However, the percentage point decline between 1986 and 2001 was very similar for men and women (14 and 12 percentage points respectively). Taking the items tapping particular aspects of control, there was little difference between the sexes on any of the measures in 1992 and this pattern remained the case in 2001, except for control over 'how to do the task' where men had a somewhat higher level of job control than women (45 per cent reporting a great deal of influence compared with 40 per cent). The decline in the overall task discretion index is, however, very similar indeed for both sexes. For men, it fell from 2.43 to 2.19 and for women from 2.44 to 2.17.

The figures for female employees, however, conceal a substantial difference by working time. On all measures and in all years, apart from the overall item on choice in 1986, female part-timers had considerably lower levels of job control than female full-timers. Taking 2001, the point difference ranged

Table 9.6   Trends in task discretion 1986–2001

	1986	1992	1997	2001
Choice over the way you do your job (%)				
Great deal	51.8	NA	44.3	38.6
Some	29.4	NA	39.0	44.3
Hardly any	9.2	NA	10.1	10.7
None	9.6	NA	6.5	6.4
Influence over how hard to work (%)				
A great deal	NA	70.7	64.4	50.6
A fair amount	NA	23.2	28.8	39.2
Not much	NA	4.9	4.7	8.6
None at all	NA	1.2	2.0	1.6
Influence over what tasks done (%)				
A great deal	NA	42.4	33.1	30.5
A fair amount	NA	33.5	36.2	35.7
Not much	NA	15.4	20.6	22.1
None at all	NA	8.7	10.0	11.7
Influence over how to do task (%)				
A great deal	NA	56.9	49.7	42.8
A fair amount	NA	30.9	34.5	40.4
Not much	NA	8.4	10.2	11.0
None at all	NA	3.9	5.6	5.8
Influence over quality standards (%)				
A great deal	NA	69.6	51.1	51.7
A fair amount	NA	23.1	28.4	32.0
Not much	NA	4.8	12.6	10.4
None at all	NA	2.6	7.9	5.9
Overall task discretion index[a]				
All	NA	2.43	2.25	2.18

[a] The task discretion index is computed as the summed average score of the four 'task influence' questions, with a highest score of 3 and a lowest score of 0.

from 6 percentage points, with respect to influence over what tasks to do, to 10 percentage points, with respect to how to do the task. Moreover, taking the trend over time, female part-timers witnessed a sharper reduction of influence over their job than female full-timers. For instance, taking the overall item on choice over the way of doing the job, there was a decline of 9 percentage points between 1986 and 2001 with respect to full-timers who reported a 'great deal' of choice, but of 17 percentage points with respect to part-timers. Similarly, the summary index for the specific aspects of control shows a decline between 1992 and 2001 of 0.24 for female full-timers compared with 0.30 for female part-timers. The period, then, has seen an increased polarisation in this respect between the work situation of women in full-time work on the one hand and part-time work on the other.

Table 9.7   **Trends in task discretion by gender and full-time/part-time status 1986–2001**

	1986	*1992*	*1997*	*2001*
A great deal of choice over the way you do your job (%)				
Male	56.0	NA	48.9	42.4
Female	46.5	NA	39.1	34.3
Female full-time	46.3	NA	42.7	37.3
Female part-time	46.8	NA	34.4	29.8
Great deal of influence over how hard to work (%)				
Male	NA	70.1	64.6	51.1
Female	NA	71.4	64.2	50.0
Female full-time	NA	73.4	66.9	53.1
Female part-time	NA	68.5	60.5	45.2
Great deal of influence over what tasks done (%)				
Male	NA	40.9	33.0	30.3
Female	NA	44.0	33.3	30.7
Female full-time	NA	47.1	38.2	32.9
Female part-time	NA	39.3	26.7	27.2
Great deal of influence over how to do task (%)				
Male	NA	57.2	51.2	45.0
Female	NA	56.5	48.1	40.3
Female full-time	NA	59.7	54.3	44.1
Female part-time	NA	51.8	39.8	34.5
Great deal of influence over quality standards (%)				
Male	NA	69.1	52.5	52.1
Female	NA	70.1	49.6	51.3
Female full-time	NA	71.8	53.8	54.3
Female part-time	NA	67.5	43.9	46.6
Overall task discretion index				
Male	NA	2.43	2.26	2.19
Female	NA	2.44	2.24	2.17
Female full-time	NA	2.49	2.33	2.25
Female part-time	NA	2.37	2.13	2.07

Conclusion

This chapter has outlined how two distinct conceptual dimensions of 'skill' can be measured using specially constructed questions for those in work at the time of interview. In doing so, the chapter has presented evidence which tracks how work skills have changed in Britain over the last fifteen years. The data show two distinct trajectories and patterns that paint a complex overall picture of skill change.

On the one hand, the data suggest a consistent upward movement in the complexity of jobs carried out in Britain. This is evident in the significant rise in the qualification requirements of jobs. Notably, the proportion of degree-level jobs rose from 10 per cent in 1986 to 17 per cent in 2001. Similarly, fewer jobs in 2001 needed a cumulative training time of under three months than in earlier years; in 1986, 66 per cent fell into this category, but by 2001 this had fallen to 61 per cent. By the same token, fewer jobs required under one month 'to learn to do well'; these jobs accounted for 27 per cent of the total in 1986 compared with 20 per cent in 2001. A rise in the complexity of jobs is also evident in the rising important ratings given to a range of generic activities carried out at work. Most notably, the importance of computer skills has risen more rapidly in the last four years than any other job skill. Movement towards greater equality is also evident in these trends. While there are substantive differences between the skills used at work by men and those used by women, the differences appear to be narrowing over time. For example, the proportions of jobs held by men requiring no qualifications fell from 31 to 24 per cent over 1986–2001, while the equivalent decline for women's jobs was from 48 to 29 per cent. Moreover, it is women part-timers who are benefiting most from the narrowing of the gender gap.

However, the rise in job complexity has *not* been accompanied by a corresponding rise in the control workers can exercise over their jobs. Rather there has been a marked decline in task discretion. For example, the proportion of employees reporting 'a great deal' of choice over the way they do their job fell from 52 per cent in 1986 to 39 per cent in 2001. The proportions reporting a 'great deal' of influence over what tasks are done fell from 42 per cent in 1992 to 30 per cent in 2001. This decline occurred for both men and women. Nevertheless, the level of task discretion in jobs declined much faster for women part-timers than for women full-timers, thereby exacerbating rather than alleviating existing inequalities in the quality of women's working lives.

Of particular interest to policy-makers is the finding of a large mismatch between the supply and demand of intermediate qualifications. There are 6.4 million people qualified to the equivalent of National Vocational Qualification (NVQ) level 3 in the workforce but only 4 million jobs that demand this level of highest qualification. There are a further 5.3 million people qualified at level 2 but only 3.9 million jobs that require a highest qualification at this lower level. The other side of this same coin is that, whereas there are now only 2.9 million economically active people aged 20–60 who hold no qualifications, there remain 6.5 million jobs for which no qualification would be required to obtain them. This aggregate imbalance suggests that previously reported deficiencies in Britain (by comparison with other countries) in the use of intermediate-level qualifications might extend to deficiencies of demand as well as of supply. On this evidence, more emphasis should be directed at increasing the qualification (skill) demands of employers in order to effectively utilise the qualifications (skills) held by workers.

More generally, the chapter has outlined how 'skills' used in the work-place can be tracked over time, in a comprehensive and affordable manner. Continuation of this type of work will necessitate sufficient resources being set aside in order to achieve a reasonable response rate from a randomly drawn and representative survey of the whole economy rather than either concentrating on just one sector or occupation, or relying on quota-based sampling. Yet, the comparative stability of many of the skills measures over relative short periods (e.g. 1997–2001) confirms that there is little added value in repeating such a national survey every year. There is less need for regular annual or quarterly information about the *stocks* of skills than there is for regular data on *flows* of skills acquired by through training and educa-tion. Thus, a survey of skill stocks every three or four years, deploying a core of unchanged questions and procedures, provides a reasonably cost-effective means of acquiring highly useful labour market information. This chapter has provided an overview of the insights the most recent of these surveys has so far produced.

Acknowledgements

The 2001 Skills Survey was funded by the Department for Education and Skills with the Centre for Skills Knowledge and Organisational Performance (SKOPE) at the Universities of Oxford and Warwick. We are grateful to Ken Mayhew (Director of SKOPE) for his continuing support and to Rosa Fernandez for research assistance. Material from the Labour Force Surveys is Crown Copyright and has been made available by the Office of National Statistics (ONS) through The Data Archive and has been used by permission. Neither ONS nor The Data Archive bear any responsibility for the analysis or interpretation of the data reported here.

Notes

1 The skills of non-standard workers are considered in more detail elsewhere (Felstead and Gallie 2002).
2 Details are given in the notes to Table 9.3. These supply and demand estimates do not take account of the supply of economically active people and the available jobs for people aged above 60 or below 20 which were outside the scope of the SCELI, EIB and the 1997 and 2001 Skills Surveys. Nor is account taken of the fact that a small proportion of people (around 6%) hold second jobs which were also outside the scope of these surveys.
3 The determinants of changing levels of discretion at work are considered in more detail elsewhere (Gallie *et al.* 2002).

4 The question format was: 'How much influence do you personally have on... how hard you work; deciding what tasks you are to do; deciding how you are to do the task; and deciding the quality standards to which you work?'
5 The index was statistically robust, with an overall alpha of 0.78.

References

Ashton, D., Davies, B., Felstead, A. and Green, F. (1999) *Work Skills in Britain*, Oxford and Warwick: SKOPE.

Blake, N., Dods, J. and Griffiths, S. (2000) *Employers Skill Survey: Existing Survey Evidence and its Use in the Analysis of Skill Deficiencies*, Sheffield: DfEE.

Blauner, R. (1964) *Alienation and Freedom. The Factory Worker and his Industry*, Chicago: University of Chicago Press.

Braverman, H. (1974) *Labor and Monopoly Capital*, New York: Monthly Review Press.

Campbell, M., Baldwin, S., Chapman, R., Johnson, S., Upton, A. and Walton, F. (2001) *Skills in England: Research Report*, London: Department for Education and Skills.

Carey, S., Low, S. and Hansbro, J. (1997) *Adult Literacy in Britain*, London: The Stationary Office.

Department for Education and Skills (2000) *Skills for All: Research Report from the National Skills Task Force*, London: Department for Education and Skills.

Department for Education and Skills (2001) *Meeting the Sector Skills and Productivity Challenge*, London: Department for Education and Skills.

Felstead, A. and Gallie, D. (2002) 'For better or worse? Non-standard jobs and high involvement work systems', *SKOPE Research Paper No 29*, Universities of Oxford & Warwick.

Felstead, A., Gallie, D. and Green, F. (2002) *Work Skills in Britain, 1986–2001*, London: Department for Education and Skills: http://www.skillsbase.dfes.gov.uk/downloads/WorkSkills1986–2001.doc.

Gallie, D. (1994) 'Methodological appendix', in R. Penn, M. Rose and J. Rubery (eds), *Skill and Occupational Change*, Oxford: Oxford University Press.

Gallie, D., Felstead, A. and Green, F. (2002) 'Changing patterns of employee involvement', *SKOPE Research Paper No 28*, Universities of Oxford & Warwick.

Gallie, D., White, M., Cheng, Y. and Tomlinson, M. (1998) *Restructuring the Employment Relationship*, Oxford: Oxford University Press.

Green, F. (1999) 'The market value of generic skills', *Skills Task Force Research Paper 13*, Nottingham: DfEE Publications.

Green, F. and James, D. (2001) 'Do male bosses underestimate their female subordinates' skills? A comparison of employees' and line managers' perceptions of job skills', *University of Kent at Canterbury Studies in Economics, Number 01/07*.

Green, F. and McIntosh, S. (2002) 'Is there a genuine under-utilisation of skills amongst the over-qualified?', *SKOPE Research Paper No 30*, Universities of Oxford & Warwick.

Green, F., McIntosh, S. and Vignoles, A. (2002) 'The utilisation of education and skills: evidence from Britain', *The Manchester School of Economic and Social Studies*, forthcoming.

Hales, C. (2000) 'Management and empowerment programmes', *Work, Employment and Society*, 14:3, 501–519.

HM Treasury (2002a) *Developing Workforce Skills: Piloting a New Approach*, London: HM Treasury.

HM Treasury (2002b) *Opportunity and Security for All: Investing in an Enterprising, Fairer Britain – New Spending Plans 2003–2006*, Cm 5570, London: HM Treasury.

Learning and Skills Council (2002) *LSC Draft Workforce Development Strategy to 2005*, Coventry: Learning and Skills Council.

NACETT (2000) *Aiming Higher: NACETT's Report on the National Learning Targets for England and Advice on the Targets Beyond 2002*, London: National Advisory Council for Education and Training Targets.

OECD and Statistics Canada (1997) *Literacy, Economy and Society*, Paris: Organisation for Economic Co-operation and Development.

O'Mahony, M. (1999) *Britain's Productivity Performance 1950–96: An International Perspective*, London: National Institute of Economic and Social Research.

PIU (Performance Innovation Unit) (2001) *In Demand: Adult Skills in the 21st Century*, London: Performance and Innovation Unit.

Spenner, K. I. (1990) 'Skill, Meanings, Methods and Measures', *Work and Occupations*, 17, 399–421.

Zuboff, S. (1988) *In the Age of the Smart Machine*, New York: Basic Books.

10
Lifelong Learning and Workplace Relations: Singing from the Same Hymn Sheet, Worshipping Different Gods?

Graham Symon

Introduction

The concept of lifelong learning is embedded in the *zeitgeist*. Official bodies, private and public sector employers, and the trade union movement have all positively associated themselves with it; but their common language has not been matched by any shared set of meanings. Both the available literature and evidence of practice show how different the approaches that these groups have adopted are. This chapter attempts to conceptualise these differences by comparing the lifelong learning agendas of two groups: employers and the trade union movement.

One of the key influences on employers' approaches to lifelong learning has been the idea of the 'learning organisation' (Senge 1990; Marquardt 1996; Pedler *et al.* 1996). Becoming one is seen as a key to combating and thriving in uncertain and adverse operating conditions. Lifelong learning becomes personal development and a component of organisational learning and development: the continual redefinition of assumptions and objectives (Argyris and Schon 1978). The anticipated result is a lean, dynamic, flexible and responsive organisation that engages its employees in high-trust, high-commitment relations with challenging and rewarding work. Yet, despite this emancipatory rhetoric, in practice, in the hands of the employers, lifelong learning becomes a means of behavioural adjustment through rhetoric and symbolism (Willmott 1993).

The trade union movement has a quite different conceptualisation of lifelong learning. The UK Trades Unions Congress (TUC) has sought to use it as a vehicle for campaigning for the 'upskilling' of its members to improve their employability and earning potential (TUC 1998; Unions 21 2000), while individual unions such as UNISON and AMICUS have supported lifelong learning through local bargaining. This focus on skills echoes the search for

170

competitiveness via high skills (see Grugulis 2003). Yet, despite the evidence that campaigns to increase training benefit employers and result in harmonious industrial relations, most employers still seem to prefer lifelong learning as an attempt to manage meaning rather than a reason to upskill. 'High' skills training in the UK is still much lower than in comparable European economies (Robinson 1996; Keep and Rainbird 2000) raising questions about the extent to which the UK can become a high skill, high wage economy. Much of the workplace training provided by employers is actually organisation-specific socialisation (Hallier and Butts 1999; Keep and Rainbird 2000) and the state's activities in vocational education and training (VET) have been called into question for its ineffectiveness (Grugulis 2003). The deregulated skilling infrastructure in the UK – a result of the neo-liberal policies of the post-1979 Administrations – has resulted in progressive skill development being retrenched and there seems little ambition to develop the UK into a high skill economy in anything other than rhetorical terms. Rather, employers and the state are content to utilise a deskilled and disenfranchised labour force (Lloyd and Payne 2002).

The tensions within lifelong learning are most apparent where trade unions seek more 'useful' training in terms of transferable skills that will increase employees' security, employability and control over work (Claydon and Green 1994). Employers' notions of lifelong learning are intended to gain greater control and induce attitudinal change to encourage the fulfilment of employers' objectives on employers' terms (Hallier and Butts 1999; Keep and Rainbird 2000). While managerialist interpretations of lifelong learning are presented in terms of 'high performance', 'new paradigm', 'partnership and unitarism', this rhetoric is often little more than another means to humanise capitalism or to obscure its more unsavoury aspects (Ramsay 1977; Cressey and MacInnes 1980; Willmott 1993). Essentially, employers' approaches to lifelong learning *deskill* and disenfranchise by gaining control from employees (see Braverman 1974; Willmott 1993). This chapter seeks to assess the nature and consequences of these tensions and considers whether an understanding of the issues of differing approaches to lifelong learning can make a contribution to our understanding of relations in the contemporary workplace. It concludes that lifelong learning is part of the 'contested terrain' of UK production.

Lifelong Learning and the UK

Lifelong learning has become virtually unavoidable in contemporary UK society. For some the focus is adult and/or community education, quality of life, leisure or self-improvement (Jones and Symon 2001). For others it is a form of civic engagement and a vital component of participatory democracy (Schuller 2000). However, arguably the most vocal institutions are those that assign economic and vocational functions to lifelong learning (O'Connell 1998).

This distinctly economic flavour has led to accusations that policy-makers have hijacked the concept of continuing and adult education (Jones and Symon 2001). A coherent vision of the potential economic *and* social uses of lifelong learning was provided by Faure and his colleagues (1972). In this work, a blueprint for a general developmental framework of continuing education intended to enable democratic engagement, and individual and societal growth, was proposed and endorsed by the UN. In countries as diverse as Japan, Australia, France, Singapore and South Africa, coherent and successful frameworks of adult and continuing education have yielded simultaneous economic and social benefits (Holford *et al.* 1998). Yet, almost three decades after Faure, the social agenda of lifelong learning has been marginalised in many nations – not least in the UK – with vocational and economic priorities dominating the agenda.

Lifelong learning has underpinned much of the previous two UK Governments' policy on skill formation and labour markets (DfEE 1995, 1998). A voluntarist framework is considered by policy-makers – however misguidedly – to be the means whereby the UK can have the skills to be a flexible and dynamic economy. Within lifelong learning, workers should have the means to update or change their skills. In this neo-liberal scenario, individual actors and institutions have agency to pursue their own fortunes. The impulse for social action, justice and progress stems from market mechanisms. Neo-liberalism as an ideology has been found wanting by numerous critics (see Streeck 1989) not least because opportunities in society are rarely 'equal' and markets – despite deregulation – generally not 'free' (Warhurst 1997).

The principal aim of the current government's lifelong learning policy is to create a 'learning society' (DfEE 1998) that is more than a system of adult education. Rather it has become an instruction to participants in the labour market that they must adopt whatever behaviours and values that employers desire. The 'learning' in lifelong learning is not education but attitudes and characteristics. The pay-off for individuals is that work will be varied, exciting and rewarding in a manner consistent with post-Fordism. It is possible to detect echoes of Charles Handy's utopian vision of the 'portfolio' career (Handy 1989). Workers can enjoy the emancipation of occupational fulfilment unconstrained by the iron cage of bureaucratic industrial organisation. This similarity extends to the fact that responsibility for skills rests with individuals.

The Government commissioned three committees – chaired by Dearing for higher education, Kennedy for further education and Fryer for lifelong learning in general – to investigate ways in which the learning society might be realised (Tight 1998). There were four principal developments that resulted from these deliberations. Firstly, there was an expressed intention to consolidate the largely ineffectual system of National Vocational Qualifications (NVQs), a strategy that is yet to yield convincing improvements (Grugulis 2003). Secondly came the foundation of the controversially named 'University for

Industry' (now referred to as LearnDirect) and the disastrous introduction of Individual Learning Accounts (ILAs); initiatives which received the backing of much of the trade union movement (e.g. UNISON 1999; MSF 2000). Finally, at the level of individual workplaces *Investors in People* (IiP) provided a seal of approval to employers judged to be implementing effective employee development practices. Accounts of its efficacy are mixed (Grugulis 2003).

For all the apparent activity surrounding 'economic' lifelong learning and the reiteration of the importance of being skilled, there have been no moves to a compulsory levied system of VET. Despite the fact that the skill levels in certain areas of the UK economy are perilously low, VET policy continues to be voluntarist with the market expected to regulate skill levels (Streeck 1989; Keep and Rainbird 2000).

Lifelong learning is dominated by economic imperatives. The government pays lip-service to the non-economic aspects but does not engage in any constructive actions to achieve them (Jones and Symon 2001). As Tight explains, policy manifestos tend to assert 'without evidence, in a taken for granted fashion – the critical importance of lifelong learning for the economy. They then quickly qualify this by referring to other, non-economic, personal or social (even…spiritual) benefits' (Tight 1998: 482–483). In practice, these non-economic benefits are marginalised or subsumed. In *The Learning Age* (DfEE 1998) the economic and the social are conflated with solutions to 'social exclusion' anticipated from economic interventions (Edwards *et al.* 2001).

Employers and Lifelong Learning

As employers and employers' interest groups have been granted a considerable input into the policy-making process, it is not surprising that they endorse the concept of lifelong learning (e.g. CBI 1998). Employers readily express concerns about the lack of skills in the labour market and often blame the systems of compulsory and post-compulsory education (Robinson 1996; Hallier and Butts 1999). Lifelong learning has underpinned a considerable amount of managerial thought, emphasising the need for adaptation and innovation in the face of environmental change, and intensified competition brought about by compelling phenomena such as 'globalisation' and the coming of the 'information society'.

The epistemology of the learning organisation can be traced back to the work of organisational theorists (Cyert and March 1963; Argyris and Schon 1978) who developed the notion of organisations as learning systems and attempted to refine the rather ethereal concepts of organisational and 'double-loop' learning. These involve the development of organisational cultures through collective interaction, sharing knowledge and challenging the status quo, allowing organisations to be creative in the face of adversity. These notions echo the classic model of the 'organic' (as opposed to 'mechanistic') organisation where looser, less hierarchical more democratic structures can facilitate innovation, especially in the face of uncertainty and macro-environmental turbulence (Burns and Stalker 1961).

This flexibility and dynamism is attractive to employers, many of whom have an insatiable appetite for the managerial techniques provided by consultants and gurus (Ramsay 1996). The ethos of contemporary discourses of lifelong learning have been encapsulated in the concept of the 'learning organisation' (Senge 1990) or 'learning company' (Pedler *et al.* 1996). The learning organisation largely embodies the spirit of lifelong learning in the sense of continuous development, adaptation and improvement. However, due to the charisma-hungry nature of the audience, the concept also embodies normative and sociologically problematic notions of trust, empowerment, unitarism and organisational effectiveness (Symon 2002).

Of course, one should not confuse or conflate the idealistic musings of managerial writers or the unrealistic aspirations of some managers with actual material developments in the workplace (Keep and Rainbird 2000). However, at the rhetorical level at least, the idea of the learning organisation is both powerful and popular. Barley and Kunda (1992) and Ramsay (1996) have offered eloquent accounts of the ways in which initiatives reflect the mood and mores of the times; 'downsizing' and 'hard' HRM in recession (Keenoy 1999) or participation and involvement when employers want consent (Ramsay 1977). Management also responds well to organisational heroism and gurus stoke their delusions with sycophantic eulogies on, for instance, the potential for inspirational leadership. However, as Carlyle argued, in order to be a hero one must counter a villain (Carlyle 1872). So corporate villains are created: the UK's poor economic performance in the 1970s and early 1980s was blamed on labour's militancy (Cutler 1992). By the mid-1980s skills shortages became the new villain, which later transformed into the unwillingness of organisations (or indeed society) to *learn* (Keep and Rainbird 2000).

As with a great deal of managerial literature, much of the writing on learning organisations is a combination of prescription and panacea supported by accounts of utopian workplaces where workers are engaged in a harmonious, rewarding and productive 'love-in' with management. Jargon and hyperbola abound and little stands up to critical scrutiny (Keep and Rainbird 2000). This is especially the case with *The Fifth Discipline* (Senge 1990) that has pretensions of being a work of philosophy and repeatedly states that the book should not merely be regarded as a business book but the blueprint for a new way of life.

Despite its shortcomings, the idea of the learning organisation has undoubtedly captured the imagination of managers. Statements such as 'we are a learning organisation' can be seen on a variety of company reports, public relations materials and policy documents while the White Paper, *Modernising Government* (Cabinet Office 1999) instructs public sector bodies to become learning organisations. There is no officially sanctioned benchmark, so employers are free to use the label whether or not they fulfil the criteria. Many claims are questionable, particularly in the public sector where recent experiences have been anything but harmonious and enriching. Ironically, much of the excellent training that does occur in the public sector, legacies of its role as a 'good employer' or the product of professional codes and qualifications, can lead to skilled workers obstructing 'learning' that is simply accepting managerial instructions (du Gay 1996).

More doubts are observed in the private sector with empirical studies questioning the learning organisation's viability (e.g. Lahteenmaki *et al.* 1997 with the UK and Finland; Huzzard 2000 with Sweden). In response, the gurus turn to their favourite tool, the anecdote:

> Rover has grown and benefited immensely over the past five years as an emerging learning organization. There has been a continuous flow of improvements initiated and generated through learning by empowered employees. Learning has indeed resulted in a better bottom line, happier employees, and a superior globalwide (*sic*) reputation. (Marquardt 1996: 208)

Marquardt (1996: 194) attributes an atypical profit made in 1994 to the company's 'journey to becoming a learning organisation'. He provides little evidence, but the language used speaks volumes about the nature of the learning organisation: it is a normative instrument of rhetoric and symbolism rather than an actual tangible process. Worryingly, Marquardt's account does not consider factors such as the state of the automotive market, levels of investment, public subsidy or trading of assets. In fact, when BMW acquired Rover in 1994, the firm's future was in some doubt and substantial investments in plant, R&D and skills were needed (Brady and Lorenz 2001). In 2000, Rover, nicknamed 'the English patient' by the German press, was sold. It may be that (in contrast to Marquardt's account) BMW's failure to turn the Longbridge plant into a little slice of Bavaria can be attributed to the lack of cultural and institutional infrastructure necessary to develop and sustain a high-performance work system (Lloyd and Payne 2002).

The normative tone of employers' lifelong learning and learning organisation discourses is noteworthy. The skills that are expected to result from employers' lifelong learning initiatives are often not *high* or transferable, but more abstract competencies such as being a 'team player' or 'coping with change'. This is even the case with the hi-tech manufacturer Motorola's 'University' (Hallier and Butts 1999). Indeed, empirical investigation has suggested that many UK employers place attitudinal attributes above technical capacity and qualifications in recruitment (Robinson 1996). Malleable attitudes will 'enable people to make the right and necessary attribution to the success of the organisations for which they work' (du Gay 1996: 41; Warhurst and Thompson 1998). Many of the skills employers demand are attitudinal characteristics such as 'punctuality' and 'following instructions' (see Robinson 1996; Keep and Rainbird 2000).

Given the voluntarist system, employers may have acted rationally by using resources that could have been spent on vocational training as surplus revenue. Many have chosen to compete on the basis of cost, used operations as 'cash-cows' (Cutler 1992) or engaged in mergers and acquisitions (Keep and Rainbird 2000). The rhetoric on competitive advantage through skills seems misplaced.

Trade Unions and Lifelong Learning

Trade union involvement with education is long-standing. The Workers' Educational Association (WEA) is a well-established source of adult education and most unions are providers of significant amounts of training (Payne 2001). Unions have also cooperated with industry and the state to coordinate apprenticeship training, a practice presently moribund in the UK (Keep and Rainbird 2000). More recently, they have developed their own lifelong learning policies, promoted skills through bargaining, distributed the state supported Union Learning Fund (ULF), deployed 'skills reps' in workplaces and engaged in 'partnerships' with employers.

Managerialists are critical of the trade union movement, accusing them of hindering enterprise (see Ackers *et al.* 1996). However, there is an increasing body of evidence that suggests the presence of a trade union can make a significant contribution to productivity by encouraging training. The trade union movement has also made significant contributions to lifelong learning internationally (ILO 2000), at national congress (e.g. TUC 1998; Unions 21 2000), and locally (Munro and Rainbird 2000; Payne 2001). Furthermore, unions have collaborated with employers, the state and other interest groups in a number of fora such as the Campaign for Learning, in the administration of the ULF and through submissions to commissions of inquiry.

Trade union concerns over the availability of education and training can be traced to its roots as a social and political movement (Flanders 1968). Given their substantial decline in membership and influence, current hopes for renewal are pragmatic and require unions to increase their appeal to employers, society in general and especially workers (Ackers *et al.* 1996; Kelly 1996). Though there is still space for rhetoric:

> The notion that learning is a peripheral union issue is gradually collapsing. Anyone questioning the merit of placing skills on the bargaining agenda need only look at some of the ideals behind lifelong learning that have always been at the heart of trade unionism: empowerment, respect, fulfilment at work and the quality of members' lives. (Unions 21 2000: 2)

Payne's consideration of strategies on lifelong learning discusses the way that unions can help their members cope with changing economic and social circumstances (see Payne 2001: 381–382). According to social theory, those who prosper during times of upheaval will be the ones with access to cultural and educational resources (Beck 1986). Payne argues that many union members lack these resources and trade unions can be useful as agents of lifelong learning. This consensus over the value of lifelong learning has advantages, but also poses problems. Despite the similarities in the rhetoric, trade unions seek different objectives from lifelong learning and these require very different approaches.

UNISON is the UK's biggest union and, as well as contributing to national policy, administers many of its own members' education and training programmes (Munro and Rainbird 2000). The white-collar union (Manufacturing, Science and Finance Union, MSF) (now part of AMICUS) has been similarly proactive (MSF 2000). Interestingly, the government has endorsed these policy initiatives by awarding funding to the TUC (Antill *et al.* 2001). Munro and Rainbird (2000) have identified this as 'managerial-servicing' unionism (cf. Heery 1996) that entails pragmatic servicing of members' needs. UNISON aims to install 'learning reps' in every workplace in order to coordinate lifelong learning and lobby management (UNISON 1999; cf. Antill *et al.* 2001). As of July 2001, there were 3240 ULF funded learning reps in UK workplaces (Antill *et al.* 2001), although unions have considerable difficulty in recruiting and retaining reps; perhaps because the impetus for collective action has subsided (Heery and Kelly 1994) or because reps have difficulty being taken seriously. Section 5 of the Employment Relations Act 1999 makes (very limited) provision for bargaining on training matters, but as with so much in that piece of legislation, expectations have not been met (Ewing 2001). One example of successful practice is Ford, UK (Payne 2001); through the Employee Development and Assisstance Programme (EDAP) scheme, access to learning and development on the shopfloor has been enhanced due to the Transport and General Workers' Union (TGWU) reps. It is doubtful, however, whether learning reps would carry out their union duties with the same charismatic fervour as the militant shop stewards portrayed by Beynon (1975) three decades ago carried out theirs.

It is not only union members who benefit from VET. Through the assertion of training, unions have directly contributed to increased skill levels and better organisational performance (e.g. Claydon and Green 1994; Heyes and Stuart 1994; Dundon and Eva 1998). It should be noted, however, that the presence of a trade union can also *depress* investment in human capital by raising wages and countering productivity gains (Metcalf *et al.* 1996). Nevertheless, these studies underline the point that skilling, skills and learning in the workplace cannot be extracted from the milieu of workplace relations or the wider political economy (Lloyd and Payne 2002).

Union rhetoric and practice on lifelong learning stress the employability and earning potential of members. These are long-standing concerns and the strategies employed to deal with them have changed over time, the means of production may have changed (see Warhurst 1997), but problems with them are likely to continue, despite new management practices and the rhetoric of post-Fordism (cf. Ramsay 1977, 1996; Ackers *et al.* 1996; Kelly 1996).

The focus on earning potential is interesting because, expressed through lifelong learning, it is startlingly similar to human capital theory (HCT) (Becker 1975). This is effective only if there is demand from employers for the skills provided or enhanced. Lloyd and Payne (2002) deftly expose the limitations of HCT by explaining the link between investment in skills (which are principally individual) and economic performance. When competitiveness is based on cost (e.g. entering low-quality product markets) rather than quality, increasing skills can be futile.

All principal institutions in contemporary industrial relations agree that the UK should become a 'competitive' economy and that the competitiveness should be based on high skills. However, the fact that in many organisations unions have to campaign for training is an indictment of British employers (Claydon and Green 1994). It is also worrying that union calls for high skills are resisted even when it has been convincingly demonstrated that investment can improve quality, productivity and performance. Employers seem to be reluctant to give workers the power that skills would bestow. Rather, employers seek more 'normative' attitudinal attributes (Hallier and Butts 1999; Lloyd and Payne 2002). That the UK economy can survive and compete – albeit in the short term – on the basis of such practices perhaps further exposes the limitations of HCT.

At a superficial level, employers and unions do appear to be 'singing from the same hymn sheet': competitiveness is important; lifelong learning is important; skills are important; and adaptability to change is important. Indeed much of the bargaining over lifelong learning can be presented as 'mutual gains' and 'social partnership' (Kelly 1996):

> The [TUC's 'Learning Services'] has addressed the TUC's priorities of competitiveness, employability, partnership and new unionism. (ADAPT 2000: 1)

> Learning is an issue on which unions can work in partnership with the Government and employers to secure the best deal for their members. (Unions 21 2000: 3)

Rhetorically, at least, the new modernised trade union movement has developed a 'stakeholding' outlook. This approach has been effective elsewhere. Streeck (1989, 1992) shows how, in high-tech/high skill workplaces, labour unions have been able to secure influence and legitimacy through the promotion of lifelong learning:

> Unions should embrace skill formation as the centrepiece of a new, co-operative and productive strategy, and at the same time insist on the unions' need for a strong independent power base giving them, just as in the past, a capacity to impose rules and obligations on employers. (Streeck 1992: 252)

The prospects that Streeck discusses are pan-European and seem more achievable from a Continental vantage point where constructive management–union relations are supported by fiscal frameworks and general cultural mores (see also Lloyd and Payne 2002). Lifelong learning is prominent in European 'social dialogue'. It will be interesting to see whether European integration has an isomorphic effect on UK policy. Streeck's reservation is also crucial: that if unions get too close to employers, they could be 'incorporated' and alienated from their members' interests (see also Kelly 1996).

Arguably, what the various perspectives on trade union lifelong learning activity have in common is the desire for legitimacy. In an era of diminished trade union movement power and status, the union bosses may need to be seen doing something high profile or 'strategic'. This is not to imply that union policy lacks integrity or efficacy. On the contrary, many initiatives have yielded benefits; although radical scholars (e.g. Ramsay 1977; Cressey and MacInnes 1980) would have been quick to point out the dangers of the acquiescence of labour to a capitalist agenda.

The 'Contested Terrain' of Lifelong Learning?

There are large areas where employer and trade union rhetoric on lifelong learning appear to be compatible, for example the recognition of the importance of 'skills' and the need for organisational effectiveness. Indeed, the moral potency of lifelong learning and skills in social and economic life is such that few would dare contest them publicly. However, any coincidence of interest is partial.

Skill and skills are words that are used widely by both camps in the lifelong learning dialectic but skill is a rather difficult concept to pin down (Gallie 1991). For the purposes of this chapter, it is perhaps most convenient to consider skill in terms of control over work. Radical labour process writers have argued that skill is *contested* (see Thompson and McHugh 2002). As Warhurst (1997: 227, 232) explains: 'Labour process analysis, concerned with the politics of production, recognises managerial control as an imperative of the capitalist (and any labour) process for both operational and ideological reasons', and 'control is manifest in a managerial prerogative (however moderated) to direct, evaluate, discipline and reward labour'. Where there are tasks in the production process that enable labour to exercise specialisms or autonomy, employers concede control. Braverman (1974) argues that employers attempt to minimise this possibility (through, *inter alia*, scientific management and pre-programmed technologies) in order to assert control.

Braverman's thesis has been criticised on a number of points; principally, the reductionist nature of his arguments and his conviction that deskilling is employers' primary labour strategy. He also missed the fact that labour has agency and can resist deskilling (Edwards 1979). Warhurst identifies further critiques and argues that deskilling is not the only strategy for the control of labour and that 'responsible autonomy' may substitute for 'direct control' (Friedman 1977); particularly in 'high-performance' work systems (see Thompson and McHugh 2002). Such practices have enjoyed periodic popularity among UK employers seeking to improve efficiency and productivity or to marginalise collectivised labour (Ackers *et al.* 1996). However, these have often not delivered either greater organisational performance or enriched work for employees; the rhetoric has not been matched by genuine autonomy (Marchington and Grugulis 2000; Ramsay *et al.* 2000). Rather, they are a normative means of workplace subordination whereby employers attempt to use symbolic and social instruments to control labour (Willmott 1993; Flecker and Hofbauer 1998; Keenoy 1999). Such initiatives by diminishing or failing to develop skills, may reduce workers' capacity to exit and seek employment elsewhere (Hallier and Butts 1999). It is possible to locate the learning organisation version of lifelong learning in this category (Symon 2002).

If the notion of skill as control is contested, then lifelong learning is a contentious element in the politics of production. The coincidences of interest aside, numerous tensions are evident in the lifelong learning agendas of employers and labour; these are summarised in Table 10.1.

Given employers' rhetoric on the need for skills, it is ironic that the learning they seek to provide could be interpreted as 'deskilling' in as much as it seeks to disenfranchise workers, increase management control and intensify labour. The emotional aspects of many of these processes can lead to workers losing control of their identity as they alter their behaviour, 'acting' to fit in with cultural norms (Fox 1989; McKinlay and Taylor 1996; Antonacopoulou 1999).

Despite the potential for insidious subjugation, it should not be forgotten that the promotion of high-quality formal learning has considerable virtue.

Table 10.1   The contested terrain of lifelong learning:
some key aspects

Dynamic	Employers	Trade union movement
General outcomes expected	Control Competitiveness (cost) Efficiency Flexibility Strong corporate culture	Employability for members Higher wages Influence in decision-making Legitimacy Social justice
Learning outcomes	Adaptability Attitudinal appropriateness	'High' technical skills Transferable skills
Organisational paradigm	The learning organisation	Social partnership

However, empirical investigations suggest that where workers are encouraged – or *obliged* – to undertake learning (e.g. part-time FE and HE study), employers are often not prepared to allow time off or reduce expected performance levels (Kinman and Kinman 2000; Symon and Fallows 2000). Line managers often show little sympathy, casting doubt on the ability of organisations to create learning cultures (Keep and Rainbird 2000; Kinman and Kinman 2000). The learning organisation in the UK may be little more than a cosmetic exercise and a means of work intensification (Ramsay *et al.* 2000). Furthermore, despite Pedler *et al.*'s (1996) insistence that *everyone* in their learning company should be 'allowed to learn', opportunities are often confined to core and managerial staff (Lahteenmaki *et al.* 1999), to the concern of the trade union movement (Payne 2001).

The learning organisation also presents opportunities for the trade union movement. Huzzard's (2000) study of Ericsson's Norrkoping plant notes that the unions were able to harness the principles of organisational learning and learning exchange to become more effective in exerting their influence over the workplace and in their resistance to management. Unions too have structures and hierarchies, and most certainly face the issue of survival.

State policy, market conditions, new production arrangements and organisational forms have contrived to make it difficult for unions in the UK to make the sort of impact on skills that their counterparts elsewhere have enjoyed. Lifelong learning is sufficiently ethereal for any interested institution to present it in the manner that suits their agenda. Employers' discourses of lifelong learning tend to focus on moulding flexible, compliant (or committed) employees who are prepared to assume the responsibility for gaining skills themselves. This use of lifelong learning as a means of cultural control and even as a component in union marginalisation does not enhance the UK's skills base or secure constructive industrial relations. Without genuine state support and investment in industrial infrastructure that is conducive to high skill work, unions' efforts to enhance skill levels will be an uphill struggle.

Conclusion

Lifelong learning continues to maintain its momentum, and employers and trade unions have been vociferous in their support. In some instances, these have been compatible and have given the impression of a move to partnership. But the most remarkable feature of these approaches is not how they coincide but how they differ.

There is no obligation on UK employers to engage with lifelong learning. It is possible to treat it as a cosmetic exercise and, in many cases, this is what happens. More worryingly, some employers see the appeal of engaging with manifestations of lifelong learning that espouse flexibility, adaptability and employee commitment. So lifelong learning and the learning organisation join the relentless barrage of 'enterprise' discourses where programmes of organisational indoctrination serve to assert control and legitimise the managerial prerogative.

The trade union movement's contributions to lifelong learning are both encouraging and worrying. On the one hand, intervention in, and endorsement of, the policy raises the profile of unions. More pragmatically, union action on training and development can have a positive impact on high skills and performance. There are also potential benefits for members through enhanced human capital, employability and higher wages. However, these good intentions cannot be assessed in isolation from the political economy or from material developments in production arrangements. The UK is not Germany and does not enjoy high skill/high-performance/high-trust production to the same extent (Streeck 1989, 1992). Rather, British industry has tended to gravitate towards deskilled, low-wage work in which skills can be rendered redundant by production arrangements and technology. Many firms have sought to compete in low-quality markets rather than those that require the use of high skills (Grugulis 2003). Any union pressure for upskilling that lacks statutory intervention, a radical overhaul of the education system and changes to the industrial infrastructure are struggles of Sisyphean proportions (Lloyd and Payne 2002).

In a broad sense, although lifelong learning is common property, employers and the trade union movement have different and largely conflicting expectations of it. The unions seek upskilling to enhance their position and that of their members; employers seek to use it as a means of socialisation with the intention of gaining greater control over workers. Much of the reality makes rather gloomy reading. It appears that, for all the time spent talking about its wonderful possibilities, employers would rather have a workforce that is low skilled and dis-empowered to secure short-term profits. Until the UK Government concentrates less on producing aesthetically pleasing glossy pamphlets such as *The Learning Age* (DfEE 1998) and undertakes some legislative intervention on training and skills, this will probably continue to be the case.

Acknowledgement

The author would like to express his thanks to the editors – and in particular Irena Grugulis – for their substantial guidance and patience.

References

Ackers, P., Smith, C. and Smith, P. (1996) 'Against all Odds? British Trade Unionism in the New Workplace', in P. Ackers, C. Smith and P. Smith (eds), *The New Workplace and Trade Unionism*, London: Routledge.

ADAPT (2000) 'Trade Unions and Learning Partnerships', *ADAPT News*, Winter.

Antill, M., Cutter, J., Brass, J., Mortimore, C., Rodger, J. and Shaw, N. (2001) *An Evaluation of the Union Learning Fund in Year 3*, Report RR282, Nottingham: Department for Education and Skills.

Antonacopoulou, E. (1999) 'Developing Learning Managers within Learning Organizations', in M. Easterby-Smith, J. Burgoyne and L. Araujo (eds), *Organizational Learning and the Learning Organization*, London: Sage.

Argyris, C. and Schon, D. (1978) *Organizational Learning*, Cambridge, MA: Addison-Wesley.

Barley, S. and Kunda, G. (1992) 'Design and Devotion: Surges of Rational and Normative Ideologies of Control in Managerial Discourse', *Administrative Science Quarterly*, 37, 363–399.

Beck, U. (1986) *Risk Society: Towards a New Modernity*, London: Sage.

Becker, G. (1975) *Human Capital Theory*, New York: Columbia University Press.

Beynon, H. (1975) *Working for Ford*, Wakefield: EP.

Brady, C. and Lorenz, A. (2001) *End of the Road: BMW and Rover – a Brand Too Far*, London: FT Prentice Hall.

Braverman, H. (1974) *Labor and Monopoly Capital*, New York: Monthly Review.

Burns, T. and Stalker, G. (1961) *The Management of Innovation*, London: Tavistock.

Cabinet Office (1999) *Modernising Government*, Cm 4310, London: The Stationery Office.

Carlyle, T. (1872) *On Heroes, Hero-worship and the Heroic in History*, London: Chapman & Hall.

Claydon, T. and Green, F. (1994) 'Can Trade Unions Improve Training in Britain?', *Personnel Review*, 23:1, 37–51.

Confederation of British Industry (1998) 'Qualified to Compete: Creating a World Class Qualifications Framework', *Human Resources Brief*, January, London: CBI.

Cressey, P. and MacInnes, J. (1980) 'Voting for Ford: Industrial Democracy and the Control of Labour', *Capital and Class*, 11, 5–33.

Cutler, T. (1992) 'Vocational Training and British Economic Performance: A Further Instalment of the "British labour problem"', *Work, Employment and Society*, 6:2, 161–183.

Cyert, R. and March, J. (1963) *A Behavioral Theory of the Firm*, Englewood Cliffs, NJ: Prentice-Hall.

DfEE (Department for Education and Employment) (1995) *Lifetime Learning: A Consultation Document*, London: HMSO.

DfEE (Department for Education and Employment) (1998) *The Learning Age: A Renaissance for New Britain*, London: The Stationery Office.

du Gay, P. (1996) *Consumption and Identity at Work*, London: Sage.

Dundon, T. and Eva, D. (1998) 'Trade Unions and Bargaining for Skills', *Employee Relations*, 20:1, 57–72.

Edwards, R. (1979) *Contested Terrain: The Transformation of the Workplace in the Twentieth Century*, London: Heinemann.

Edwards, R., Armstrong, P. and Miller, N. (2001) 'Include Me Out: Critical Readings of Social Exclusion, Social Inclusion and Lifelong Learning', *International Journal of Lifelong Education*, 20:5, 417–428.

Ewing, K. (ed.) (2001) *Employment Rights at Work: Reviewing the Employment Relations Act 1999*, London: Institute of Employment Rights.

Faure, E., Herrera, F., Kaddowa, A., Lopes, H., Petrovsky, A., Rahnema, M. and Ward, F. (1972) *Learning to Be: The World of Education Today and Tomorrow*, Paris: UNESCO.

Flanders, A. (1968) *Trade Unions*, London: Hutchinson.

Flecker, J. and Hofbauer, J. (1998) 'The "New Model Worker" and the Importance of Being Useful', in P. Thompson and C. Warhurst (eds), *Workplaces of the Future*, Basingstoke: Macmillan.

Fox, S. (1989) 'The Panopticon: From Bentham's Obsession to the Revolution in Management Learning', *Human Relations*, 42:8, 717–739.

Friedman, A. (1977) *Industry and Labour*, London: Macmillan.

Gallie, D. (1991) 'Patterns of Skill Change: Upskilling, Deskilling or the Polarization of Skills?', *Work, Employment and Society*, 5:3, 319–351.

Grugulis, I. (2003) 'Putting Skills to Work? Learning and Employment at the Start of the Century', *Human Resource Management Journal*, 13:2, 3–12.

Hallier, J. and Butts, D. (1999) 'Employers' Discovery of Training: Self-development, Employability and the Rhetoric of Partnership', *Employee Relations*, 21:1, 80–95.

Handy, C. (1989) *The Age of Unreason*, London: Arrow.

Heery, E. (1996) 'The New New Unionism', in I. Beardwell (ed.), *Contemporary Industrial Relations*, Oxford: Oxford University Press.

Heery, E. and Kelly, J. (1994) 'Professional, Participative and Managerial Unionism: An Interpretation of Change in Trade Unions', *Work, Employment and Society*, 8:1, 11–22.

Heyes, J. and Stuart, M. (1994) 'Placing Symbols before Reality? Re-evaluating the Low Skills Equilibrium', *Personnel Review*, 23:5, 34–49.

Holford, J., Jarvis, P. and Griffin, C. (1998) (eds) *International Perspectives on Lifelong Learning*, London: Kogan Page.

Huzzard, T. (2000) *Labouring to Learn*, Umeå: Boréa.

ILO (2000) Report on the Committee on Sectoral and Technical Meetings and Related Issues (GB.279/14), Geneva: ILO.

Jones, I. and Symon, G. (2001) 'Lifelong Learning as Serious Leisure: Policy, Practice and Potential', *Leisure Studies*, 20:4, 269–283.

Keenoy, T. (1999) 'HRM as Hologram: A Polemic', *Journal of Management Studies*, 36:1, 1–23.

Keep, E. and Rainbird, H. (2000) 'Towards the Learning Organization?', in S. Bach and K. Sisson (eds), *Personnel Management*, Oxford: Blackwell.

Kelly, J. (1996) 'Union Militancy and Social Partnership', in P. Ackers, C. Smith and P. Smith (eds), *The New Workplace and Trade Unionism*, London: Routledge.

Kinman, R. and Kinman, G. (2000) ''What's that got to do with making Motor Cars?' The Influence of Corporate Culture on 'in-company' Degree Programmes', *Journal of Education and Work*, 13:1, 5–24.

Lahteenmaki, S., Holden, L. and Roberts, I. (eds) (1999) *HRM and the Learning Organization*, Turku, Finland: TSEBA.

Lloyd, C. and Payne, J. (2002) 'Developing a Political Economy of Skill', *Journal of Education and Work*, 15:4, 365–390.

Marchington, M. and Grugulis, I. (2000) 'Best Practice Human Resource Management: Perfect Opportunity or Dangerous Illusion', *International Journal of Human Resource Management*, 11:6, 1104–1124.

Marquardt, M. (1996) *Building the Learning Organization*, London: McGraw-Hill.

McKinlay, A. and Taylor, P. (1996) 'Power, Surveillance and Resistance: Inside the Factory of the Future', in P. Ackers, C. Smith and P. Smith (eds), *The New Workplace and Trade Unionism*, London: Routledge.

Metcalf, D., Hansen, K. and Charlwood, A. (1996) 'Unions and The Sword of Justice: Unions and Pay Systems, Pay Inequality, Pay Discrimination and low pay', CEPR Discussion Paper, London: LSE.

MSF (2000) 'Individual learning accounts', *Research Brief 48*, London: MSF.

Munro, A. and Rainbird, H. (2000) 'The New Unionism and the New Bargaining Agenda: UNISON-Employer Partnerships and Workplace Learning in Britain', *British Journal of Industrial Relations*, 38:2, 223–240.

O'Connell, P. (1998) *Adults in Training: An International Comparison of Continuing Education and Training*, Paris: OECD.

Payne, J. (2001) 'Lifelong Learning: A National Trade Union Strategy in a Global Economy', *International Journal of Lifelong Education*, 20:5, 378–392.

Pedler, M., Burgoyne, J. and Boydell, T. (1996) *The Learning Company*, London: Sage.

Ramsay, H. (1977) 'Cycles of Control: Worker Participation in Historical and Socio-logical Perspective', *Sociology*, 1:3, 481–506.

Ramsay, H. (1996) 'Managing Sceptically: A Critique of Organisational Fashion', in S. Clegg and C. Hardy (eds), *The Politics of Management Knowledge*, London: Sage.

Ramsay, H., Scholarios, D. and Harley, B. (2000) 'Employee and high-performance work systems: testing inside the black box', *British Journal of Industrial Relations*, 38:4, 501–531.

Robinson, P. (1996) 'Skills, Qualifications and Unemployment', *Economic Affairs*, 16:2, 25–30.

Schuller, T. (2000) 'Social and Human Capital: The Search for Appropriate Techno-methodology', *Policy Studies*, 21:1, 25–35.

Senge, P. (1990) *The Fifth Discipline*, New York: Doubleday.

Streeck, W. (1989) 'Skills and the Limits of Neo-liberalism: The Enterprise of the Future as a Place of Learning', *Work, Employment and Society*, 3:1, 89–104.

Streeck, W. (1992) 'Training and the New Industrial Relations: A Strategic Role for Unions?', in M. Regini (ed.), *The Future of Labour Movements*, London: Sage.

Symon, G. (2002) 'The 'reality' of Rhetoric and the Learning Organization', *Human Resource Development International*, 5:2, 155–174.

Symon, G. and Fallows, S. (2000) 'Part-time HE Study in Luton and Its Environs', *Journal of Access and Credit Studies*, 2:1, 112–123.

Thompson, P. and McHugh, D. (2002) *Work Organizations*, Basingstoke: Palgrave.

Tight, M. (1998) 'Education, Education, Education! The Vision of Lifelong Learning in the Kennedy, Dearing and Fryer Reports', *Oxford Review of Education*, 24:4, 473–485.

Trades Union Congress (1998) *Evidence from the TUC to the House of Commons Education and Employment Committee Inquiry: Access for All? A Survey of Post -16 Participation*, London: TUC.

Unions 21 (2000) *Lifelong Learning – A, 21st Century Union Challenge*, London: Unions 21.

UNISON (1999) *Lifelong Learning Policy*, London: UNISON.

Warhurst, C. (1997) 'Political Economy and the Social Organisation of Economic Activity: A Synthesis of Neo-institutional and Labour Process Analyses', *Competition & Change*, 2, 213–246.

Warhurst, C. and Thompson, P. (1998) 'Hands, Hearts and Minds: Changing Work and Workers at the End of the Century', in P. Thompson and C. Warhurst (eds), *Workplaces of the Future*, Basingstoke: Macmillan.

Willmott, H. (1993) 'Strength is ignorance, slavery is freedom: managing culture in modern organizations', Journal of Management Studies, 30:5, 515–552.

11

Skill and the Renewal of Labour: The Classical Wage-Earner Model and Left Productivism in Australia

John Buchanan, Ian Watson and Chris Briggs

Introduction

What are the skills that matter? Scholars and policy-makers who have sought to answer this question have often assumed there is a single, objective 'logic' of skill waiting to be discovered which can then be measured and used for cross-national and historical comparisons. An alternative perspective views skill as a social relation (Braverman 1974; Cockburn 1983; Smith and Thompson 1998). In Mournier's (2001) framework, skill has three dimensions or 'logics' that are embedded in historically specific economic and political settings. Using this perspective, the focus and concerns also change. The primary question is not whether or not skill requirements are increasing. Instead the key questions are:

- How are the three dimensions of skill being socially redefined as post-war 'social settlements' unravel?
- What role skill can play in economic and social renewal?

Additional questions then become:

- How do sustainability and equality mesh within different regimes of skill?
- What role can skill policy play in the renewal of the labour movement as a force for progressive change and the development of policy alternatives to neo-liberalism?

The answer to these questions is developed here from an analysis of Australian skill politics, especially the fortunes of a skill-centred 'left-productivist' trade union strategy[1] following the breakdown of the Australian social settlement.

Skill policy was a key element in the Australian social settlement. The 'new protection' settlement in place from the early twentieth century centred

186

around tariff protection, union recognition before the arbitration tribunals which were the primary mechanism for setting wages and employment conditions and controls on labour supply through the 'white Australia' immigration policy. The skills regime, constructed around apprenticeship training and trade skills, was effective in reproducing skills that mattered economically but socially excluded women, migrants and aborigines. During the 1980s, a skill-centred left productivist strategy to modernise the skill regime and remove inequitable barriers became the focal point of union policy. The left productivists succeeded in dismantling the old skill regime but amidst the broader dominance of neo-liberals in other policy domains, they were swept aside as a state-engineered training market became the focal point of skills policy. The neo-liberal 'training market' is neither sustainable nor equitable, characterised by declining employer investment in training, deepening inequality and the growth of employment low in technical skill.

Both too much and too little has been expected of skill formation policies as a vehicle for economic and social renewal. Whilst some advocates spoke of a 'skill-led recovery' in the 1980s, skill formation was always only a secondary element in the policy mix, expected to accommodate economic restructuring and other policy developments. On the basis of the Australian experience, whilst current political and economic challenges cannot primarily be solved through reforms to skill formation, there cannot be lasting, desirable social change without a profoundly different approach to skill development and utilisation – a new vision of skill policy based upon the promotion of 'work', instead of passively accepting any opportunity to 'labour' (Standing 1999) and actively shaping instead of merely accommodating the character of economic development.

This chapter firstly clarifies the concepts that guide the analysis. The skills regime within the post-war social settlement will be outlined before analysing the emergence of the left productivist approach, its subsequent transmutation into a neo-liberal 'training market' and policy outcomes. The final section delineates a new approach for defining the skills that matter through a critical analysis of left productivism. In so doing, the elements of a skills regime that aims at both sustainability and equality is outlined.

Skill Regimes: The Logics of Skill and Skills Ecosystems

Before analysing the level of skills embedded in any particular task or setting, the issue of what constitutes skill needs to be examined. Mournier (2001: 28) argues that this issue should not be approached from a substantivist viewpoint. As he argues;

> In searching for a homogeneous and substantive definition of skills, most attempts have only looked for one single logic, which has led them to

neglect the social process of defining skills and to assume that skills could be compared through time and space.

What Mournier offers instead is the notion of the 'three logics' of skill, a logic being defined as 'a social force (the interaction between social actors, institutions and social values and norms) acting in a given direction'. The three major components that constitute skill are:

- *technical*, related to the exercise of labour power, and determined by equipment and productive methods;
- *behavioural*, related to the subordination aspects of employment relationships, and reflecting the 'personal qualities of the worker to deal with interpersonal relationships in dependent and subordinated labour'; and
- *cognitive*, related to the level and kind of general education and training undertaken by a population to help it understand and act in the world (p. 28).

Indeed, Mournier anchors his concepts in notions of citizenship and employment. The state's interest in the underlying capacity of its citizens is the primary force shaping the development of cognitive skills. The development and use of technical and behavioural skills are anchored in the open-ended nature of the employment relationship in capitalist societies (Braverman 1974; Fox 1974). Technical skills primarily concern the development of workers' potential to perform. Behavioural skills primarily concern issues associated with the realisation of labour potential on the job. The combination of these three logics is always time and space-specific, 'because these logics are embedded in labour relationships and broader social structures' (Mournier 2001: 28). This approach to the definition of skill emphasises the interface between skill and work, education and social structures as a *skills regime*. The skills link in this configuration can be unpacked analytically into these three logics and then recombined into a historical narrative.

This configuration can also be theorised more usefully by recourse to the concept of skills ecosystems, which emphasises both the spatial and economic context in which such a configuration operates and the political mobilisations which form part of that context. In its original conception, 'skills ecosystems' referred to high skill regions underpinned by interlocking networks of firms, markets and institutions (Finegold 1999). In their extension of the concept, Buchanan *et al.* (2001) included 'clusters of high, intermediate or low-level competencies in a particular industry or region' and reinforced the emphasis on the interlocking networks of firms, markets and institutions, conceived as a form of 'interdependence' (hence the biological metaphor). Such ecosystems do not settle at some level of equilibria but continue 'to evolve and adapt in response to external and internal stimuli' (pp. 21–22). These stimuli include patterns of political mobilisation that shape processes of economic restructuring.

Processes of economic restructuring never happen autonomously but are invariably shaped by processes of political mobilisation as the social actors aligned to different economic interests develop new strategies to deal with these economic challenges.

This approach leads to a triple formulation and a particular methodology. In the discussion that follows, the term 'skills regime' will be used as short-hand for the phrase 'configuration of skills-work-education-social structure'.

The Skills Regime of the Classical Wage-Earner Model

Central to Australia's post-war skills regime were the skilled trades, the backbone of manufacturing and the heart of the labour movement. Their embeddedness in the social structure was based on long-standing divisions within the working class and on the peculiar industrial relations institutions developed in Australia at the turn of the twentieth century. The skilled trades formed part of a 'labour aristocracy', defined largely by a key role in the labour process, a pride in craft skills and by social values that emphasised respectability and exclusiveness. Historians to explain cultural divisions within the working class have long used the notion of the labour aristocracy. Hobsbawm, for example, has argued that in nineteenth-century Britain skilled craftsmen saw themselves as a stratum of the working class superior and separate to the 'labourers'. Despite attempts by the ruling class to patronise them as a kind of lower middle class, the labour aristocracy 'saw itself as a working class, even in some respects as the spokesmen and leaders of the rest of the manual workers' (Hobsbawm 1989: 183). For Hobsbawm, its status and economic power was based on its capacity to organise, both in the trade unions and also in cooperatives and other self-help organizations.

While there have been debates about the appropriateness of the term 'labour aristocracy' in the Australian context (Patmore 1991: 66), the term 'labour aristocracy' does highlight an important social division within the working class between labourers and skilled craftsmen, a division which was always evident on the factory shop floor and in the tensions between their respective unions. Social divisions between labourers and skilled craftsmen were reinforced economically by Australia's unique industrial relations system. The system of apprenticeships ensured control by the craft unions over the supply of skilled tradespersons available for industry while the pay setting arrangements established under the arbitration system were based on a complex set of relativities in which skill was privileged. The principle of a 'basic wage' and 'a margin for skill' served to institutionalise the concept of 'skills within the labour process'. Pay setting was never left to the market, to the supply and demand of particular kinds of skilled labour, but was enshrined in a notion of comparative wage justice in which a skills premium was integral.

In terms of the 'three logics of skills', the skilled trades in post-war Australia were based on a technical component under the control of the craft unions; a behavioural component reflecting a balance of power between management, skilled workers and semi-skilled workers; and an education/training component derived from a guild tradition of time-based apprenticeships in which control was split between the technical colleges and the shop floor. The hierarchical dimension of the behavioural component was particularly noteworthy. Race and gender were central to its exclusionary framework. For most of the post-war period women, non-English speaking migrants and Aborigines were effectively excluded from the skilled trades. Furthermore, even within the Anglo-Celtic male working class, these sharp divisions between skilled, semi-skilled and unskilled were prominent in the workplace and then carried over into the wider community as divisions in social status. These various elements marked the skills regime linked to the classical wage-earner model as inherently unequal.

At the same time, however, this skills regime was economically sustainable. Skills were effectively reproduced from generation to generation. This reproduction was partly the result of the attraction of status and its economic rewards: it was common in working class households for parents to urge their children to protect their futures by entering a trade. More importantly, however, the sustainability came from the influence of the craft unions, the arbitration system and the state-based education system. A systematic, highly regulated mode for the transition of technical skills was fixed by colleges of technical education, industrial awards and a vigilant union presence in the workplace.

By the early 1970s these relationships and the sustainability of the skills regime had begun to unwind. In particular, the attractiveness of the manual trades for working class youth began to wane. Middle class occupations, accessible through the universities, became increasingly attractive to working class youth from the mid-1980s onwards. Previously, teachers' college had been the main avenue out of the manual working class. University was available to only a tiny fraction of working-class youth, those who won scholarships or gained entry as returned soldiers. During this period, the nexus between skill and education was captured in the observation that the 'cream of the working class' formed the bulk of the skilled trades. The small overflow into non-manual higher education (HE) had little impact on the overall composition of the working class for most of this period. Consequently, access to education and the development of cognitive skills mainly lay within the realm of working class self-education, buttressed by a century's old tradition of mechanics' institutes, Schools of Arts, railway institutes and movements such as the Workers' Education Association. The expansion of Colleges of Advanced Education and the steady growth in teacher's college enrolments allowed far larger numbers of working-class youth to escape a future based on manual labour. Figure 11.1 demonstrates the dramatic changes of the 1970s.

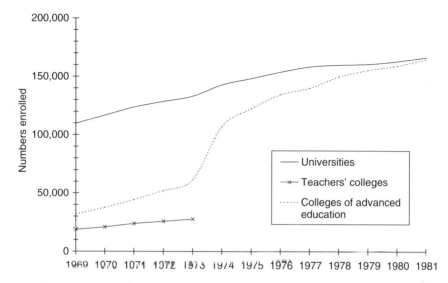

Figure 11.1 Students enrolled in tertiary education, Australia 1969–1981
Source: Vamplew (1987).
Note: After 1973, teachers colleges were classified as Colleges of Advanced Education.

As a consequence of these new opportunities, the skilled trades became less attractive to the more able working class youth. As university education expanded dramatically during the 1980s, particularly after the Dawkins 'reforms' of the late 1980s, this trend accelerated. In 1984 the Australian National Opinion Polls (ANOP) surveyed 15–24-year-olds about their further education (FE) plans, and found that 22 per cent were interested in Technical and Further Education (TAFE), while 19 per cent were interested in university. By 1990, just 12 per cent were interested in TAFE while 31 per cent were interested in university (Dawkins 1992: 8).

These changes in the nexus between skills and education were reflected in the changing occupational structure during this period. As Table 11.1 shows, all of the (male) skilled trades fell below the growth in the labour force from the 1970s onwards, whilst the professions grew at several times the labour force growth. Only two trade areas (electrical/electronic trades and vehicle trades) continued to grow strongly during the 1980s. By contrast, the teaching professions grew very strongly, as did business professionals.

The fact that many of these changes emerged during the late 1960s and early 1970s was no accident. While some of these educational changes were relatively autonomous, the overall dynamic for change was grounded in processes of economic restructuring and political mobilisation. In particular, a crisis in capitalist profitability – induced by problems of excess capacity in manufacturing and an intensification of global competition – became a major force for economic restructuring during the 1970s (Brenner 1998). A political

Table 11.1   Growth in employment in occupations, Australia 1961–1991

Occupations	1961	1966	1971	1976	1981	1986	1991
Skilled trades (males)							
Metal fitting and machining	100	115	114	119	124	123	121
Other metal	100	115	116	119	121	115	117
Electrical and electronic	100	113	126	132	140	143	164
Building	100	104	104	105	106	106	129
Printing	100	108	111	106	108	107	119
Vehicle	100	114	115	118	120	120	152
Food	100	105	98	103	101	117	137
Horticulture	100	91	80	70	71	66	85
Professions (persons)							
Scientists	100	122	136	166	208	230	303
Engineers	100	115	105	148	178	173	223
Health professionals	100	108	122	159	205	240	315
School teachers	100	133	154	214	264	294	353
Other teachers	100	129	148	192	232	259	400
Social professionals	100	118	120	144	183	212	322
Business professionals	100	128	161	187	237	296	489
Artists	100	116	134	149	191	222	316
Labour force (persons)	100	115	125	139	151	152	180

Source: Unpublished Census data 1961–1986 (ABS 1991).
Note: Index of Employment Growth (1961 = 100).

mobilisation – centred on the ideology of neo-liberalism – targeted those aspects of the Australian 'social settlement' that were seen as impeding the revival of capitalist profitability. Australia's unique industrial relations system and the arrangements within the world of work that it underpinned, were particularly vulnerable to this neo-liberal onslaught (ACIRRT 1999). At the same time, the inequality, status divisions and exclusiveness inherent in the post-war skills regime became a target for left-productivist 'reformers'. Ironically, by dismantling the old skills regime, these proponents of equality (progressive unionists, trainers and educators) ultimately paved the way for a neo-liberal 'training market'.

Struggles and Debates during the 1980s and 1990s

Australia's education and training policy framework and its practices of skill formation consequently became one of the key sites of political struggles to reconfigure the Australian 'social settlement'. Throughout the 1980s and 1990s, skill, education and training policy settings were restructured and 'modernised' in a series of waves that reflected the trajectory of broader political changes. The failure of union ambitions to push the newly elected federal Australian Labor Party (ALP) Government to implement interventionist industry policies led the pivotal Australian Manufacturing Workers' Union (AMWU) to focus upon award restructuring and 'skill-based restructuring' as an alternative point of intervention. However, the 'left productivist' focus on skill as the pivot for progressive change floundered amidst the broader influence of neo-liberals upon economic and social policy-making: neo-liberalism ultimately wrested control over skills and training policy, sweeping aside award restructuring and the National Training Reform Agenda (NTRA) in favour of a state-engineered 'training market' (see also Hampson in Chapter 5).

In the early neo-Keynesian phases of the Prices and Incomes 'Accords' between the Australian Council of Trade Unions (ACTU) and federal ALP Government (1983–1986), skill formation was a low priority. The focus of economic policy-making was centralised wage discipline negotiated between the ACTU and the ALP under the Prices and Incomes Accord combined with mildly expansionary fiscal/monetary policies and industry plans for sectors in crisis (e.g. steel and cars). Within this neo-Keynesian project, skill formation played a secondary role; retraining measures were included in industry plans to facilitate labour market adjustment and as a 'safety net' to ameliorate the social impact of industry restructuring (ALP-ACTU 1983; Ewer *et al.* 1991).

Skill, training and education became the pivot for a left productivist project centred on the AMWU during the mid-1980s. The antecedents for the AMWU's productivist strategy can be found in the industrial democracy interventions of the 1970s. Influenced by the worker control and Euro-Communist debates in the Communist Party of Australia, the AMWU promoted workplace interventions to challenge the managerial prerogative and an alternative economic strategy to regenerate manufacturing and build momentum for socialist change (AMWU 1978; Rushkin 1986). During the second developmental phase of the AMWU's interventionist strategy, the political unionism of the early Accords, the focus of AMWU interventions was the state, tripartite forums and industry policy. However, the limited policy and institutional advances of political unionism (Bell 1991; Ewer *et al.* 1991) combined with the weaknesses of Australian manufacturing (e.g. skill gaps) unearthed by union campaigns to increase local content in manufacturing projects led the AMWU to focus on skill formation and workplace restructuring as a new point of intervention to regenerate manufacturing, politicise workers and open up access to skills and career paths for disadvantaged labour market groups (Ewer *et al.* 1987).

The AMWU, in conjunction with the ACTU following the *Australia Reconstructed* mission,[2] developed a blueprint for restructuring the award system as a vehicle to drive the productivist strategy. The AMWU model envisaged restructuring the metal industry award by broadbanding the 300-plus job classifications into 14 skill levels, attaching a wage rate and relativity as a percentage of the basic trade level to each skill level and creating a career path for the first time with a clear schedule of rewards and incentives for skill acquisition. The privileged status of the trades and apprenticeship front-end training would be diluted under this model of lifelong learning and career paths spanning from entry-level jobs to trades-level and post-trades occupations would be constructed. Skills would be devolved to sub-trades employees, training resources would be redistributed from 'front-end' trades-based training to be more equitably shared across the workforce throughout their working lives and demarcation barriers would be diluted to facilitate multi-skilling. Job classifications would be defined by skill and competence instead of time served or narrowly defined tasks. The ACTU moved to extend the metals restructuring model across the award system. The ACTU developed a 'blueprint' for award restructuring, which combined a solidaristic wages policy (large increases to minimum award rates and aggregate wage discipline) with the metals restructuring model of redesigned awards to facilitate skill-based career paths, multi-skilling and labour flexibility (ACTU 1989). Political dimensions of the earlier 'left productivist' project which envisaged using skill as a lever for workplace mobilisation and union training leave to revitalise the political education courses of the 1970s faded as award restructuring became a more narrowly productivist strategy to develop a high skill, high wage economy. The key elements of the ACTU blueprint were transplanted into the national wage principles during 1988–1989 by the Federal Industrial Relations Commission (ACAC 1988; AIRC 1989a,b). Subsequently, during the late 1980s, unions and employers began negotiating changes to their awards from a template based upon the ACTU blueprint.

Award restructuring was the catalyst for reforms to the training system. A series of reports published by the Federal Minister for Education and Training, John Dawkins (Dawkins 1987, 1988, 1989) identified training reforms necessary to remove supply-side constraints to labour market adjustment (e.g. skill shortages and mismatches), develop competency-based training infrastructure to bridge award restructuring and the vocational education and training (VET) system and re-orient training to also incorporate behavioural skills (e.g. teamwork skills) in addition to technical skills. The core elements of the Labor Government's National Training Reform Agenda (NTRA) were:

- a major increase in the level of national investment in training;
- a competency-based training system: new competency-based skill standards for award classifications and training courses were to be established at industry and occupational level related to each other through the Australian Standards Framework (ASF) spanning from a Level One certificate (entry-level skills and knowledge) through to Level Eight (degree or higher degree); and
- the establishment of new bureaucratic institutions such as the Australian National Training Authority (ANTA) and the National Training Board (NTB) to improve the coordination of national training arrangements.

The objective of the NTRA was to create a nationally integrated formal system of skill formation based on competencies (instead of time-serving), modules (instead of fixed sequencing of training) and flexible delivery of training (on- and off-the-job).

Before award restructuring and the NTRA were bedded down, policy moved on to the neo-liberal training market and enterprise bargaining via third-way style experimentation with marketisation in the early 1990s.[3] The ascendancy of the trades-based training system was dismantled but the alternative – a vision of 'lifelong learning' – never materialised as policy-makers turned their attention to constructing an 'industry-led' system and a 'training market'. The logic of the training market was that the reform agenda had to shift from the supply-side to the demand-side to eradicate the mismatch between market demand and training supply by:

> developing a training market centred round direct client relationships between training providers on the one hand and enterprises and individuals on the other, and in which the skills held by individuals are publicly recognised and portable to the maximum extent possible (Allen Consulting Group 1994: 111).

In November 1990, Commonwealth and State Governments determined that the policy framework should be geared towards establishing an 'open market' incorporating a variety of private training providers, community and volunteer groups, employer's in-house schemes and professional organisations alongside the publicly funded TAFE sector.

But whereas injecting market competition to improve the responsiveness of the training system to employer and industry, demand was initially viewed as a complement to the creation of a high skill, high wage economy through the NTRA and award restructuring, market flexibility increasingly became the central organising principle of reform throughout the 1990s. The focus of policy was the construction of the institutional infrastructure to support the training market (e.g. national recognition framework for private providers), the introduction of a training levy to create a pool of capital to 'kick-start' the market and the commercialisation of the TAFE sector to integrate the public providers into the training market (Marginson 1997). The pre-occupation with flexibility is blind or indifferent to skill levels: the focus of policy is simply to create institutions and incentives to replicate and encourage markets wherever possible. With the emergence of the 'training market' policy framework, the normative orientation of a 'high skill, high wage' economy was swept away.

The Transformation of Skills Ecosystems and the Emergence of a New Skills Regime

These training and skill policy reforms were introduced amidst profound economic restructuring and change. The end of the post-war boom and emergence of global excess capacity (see Brenner 1998) severely impacted upon

Australia – a small economy with a dependence upon the export of bulk commodities – leading to a crisis of profitability, soaring current account deficits and foreign debt. Within the Australian economy, there was a shift to a growth path based on deepening levels of market inequality similar to other English-speaking nations (Froud *et al*. 1997). The ascendancy of short-run maximisation of 'shareholder value' as a guiding principle for investment and corporate decision-making triggered waves of retrenchments, labour intensification and the growth of 'non-standard' work such as casuals, contractors and labour hire. In this context, whilst there were some substantial achievements associated with the training and skill policy reforms (e.g. increased availability of structured training), the key outcomes were declining levels of employer investment in training and lower standards of skills attainment. The legacy of two decades of third-way and neo-liberal 'reforms' has been deepening market inequality, an increase in low skill employment, and a new skills regime whose sustainability is highly questionable (Watson *et al*. 2003).

Australian training investment and standards are low by international standards and continue to fall. Between 1990 and 1995, the number of apprentices fell by approximately one quarter, primarily due to falling investment in large workplaces, especially in the public sector (Toner 1998). Whilst public funding for higher education and especially VET has declined markedly (Burke 2001; Marginson 2001), the private sector has not filled the gap left by the disengagement of the public sector from apprenticeship training. Between 1990 and 1996, annual average training hours per employee declined from 5.7 to 4.9 (ABS 1997) – notwithstanding a temporary increase in the early 1990s as a result of the Training Guarantee Levy (TGL) which was abandoned following employer pressure (DEETYA 1996a,b). The number of organisations that spent less than 2.5 per cent of payroll on training increased from 51 per cent (1991) to 52 per cent (1996) to 61 per cent (2001). Not only is employer training investment low, surveys of employees have found that the vast majority of employer-funded skill acquisition is low quality – ad hoc, task-specific on-the-job training ranging from 'being shown how to do the job' to 'teaching self' (Hall *et al*. 2002: 10–11). Overall, Australian investment in knowledge-based ventures (training, research and development and technology expressed as a proportion of GDP) fell by 10.8 per cent between 1985 and 1995 – and a further 3.3 per cent relative to other Organisation for Economic Cooperation and Development (OECD) nations between 1995 and 1998: Australia is now ranked third-last amongst 13 OECD nations in terms of investment in knowledge-based ventures (Marginson 2001). At the same time, inequality in access to training increased during the 1990s. About 92 per cent of employees in high-skilled managerial, professional and paraprofessional occupations participated in some form of training compared to 69 per cent of low-skilled workers such as salespersons, plant and machine operators/drivers and labourers (ABS 1997). Finally, the withdrawal of employer and public funding shifted the burden of responsibility to individuals for their own training. A new enthusiasm for 'lifelong learning' emerged from within the education and training industries and turned what had once been a progressive strand within working class adult education into a bland formula for a new user-pays philosophy within those industries.

Declining levels and standards of training were closely intertwined with labour market changes, particularly the growth in low skill and non-standard work. A recent Australian study (Borland *et al.* 2001) found only one quarter of all new jobs added in the 1990s were full-time jobs and the rate of growth for full-time jobs was only about one quarter of what it had been during the 1980s. This growth in part-time work was also a growth in low paid and less-skilled jobs: the average earnings from part-time jobs, relative to full-time jobs, declined during the 1990s. Using an innovative approach to measuring the knowledge intensity of jobs, this study also concluded that part-time jobs were much less knowledge intensive than full-time jobs. Overall, the Australian growth rate in low-skilled jobs (1.2 per cent per annum) was higher than any other OECD nation (where there had actually been a decline in the number of low-skill jobs in 10 of the OECD nations). Conversely, Australia ranked 16th out of 21 OECD nations in relation to annual average percentage growth in white-collar high-skilled workers between 1980 and 1998 (OECD 2001). By the end of the 1990s, just over half of the workforce was employed on a full-time permanent basis, with growth in casual employment and contractor arrangements outstripping the 'classical' mode of engaging labour. While not all non-standard work engagements were associated with poor training and skill outcomes, it remained the case that over one half of casual employees received no training compared to 30 per cent of permanent employees (ABS 2000).

These trends and the dynamics underpinning the breakdown of skill formation were most advanced in the manufacturing sector. A recent study by Buchanan *et al.* (2002) found manufacturers in the state of Victoria had articulated their skill requirements for more highly developed cognitive and behavioural skills, and had identified skill shortages, but they faced a systemic incapacity to meet new and emerging skill needs. Excess capacity, intense competition and pressures on margins were leading, on the one hand, to reduced intakes of apprentices and reliance on an aging workforce for skills, and on the other hand, to new forms of business organisation and non-standard labour. There were four dimensions to the problem.

1. Labour intensification and a preoccupation with ensuring labour was fully deployed on-the-job undermined the capacity of workplaces to conduct skills development. The stock of skills required for growth and longer-term survival were diminishing in a fashion akin to 'farmers eating their seeds'. For example, while it takes seven years to train an aircraft engineer, the average age of a Licensed Aircraft Mechanical Engineer in Australia is now greater than 55 years.

2. Systemic approaches to on- and off-the-job training were breaking down. For example, under pressure from head office to defend shareholder value, one site engaging in food-processing that had been an industry leader in broad-based training, now trained only in competencies directly relevant to the job. This was just typical of many examples in sectors as diverse as biotechnology, engineering, chemicals and plastics.

3. Declining skill formation capacity was linked to new forms of business organisation and rising usage of non-standard employment. Labour hoarding in the 1960s and 1970s, a device to enable firms to respond quickly to market upturns, had been replaced by lean workforces, supplemented by casuals, contractors and labour hire workers as required.

4. Whereas larger firms previously had regularly taken responsibility for nurturing appropriate levels of skilled labour for particular local and occupational labour markets, larger firms and workplaces now tightly controlled the levels of labour required for production, and this control led directly to a large drop in apprenticeship numbers (Buchanan *et al*. 2002).

In summary, the skills regime that emerged during the 1990s was one that cemented in place new forms of labour market inequality whilst failing to provide any coherent framework for long-term sustainability.

Policy Challenges Arising from the New Skills Regime

The emergence of low skill ecosystems and the pressures driving change represent a major challenge for policy-makers: old policy instruments, crafted for a different labour market, are no longer appropriate but skill formation capacity is being eroded under current policy settings. It is to new policy approaches that this chapter now turns.

  If the concern is the renewal of labour (at work and in society at large), returning to the past or continuing with current arrangements are neither possible nor desirable. The status divisions inherent in the classical wage-earner model were especially undesirable for women, the less-skilled and other marginalised groups. This situation arose because exclusivity was integral to its definition of skill. Besides, it is not possible to return there now even if desired. Times have changed – especially the way employers organise production. Equally, the current neo-liberal regime with its roots in proto-third way arrangements is equally unhelpful. Training levels are falling amongst key areas of skill demand, and reform has not resulted in a demand-driven system, but instead a system of business welfare: employers have merely shifted training costs to the state, not improved their contribution to skill formation (Hall *et al*. 2002; Watson *et al*. 2003).

  Most importantly, analysis of the evolution of labour enhancing left productivism reveals that it was unable to offer viable alternatives to the neo-liberal challenge. The limits of this form of left productivism were not confined merely to a lack of political clout. This policy model had several fundamental design flaws. In its accommodations with neo-liberalism, the left productivists retreated from other policy domains such as industry and tax policy, becoming preoccupied with the *content* of *technical* skill as is evident in the time and resources spent by key union officials on competency standards and competency-based training. As such it became increasingly economistic and technicist in orientation, neglecting two key issues:

1.   Because it became preoccupied with technical skill, it neglected other dimensions of skill, especially those of a cognitive and behavioural nature. This neglect allowed management to hijack these other aspects of skill without any serious contest. This was first evident in their push for 'team skills' in the later 1980s and early 1990s. More recently, it has manifested itself in the push to increase 'generic' and 'employability' skills (Buchanan and Hall 2002.)

2.   It neglected to address the settings in which skills are developed and deployed. Arguably more union time was spent attacking the system of publicly funded TAFE than addressing what management was up to in the workplace. The classical wage-earner model was not just (or even primarily) a skills package (Ewer *et al.* 1991). It was a model of engaging labour in production, which offered security and guaranteed the reproduction of labour power and of the skills that underpinned that labour. Left productivists implicitly assumed that all that needed to change was skill content, while the rest of the model would remain in tact. In fact, other elements of the model were breaking down even faster than the skill element, as evidenced by the rise of non-standard employment and changing forms of business organisation.

These weaknesses have serious implications. Skills are important for defining humans as a collective force in production and in politics (i.e. at work and in society). If too much attention is devoted to the content of technical skill, then the importance of the other dimensions are neglected. The behavioural dimension, for example, is integral to defining people as workers, and not merely as labour. And the cognitive dimension deals with people as citizens, not merely as productive beings. In addition, neglect of the workplace settings in which skills are developed and deployed means management ends up with a free hand in controlling most of the key processes and outcomes associated with skill development and use.

   In our view, the debate on skill needs to move into a different conceptual and policy space: beyond a preoccupation with humans conceived primarily in terms of 'labour' and economic development defined primarily in terms of 'growth'. It must move the focus onto the more encompassing ideas of sustainability and of promoting fair and enduring social relations. These will only be achieved if new political-economic settings at national, sectoral and workplace level to sustain current and nurture emerging skill needs are established (Buchanan *et al.* 2002). Effective change will also require the development of sustainable consumption aspirations. Education is needed on how to live rewarding lives without aspiring to ever higher levels of material consumption (Lane 2000). As such, the notion of skills needs to embrace cognitive and behaviour capacities in the broadest possible sense – not just a broader notion of technical skill development and deployment. Consequently, our major finding is that the key problem with left productivism is its *productivism*. A vision of life is needed beyond productive activity to guide political calculation and mobilisation. Left productivism without such a vision becomes economistic and technicist in outlook.

Skills and the Renewal of Labour

This conclusion raises a major challenge: how are we to successfully move beyond current policy choices? We believe that to move beyond the limitations of current policy offerings it is necessary to reconsider fundamental issues: objectives concerning economic and social priorities and categories to provide guidance for thinking through effective institutional reform. Three issues then become important:

1. notions of sustainable economic development;
2. the place of competition in economic development; and
3. the notion of enhancing citizen's choices over their working lives.

Objectives concerning fundamental economic and social priorities: sustaining life vs. sustaining markets

As the Canadian philosopher, McMurtry (1999) recently argued, the current stage of economic development is best characterised as the 'cancer stage of capitalism'. Destruction of social and natural infrastructure (what he calls the civil commons) creates new 'market opportunities' (p. 366). For example, the erosion of standards of service in public education, public health and public transport as well as emerging environmental problems create new markets for 'growth'. As a result, 'money is not used for life. Life is used for money. The final measure of the Good is an increase or decrease in money sums' (p. 299). As McMurtry (1998: 356) further puts it: 'The problem is not one of being unable to tell the difference between good and bad [but rather in distinguishing] between what disables and what enables life.' Public policy should be oriented to sustaining life – not the current goal of sustaining markets as ends in themselves. These insights are particularly relevant for skill formation policy and practice. Our own research confirms what growing numbers of studies are revealing: in sectors as diverse as engineering and nursing growing numbers of workplaces do not provide settings that allow for the coherent development, transmission and deployment of skill (Buchanan and Considine 2002; Buchanan *et al.* 2002). Growing numbers of sectors are relying on skills inherited from a previous skill regime or skilled labour imported from elsewhere. Such arrangements are clearly unsustainable in the longer run and require policy responses in which the issue of sustainability is one of central concern.

Criteria for institutional design: disciplining competition, not being disciplined by competition

The driving force behind most of the negative skills outcomes noted earlier is competition. It is widely accepted that market arrangements systematically result in the under-provision of public goods such as skills. What is less widely accepted is the need to move beyond reliance on mechanisms based on competition to solve this problem. The project of constructing a national training market is based on the assumption that market-based institutions are part of the solution, not part of the problem. A growing literature is, however, highlighting the need for a more critical approach to the question of markets and competition building upon a long tradition of classical and Marxian political economy (e.g. Botwinick 1993).

The problem of excess capacity in the sphere of production has been convincingly traced back to excessive inter-capitalist competition by Brenner (1998). Within the financial sector a lemming-like pursuit amongst funds managers (and their customers) for maximising shareholder value has resulted in an economy based on the pursuit of higher and higher rates of return that are both unattainable and disruptive to organisational stability (Henwood 1997). Finally Schor (1998) has noted the emergence of a culture of competitive consumption that has emerged since the 1970s that has driven much consumer behaviour since that time. This behaviour has played a major role in contributing to a deteriorating situation in hours of work, especially amongst upper decile workers, and has fuelled demand for cheap household services. Clearly, competition needs to become a servant and not the master of economic development if dynamics such as these are to be arrested. The promotion of competition as the defining feature of Australia's newly emerging training market is likely to make a deteriorating situation worse, not better.

Categories that can provide criteria for designing institutions concerning work

Our analysis in the previous section and elaborated elsewhere in more detail (ACIRRT 1999) has established the need to move beyond the classical wage-earner model of employment. Equally, it is important to move beyond the neo-liberal notion of the 'free individual agent' in the economy and the 'autonomous family' vision of the household (Buchanan and Pocock 2002; Watson *et al.* 2003). Instead, it is more useful to work with the notion of promoting fairness and efficiency by enhancing the choices of citizens over the life cycle. In particular, our analysis has highlighted the importance of moving beyond the traditional assumptions about the settings in which skills are developed and used, namely 'individuals', 'firms' and 'classrooms'. On the demand side there is need to focus on the structure of jobs and especially on their location in skill ecosystems. The idea of skill ecosystem also raises important implications. How well do different elements of such systems cohere both within themselves and between different systems? The beauty of this concept is that it highlights how skills are deployed as well as how they are developed. As such it highlights the importance of how well the risks of skill formation are shared and rewarded. Clearly, questions of pooling risk and the sustainability of different skill regimes move to centre stage given this analytical category. The central task of policy must be to create new institutional capacity that can simultaneously meet the needs for full labour capacity utilisation and the development of skills. If deployment issues prevail then clearly no space is available for the development of skill.

The idea of skill ecosystem is very helpful for thinking through issues of labour demand. It is also important, however, to reconceptualise labour supply. This supply is an issue that has been receiving increasingly significant attention amongst social researchers, especially in Europe. Schmid (1995), for example, has noted that not only is the nature of jobs changing but so too are workers' preferences and working life choices. Increasing numbers no longer want 'standard' jobs at every stage of their life. He argues that there are five common transitions people move through:

1. education, training and employment;
2. domestic work or private activities and gainful employment;
3. short-time work and full-time work;
4. unemployment and employment; and
5. full-time work and retirement.

Schmid's framework of 'transitional labour markets' provides a far more realistic framework for thinking through issues of labour supply than do rival theories, particularly those of the generic rational maximising individual at the core of human capital theory. Skills policy therefore needs to deal with issues of skill ecosystems on the demand side and working life transitions on the supply side.

Political implications

Our analysis is not merely of analytical interest or policy relevance in offering solutions for a particular area of policy concern. It also has significant political implications. Most labour movements (especially unions) are having real difficulty in responding successfully to the current situation. Historically, the classical wage-earner model of employment and skill has been the ideological and organisational glue that has held them together. It is not stretching the analysis to say that a tightly defined (vocational/technical) notion of skill has been the central element in constituting union movements. To this day in Australia mass organisations of workers are called *trade* unions. And currently, the most coherently defined unions in vocational terms are consistently the strongest: the nurses, the teachers, the coal miners, the electricians – not to mention the doctors and the lawyers. In the past, the skills that mattered were 'trade' skills – or specialised skills (e.g. margin skills); that is, differentiation based on skill was important for establishing and maintaining power in the labour market. Power was based on control and exclusion of others – on establishing labour market shelters at the expense of labour market inequality. This skill regime has been breaking down for some time. Progressive social change needs a conception of skill appropriate to the current situation: notions such as skill ecosystem on the demand side and transitional labour markets on the supply side are helpful here. In framing new ideas about skill, it is important to remember not to oversell or undersell the importance of skill. While skills are not the answer there can be no answer without skill. In short, a vision of skill is needed to shape the character of economic development and not merely accommodate economic development (Buchanan *et al.* 2001).

Our ultimate conclusion is that any thinking about the skills that matter must move beyond the limitations of the classical wage-earner, neo-liberal and left productivist notion of skill. In particular, it must encompass broader notions of skill than technical competence and include a concern with deepening peoples' cognitive and behavioural capacities. In so saying, we are not supporting the current push for 'employability' or 'generic' skills with their tacit visions of responsible lifelong learners acquiring the skills that employers need, when they need them. Rather, we have in mind skills such as the capacity for disciplined contemplation, critical analysis and collective self-management at the workplace and beyond. But skills such as these cannot be developed in isolation or in the abstract. They will only emerge and, more importantly, be used if particular institutional arrangements are established. It is for this reason that we believe any notion of the 'skills that matter' must also encompass notions of sustainability at work and enhancing people's capacity to exercise choice over when and how they develop skills through the course of their working lives in the context of diverse and changing skill ecosystems. Developing such skills and settings is not just of analytical or policy concern. By moving beyond the limitation of current policy settings such an approach to the question of the skills that matter could help the agents committed to progressive social change grapple more effectively with current realities. It would also help redefine their objectives in ways relevant to the current situation. As such it would, hopefully, contribute to the renewal of the social forces necessary for achieving their implementation.

Notes

1   The Australian union movement's strategy from the mid-1980s into the 1990s is very similar to the left productivism advocated by Rodgers and Streeck. Moving beyond the post-war Keynesian focus on the 'politics of redistribution' to a 'politics of production' (Rodgers and Streeck 1994: 129), Australian trade unionism committed themselves to 'wealth creation' (ACTU-TDC 1987) by developing the 'social infrastructure of collective goods' (Rodgers and Streeck, 1994: 134) – public goods such as transferable worker skills essential for international competitiveness that capitalists cannot themselves construct. The intellectual schools of thought influencing the labour movement during this period were flexible specialisation and post-Fordism (Curtain and Mathews 1990; Ewer *et al.* 1991). These ideas were diffused throughout the union movement by a group of left-wing union officials (especially in the metal workers unions), academics and policy-makers in labour market and training departments. The ideas were particularly influential in reforming wage, skill formation and labour market institutions during this period.
2   The *Australia Reconstructed* mission, a tour of small Western European economies by leading union officials, was the catalyst for the official embrace of productivism by the union movement. *Australian Reconstructed* (ACTU/TDC 1987) advocated unions move beyond a narrow focus on wages to shape macroeconomic, labour market, industry and skill policies to influence wealth creation as well as distribution.
3   The term 'third way' only emerged later. During the 1980s, however, Federal ALP governments pioneered many policies that were subsequently more broadly celebrated as 'third way' solutions to the alleged failings of both traditional social democracy and new right policy prescriptions. For more details see Buchanan and Watson (2001).

References

ABS (Australian Bureau of Statistics) (1991) Labour Force Survey for 1991, Cat. No. 6204.

ABS (Australian Bureau of Statistics) (1997) *Employer Training Expenditure*, Cat. No. 6353.

ABS (Australian Bureau of Statistics) (2000) *Employment Arrangements and Superannuation*, Cat. No. 6361.

ACAC (1988) *National Wage Case. Reasons for Decision*, Print GH4000.

ACIRRT (1999) *Australia at Work*, Sydney: Prentice Hall.

ACTU (1989) *ACTU Blueprint for Changing Awards and Agreements*, Melbourne: ACTU.

ACTU/TDC (Australian Council of Trade Unions/Trade Development Council Secretariate) (1987) *Australia Reconstructed*, Canberra: AGPS.

AIRC (1989a) *February 1989 Review. Statement by the Full Bench*, Print H8200, 25 May.

AIRC (1989b) *National Wage Case. Reasons for Decision*, Print H9100, 20 August.

Allen Consulting Group (1994) *Successful Reform: Competitive Skills for Australians and Australian Enterprises*, Report to the Australian National Training Authority, Sydney: Allen Consulting Group.

ALP-ACTU (1983) *Statement of Accord by the Australian Labor Party and the Australian Council of Trade Unions Regarding Economic Policy.*

AMWU (1978) *Australia Ripped-Off*, Sydney: AMWU.

Bell, S. (1991) 'Unequal Partners: Trade Unions and Industry Policy under the Hawke Government', *Labour and Industry*, 4:1, 119–137.

Borland, J., Gregory, B. and Sheehan, P. (eds) (2001) *Work Rich, Work Poor, Inequality and Economic Change in Australia*, Centre for Strategic Economic Studies, Victoria University.

Botwinick, H. (1993) *Persistent Inequalities*, Princeton: Princeton University Press.

Braverman, H. (1974) *Labor and Monopoly Capital*, New York: Monthly Review Press.

Brenner, R. (1998) 'The Economics of Global Turbulence: a Special Report on the World Economy 1950–1998', *New Left Review*, 1, 229–265.

Buchanan, J. and Considine, G. (2002) *Stop telling us to Cope! NSW Nurses explain Why they are Leaving the Profession*, NSW Nurses Association (available as a working paper at www.acirrt.com).

Buchanan, J. and Hall, R. (2002) 'Teams and Control on the Job: Insights from the Australian Metal and Engineering Best Practice Case Studies', *Journal of Industrial Relations*, 44:3, 397–417.

Buchanan, J. and Pocock, B. (2002) 'Responding to Inequality Today: Eleven Theses Concerning the Redesign of Policies and Agents for Reforms', *Journal of Industrial Relations*, 44:1, 108–135.

Buchanan, J. and Watson, I. (2001) 'The Failure of the Third Way in Australia: Implications for Policy about Work', *Competition and Change*, 5:1, 1–37.

Buchanan, J., Briggs, C. and Evesson, J. (2002) *Renewing the Capacity for Skill Formation: the Challenge for Victorian Manufacturing*, A Report for the VLESC/MICC: Melbourne (available at www.det.vic.gov.au/otte).

Buchanan, J., Schofield, K., Briggs, C., Considine, G., Hager, P., Hawke, G., Kitay, J., Meagher, G., Macintyre, J., Mounier, A. and Ryan, S. (2001) *Beyond Flexibility: Skills and Work in the Future*, Sydney: NSW Board of Vocational Education and Training (BVET) and published at www.bvet.nsw.gov.au.

Burke, G. (2001) 'Trends in Educational Expenditure', *Paper Presented at the AVETRA 2001 Conference*, Adelaide.

Cockburn, C. (1983) *Brothers: Male Dominance and New Technology*, London: Pluto Press.

Curtain, R. and Mathews, J. (1990) 'Two models of Award Restructuring', *Labour and Industry*, 3:1, 58–75.

Dawkins, J. (1987) *Skills Formation in Australia*, Canberra: AGPS.

Dawkins, J. (1988) *Industry Training in Australia: the Need for Change*, Canberra: AGPS.

Dawkins, J. (1989) *Improving Australia's Training System*, Ministerial Statement, Canberra: AGPS.

Dawkins, J. (1992) 'Post-Compulsory Education and Training: the National Challenge', *Unicorn: Bulletin of the Australian College of Education*, 18:1, 6–12.

Department of Employment, Education, Training and Youth Affairs (DEETYA) (1996a) *The Training Guarantee: Its impact and legacy, 1990–1994. Main Report*, Canberra: AGPS.

Department of Employment, Education, Training and Youth Affairs (DEETYA) (1996b) *The Training Guarantee: Its Impact and Legacy, 1990–1994. Summary Volume*, Canberra: AGPS.

Ewer, P., Hampson, I., Lloyd, C., Rainsford, J., Rix, S. and Smith, M. (1991) *Politics and the Accord*, Sydney: Pluto.

Ewer, P., Higgins, W. and Stevens, A. (1987) *Unions and the Future of Australian Manufacturing*, Sydney: Allen and Unwin.

Finegold, D. (1999) 'Creating Self-Sustaining High-Skill Ecosystems', *Oxford Review of Economic Policy*, 15:1, 60–81.

Fox, A. (1974) *Beyond Contract*, London: Faber and Faber.

Froud, J., Haslem, C., Johal, S. and Williams, K. (1997) 'From Social Settlement to Household Lottery', *Economy and Society*, 26:3, 340–372.

Hall, R., Buchanan, J. and Considine, G. (2002) '"You Value What You Pay For" – Enhancing Employers Contribution to Skill Formation and Use', *A Discussion Paper for the Dusseldorp Skills Foundation*, Sydney.

Henwood, D. (1997) *Wall Street: How it Works and For Whom*, London: Verso.

Hobsbawm, E. (1989) *Worlds of Labour*, London: Weidenfeld and Nicolson.

Lane, R. E. (2000) *The Loss of Happiness in Market Democracies*, New Haven: Yale University Press.

Marginson, S. (1997) *Markets in Education*, Sydney: Allen and Unwin.

Marginson, S. (2001) 'Investment in Knowledge in Australia – Some Year 2001 Policy Issues', paper presented at the *NSW BVET/DET Conference on The Future of Work*, Sydney.

McMurtry, J. (1998) *Unequal Freedoms: The Global Market as an Ethical System*, Connecticut: Kumarian.

McMurtry, J. (1999) *The Cancer Stage of Capitalism*, London: Pluto.

Mournier, A. (2001) 'The Three Logics of Skill', *ACIRRT Working Paper* No. 66, ACIRRT, Sydney.

OECD (2001) *Education Policy Analysis: 2001*, Paris: OECD.

Patmore, G. (1991) *Australian Labour History*, Melbourne: Longman Cheshire.

Rodgers, J. and Streeck, W. (1994) 'Productive Solidarities: Economic Strategy and Left Politics', in D. Miliband (ed.), *Reinventing the Left*, Cambridge: Polity.

Rushkin, N. (1986) 'Union Policy on Industrial Democracy: The Case of the AMWU', in E. Davis and R. Lansbury (eds), *Democracy and Control in the Workplace*, Melbourne: Longman Cheshire.

Schmid, G. (1995) 'Is Full Employment Still Possible? Transitional Labour Markets As a New Strategy of Labour Market Policy', *Economic and Industrial Democracy*, 16:3, 429–456.

Schor, J. (1998) *The Overworked American*, New York: Basic Books.

Smith, C. and Thompson, P. (1998) 'Re-Evaluating the Labour Process Debate', *Economic and Industrial Democracy*, 19:4, 551–578.

Standing, G. (1999) *Global Labour Flexibility: Seeking Distributive Justice*, London: Macmillan.

Toner, P. (1998) 'Trends in NSW Government Apprentice Intake: Cause and Implications', *Australian Bulletin of Labour*, 24:2, 141–157.

Vamplew, W. (1987), *Australians: Historical Statistics*, Sydney: Fairfax, Syme and Weldon Associates.

Watson, I., Buchanan, J., Campbell, I. and Briggs, C. (2003) *Fragmented Futures: New Challenges in Working Life*, Sydney: Federation.

12

The Political Economy of Skill: A Theoretical Approach to Developing a High Skills Strategy in the UK[1]

Caroline Lloyd and Jonathan Payne

Introduction

A common policy discourse has emerged across advanced capitalist econ-omies stressing the pursuit of competitive advantage on the basis of high skill, high value-added approaches. The present UK Labour government is no exception. It is committed to creating a 'knowledge-driven' economy and a culture of lifelong learning as solutions to a wide range of economic and social problems (DfEE 1998; DTI 1998). Critics, however, have pointed to the limitations of policy that rests upon simplistic notions of human capital theory and a skewed emphasis upon a very narrow and limited set of interventions aimed at boosting the supply of skills (Keep and Mayhew 1998).

More recently, there has been recognition within the vocational education and training (VET) field of the need to develop better theory (Ashton 1999) in order to understand the relationship between institutions, skill formation and economic competitiveness, particularly in a comparative context (Ashton and Green 1996; Crouch *et al*. 1999). According to Ashton (1999: 347), 'a para-digm shift in theoretical approaches to skill formation' is occuring, with some commentators explicitly trying to develop a 'political economy of high skills' (Brown 1999). Starting from a rejection of human capital theory, they stress the need for a holistic and multi-disciplinary approach to theorising skill formation, emphasising both the demand for, and supply of, skills. While these accounts have undoubtedly added to an understanding of skill formation issues, it is argued here that there is still some way to go in theoris-ing a 'political economy of skill', and that this theorising is essential if current debates are to be moved forward.

First, given the origins of the skills debate in theories of post-Fordism, there is a need to consider whether or not a fundamental transformation, or para-digm shift, has taken place in the *nature* of contemporary capitalism, the employment relationship and waged labour. Second, there is still some confusion over certain fundamentals, such as what is to be achieved or even meant by a 'high skill economy/society', the particular capitalist model (be it the US, German or Scandinavian) that informs these judgements, and, then, how the UK might actually arrive 'there' (Keep 2000a; Lloyd and Payne 2002b). Third, although some commentators equivocate on whether skills are the answer or not (Crouch *et al.* 1999), others hint that the underlying issue revolves around how to 'modernise' British capital and state institutions without specifying what this modernisation would entail (Ashton and Green 1996; Keep and Mayhew 1999; Lauder 1999).

The first part of this chapter addresses the central question of capitalist change and finds little supportive evidence for a paradigm shift. This implies that a broad and active range of policies would need to be implemented to shift any economy away from predominantly low skill forms of competition. A number of commentators have argued that for the UK to move towards a higher-skilled economy, it is essential to tackle the low levels of employer demand for skill. The second section considers the limitations of this approach, both in terms of policy proposals and the underlying method of analysis. The final section outlines the main elements that are necessary to progress beyond existing attempts to theorise a 'political economy of skill'. First, there is a need to deal more effectively with the workplace by incorporating elements of labour process theory into an analysis of work organisation and skills. Second, any such theory must contain an adequate conception of the capitalist state, recognise the centrality of conflict and power in skill formation, and make some reference to possible agencies for transformation. Without confronting these issues, there is little possibility of an effective and realistic evaluation of what a high skills strategy for the UK would mean and what would be required to implement it.

A Paradigm Shift?

A key theme underlying the current policy rhetoric on skills, and the assumed linkages with economic performance and competitiveness, is the nature of changes said to be taking place within capitalist economies, and in particular the workplace. The first step of any political economy of skill, therefore, is to question the assumption of a new phase of capitalist development qualitatively different from the past and that promises a new, progressive paradigm of work. Three broad positions are taken by commentators that can be labelled 'the knowledge economy optimists', 'the knowledge economy pessimists' and 'the sceptics'. It is important to note at the outset that such an exercise is not unproblematic. It is not just that many commentators shift their position over time, but they can often hold what appear to be completely opposing views even within the same piece of writing (see Crouch *et al.* 1999).

As such they can be placed in more than one camp depending upon which part of their analysis is emphasised – which itself highlights the confusion about the precise nature of the changes taking place in advanced capitalist economies.

The knowledge economy optimists

It is clear that many writers and policy-makers in the area of VET accept some sort of 'paradigm shift' in the nature of contemporary capitalism and work. These claims are often linked to a series of theoretical 'post-Fordist' or 'neo-Fordist' perspectives, notably 'flexible specialisation' (Piore and Sabel 1984) and regulation theory, which have evolved into the looser approaches of the 'information society' and the 'post-industrial', 'knowledge-driven' or 'learning' economy (Leadbeater 1999; Giddens 2000). Intensifying 'global' competition, combined with the rapid pace of technological change, is said to require a new organisation geared towards 'continuous improvement' in product quality, design and innovation. This organisation, in turn, calls for a more adaptable, better-educated and highly skilled workforce than was the case within Fordist mass production. Organisations, it is claimed, will also need to become 'flatter', less hierarchical and more 'trust-based' if they are to embrace autonomous forms of working and tap the creative, value-adding potential of the human resource that holds *the* key to competitive success. The more optimistic of these approaches emphasises the potential to change the very nature of society itself. Leadbeater (1999: ix), for example, argues that the move from manufacturing to 'thin-air business' 'should allow our economies, in principle at least, to become more humane...our children...will make their livings through creativity, ingenuity and imagination'. Similarly, Carnoy (1998: 124) asserts that the transformation of work has 'created the basis for reintegrating the individual into a highly productive, more egalitarian social structure'.

These well-known interpretations of current trends have also found favour amongst a number of educationalists enthused over the 'progressive' educational implications of the new production concepts and the opportunities they create to develop the talents and capabilities of all. On this basis, new 'possibilities' are opened up for everything from a more inclusive society, a more meritocratic education system (Brown and Lauder 1991) and new concepts of schooling (Bentley 1998), to a post-compulsory curriculum informed by the principle of 'connectivity' that breaks down the old academic/vocational divisions (Young 1998).[2] For the optimists there is a tendency either to assume that an inevitable shift is taking place towards a knowledge economy that will automatically raise the level of skills, knowledge, education, training and learning required of all employees or, alternatively, to advance educational reform proposals around the promise of new production processes that are said to be 'emerging' (Young 1998).

The knowledge economy pessimists

For others, however, such heady optimism requires careful qualification. Several commentators point out that despite the furore surrounding the new 'knowledge economy' or 'learning society', high skill sectors are only ever likely to create a limited number of high skill jobs (Brown and Lauder 2001). Crouch *et al.* (1999) claim there are 'clear limits on who can enter utopia' (p. 3), as 'an important minority of the workforce will be unable to participate in the employment provided by the learning society' (p. 238). Green and Sakamoto (2000) are even less sanguine about the UK version of the high skill economy, suggesting that the vast *majority* will find themselves excluded. Even Giddens (2000), who clearly welcomes the opportunities afforded by the knowledge economy, acknowledges that it will mean greater uncertainty and insecurity in the area of employment.

While these visions of the knowledge economy accept that not everyone can be in high skill jobs, it is still assumed that those in lower-skilled employment will need to develop new skills and become more flexible as a result of the changed nature of competition. Teamworking, communication, initiative and a variety of behavioural skills, such as motivation and the ability to deal with customers, are said to be required across all sectors even for low-skilled workers (DTI 1998). These requirements, in turn, have led to widespread calls for the general improvement of VET for all employees, particularly with regard to the provision of generic skills. For Brown (1999: 236), the issue is one of 'how to harness the emotional and creative energies of a large proportion of the workforce to produce quality goods and services'. At the same time, the assumption is often made that the new forms of competition will require a high trust work environment, greater employee commitment and higher levels of cooperation (Brown 1999; Leadbetter 1999).

In contrast to the optimists, these more pessimistic commentators have tended to recognise the severe problems facing the UK in making a successful transition to a knowledge economy. Attention has, therefore, focused on how to shift the UK from its 'low skill equilibrium' (Finegold and Soskice 1988) in an effort to capture the growing number of high skill market segments (Finegold 1999). Policy proposals have concentrated mainly on increasing the supply of skilled and educated labour, particularly on the basis of an expanded post-compulsory and higher education system (Soskice 1993). Others have stressed the need to address the growth of insecure low skill service jobs in a deregulated UK labour market (Brown and Lauder 2001). What tends to unite these writers, however, is the assumption that skill needs are increasing and that the only way advanced economies can secure *long-term* competitive advantage is by adopting high skill approaches.

The sceptics

More sceptical writers have questioned whether the rules of international competition have changed so fundamentally that there exists only one viable 'high skills' route to competitiveness and profitability for advanced capitalist economies (Ashton and Green 1996). Keep and Mayhew (1998) argue that alternatives to the high skills option have been prominent in the UK, including growth through takeovers, shifting investment aboard, acquiring monopoly power, as well as various forms of 'neo-Fordism' and 'cost-cutting'. Across large tracts of employment, in areas such as retail, banking, insurance, hospitality and catering, they highlight the number of firms that still choose to compete primarily on the basis of low price, standardised goods and services and a predominantly low skill, low wage and casualised workforce. Others have stressed the polarisation of skills that appears to have developed both in the UK and the US, which nevertheless still provides the basis for competitive success (Lauder 1999; Green and Sakamoto 2000).

Thus, in the UK, the fastest growing areas of employment are not just professional and managerial jobs, software analysts and business consultants, but also waitresses, security guards, care assistants, salespersons, shelf-fillers and cleaners (Nolan 2000). Even in the new knowledge-intensive sectors, work may not always be 'high skill'.[3] Research from within the British labour process tradition has also contributed powerfully to dispelling many of the myths surrounding 'the new workplace' and the rhetoric of universal up-skilling (Thompson and Warhurst 1998). As Warhurst and Thompson (1998: 8) note, the overall picture that emerges suggests 'continued variability in workplace trends', alongside a general underlying shift towards work intensification.

Further concerns surround the spread of the much vaunted high performance workplace model, usually taken to mean a varied 'bundle' of human resource management practices, including team working and forms of employee involvement. Keep (2000a) stresses that the 'high-performance workplace' displays only a very limited presence on UK soil. He cites the 1998 Workplace Employee Relations Survey (WERS) findings which found that only one-fifth of the organisations sampled had half or more of the 16 practices which when combined together are thought to comprise a coherent, strategic approach to managing the human resource (Cully *et al.* 1998: 11). More recently, Keep and Mayhew (2001) have suggested a fundamental incompatibility between the high performance workplace and the Anglo-Saxon model of capitalism, the former being hard to nurture in a business environment characterised by deregulated labour markets, cost-based competitive strategies, and short-term pressures on management to satisfy shareholders (see also Brown and Reich 1997; Hillard and McIntyre 1998). Not surprisingly, such findings are echoed in the US context (Milkman 1998; Cappelli 1999).

Despite the existence of alternative forms of competition and a more constrained perspective on how capitalism is changing, the sceptics insist that the 'high skills route' remains a viable option, as well as a more desirable one, given the social and distributional outcomes. Ashton and Green (1996), for example, claim that the high skill route offers 'a substantial expansion of freedoms that accrue to a well-educated and highly trained population' (p. 191). Although this route would not be 'free from contradictions', they argue that space exists for 'a medium-term successful period of capital accumulation, relatively free from crises' (p. 177). However, moving the UK economy onto such a high skills trajectory is generally seen to be extremely difficult requiring major shifts in the 'demand for skill' as part of more proactive industrial policy (a point returned to later).

A changing paradigm?

Many of the sceptics' observations concerning the continued viability of alternative routes to profitability, the trend towards increasing labour market and skill polarisation in the UK and the USA, and the constraints imposed by the Anglo-Saxon model in limiting firms' ability to compete on skills are correct.[4] However, sceptics have also stressed the lack of evidence of new forms of work organisation in particular the high performance workplace,[5] as an indicator of the limited progress being made towards a high skills society in the UK and US. It could be argued, in contrast, that these 'new' practices do not necessarily have a positive impact on employees' skills or their quality of working life.

Even a cursory glance at the literature shows that these types of practices vary hugely in their definition, rationale and implementation, and many have a long and chequered history (Ramsay 1977; Geary 1994). Not surprisingly, then, research has found numerous examples of teamworking that involve work intensification and 'more insidious forms of control' (Marchington and Grugulis 2000: 1105–1106), particularly in the form of peer pressure (Geary and Dobbins 2001). An evaluation by Godard and Delaney (2000) of the largely US literature, discovered little evidence of positive benefits accruing to employees and warns instead of a growing catalogue of negative effects. These effects include: work intensification, increased stress, the use of peer pressure to control workers, and the undermining of trade unions. There remains a serious question mark, therefore, over both the extent to which these new management practices are spreading and whether they represent positive gains for employees.

What about the impact of these new work practices on skill? A common assertion is that they require employees even at the lower reaches of the labour market to develop the requisite 'social skills' of communication, teamworking and adaptability (Crouch *et al.* 1999; Green *et al.* 1999). Evidence from the UK skills surveys seems to support the view that these types of skills are on the increase (Green *et al.* 2000; Felstead *et al.* 2002). However, it is important not to exaggerate the changes. Other surveys have found that UK employers are demanding generic skills, including literacy and numeracy, but that for the majority of employees this requires competency only at very low skill levels in jobs offering little scope for autonomy (Dench *et al.* 1998; McIntosh and Steedman 2001). This picture is confirmed by the latest UK Skills Survey (Felstead *et al.* 2002: 42), which estimates that there are currently around 6.5 million jobs in the UK that do not require a single qualification to gain entry, while also noting that levels of reported discretion had fallen significantly.

To sum up, there is little conclusive evidence to support the view that a major 'paradigm shift' has taken place in the nature of capitalist competition resulting in a universal trend towards higher skills and a qualitative transformation in the nature of the employment relationship. There are ongoing changes in patterns of work organisation (a process that has always taken place, albeit one which may have speeded up in the last 20 years), but it would seem dangerous to advance policy on the basis of a 'hoped-for' post-Fordist transformation in the nature of capitalism. By rejecting the assumption that skills are inevitably increasing, the process of how to move towards a 'high skills society', as well as what that society will look like, becomes of central importance. This has been recognised by a number of more critical commentators within the UK VET debate who have called on policy-makers to tackle the level of employer demand for skill. The next section assesses what doing something about 'the demand side' really means for UK policy and, as a result, why it has been inadequately theorised.

Tackling 'the demand side'

A number of commentators have argued that constructing an inclusive, high skill society in the UK would require tackling the low level of employer demand for, and usage of skills, across the economy in general (Ashton and Green 1996; Keep and Mayhew 1999; Green and Sakamoto 2000; Brown and Lauder 2001). Keep and Mayhew (1999) argue, for example, that the UK VET policy approach, by focusing on expanding the *supply* of skills, fails to get to grips with the critical issue of the firms' choice of product strategy, job design and people management approaches which currently limit many firms' ability to make use of the skills available. Shifting the skills trajectory of an economy has to address how the demand for skill is constructed and what can be done to ensure that firms demand higher level skills.

The need for a 'demand side' approach to tackling the UK's skills problem has led some of these commentators to emphasise the importance of developing an active industrial policy (Finegold and Soskice 1988; Ashton and Green

1996). However, when investigating what such an industrial policy will look like, there is a general failure to flesh out the sort of intervention that might be sufficient to tackle the problem. Brown and Lauder (1999: 56) cite the need for an active developmental state involved in 'investment, regulation and strategic planning in the economic infrastructure'. Lauder (1999) goes even further highlighting in the UK context the necessity of confronting the vested interests of 'the City' and business short-termism, in addition to calling for the global regulation of capital movements. Nevertheless, what this means in practical terms is left unstated.

By contrast, Finegold (1999) and Keep (2000a,b) do offer policy prescriptions, although they attack the problem differently both in terms of the way they analyse current difficulties but also with respect to their 'high skills vision'. Drawing upon the example of the high-tech clusters of California's Silicon Valley, Finegold's policies are aimed at expanding the existing high skill sectors of the UK economy (dubbed 'high skill ecosystems'), which he claims are essential for wealth creation and development. The problem, as Finegold concedes, is that these sectors will only ever employ a small minority and, as such, offer no solution to the problem of the 'low skills equilibrium' (Finegold and Soskice 1988). Nevertheless, there is scope for the wealth generated by high-tech sectors to be redistributed in ways that improve the employment conditions of those in 'peripheral', low skill, low wage and insecure jobs (see also Crouch *et al.* 1999). Policy proposals then focus on state funding for research in science and technology and for pre-venture capital investment, alongside measures to encourage the supply of entrepreneurial skills and the fostering of regional and individual networks. Such an approach avoids the need for fundamental shifts in the model of British capitalism but it does suggest major changes in the redistributive policies of the state.

Keep's (2000a: 8, 2000b: 15) vision of a relatively egalitarian, high skills economy and *society*, 'where all share in country's economic success', is both broader and more demanding. His vision 'draws more upon a North European, and particularly Scandinavian tradition, rather than the Anglo-Saxon models of England and the US'. Policy proposals include a measure of income redistribution to 'reduce the incidence of acute poverty in the UK population', with the explicit aim of blocking-off a market for cheap, standardised goods and services, and engineering a Scandinavian-style broad 'high-income consumer base' to support more expensive, quality-based production. If companies are to engage in expansive work reorganisation and job redesign programmes, consistent with the high performance workplace model, they will also need access to long-term 'competent and patient capital' (Keep 2000a: 14). Keep (2000a) also envisages a new role for government in championing better quality working environments, with the public sector leading the way in terms of the adoption of the high performance work model. Moreover, as a major purchaser of private-sector goods and services, government is uniquely positioned to set thresholds in terms of levels of research and development investment and the *range* of high involvement work practices to be expected from those firms with whom it is willing to do business.

A deficient agenda?

Two key issues are raised by these types of policy proposals. The first is whether, in themselves, they would be *sufficient* to move the UK off its low skill trajectory. The second concerns what changes would be required for the appropriate policies to be implemented. As noted above, many commentators acknowledge, at least implicitly, that moving the UK economy on to the 'high road' would require tackling the systemic weaknesses of the UK model of 'stockholder' capitalism and its dominant 'regime of competition' (Green and Sakamoto 2000). In addition, it has also been argued (Brown 1999; Keep 1999) that there needs to be major reforms to the industrial relations system to provide a more supportive infrastructure to a high skills project. These reforms would require a central and strong role for trade unions, more along the lines of German or Scandinavian social partnership. Finegold's policy proposals are never aimed at this type of major institutional change, while Keep's are simply a series of initial starting points that only scratch the surface of how to deal with the long-term structural weaknesses of UK capitalism.

When seen in these terms, it is clear that the skills debate is really pushing in the direction of a much older one concerning the roots of UK relative economic decline, the complex relationship between financial and industrial capital, and the absence of an industrial policy aimed at modernising Britain's manufacturing base and redressing its bias towards under-investment (Fine and Harris 1985). Given the kind of *radical* institutional changes, this is likely to require in terms of City reform, fiscal policy, the labour market and industrial relations, it begs the crucial question of where change will come from.

Such matters inevitably lead us to a consideration of the *role of the state* as the key transformative agency cited within the skills literature. Many commentators acknowledge that not all capitalist states are the same, that some have developed a greater historical capacity to shape the process of economic restructuring than others, graphically illustrated by a comparison of the Japanese, German and British industrial policy approaches (Ashton and Green 1996; Green and Sakamoto 2000). Beyond that, however, 'the state' often remains an untheorised concept. In some accounts, the state approximates to some kind of vague, 'neutral' entity that encapsulates the 'common good' of society, while being constrained by the forces of capital to limit forms of regulation (Crouch *et al.* 1999). In others, there is the implicit belief that it acts, or at least desires, to secure the long-term interests of the economy and society, and that it might be *persuaded* to 'tackle the demand side' (Keep and Mayhew 1999). Finegold (1999) rejects major institutional change for the UK.

Nevertheless, he still calls for the state to redistribute wealth without offering any indication of how or why this should happen.

Ashton and Green (1996: 39) are among the few VET contributors who directly address the issue of the state, arguing that it is essential to have an 'adequate conception of the nation state'. They view the state as an arena 'where different class interests are struggled over, with capitalist interests...normally dominant' (p. 40). Without such an analysis, which recognises the conflict and power relations operating within the state, it is difficult to grasp what forces influence the state or how change can take place. Despite their observation that 'skill formation issues are inherently subject to conflict', Ashton and Green insist that a 'high skills route to accumulation' would have as its *sine qua non* a 'workable consensus' embracing the ruling political elite and leading employers (p. 190). Similar conclusions have been reached by Coffield (1999) and Brown and Lauder (2001), yet there is failure to take the next logical step of exploring the possibilities for such a political settlement emerging in specific national contexts such as the UK.

The lack of detailed policy proposals and the limited exploration of the role of the state reflect the problem that existing frameworks have in adequately theorising a political economy of skills, in particular the relations between state, capital and labour. The next section outlines some of the key elements that are required to develop such a theoretical approach. The first part focuses on the need to integrate an analysis of the workplace into the skills debate in order to appreciate the extent and type of change that would be required to ensure high skill production. The second part stresses the importance of a theory of the state in identifying how and whether change can take place.

Towards a Political Economy of Skill

The workplace

Central to theorising a political economy of skills, and often absent from much of the skills literature, is the integration of workplace dynamics with the type of institutional changes outlined in the previous section. Taking Keep's (2000b) broader vision of a high skills economy, the aim is not just competitive strategies based on high quality goods and services, but a more democratic, egalitarian and socially inclusive society, with forms of work organisation that give workers greater autonomy, discretion and skill. Having accepted that there is no major transformation occurring in the nature of capitalism and, as a result, employers are not automatically going to require more highly skilled workers, it becomes clear that any policy agenda to reach such a goal must impact radically on employers' business strategies and workplace relations. In the first instance, a large number of employers will have to shift their business strategies, adopting long-term approaches and focusing on higher quality product markets or innovative/differentiated markets. Second, employers will have to use forms of work organisation that require more, not less, skill and provide greater levels of autonomy at all levels within the company. The example of many firms in France provides a warning that institutional arrangements which offer labour market protection, formal training systems and long-term approaches to investment can coexist with hierarchical, Taylorist forms of work organisation (Saglio 1995). In contrast, workplace trade union organisation is central to the German model, in terms of ensuring that regulations are enforced and that works councils can operate effectively.

Major shifts in the institutional and industrial policy framework are a *necessary*, but not *sufficient*, condition for the achievement of a high skill economy. Institutional change would provide a range of constraints and incentives to encourage firms to shift towards high quality production approaches and to block-off low wage, 'flexible' routes to capital accumulation. Yet for firms operating in high quality markets, there remain real choices at the point of production over how jobs are designed and work is organised. Employers, for example, could select a high quality route, but with the vast majority of employees undertaking a relatively narrow range of tasks, with limited job autonomy and little real involvement in work. This type of approach has already been adopted by some companies in the UK operating in high value-added markets (Lloyd 2000) and in the USA, where large numbers of graduates supplement the limited skills and autonomy of workers on the shop floor (Mason 1999). Evidence indicates that power relations within the firm, in conjunction with wider institutional constraints, play a key role in explaining the variation in forms of work organisation and skill levels both across companies and countries (Senker and Senker 1994; Thompson *et al.* 1995; Mason and Finegold 1997).

The principal relations within the workplace are between managers, workers and, where they exist, trade unions over the design, autonomy and definition of work. Important too are the relations between groups of workers, especially with regard to issues over who has access to higher-skilled jobs. It is vital, therefore, to reassert that the definition of skill and the skills associated with a particular technology (and product market strategy) are negotiated and rewarded through social processes, including gender and power (Cockburn 1985). As a result, it can be argued that ensuring jobs are redesigned to produce a wider spread of benefits that requires a strengthening of labour vis-à-vis capital within the firm, as well as confronting the sexual division of labour. Without a strong role for workers' organisations, alongside regulatory measures such as job security protection (see Lloyd 1999) and incentives for training and education, there is likely to be little internal pressure on employers to ensure that high quality product strategies are associated with a broad range of skills and development opportunities. Whether trade unions are capable or willing to pursue such an approach depends ultimately, however, on radical shifts in their own organisational structures and strategies towards skill formation at the workplace.

A further factor in the analysis here is a rejection of the notion that high skills constitute a 'common good' and that firms can be persuaded to utilise employees to maximise those skills. In an environment where firms are being pushed to move upmarket to compete on high skills, those already occupying such markets may not welcome the added competition from new entrants, while those pursuing cost-based strategies may be unable to respond and, therefore, survive. Evidence also exists that some managers, particularly in the UK, have found that employing skilled workers presents a number of problems in terms of higher costs, training and recruitment issues and the challenges they pose to managerial control. These types of issues have provided a rationale for deskilling in a number of UK industries, particularly in relation to workers in craft occupations (Senker and Senker 1994; Thompson *et al.* 1995). In addition, there are distributional issues that may arise amongst employees with a move to a more equal distribution of skills. Such change may be perceived as a threat by those already in higher-skilled jobs, as opportunities, advantages and resources are redistributed to the lower-skilled workers.

Integrating institutional structures and workplace relations into an analysis of the political economy of skill, starkly presents what 'doing something about demand' involves. The institutional and workplace changes that would be required to shift the UK from its current growth trajectory represent fundamental challenges to the existing organisation of the UK economy. If this analysis is accepted, then the central question becomes one of how could change come about and what would be its agency?

State, consensus and agency

The section 'A Paradigm Shift?' demonstrated that much of the VET literature either ignores the process of how change takes place or gives the principal role to the government in instituting a range of policy interventions. The tendency has often been to draw back from confronting difficult issues concerned with the understanding of the state, the formation of a political consensus/strategy in favour of radical capitalist modernisation and, most problematic of all, where 'the agency of change' itself will come from. A similar approach is adopted here to that of Ashton and Green, who view the state as an arena of conflict and political struggle but with a core function of maintaining an environment for profitable capitalist accumulation. If many routes to competitive success do exist, there is no automatic reason to believe that the *long-term* interests of UK capital, or the state, lie in the direction of the 'high skills road'.

The problem for Ashton and Green is that they fail to draw out the implications of their theory of the state and instead adopt the position that progress requires the development of a workable political consensus involving the state, capital and labour in support of a high skills strategy. Applying this perspective to the UK, the main problem is the tendency to underestimate the enormous difficulties of forging such a consensus around what amounts to a radical project of capitalist restructuring and institutional modernisation. If low cost routes to profitability are to be curtailed and mechanisms put in place to encourage the development of a more even distribution of skills within the workplace, then such a strategy would have to incorporate at least three key elements. First, it would require fundamental institutional resetting aimed explicitly at reforming a City-driven model of capital accumulation, geared primarily to the maximisation of short-term 'shareholder' value and destructive of long-term investment in people, plant and technology.[6] Second, it would need to reform the structure of the UK state itself, tackling the 'City–Bank Treasury' nexus that has long pursued policies of monetary and fiscal orthodoxy to the detriment of the UK's manufacturing base (Coates 1996). Third, there would need to be strong regulation of employers and labour markets, as well as the development of collective institutions (both of employers and trade unions) at state and workplace level to deliver training commitments, minimum standards and measures to push firms 'upmarket'.

Developing an inclusive high skills economy in the UK, therefore, represents an explicit challenge to the current UK model of deregulated shareholder capitalism and the neo-liberal political consensus that helps sustain it. The question then becomes: under what conditions might sections of capital and the state line up behind such a project? It is far from clear that UK domestic capital has a genuine 'stake' or interest in the high skills project, given the availability of alternative routes to profitability. As for UK multinationals, they are increasingly shifting more of their assets overseas (Temple 1998), questioning their commitment to the UK. Eighteen years of Conservative government left a severely weakened trade union movement, ill-placed to pressure for radical capitalist modernisation. At the same time, they confront hostile employers steeped in laissez-faire ideology that would resist tooth and nail the kind of policy regime sketched above. Such a project could also expect massive opposition from the City, along with its main ally within the state apparatus, namely the Treasury, and would also have to work hard to calm punitive international money markets. Finally, as argued elsewhere (Lloyd and Payne 2002c), New Labour's accommodation within the neo-liberal growth paradigm, coupled with its concern not to offend business interests or the City, make it an unlikely candidate to pursue such an ambitious project.

If, as has been argued here, the high skills project in the UK amounts to one of radical economic, institutional and social modernisation, then there is a need to look beyond easy notions of consensus and confront the thorny problem of *agency*. For, in the end, the pursuit of such a strategy comes down to issues of *power* and whether other social actors are strong and determined enough to exert pressure on the state and force capital's hand. Critical is the balance of social forces between capital and labour and whether labour is in a position to command a new social settlement centred on a more democratic and egalitarian high skills growth model. For these reasons, 'labour' is the crucial agency of change. The strengthening of labour vis-à-vis capital is vital, as trade unions (and other forms of labour organisations) are the only social actors that have the potential to exert power in favour of the high skills project, as well as an interest in doing so. However, no claim is made that organised labour would *necessarily* choose to act in this way, even allowing for more favourable conditions, or that they could unilaterally impose a high skills strategy. Such an outcome remains but one possibility amongst others that might emerge were the current model to enter a major period of crisis and labour finds itself with a stronger bargaining hand than at present.

Conclusion

The political economy of skill has moved on significantly from the self-limiting assumptions of human capital theory that improving the supply of skills will create its own demand and solve the problems of low skill economies. Those commentators who have been at the forefront of attempts to theorise a political economy of skill have all tended to concur on the need for a more holistic, 'societal' approach to skill formation issues. Attention has been focused on the institutional linkages between government agencies, the education and training system, labour market regulation, employment structures, and systems of finance and industrial relations that make up distinctive 'national business systems', and help shape the dominant growth or skill trajectory of a particular country. There is broad agreement that international comparisons of skill formation need to take account of this wider picture, and require a multi-disciplinary approach drawing upon the insights from fields as diverse as economics, politics, industrial relations, sociology, history and cultural studies.

Yet differences inevitably persist. Some analyses are framed in terms of 'post-industrial possibilities', suggesting a qualitative shift in the nature of capitalism and work, which creates new opportunities for progressive change even where such change is absent from the political agenda (Brown and Lauder 2001). Others, such as Ashton and Green (1996), have stressed the contradictions and uneven development of capitalist societies, and the need for a materialist analysis of the state as an arena of class conflict, whilst holding out hope of a feasible 'high skills route to accumulation' as the best option currently available.

This chapter has sided more with the latter approach, questioning the usefulness of terms such as 'post-Fordism', 'post-industrial' and the 'new knowledge economy' for describing the changes currently taking place in advanced capitalist societies. As a corrective to this tendency, an integration of labour process research into mainstream education and training debates around the knowledge economy and the learning society is necessary to bring back the reality of what is happening in the workplace. Moreover, a radical political economy of skill must recognise the fundamental conflicts of interest between labour and capital, both within the firm and wider social formation, and the role the state plays within these conflicts.

In applying this perspective to the UK, this chapter has focused on the central question; namely, what would be required to shift the economy off its existing low skills trajectory and onto a high skills route to accumulation? It is significant that, despite a growing acceptance of the need to 'do something about the demand side', few commentators have been prepared to discuss in any detail what this approach might mean, beyond hinting at some form of industrial policy. This retreat into the vagueness of 'the demand side' may well reflect the sheer scale of the economic and social modernisation project required in the UK, as well as the difficulty of selling such a radical project to policy-makers and politicians wedded to the prevailing 'neo-liberal' consensus.

In addition to radical industrial policies, if firms are to be pushed into pursuing a high skills approach, there is a requirement for a major strengthening of the position of employees and their organisations. Accepting a stronger role for trade unions, instituting reforms to strengthen the 'voice' of workers and their influence, and providing elements of codetermination represent considerable 'threats' to British capital as currently constituted. Framing the problem in these terms identifies what such a high skills/modernisation strategy would mean for many employers and why fierce resistance would be expected.

Once it is accepted that the skills debate in the UK boils down to 'how you change the model', then it is necessary to confront the fact that a high skills/radical modernisation project in the UK is a *class project* that aims to shift the balance of power between capital and labour, both at the level of state policy and the workplace. The conceptualisation of the state as an arena of conflict and political struggle accepts that the state has a key role to play in a Left modernisation project, but insists that it will do so only under specific political, economic and social conditions. In the end, however, this depends *not* on the construction of some nebulous 'consensus' but on a fundamental shift in the existing balance of social forces and a strengthened labour movement capable of imposing a new competitiveness contract on reluctant capital. Whilst a radical political economy of skill does not make the issue of finding a viable Left political strategy any easier under existing economic, social and political conditions, it may at least make clearer the real limits and possibilities for an inclusive high skills project in the UK.

Notes

1 A version of this chapter appeared in the *Journal of Education and Work* (see Lloyd and Payne 2002a).
2 These arguments are dealt with critically elsewhere (see Lloyd and Payne 2003).
3 See Green and Sakamoto (2000) on the UK's banking and financial services sector and Keep 2000a on the software industry.
4 For more detailed evaluation see Lloyd and Payne (2003).
5 Despite frequent reference in both the academic and policy literature, there remains no agreed definition of the high performance workplace. It remains a shadowy entity whose presence is assumed to be growing.
6 For detailed policy proposals see Hutton (1997).

References

Ashton, D. (1999) 'The Skill Formation Process: A Paradigm Shift?', *Journal of Education and Work*, 12:3, 347–350.

Ashton, D. and Green, F. (1996) *Education, Training and the Global Economy*, London: Edward Elgar.

Bentley, T. (1998) *Learning Beyond the Classroom*, London: Routledge.

Brown, C. and Reich, M. (1997) 'Micro-macro Linkages in High-performance Employment Systems', *Organization Studies*, 18:5, 765–781.

Brown, P. (1999) 'Globalisation and the Political Economy of High Skills', *Journal of Education and Work*, 12: 3, 233–251.

Brown, P. and Lauder, H. (1991) 'Education, Economy and Social Change', *International Studies in the Sociology of Education*, 1, 3–23.

Brown, P. and Lauder, H. (1999) 'Education, Globalization and Economic Development', in J. Ahier and G. Esland (eds), *Education, Training and the Future of Work*, London: Routledge.

Brown, P. and Lauder, H. (2001) *Capitalism and Social Progress*, Basingstoke: Palgrave.

Cappelli, P. (1999) 'Introduction', in P. Cappelli (ed.), *Employment Practices and Business Strategy*, Oxford: Oxford University Press.

Carnoy, M. (1998) 'The Changing World of Work in the Information Age', *New Political Economy*, 3:1, 123–128.

Coates, D. (1996) 'Labour Governments: Old Constraints and New Parameters', *New Left Review*, 219, 62–77.

Cockburn, C. (1985) *Machinery of Dominance*, London: Pluto.

Coffield, F. (1999) 'Breaking the Consensus: Lifelong Learning as Social Control', *British Educational Research Journal*, 25:4, 479–499.

Crouch, C., Finegold, D. and Sako, M. (1999) *Are Skills the Answer? The Political Economy of Skill Geation in Advanced Industrial Societies*, Oxford: Oxford University Press.

Cully, M., O'Reilly, A., Millward, N., Forth, J., Woodward, S., Dix, A. and Bryson, A. (1998) *The 1998 Workplace Employee Relations Survey: First Findings*, London: ESRC/ ACAS/PSI.

Dench, S., Perryman, S. and Giles, L. (1998) *Employers' Perceptions of Key Skills*, Report 349, Brighton: Institute for Employment Studies.

DfEE (Department for Education and Employment) (1998) *The Learning Age*, London: HMSO.

DTI (Department of Trade and Industry) (1998) *Our Competitive Future: Building the Knowledge-Driven Economy* Cm 4176, London: HMSO.

Felstead, A., Gallie, D. and Green, F. (2002) *Work Skills in Britain 1986–2001*, Nottingham: DfES.

Fine, B. and Harris, L. (1985) *The Peculiarities of the British Economy*, London: Lawrence & Wishart.

Finegold, D. (1999) 'Creating Self-sustaining, High-Skill Ecosystems', *Oxford Review of Economic Policy*, 15:1, 60–81.

Finegold, D. and Soskice, D. (1988) 'The Failure of Training in Britain: Analysis and Prescription', *Oxford Review of Economic Policy*, 4:3, 21–53.

Geary, J. (1994) 'Task Participation: Employees' Participation Enabled or Constrained', in K. Sisson (ed.), *Personnel Management*, Oxford: Blackwell.

Geary, J. and Dobbins, A. (2001) 'Teamworking: A New Dynamic in the Pursuit of Management Control', *Human Resource Management Journal*, 11:1, 3–23.

Giddens, A. (2000) *The Third Way and its Critics*, Cambridge: Polity.

Godard, J. and Delaney, J. (2000) 'Reflections on the "High Performance" Paradigm's Implications for Industrial Relations as a Field', *Industrial and Labor Relations Review*, 53:3, 482–502.

Green, A. and Sakamoto, A. (2000) 'The Place of Skills in National Competition: Strategies in Germany, Japan, Singapore and the UK', *The High Skills Project Working Paper*, London: Institute of Education.

Green, A., Wolf, A. and Leney, T. (1999) *Convergence and Divergence in European Education and Training Systems*, London: University of London, Institute of Education.

Green, F., Ashton, D., Burchell, B., Davies, B. and Felstead, A. (2000) 'Are British Workers Getting More Skilled?', in L. L. Borghans and A. D. Grip (eds), *The Over Educated Worker?*, Cheltenham: Edward Elgar.

Hillard, M. and McIntyre, R. (1998) 'The Ambiguous Promise of the High Performance Work Organization', *Review of Radical Political Economics*, 30:3, 25–33.

Hutton, W. (1997) *The State To Come*, London: Vintage.

Keep, E. (1999) 'UK's VET Policy and the "Third Way": Following a High Skills Trajectory or Running Up a Dead End Street?', *Journal of Education and Work*, 12:3, 323–346.

Keep, E. (2000a) 'Creating a Knowledge-driven Economy – Definitions, Challenges and Opportunities', *SKOPE Policy Paper* 2, University of Warwick.

Keep, E. (2000b) *Upskilling Scotland*, Edinburgh: Centre for Scottish Public Policy.

Keep, E. and Mayhew, K. (1998) 'Was Ratner Right?', *Economic Report* 12:3, London: Employment Policy Institute.

Keep, E. and Mayhew, K. (1999) 'The Assessment: Knowledge, Skills and Competitiveness', *Oxford Review of Economic Policy*, 15:1, 1–15.

Keep, E. and Mayhew, K. (2001) 'Globalisation, Models of Competitive Advantage and Skills', *SKOPE Working Paper*, No 22, University of Warwick.

Lauder, H. (1999) 'Competitiveness and the Problems of Low Skills Equilibria: A Comparative Analysis', *Journal of Education and Work*, 12:3, 281–294.

Leadbeater, C. (1999) *Living on Thin Air*, Harmondsworth: Penguin.

Lloyd, C. (1999) 'Regulating Employment: Implications for Skill Development in the Aerospace Industry', *European Journal of Industrial Relations*, 5:2, 163–185.

Lloyd, C. (2000) 'High Involvement Work Systems: The Only Option for UK High Skill Sectors?', *SKOPE Research Paper* 11, University of Warwick.

Lloyd, C. and Payne, J. (2002a) 'Developing a Political Economy of Skill', *Journal of Education and Work*, 15:4, 365–390.

Lloyd, C. and Payne, J. (2002b) 'In Search of the High Skills Society: Some Reflections on Current Visions', *SKOPE Research Paper No. 32*, University of Warwick.

Lloyd, C. and Payne, J. (2002c) 'On 'The Political Economy of Skill': Assessing the Possibilities for a Viable High Skills Project in the UK', *New Political Economy*, 7:3. 367–395.

Lloyd, C. and Payne, J. (2003) 'The Political Economy of Skill and the Limits of Education Policy', *Journal of Education Policy*, 18:1, 85–107.

Marchington, M. and Grugulis, I. (2000) ''Best Practice' Human Resource Management: Perfect Opportunity or Dangerous Illusion?', *International Journal of Human Resource Management*, 11:6, 1104–1124.

Mason, G. (1999) 'Product Strategies, Work Force Skills, and "High Involvement" Work Practices', in P. Cappelli (ed.), *Employment Practices and Business Strategy*, Oxford: Oxford University Press.

Mason, G. and Finegold, D. (1997) 'Productivity, Machinery and Skills in the United States and Western Europe', *National Institute Economic Review*, 162, 84–97.

McIntosh, S. and Steedman, H. (2001) 'Learning in the Workplace: Some International Comparisons', in F. Coffield (ed.), *What progress are we making with lifelong learning: the evidence from research*, University of Newcastle: Department of Education.

Milkman, R. (1998) 'The New American Workplace: High Road or Low Road?', in P. Thompson and C. Warhurst (eds), *Workplaces of the Future*, London: Macmillan.

Nolan, P. (2000) 'Back to the Future of Work', *Paper presented to BUIRA Conference, University of Warwick*, mimeo.

Piore, M. and Sabel, C. (1984) *The Second Industrial Divide*, New York: Basic Books.

Ramsay, H. (1977) 'Cycles of control: Worker participation in sociological and historical perspective', *Sociology*, 11:3, 481–506.

Saglio, J. (1995) 'Industrial Relations and Human Resources in France', in R. Locke, T. Kochan and M. Piore (eds), *Employment Relations in a Changing World Economy* Massachusetts: MIT.

Senker, J. and Senker, P. (1994) 'Information Technology and Skills in Manufacturing and construction', in K. Ducatel (ed.), *Employment and Technical Change in Europe*, Aldershot: Edward Elgar.

Soskice, D. (1993) 'Social Skills from Mass Higher Education: Rethinking the Company-based Initial Training Paradigm', *Oxford Review of Economic Policy*, 9:3, 101–113.

Temple, P. (1998) 'Overview: Growth, Competitiveness and Trade Performance', in T. Buxton, P. Chapman and P. Temple (eds), *Britain's Economic Performance*, London: Routledge.

Thompson, P., Wallace, T., Flecker, J. and Ahlstrand, R. (1995) 'It Ain't What You Do, It's the Way that You Do It: production organisation and skill utilisation in commercial vehicles', *Work, Employment and Society*, 9:4, 719–742.

Thompson, P. and Warhurst, C. (eds) (1998) *Workplaces of the Future*, London: Macmillan.

Warhurst, C. and Thompson, P. (1998) 'Hands, Hearts and Minds: Changing Work and Workers at the End of the Century', in P. Thompson and C. Warhurst (eds), *Workplaces of the Future*, London: Macmillan.

Young, M. (1998) *The Curriculum of the Future*, London: Routledge.

13
'Old Nurses with New Qualifications are Best': Competing Ideas about the Skills that Matter in Nursing in Estonia, France, Germany and the UK

Alan Brown and Simone Kirpal

Introduction

The skills that matter in health care could be regarded as unproblematic: above all, patients want staff who 'really care'. However, lists of required skills or behaviours related to the tasks to be performed in nursing can be never-ending and still not get to the heart of professional practice, according to Benner (1982). A distinction can be made between the technical skills required and the need 'to develop and sustain therapeutic caring relationships with patients and clients which are conceptualised and practised in an integrated and holistic fashion' (McAleer and Hamill 1997: 99). Playle (1995) identifies the shift in the caring professions away from illness-cure models and the objectification of patients towards a more holistic, person-centred approach that 'promotes mutual respect, genuineness and joint partnership in the achievement of patient-centred goals' (McAleer and Hamill 1997: 5). Furthermore, Wright (1994) highlights the value of expressive rather than instrumental care: caring about the patient not just caring for the patient. Expressive caring means professional activities should reflect the value of each individual person, and be imbued with the values of respect, dignity and individuality. Expressive caring contains a more explicit affective dimension compared to instrumental caring in which actions are predetermined in the form of a technique or strategy.

Expressive caring drives the idealised model of the skills that matter in health care. This chapter looks at competing ideas about the skills that matter in nursing and changing attitudes towards the formation, development and utilisation of the skills of health care professionals, especially nurses, in Estonia, France, Germany and the UK. The analysis is drawn from a European research project (FAME)[1] and is based upon qualitative material generated, principally through interviews with over one hundred health care professionals with varying levels of qualification, specialisation, skill profiles and functional responsibilities. Mainly nurses were interviewed but also smaller numbers of midwives, radiographers, physiotherapists and managers. The skill formation, development and utilisation of the skills of nurses have been accompanied by continuity and change in attitudes towards the skills and attitudes nurses should (ideally) display in practice.

Technological change, changing patterns of work organisation and changing demands for health care services have triggered significant changes in the skill needs and labour market demands for health care professionals, including nurses. Many occupational roles have been transformed, along with parallel shifts in the processes of occupational socialisation, and many work identities have become unstable (Sennett 1998; Carruthers and Uzzi 2000). However, the nursing profession has a long-standing occupational tradition with related skill development patterns. For centuries, religious and charitable organisations ran health-care services, and these historical roots have influenced work profiles and have established a more or less universal image of what qualities and skills a 'good' nurse should possess. Since the 1980s changing work requirements, new skills profiles and a strong tendency towards professionalism have been eroding this traditional image. Health care services have been expanding, partly due to demographic shifts and an ageing population, but their nature has been changing too with a shift in focus from simply providing care to prevention, counselling and the support of a patient-oriented self-help approach. All these changes mean understandings of the skills required for nursing are much more open to change and there are different discourses about the skills, qualities and attitudes required. However, before looking at changing skill requirements, some of the distinctive and common features of the skills involved in nursing in the different national contexts will be outlined.

The Nursing Profession in National Perspective

Estonia

Estonia is a country where the post-Soviet transition (Loogma and Vilu 2001) represents a 'civilisation shift' (Lauristin 1997) and a 'return to the Western World' (Lauristin and Vihalemm 1997). In such a context, Estonia faces the challenge of redefining the skills requirements and related occupational profiles of the nursing profession. Human resources policies in hospitals have been transformed with the loss of employment security and new medical technologies have been introduced. For the nursing profession the driving force for change has been the implementation of a new curriculum for their education and training, and nurses who trained during Soviet times have had to undergo retraining and pass examinations according to the new curriculum. Newly introduced private hospitals have pioneered more modern and flexible ways of working and have updated the skills profiles of nurses. These changes include greater responsibility and independence of nurses, a stronger emphasis on the quality of care and working in small teams. But even in private hospitals a new partnership model based on cooperation between doctors, nurses and patients is still far from being realised in practice.

Public hospitals are still to a certain extent characterised by the structural, organisational and habitual features of Soviet times. With regard to professional development, nursing has established itself as an independent discipline with the possibility of following an academic career in nursing. But the dominant opinion in society, and of employers, about the qualities and skills of a 'good' nurse still adheres to the traditional image of a devoted carer working under the supervision of doctors. In the changed, and rather unstable, economic environment, stability in respect to the work and the workplace is increasingly valued and there is a general feeling that, in a changing world, at least the public has a clear image of nurses, the skills they have, and the work they (should) do.

Germany

After a period of expansion, specialisation and implementation of the latest technologies during the 1980s, the costs of the German health care system spiralled. The government then enacted legislation in the 1990s to restrict and control expenditure for health care services, a move that resulted in major organisational changes for health care providers. The structural reforms meant subsidies for public hospitals are now determined according to medical case and outcomes, with less flexibility in how long patients stay in hospital. Hospital wards are organised as profit centres and each medical treatment and service has to be documented and justified in order to be reimbursed through the health insurance system. Social interaction and communication with patients suffer, as staff are exposed to the conflicting demands of health insurance restrictions and patients' expectations. Customer orientation, quality of care and economic efficiency are the key criteria for how hospitals should be run.

With the cutback of inpatient treatment and care, more responsibility is transferred to the individual patient, and nurses are required to develop new attitudes and knowledge as to how best to support patients in activating their potential for self-care. Patients are also better informed about health issues. They have higher demands on the quality of care and treatment, and have become much more involved in making decisions regarding their medical treatment, bringing a greater focus on consultation, and introducing guidance and counselling into the health care process. As a consequence, staff are challenged to meet these expectations, and counselling methods have become an important aspect of nurse training. The professional profile has shifted from a hierarchically oriented structure towards a model that emphasises self-organisation and independent action by patients and nurses.

The job profiles, and associated skill demands, of staff are changing insofar as institutions and management increasingly emphasise efficiency, quality control and documentation. Work intensification, time constraints and, in particular, not having enough time to care for individual patients have become major issues. Information and communication technologies, coordination and the management of complex data processing combined with a new approach towards customer orientation have redefined the traditional skills profiles in health care services. Yet skill requirements and patient-related core activities in nursing change slowly as many work processes are highly ritualised. Thus, innovation and the introduction of new approaches in health care are difficult to put into everyday practice.

France

According to the 2002 World Health Organisation assessment, the French health care system is one of the best in the world in terms of overall health of the population; (limited) extent of health inequalities; responsiveness towards change and patient satisfaction; and distribution of the financial burden. Within this system, nurses form a well-established occupational group, although as elsewhere, they are lacking in social recognition compared to doctors. They also have comparatively poor salaries considering their increasing workload and responsibilities. Doctors primarily have functional (medical) responsibilities whereas health care services and the daily work in hospital wards are mainly organised by senior nurses.

Nurses have a strong professional identity based on the ethics of their profession in two ways: first, through the *acte propre* that relates a nurse's caring mission with autonomy, responsibility and a high level of interaction with the patients; second, through the *acte prescript* that relates to the medical mission characterising a nurse's daily work-related interactions with doctors within hospitals or clinics. Morale was reported as generally high, and skills profiles were seen as supportive of continuing learning, the introduction of innovations in health care and the use of modern medical technology, but they were not seen as supportive of changes in work organisation. Nurses working in the public sector (mostly in hospitals) are employed as civil servants with a high level of job security.

The health care system is, however, undergoing structural change. The emergence of outpatient medical treatment, auto-diagnostics and home care services has effectively decreased patients' short-term stays in hospitals. Concurrently, the need for long-term hospitalisation has increased due to partially or fully dependent patients. Regional hospital authorities have been attempting to create pools of excellence by merging hospitals and closing down, if necessary, hospitals with occupancy rates of less than 60 per cent. Staff are then transferred between hospitals. The introduction and implementation of the national 35-hour maximum working week has significantly affected work organisation in hospitals. This regime, although welcomed elsewhere, has increased the work burden and involuntary time allocation for hospital staff, especially for nurses.

The 'Compensation and Replacement Pool' (*Service de Compensation et de Suppléance*) facilitates flexibility in the use of health care professionals. It is used to compensate for temporary staff shortages in hospitals. Although staff are drawn from the pool as required, the use of the 'list' is pre-planned from the individual's perspective and staff have permanent work contracts. It is a voluntary system and the pool recruits nurses in a similar way to other departments. Mostly, basic grade nurses are then functionally and horizontally mobile on demand between different departments. In the light of different departmental needs for temporary work or replacement, the pool distributes them between its members according to their profile and their pre-planned time for shift work (proposed two months in advance). It might be thought that individuals just move from the list to work on permanent attachment to particular departments. In fact, there are some advantages to being in the pool, most notably that nurses are much more in control of their own working time, whereas those working in departments will have to agree rotas. Also outside the 'supplementary pool', the internal mobility of nurses is usually still limited to the units of a single department.

Although the above mentioned developments do considerably affect work structures and organisation, they do not seem to induce major shifts within the French health care system. There is no sense that the nursing profession is undergoing a redefinition process. The health care system, as currently established, is financially well-equipped and is generally held in high regard by staff, patients and the public.

The UK

In the UK, flexibility in work organisation had been a major goal of employers in pursuing the National Health Service (NHS) modernisation agenda from the mid-1990s (Department of Health 1997). However, since the 2001 general election the emphasis is upon recruiting and retaining more staff through making the approach to flexibility more employee-centred in some respects. Significantly, there is less talk of driving through change and more attention given to staff as if they are part of the solution rather than being the problem. One example of the previous approach occurred at the height of attempts to impose greater flexibility in work and expectations that staff would accept resulting changes in patterns of work organisation, and involved a single radiographer being on-call all night for the full range of possible duties across a hospital. This practice proved problematic, as many of the radiographers did not feel confident to undertake the full range of duties that may be required of them when they were on-call alone and had no-one with whom they could consult over possible problems.

In the UK nurses and professions allied to medicine have strong occupational identities, and in many hospitals recruitment and retention of these groups of staff are major concerns. Managers have used access to further training as a means to encourage applicants. The possibility for promotion as extended scope practitioners (promotion that involves continuing in practice rather than moving into management) is also seen as an aid to retention of staff. In nurse training there have been attempts to move from a directive 'control' approach towards an 'empowering' approach to care that relies upon the establishment of trust, with a focus on support and development.

The organisational changes in hospitals, changes to professional training and development, changing ideas about the nature of practice and philosophies of care, changing patterns of work and demand for services, and the adoption of new technologies and new techniques have created a turbulent environment for practice for health care professionals. These changes mean that the skills to be used by nurses in practice following initial qualification need to be refined. Newly qualified nurses still have much to learn in an environment characterised by flexibility and work intensification. In order to make a successful transition to becoming an experienced practitioner, the 'novice' will need to negotiate six major learning challenges involving: successful engagement with major work activities; successful interaction with others; successful learning from experience; alignment of professional and personal values; commitment to continuing professional development; and coping with the demands for flexibility, transferability and work intensification in the workplace.

The context in which the work takes place, a hospital department with demanding performance targets, itself acts to reinforce some tensions between working and learning. For example, decisions about balancing the competing requirements for service delivery and how to support skill development most effectively have a number of dimensions. These influences upon service delivery include professional judgement about the most appropriate approach to care and practice; organisational issues about how to cope with the particular context in which health care is provided; caseload management; and departmental management. This means that in any particular setting there is not a single model of best practice about how health care professionals should act. Rather hospital departments have to make contextualised decisions about how best to optimise service delivery and skill development in the settings in which their practice is grounded (Brown *et al.* 2000).

The skills required of nurses are undergoing significant change, partly in response to 'modernisation', changing patterns of work organisation and education and training, technological change and increasing demand for their services. However, alongside these pressures for change, there are very strong continuities with the past and images of the skills and qualities nurses should ideally possess.

Constraints upon the Exercise of Caring Skills in Practice in Estonia, France, Germany and the UK

The above national contexts have clearly illustrated that the social construction of the skills of nursing is a complex process with explicit social, economic, political, psychological and organisational dimensions. Clearly, it is not a simple technical process. Looking at commonalities in developments in Estonia, Germany and the UK, it might appear plausible to construct a model with 'imperatives' leading to the 'modernisation' of nursing according to the demands of marketisation, economic efficiency and effective organisation. The problem with this model is that it clearly does not apply to France. Rather the French experience shows that these factors are not 'imperatives' but are grounded in 'choices', values and a willingness of staff to act collectively in support of their goals.

Indeed one of the most interesting aspects of the discussions with French managers was not that they did not wish to shape patterns of skill utilisation and work organisation of nurses in a more radical way. They did, but this was effectively a non-issue precisely because of public support and the existence of strong and highly regulated patterns of work-related identities. Managers complained that aspects of the French system are bureaucratic and rather inflexible. They were frustrated by their failure to be able to exercise control over significant aspects of work organisation and skill utilisation. Even for nurses there are some disadvantages in that transfer between departments is difficult and some nurses might wish for greater variety in their work. For most nurses, however, these disadvantages are outweighed by the social stability and stability in outlook the system generates. Overall, managers felt constrained, and nurses felt secure, in how the skills of nurses would be utilised in public hospitals in France. This is all the more striking if a comparative perspective is adopted. In the other three countries there is a sense of a 'profession under pressure' and many nurses as individuals are facing much greater uncertainty and stress than their French colleagues.

This is not, however, an argument for a simple transfer of the French model to other countries. Indeed some British radiographers liked the greater degree of individual control over their work they had and felt there was more opportunity to exercise a fuller range of skills in their work than their French counterparts had (certainly in taking over more clinical responsibilities from doctors). However, there is the rub – it is an individual form of coping and control. In France, nurses exercise a stronger degree of collective control and processes of skill utilisation are being changed in a more controlled way. In particular, the traditional caring skills of nursing are not viewed as under threat.

The contrast with Germany is marked, where there are three main challenges to the traditional exercise of caring skills. First, there is an increase in the administrative tasks to be performed that can take up to two thirds of the total working time of nurses in hospitals. This results in nurses having less, and often not enough, time for direct patient care. Most nurses feel over-qualified for performing administrative tasks and would prefer to concentrate on working with patients. Second, there is the drive for efficiency and a new division of labour. There is, in some respects, a mismatch between a modern approach to performing integrated, high quality health care (supported by theory and science) and severe time constraints and very demanding efficiency criteria. Financial constraints point to future work processes being dichotomised between simple tasks carried out by lower qualified assistants and coordinating or supervisory tasks carried out by higher qualified nurses. However, nurses would then interact less with patients and this type of division of labour would contradict the aim of providing integrated high quality health care services.

The third challenge concerns developing a more 'professional' work attitude that overcomes the idealised model of a nurse as 'an always friendly and smiling woman who is devoted and willing to perform a large variety of services on demand', as one respondent put it in Estonia. This tendency towards professionalism is linked to attempts to establish nurses as independent professionals with their own expertise, not just subordinate to doctors. A stronger academic path and opportunities for continuous professional development play a key role in striving to position care in equal partnership with medicine. The increasing proportion of male nurses (currently approximately 15–20 per cent) and a more professional work attitude of recently trained nurses fuel this trend.

In Germany, skill requirements are influenced by the formal regulations and occupational profiles that govern nurse training. Most managers believed strongly in nursing as a vocation but recognised nursing is changing and now look for different personality profiles when recruiting from say seven years ago. Individual characteristics required included communication skills; flexibility; ability to learn and a willingness to keep up with knowledge requirements; need to manage work and work environment efficiently; commitment and motivation; and being able to cope with a challenging profession that has a high potential for pressure and strain. The last attribute shows a significant shift from the traditional 'ideal', which made no mention of the ability to survive in an audit-driven culture.

However, in a comparative perspective, there was another interesting challenge to the 'traditional' image of nursing occurring in Germany: that was the relatively high number of young men going into nursing (up to one in five entrants). This was partly attributable to the large number of young men opting for community service rather than military service when 'called up' for national service. A significant number of these young men find out from experience that they do have the skills, qualities, attitudes and values necessary for 'caring' work and subsequently enrol for nurse training.

In Estonia, managers held similar views about how the modern skills profiles for nurses still include a sense of vocation. A head nurse believed nurses in smaller town hospitals may be just as good or even better at nursing than their colleagues at technically more developed Tallinn hospitals: 'this is because tools are nothing but tools, and without empathy, intuition and a good hand, there can be no nursing', she explained. This mixing of role and personality informed the analysis of other respondents too. Where managers identified skill gaps, these were attributed to employees having the 'wrong personality' or failing to realise that 'nursing is a mission. It is hard for people to work as nurses because of the low wages if they don't understand the work as a mission' one manager argued. Unlike in other sectors, being tainted by the past is not a problem for nurses who trained in Soviet times. Indeed those who retrained, but who retained their 'old' attitudes, were well regarded by managers. This approbation was because only those with a really strong nursing-centred identity were likely to invest their time and money in retraining for such a poorly paid vocation, with the result that many managers would probably agree with the view expressed by one of their number that 'the old nurses with new qualifications are the best'. Interestingly, younger nurses with Western values still train, but their behaviour is attributed to the fact that their qualifications are accepted elsewhere in Europe and therefore enables geographical labour mobility.

Many hospitals in the UK are experiencing staff shortages and face challenges retaining staff. Staff shortages have resulted in hospitals recruiting nurses from overseas, introducing greater flexibility in work organisation, changing the skill mix between doctors and nurses, and making greater use of assistants. These developments were occurring where there was an explicit attempt to put greater emphasis upon team working involving doctors, nurses and other support staff. Nurses were being given more autonomy and responsibility in a context of increasing demand for services. Individual commitment has always been strongly identified with the occupation and the department or service but some managers were consciously trying to reshape the focus of commitment more towards the inter-departmental team so as to improve overall quality of service to patients.

In three of the four countries, the discourse about nursing skills had changed from a search for individuals with 'ideal' caring skills to a search for the optimal 'practical' mix of skills in staff as a whole. The 'ideal' was presented as a mix of 'anchors' and 'new blood', the former representing traditional caring values, while the latter were better able to cope with stress, change and increasing work intensity. An example of the personal consequences of 'really caring' is given below.

Marianne has been working in the same German hospital for 28 years. She helped establish the urology ward and has been its director since 1979, supervising around 15 nurses. When Marianne was around 40 years old, she experienced a personal crisis. She felt burnt out. She felt that she had been 'caring too much', putting a lot of her personality and energy into her professional life. Marianne realised that since the beginning of her career she had been too close to the patients, which was 'good for them, but not for myself'. She identified with the sufferings of the patients to the extent that she often felt exhausted and fell sick herself. She considered leaving the profession but through her own initiative and with the help of a series of seminars she learnt how to maintain an emotional distance from the patients and to cope with psychological stress caused, for example, by deaths of patients. Marianne learnt to redefine her own role in terms of support rather than 'really caring' and with this more professional approach is now very happy with her work and responsibilities.

The alternative pole of 'thriving on change' is presented through the case of Juliette, a regular nurse who is a member of the 'Compensation and Replacement Pool' in a French public hospital. After about three years of work within the intensive care unit of the cardiology department, she joined the 'pool' that allows her flexibility and mobility in work between different departments within public hospitals belonging to the same corporate group. As with any regular nurse, Juliette's work is organised on a moving-shift basis. But being a member of the 'pool', she usually only works on the first two shifts in the morning and afternoon. In either shift, she works in a team (usually composed of an assistant nurse and a doctor) in charge of about a dozen patients.

Her working time flexibility is voluntarily pre-planned within each work assignment by the pool. For her, this mobility and flexibility has advantages and disadvantages. The advantages relate to spontaneity, versatility and openness to change, with fewer conflicts, tensions and stress linked to being attached to regular (long-term) working teams in a single department; and more independence and freedom of choice at work. However, as a temporary replacement, she does not give priority to professional development and knowledge in one particular domain. Also, the lack of real and lasting work-related interactions within working teams can be regarded in a negative light – leading to the development of 'individualism' or even introversion.

Reflections on the Changing Patterns of Skill Development and Utilisation in Health Care

Expressive caring as an ideal

The above commentary indicates that views on the most appropriate staff attitudes and qualities for working in the caring professions often have a temporal dimension that includes both past and future perspectives in attitudes towards the importance of 'really caring'. Many of those engaged in health care philosophy, policy and practice are trying to come to terms with changing ideas about relational and caring constructs, and there is a recognition that there are major social, economic and political dimensions to attempts to pay greater attention to therapeutic caring relationships.

Ethics and values are therefore necessarily involved in judgements about service delivery and skill utilisation and development in health care. That is, ideas about the skills and attitudes of staff required for effective and caring service delivery are inevitably connected to views about how the service should be delivered, and patients, professionals, managers and the general public all have views on this matter. Wright (1994) emphasises how expressive care involves caring about the patient not just caring for the patient. Expressive caring means professional activities should reflect the value of each individual person, and be imbued with the values of respect, dignity and individuality. Expressive caring contains a more explicit affective dimension compared to instrumental caring in which actions are predetermined in the form of a technique or strategy.

Expressive care for all patients then represents an ideal but any shifts in practice towards more expressive caring are at least partly dependent upon the personal meanings and the degree of commitment of staff. However, Oakley (1993) draws attention to the paradox that the increasing technical competence associated with greater professionalisation may serve to distance practitioners from those for whom they care. Managers in several countries were explicitly concerned about this perceived distance, and in Estonia particularly there was the almost plaintive cry that younger nurses do not *really* care like some of the older nurses. In any case the policy response of emphasising more person-centred models of care has not always been in step with how to facilitate this model in training and implementing it in practice.

At the professional level therefore, decisions to opt for particular models of care to underpin practice could affect skill utilisation and development profoundly. These decisions could be taken in one respect at an individual level, whereby an individual opts to approach her or his practice in a particular way. Departments or hospitals too may favour particular models of care, although there may be disjunctions between the policy as espoused and how it is represented in practice. Practitioners and managers in some settings were acutely aware of these tensions. For example, several respondents in

UK hospitals pointed to the consequences that follow if a physiotherapy department encourages an 'empowering' approach to care. Such an approach requires the individual patient to take increasing responsibility for her or his own care, and this can be very time intensive in the early stages, even if it eventually requires fewer interventions. The 'empowering' approach relies upon the establishment of trust, with a focus on support and development; taking time; listening to and dealing with problems, as the patient takes on greater responsibility. The 'control' approach, where the practitioner is much more directive, focuses upon what the client has to do, but with 'ownership' of the process resting with the practitioner. Tensions may arise between the two approaches, as the controlling approach may be used as a means to meet targets and cope with larger numbers of patients. In nursing too, crucially, the 'empowering' approach means giving patients time, which is often scarce as work intensifies.

One important question though is, even if everybody agrees on the need for more expressive caring, how will practitioners learn to exemplify expressive values? Dench *et al.* (1998) report that trainers working with carers found difficulties working with values, and Bradshaw (1994) points out that it can be quite difficult to confront the tension between personal values and meanings and caring for others. Furthermore, McAleer and Hamill (1997) found that nurse tutors themselves often lacked confidence in exploring this tension, partly because they had difficulty articulating the concepts of caring and its attributes. Values and meanings need to be discussed, and their application modelled in practice. Individuals too should receive support within educational and organisational structures to think about the value frameworks of themselves and others. Some engagement with these issues could take place through discussions associated with reflective practice. Some attention then needs to be given to ensure there are explicit discussions about caring and values because it could lead staff to arrive at a richer understanding of expressive knowledge, practice and their own self-understanding. By that means it should be possible to facilitate the development of a richer discourse about feelings, emotions and care rather than just positing an ideal model. McAleer and Hamill (1997) argued that tutors in supporting the learning of health care professionals needed to engage with a much wider variety of discourses about caring in order to help practitioners discuss their experience of care.

Staff also have to come to terms with the personal costs of caring for them as individuals. For example, one unintended consequence of the emphasis upon authenticity of feelings and that health practitioners should always 'really care' (and give of themselves) is that this approach could result in many otherwise capable practitioners feeling that they do not live up to the model. For this reason Taylor (1992) argues that due account needs to be taken that nurses are perceived as people with everyday human qualities and not just in terms of their professional role. This need is perhaps most evident in the balance required of staff for their own psychological well-being of caring about their patients but, at the same time, not caring too much. This was vividly illustrated by the case of Marianne described earlier. Also it is by no means clear that unconditional service to others is always the most desirable course of action. Empathy and support may be inhibiting in some circumstances, as they could be disempowering in the sense of restricting patient autonomy and cutting down on opportunities for recovery to be more self-directed.

Expressive care for all patients may represent an ideal but it is important that any attempt to implement this approach is informed by what happens in practice. For example, Stockwell (1972) pointed out that, in practice, some patients are more popular with staff than others and that practitioners use their power in a discriminatory fashion. This practice would suggest that the values underpinning expressive care need to be developed during initial training. However, some nurse tutors, interviewed by McAleer and Hamill (1997), believe that the increasing cognitive demands made in nurse training mean that such developments may be squeezed out of the curriculum as nurses become more professional.

Overall then, those working in health care need to display 'caring' qualities, as well as being technically proficient and being aware that ideas about professional competence and caring are constantly evolving. Ideas of care therefore need to be framed in a particular context and at a given time, but it nevertheless remains important that personal and professional values are in broad alignment. Some of the managers interviewed were somewhat unrealistic in this respect arguing (or just wishing?) for staff with attitudes from one era coupled with skills from another. It is interesting, however, that technical proficiency is often taken as a given, and little attempt is made to examine the interplay of trying to develop both caring and technical competence at the same time. Yet there are clearly tensions here.

Tensions in the interplay of the development and utilisation of technical skills and caring abilities in work

One problem for those with responsibility for training and development of health care professionals is that it can be very difficult to be explicit about what it is to be achieved. A trainer or manager may be able to draw up profiles of the skills, knowledge and understanding, and even the appropriate values and attitudes, required. However, it remains particularly difficult to map these against the full complexities of performance in practice (McAleer and Hamill 1997). UK hospital managers who regularly recruit newly qualified staff emphasised that the pressure was to appoint staff who would rapidly be able to contribute fully to achieving performance targets. Here there was an inbuilt bias towards technical proficiency rather than the encouragement of the development of more rounded (and caring?) performance. In these settings, the quality of mentoring, supervision or other support is critical.

The interviews in all countries support the observation of Webb (1996) that current discussions about health and social care are intimately bound up with ideas about practice as it is, how it might or should be, and relations between occupational groups. The latter point was clear in that most respondents discussed aspects of relations with medical staff as having a significant impact upon the performance of nurses and of the professions allied to medicine. This tension was most evident in attempts to offer a more holistic approach to health care, which had implications for intra-team training, if the goal of multi-disciplinary working was to be achieved.

Demonstrating commitment through caring as well as exercising technical skills adds complexity to the performance of a role but, in addition, it can make the role much more demanding. Morrison (1992) points out that those working in the caring professions have to deal with issues of emotional involvement, stress, work constraints and role uncertainty. These pressures reinforce the importance in such circumstances of having mechanisms where individuals can talk these issues through with colleagues. Taylor (1992) argues that such an approach is vital as those working in the caring professions needed to relate to each other as people, not just in terms of their professional roles. McAleer and Hamill (1997: 7) emphasise that professionals need to be regarded 'as people who share the everyday common human qualities of their patients' and not be regarded as carriers of a range of superhuman skills, qualities, attitudes and values.

For the foreseeable future, the supply of 'natural carers', with highly developed cognitive and technical skills, wishing to work in nursing or the professions allied to medicine, is likely to be less than the demand. If so, and the promotion of expressive caring remains a goal, an interesting question arises. Can certain affective responses themselves be incorporated into patterns of behaviour whereby individuals give the appearance of caring: can one person learn to give the impression of being genuinely interested in another person? This is an issue explored in part by Bolton in Chapter 2 and elsewhere by Callaghan and Thompson (2002) and, of course, Hochschild (1983).

So, balancing the development of technical skills and caring abilities is a considerable challenge in training and development. However, even if it is successful, a further challenge remains – that of coming to terms with the social organisation of work. One point emphasised in the preceding arguments was how health care professionals may come to a richer understanding of expressive knowledge, practice and their own self-understanding. This recognition of the value for staff of organised reflection upon their own role, however, has to be complemented by recognition that their individual practice takes place within particular social contexts. Perhaps the most obvious influence upon how nurses operate in practice is the social organisation of work, and variations in this within and between the four countries studied emphasises this point. May (1990) points out that focusing upon the dynamics of nurse–patient relationships takes little account of how the social organisation of care influences caregiving, not least by assuming that nurses have a relatively high degree of autonomy in how they carry out their work. The increasing drive for efficiency and performance within health care systems limits the time nurses have for activities that convey caring.

An example of the competing pressures for demonstrating care and increasing patient throughput can be taken from radiography. Recent changes in work routines in the UK are giving radiographers more responsibility but they are often allied to other changes that are increasing the pressure on staff. Radiographers are expected to do more for each patient (checking allergies, giving injections, scanning) but they are still expected to see the same number of patients as previously. Patient throughput must be maintained. Another example of work intensification is where previously six minutes were allocated per patient for a standard chest X-ray, now only three and a half minutes are allocated. To compensate for this reduction, radiographers have to talk faster, with the patient possibly losing out on receiving information, and act faster (e.g. when patients have to lie down, staff are told to 'tell patients there is no need to take their shoes off').

Conclusions

This review of competing ideas towards the formation, development and utilisation of the skills that matter in health care in four countries shows that one recurring theme is the challenge of finding enough people with the full range of skills and qualities believed to be desirable. In particular, there is a tension between technical and cognitive skills development and the inculcation of the values associated with expressive caring. It remains easier to erect an ideal skills profile than to effect change in practice. This difficulty exists perhaps partly because, particularly for nursing, these tensions appear to be affecting beliefs as to what should constitute the core of nurses' practice.

Should nursing be primarily based upon mastery of a distinctive body of (scientific and clinical) knowledge similar to doctors and other professions allied to medicine? Or does a nursing identity principally derive from the role of expressive specialist, with particular skills, knowledge and understanding of therapeutic relationships? If it is to be the latter then it is important that the curriculum for nurse training should be opened up in ways that would facilitate the development of a richer discourse about feelings, emotions and care. McAleer and Hamill (1997) point out that tutors as well as students can struggle in this respect. They argue that 'there is a danger that, in the absence of a fully developed and respected body of language to enable nurses to discuss their experience of care, they will be forced to accept accounts of nursing which are restricted to the technical and instrumental aspects of care and are unable to fully deal with alternative forms of human experience expressed in moral, political and cultural dimensions' (p. 100). Their remedy includes a new approach to curriculum construction and assessment that acknowledges ways of knowing which embrace interpretivist, constructivist and feminist research, critical theory, and could draw upon the humanities and philosophy in trying to develop the reflective capacity of both tutors and students.

Given the radical nature of such suggestions and the length of time it might take to train nurses in such an approach, it might allow for a completely different interpretation of the view that 'old nurses with new qualifications are best'. On a more serious note, the extent of engagement of managers and practitioners in changing ideas about the skills that really matter in health care is symptomatic of some fundamental challenges facing all with an interest in health care policy and practice. What is also clear from this review is that current changes in the formation, development and utilisation of the skills of nurses are promoting a much wider discourse about the skills that really matter in nursing and the delivery of health care more generally.

Note

1   See FAME Project Team (2001) for further details.

References

Benner, P. (1982) 'Issues in Competency-based Testing', *Nursing Outlook*, 30, 303–309.

Bradshaw, A. (1994) *Lighting the Lamp: The Spiritual Dimension of Nursing Care*, London: Royal College of Nursing Scutari Press.

Brown, A., Green, A., Pitcher, J. and Simm, C. (2000) *Employers Skill Survey: Case Study – Health and Social Care*, National Skills Task Force Research Report 35, Nottingham: DfEE.

Callaghan, G. and Thompson, P. (2002) 'We Recruit Attitude: The Selection and Shaping of Routine Call Centre Labour', *Journal of Management Studies*, 39:2, 233–254.

Carruthers, B. and Uzzi, B. (2000) 'Economic Sociology in the New Millennium', *Contemporary Sociology*, 29:3, 486–494.

Dench, S., La Valle, I. and Evans, C. (1998) *Supporting Skills for Care Workers*, Brighton: Institute for Employment Studies.

Department of Health (1997) *The New NHS: Modern, Dependable*, Cmd 3807, London: HMSO.

FAME Project Team (2001) *Decomposing and Recomposing Vocational Identities: A Survey of Theoretical Approaches and Investigations*, ITB Working Paper, Bremen: University of Bremen.

Hochschild, A. R. (1983) *The Managed Heart*, Berkeley: University of California Press.

Lauristin, M. (1997) 'Contexts of Transition', in M. Lauristin and P. Vihalemm with K.-E. Rosengren and L. Weibukk (eds), *Return to the Western World: Cultural and*

Political Perspectives on the Estonian Post-Communist transition, Tartu: Tartu University Press.

Lauristin, M. and Vihalemm, P. with K.-E. Rosengren and L. Neibukk (eds) (1997) *Return to the Western World: Cultural and Political Perspectives on the Estonian Post-Communist Transition*, Tartu: Tartu University Press.

Loogma, K. and Vilu, R. (2001) 'Institutional Development and Work-related Identity in the Context of Post-socialist Transition', paper presented to *Journal of Vocational Education and Training (JVET) Conference*, Telford.

May, C. (1990) 'Research on Nurse-patient Relationships: Problems of Theory, Problems of Practice', *Journal of Advanced Nursing*, 15, 307–315.

McAleer, J. and Hamill, C. (1997) *The Assessment of Higher Order Competence Development in Nurse Education*, Research Report, Newtownabbey: University of Ulster.

Morrison, P. (1992) *Professional Caring in Practice: A Psychological Analysis*, Aldershot: Avebury.

Oakley, A. (1993) *Essays on Women, Medicine and Health*, Edinburgh: Edinburgh University Press.

Playle, J. (1995) 'Humanism and Positivism in Nursing: contradictions and conflicts', *Journal of Advanced Nursing*, 23, 979–984.

Sennett, R. (1998) *The Corrosion of Character*, New York: Norton.

Stockwell, F. (1972) *The Unpopular Patient*, Nursing Project Reports, Series 1, Number 2, London: Royal College of Nursing.

Taylor, B. (1992) 'From Helper to Human: A Reconceptualisation of the Nurse as a Person', *Journal of Advanced Nursing*, 17, 1042–1049.

Webb, G. (1996) *Understanding Staff Development*, Buckingham: Society for Research in Higher Education and the Open University Press.

Wright, S. (1994) *The Foundations of Nursing – The Values and Essential Concepts for Nursing Practice*, London: The European Nursing Development Agency.

14

Skill Trends Under Capitalism and the Socialisation of Production

Paul S. Adler

Defining and understanding skill is, as several contributors to this volume have shown, a difficult task – and empirical data often do not resolve the problem. Very complex practices are often categorised as unskilled because the groups performing them are of low status (Bolton in Chapter 2). Conversely, collective action can result in job designs that call for more skill and force management to upgrade categorisations for existing jobs (Turner 1962). Analysis is further complicated when the focus is broadened to the host of economic, institutional, and political factors involved in shaping work and defining skill (as discussed in Chapter 8 by Clark and Herrmann; Chapter 4 by Darr; Chapter 6 by Rainbird *et al.* and Chapter 12 Lloyd and Payne).

When confronted with such a puzzling set of problems, a return to theory is often useful. This chapter returns to the roots of one of the most prominent theories of skill, Labour Process Theory (LPT) (see Thompson 1989; Wardell *et al.* 1999; Grugulis *et al.* 2001). Much of LPT has sought its grounding in Marxist theory, although Marxist ideas have become less central to LPT in recent years. This chapter argues that LPT has frequently been one-sided in its reading of Marx and that this one-sidedness has hobbled our ability to understand trends in skill. In turn, this handicap has encouraged scholars to abandon Marxist ideas (although this reason is far from the only factor behind that shift). This chapter proposes an alternative reading of Marx, one that helps generate a better understanding of the nature of skill and the changes in skill associated with the development of capitalism.

Confronting Upgrading

From its inception, LPT has been critical of those writers who claim to see upgrading trends in skill (e.g. Bell 1973) and the emergence of 'new paradigms' in work organisation (e.g. Kern and Schumann 1984; Piore and Sabel

1984; Mathews 1994). The first wave of LPT adopted what can be termed a 'neo-Marxist' viewpoint. At first, it was argued that capitalist imperatives of profit and control led inexorably to deskilling. Numerous studies compellingly described cases of deskilling in various occupations. Over the years, and confronted with conflicting examples and arguments, its proponents have nuanced their positions, and neo-Marxist LPT now entertains three main alternatives: deskilling, polarisation, and a contingency view.

One reason for the loss of the centrality of Marxist ideas in LPT is that, due to the specific form of Marxist theory that has been invoked, it is inconceivable that over the longer term and in the aggregate, the skills of the workforce could have trended upward. Yet not only are upgrading counter examples common in the literature, but the overall path of development of capitalism in the last century is arguably one of upgrading.

Consider, first, the evolution of the occupational distribution of the workforce. Table 14.1 shows data on the case of the US over the twentieth century. There are, of course, many difficulties in interpreting these data, not least of which is what is meant by skill – a point taken up again below. But whatever is meant by skill, it is difficult not to see in this mutation of the occupational structure an important upgrading, notably in the massive contraction of the unskilled farm and non-farm labourer category, the more recent contraction of the operative category, and the growth of the professional and technical

Table 14.1   Evolution of the US occupational structure

	1900	1970	2000
Clerical	0.03	0.18	0.16
Professional, technical	0.04	0.14	0.16
Service workers, excluding private household	0.04	0.11	–
Private household workers	0.05	0.02	–
Total service, including private household	0.10	0.13	0.14
Salesworkers	0.05	0.07	0.12
Operative and kindred	0.13	0.18	–
Labourers, excluding farm and mine	0.13	0.05	–
Total operatives plus labourers (excluding farm)	0.26	0.23	0.12
Managers, administrative proprietors	0.06	0.08	0.11
Craftsmen, foremen	0.11	0.14	0.12
Farmers	0.20	0.02	–
Farm labourers and foremen	0.18	0.01	–
Total farmers plus farm labourers	0.38	0.03	0.04

Source: Data for 1900 and 1970 from US Bureau of the Census (1975). Data for 2000 are author's imputation from US Bureau of Census (2000). Census data after 1970 combine operatives and labourers, do not distinguish private household workers and do not distinguish farm labourers from farmers and farm managers.

category. (It should be noted too that many people classified in the growing category of managers and administrators have very little managerial authority and arguably belong to the working class broadly construed.) Chapter 11 offers similar data for Australia, suggesting that these changes have been a broad development.

How do Marxist-inspired labour process theorists respond to this kind of data? Braverman (1974) anticipated the most common responses. He recommends ignoring such occupational data because, firstly, they do not recognise the many experience-based skills of farmers and farm labourers; secondly, by classifying manufacturing operatives as semi-skilled just because they work with machinery, they inflate these skills compared to those of labourers, classified as unskilled; thirdly, they ignore the class difference between middle-class professional/technical categories and the working class narrowly construed; and fourthly, they ignore the dilution over time of skills in the craft category. While there is some truth to all these objections, it nevertheless takes a huge effort of imagination to see the shift registered in these statistics as compatible with an aggregate deskilling story. And where scholars have been able to use independent measures of skill such as the Dictionary of Occupations, none has found evidence of aggregate deskilling or meaningful polarisation: a modest upgrading trend is the almost universal conclusion (see the comprehensive review of US studies by Spenner [1988]; for more recent UK data, see Felstead *et al.* Chapter 9. 'Meaningful polarisation' refers to the possibility discussed by Braverman [1974: 425] that a sizeable minority of the workforce experience deskilling while others, and perhaps the overall average, experienced upgrading).

Second, consider the average education level of the workforce – arguably an important indicator of skill: it, too, has increased dramatically. The fraction of US 17-year-olds who had completed high school grew from 6 per cent in 1900, to 57 per cent in 1950, to over 80 per cent by the end of the century. Braverman (1974) suggests ignoring this evidence too, since, firstly, it reflects the demands of urbanisation rather than industry; secondly, it is biased by the inclusion of non-working class categories; thirdly, school is a way to keep unemployed youth off the streets; and, fourthly, many workers' education is under-utilised in the workplace. Again, all these points have some validity. However, despite this huge increase in the supply of more-educated labour, high school and college education has continued to yield a sizeable positive economic return in the labour market (Goldin and Katz 1999), and this result is difficult to understand unless at least some of this increase in education levels reflected increasing skill requirements rather than pure screening and credentialism (Abramowitz and David 1996). As Goldin and Katz (1999: 25–26) write, the most plausible explanation for this pattern is that 'technological change and capital deepening have both served to increase the demand for more-skilled labour over the long run'. A considerable body of economic research has consistently found that capital equipment and worker skills are complements rather than substitutes.

Faced with evidence such as this, it is not surprising that LPT has shifted away from broad trend generalisations towards a contingency view:

> LPT is not dependent on deskilling or Taylorism as the characteristic form of the capitalist labour process. Its core theory merely recognises that competitive relations compel capital to constantly revolutionise the labour process and that within that framework, capital and labour will contest the character and consequences of such changes. (Smith and Thompson 1999: 211)

Compared to the deskilling argument, such a contingency view is easier to reconcile with the murky data but it is harder to reconcile with LPT's ostensible Marxist grounding. It is one thing to argue that workers sometimes succeed in forcing management to upgrade jobs and in forcing government to provide greater access to education. But the idea that the balance of class power should be so favourable to workers over such large aggregates and over such a long period is difficult to reconcile with any theory that characterises contemporary society as capitalist. If the data do show a long-term, aggregate upgrading trend, surely the more basic driving factor must be industry's needs for skilled labour.

To date, those who have seen an upgrading trend have usually distanced themselves from Marx. Moreover, many have simply ignored the large mass of relatively low-skilled workers that still anchors the bottom of the occupational skill distribution. They write about the long-term trends they claim to discern as if this mass were about to disappear overnight. Many recent champions of the 'knowledge society', for example, write as if we will all shortly be 'symbolic analysts' (Reich 1993) while, in reality, low-skilled, routine jobs continue to proliferate (Warhurst and Nickson 2001).

Thus on the one side there is a utopianism that ends up masking a scandal, and on the other a polemical denunciation that seems unable to acknowledge some basic facts. There is, however, a version of Marx – one that can be termed 'palaeo-Marxist' – that is easy to reconcile with *both* a broad pattern of upgrading *and* a multitude of counter-examples of deskilling. (I call this view 'palaeo' because it was common prior to First World War but was subsequently eclipsed by neo-Marxism.) This chapter attempts to explicate that palaeo point of view, arguing that capitalism progressively upgrades skills as part of the process Marx called the socialisation of the forces of production.

My thesis is that this paleo-Marxist view provides us a powerful conceptual tool for analysing skill and its evolution (see also Hirschhorn 1984; Engeström 1987, 1990; Kenney and Florida 1993). The form of argument used in this chapter is assertion rather than demonstration. I would beg readers' indulgence and ask them to try to see the skill problem through these palaeo lenses, in the hope that this effort will be rewarded by a richer understanding of skill.

Two Components of Skill

Skill, it is widely acknowledged, has two basic components: mastery of the complexity of the tasks required of workers in their jobs, and mastery of the relations that coordinate activity across these tasks. (Littler [1982] identifies a third component, the social construction of skill, which can be treated as a superstructural overlay over the two basic components.) There is broad agreement that task complexity can be measured (in principle) by the amount of required education and training. But the measurement of the relational component is more difficult. Many argue that the key aspect of work relations is the autonomy and discretion they afford. The premise of my argument is that autonomy/discretion is precisely the wrong yardstick. As others have pointed out, it is entirely backward-looking, reflecting nostalgic regret for the passing of the autonomous craftsman (or alternatively, reflecting the ideal of alienated, self-sufficient individualism that is the spontaneous ideology of market society). This yardstick allows a measurement of what has often been lost in the development of the capitalism; but there is also a need to understand what has replaced that lost autonomy.

Autonomy is merely the converse of interdependence, and to understand the changing nature of work relations and of skill more generally, we need to understand the changing forms of interdependence. Much work in LPT, starting with Braverman, has implicitly assumed that this interdependence can, under capitalist conditions, only be one of coercive dependence. If that were the case, then loss of autonomy might indeed be a useful yardstick. In reality, however, interdependence can take either coercive or collaborative forms, and therefore, a useful theory of skill must help to understand these forms and the relations between them.

I submit that Marx's theory of the socialisation of production provides a strong theoretical foundation for this task. But in order to make this argument, the palaeo reading of Marx needs first to be explained.

Reading Marx

Scholars working in the Marxist tradition all accept as their point the proposition that: 'the development of the contradictions of a given historical form of production is the only historical way in which it can be dissolved and then reconstructed on a new basis' (Marx 1977: 619). However, Neo- and palaeo-Marxists offer conflicting interpretations of 'developing contradictions'.

For neo-Marxists, class struggle is the motor of history and the development of the contradictions of capitalism consists of intensified worker struggles in reaction to exacerbated exploitation and misery. For palaeo-Marxists, by contrast, the basic contradiction is between the forces and the relations of production. (The forces of production are composed of instruments, raw materials, workers' productive faculties, and organising principles; the relations of production are the relations of control over the productive forces.) Under capitalism, the progressive socialisation of the forces of production comes into escalating conflict with the persistence of relations of production based on private property. In the palaeo view, the long-term path of development of the class struggle is determined by the evolution of the underlying contradiction between forces and relations of production. (This reading is based on Cohen's [1978] exposition of Marx's theory of history. This chapter takes Cohen's interpretation from the general societal plane into the production process.)

Socialisation plays a pivotal role in this palaeo reading of Marx's analysis of the dynamics of capitalist development. Socialisation is commonly construed as the process whereby people new to a culture internalise its norms: Marx's use is broader. Marx's (1973) discussion of the socialisation of the forces of production (as distinct from his arguments in favour of the socialisation of property relations) suggests that this psychological internalisation is just one form of a more general phenomenon: elements of the labour process are socialised insofar as they come to embody the capabilities and constraints developed in the larger society rather than only those that emerge from the isolated, private experience of local contexts. The 'objective' socialisation of the forces of production is thus visible in the complexification of the social division of labour – the specialisation of industries and regions, and their increasing global interdependence (see also Engels 1959; Sohn-Rethel 1978; van der Pijl 1998).

To these 'objective' dimensions of socialisation corresponds a subjective dimension. The civilising mission of capitalism is not only to stimulate enormously the quantitative development and qualitative interdependence of the objective components of the forces of production but also, and more fundamentally, to take a decisive step in the realisation of humankind's social nature – in our socialisation. As the objective features of these relations are transformed, so too are the subjective ones:

> The bourgeoisie, historically, has played a most revolutionary part. The bourgeoisie, wherever it has got the upper hand, has put an end to all feudal, patriarchal, idyllic relations ... In place of the old local and national seclusion and self-sufficiency, we have intercourse in every direction, universal interdependence ... And as in material, so in intellectual production. The intellectual creations of individual nations become common property. National one-sidedness and narrow-mindedness become more and more impossible ... The bourgeoisie ... has rescued a considerable part of the population from the idiocy of rural life ... [W]ith the development of industry, the proletariat not only increases in numbers; it becomes more concentrated in greater masses, its strength grows, and it feels that strength more ... The union is helped on by the improved means of

communication that are created by modern industry and that place the workers of different localities in contact with one another...The advance of industry, whose involuntary promoter is the bourgeoisie, replaces the isolation of labourers, due to competition, by their revolutionary combination, due to association...What the bourgeoisie, therefore, produces, above all, is its gravediggers. (Marx and Engels 1959: 9–20)

The development of the forces of production pulls workers out of what Marx and Engels call 'rural idiocy'. In the *Poverty of Philosophy*, Marx (1884) similarly celebrates the end of 'craft idiocy'. Here the term idiocy preserves both its colloquial sense and the meaning from the Greek *idiotes*, denoting an asocial individual isolated from the polis.

Under capitalism, this socialisation tendency is simultaneously stimulated, retarded and distorted by the prevailing relations of production. Competitive pressures force firms to breakdown parochialisms and to stimulate techno-logical progress; but the 'universal interdependence' thus created appears, in the first instance, only behind the twin veils of commodity fetishism and bureaucratic employment relations. Instead of a broadening association of producers progressively mastering their collective future, capitalism imposes the coersion of 'laws' of the market and of corporate bureaucracy. Whence capitalism's inability to manage public goods and externalities – issues whose importance grows with the increasing complexity of technology and knowledge-intensity of the economy. As a result, the path of socialisation, both objective and subjective, is halting and uneven. It should be noted too that even progressive change has social costs: far too many workers bear the burdens of structural unemployment; old union craftsmen are pitted against young non-union technicians; contracting out and globalisation undermine old solidarities.

However, in the overall dynamics of capitalism, these various 'counter-tendencies' must and do cede to the overall progress of socialisation. In modern industry, competitive advantage often flows from skill upgrading and greater collaborative interdependence within and between firms, and the pursuit of those sources of competitive advantage makes capitalists the 'involuntary promoters' of socialisation.

In analysing the evolution of skill and work organisation, LPT has too often truncated this dialectic. Marx writes:

It capitalist direction [of work] is thus twofold in content, owing to the twofold nature of the process of production which has to be directed – on the one hand a social labour process for the creation of a product, and on the other hand capital's process of valorisation – in form it is purely despotic. (Marx 1977: 450)

Neo-Marxist LPT interprets this passage to mean that the historical develop-ment of capitalist work organisation reflects above all the balance of class forces – despotism versus resistance. Palaeo-Marxists, by contrast, recall that in Marx's Hegelian discourse, content and form can be in contradiction with each other (the paradigmatic case for Marx being that of the contradiction between use value and exchange value of the commodity). The palaeo reading of this passage thus highlights the growing contradiction between an increasingly socialised labour process (the content) and the barriers posed to further socialisation by the persistence of valourisation constraints (the form). Three short cases help illustrate this point.

Case 1: Taylorism and scientific management

Taylorism and the broader scientific management movement to which it was central are depicted in much LPT as an offensive in the class struggle. The palaeo view acknowledges this reality, but identifies a second aspect as more fundamental: Taylorism was also a progressive step in the socialisation of the forces of production, both objective and subjective (Sohn-Rethel 1978). Indices of socialisation include the following:

- Under scientific management, planning replaces anarchy in enterprises of growing scale: the planning department helps assure an efficient flow of materials through more tightly interdependent operations.
- The determination of work methods and standards is no longer only a function of isolated, local struggles between workers and their bosses – it is informed by a body of socialised knowledge, Taylor's 'science' of work. In reality, this science took the form of a largely inductive and empirical 'engineering', often subject to management bias; but even in this form, the 'mysteries' of work are dissolved and knowledge of the labour process is socialised. Workers can and often do refer to this knowledge to buttress their claims in negotiations with management.
- The 'collective worker' is broadened by the development of a more differentiated and integrated division of labour. A specialised planning staff is formed, as are numerous types of 'functional foreman'. The functional foremen roles advocated by Taylor were subsequently transformed into distinct support and staff functions, expanding technical occupations that are also part of the working-class broadly construed.
- The object of work expands in a socialised direction, so that individual workers' tasks expand from assuring production at their own workstations to include more deliberate coordination with others and more planned performance-improvement efforts. When mobilised in these tasks, workers find their horizons broadened.

Neo-Marxist LPT theory is correct to insist that this all happens under capitalist authority. The resulting socialisation is therefore one-sided and distorted. But it is no less real. On the one hand, Taylorism had profoundly revolutionary effects on the management of large-scale production, with important positive effects for workers: higher productivity facilitating higher wages, fewer accidents, more promotion opportunities into technical occupations, a drastic reduction in the exercise of arbitrary personal authority in the 'foreman's empire', the experience of disciplined collective work on a large scale, and the opportunity to broaden trade union structures from narrow crafts to whole industries. On the other hand, capitalist use and abuse of Taylorism sometimes undermined or distorted these gains by turning Taylorism against workers with a loss of autonomy to remote planning departments, some job losses, the creation of some very repetitive, short-cycle jobs and a disruption of traditional craft bases of working class resistance. Taylorism may well have been negative for craft workers; but just as plausibly it consti-tuted a net improvement for the far greater mass of less-skilled labourers and operatives. The overall effects on workers were mixed; but on balance social-isation advanced.

The palaeo view can call several witnesses for this more dialectical reading of Taylorism. In the US, the Amalgamated Clothing Workers under Sidney Hillman encouraged the adoption of scientific management techniques, even conducting seminars for workshop owners, in order to rationalise production and pay (Fraser 1991). Progressive Taylorites such as Morris L. Cooke broadened the scope of scientific management to city and national economic planning (see Nyland 1998; Schachter 1989). In Sweden, trade unions in the metal trades and the textile industries gained considerable influence over wages and conditions as a result of the (management-driven) introduction of time-and-motion studies (De Geer 1982).

Case 2: Lean production

Lean production takes Taylorism to new heights. Its effects are still under debate: many critics argue that it represents an intensification of work and of managerial control (Babson 1995). But one aspect of lean production that has not received enough attention is its contributions to the socialisation of production.

This argument can be illustrated with excerpts from interviews that I conducted with workers at NUMMI. NUMMI is a unionised auto assembly plant in Northern California, jointly owned by GM and Toyota, but operating under Toyota's day-to-day control. The plant inherited its facility and almost its entire workforce (but none of its managers) from the old GM–Fremont organisation in 1983. It quickly reached 'world-class' levels of productivity and quality, relying on a rigorous implementation of the Toyota Production System, in particular, its 'standardised work' policy (Adler 1993). Standardised work is a process for determining the 'one best way' to perform a job, but whereas under traditional Taylorism this determination was made by a spe-cialist, here workers themselves hold the stopwatch and analyse alternative methods. Reflecting the added complexity of workers' tasks, new hires at NUMMI receive more than 250 hours of training during their first six months on the job, while a typical new hire in the Big Three receives 42 hours.

Interviews revealed a number of dimensions in which socialisation seemed to be at work at NUMMI. Quoting several union production workers comparing NUMMI and GM–Fremont:

- *Collective rationality tends to supercede power relations*: 'The GM system relied on authority. People with rank – the managers – ruled regardless of their competence or the validity of what they were saying. It was basically a military hierarchy. At NUMMI, rank doesn't mean a damn thing – standard-ised work means that we all work out the objectively best way to do the job, and everyone does it that way. I might make some minor adjustments because of my height, for example, but I follow the procedure we've laid out because it makes sense.'

- *Task knowledge is socialised*: 'The great thing about standardised work is that if everyone is doing the job the same way, and we run into a problem, say a quality problem, we can easily identify where its coming from and fix it. If everyone is doing the job however they feel like, you can't even begin any serious problem-solving.'

- *The collective worker is broadened to the plant*: 'The work teams at NUMMI aren't like the autonomous teams you read about in other plants. Here, we're not autonomous because we're all tied together really tightly. But it's not like we're just getting squeezed to work harder, because it's us, the workers, that are making the whole thing work – we're the ones that make the standardised work and the kaizen suggestions. We run the plant – and if it's not running right, we stop it.'

- *The collective worker is broadened to include supplier firms*: 'In 23 years working for GM, I never met with a supplier. I never even knew their names except for the names on the boxes. Now, we're working with suppliers to improve our products. Workers sit down with our engineers and managers and the suppliers' people and we analyse defects and develop improve-ment proposals. We even do that with equipment vendors. Stuff like that really gives us a better perspective on how our jobs relate to the whole process. We're not just drilling holes and slamming nuts onto bolts anymore. Now we have a say in how the product should be made.'

- *Collaborative interdependence becomes a norm beyond work*: 'I wish you could talk to the guys' wives about the changes they've seen. I was a typical macho horse's ass when I worked at Fremont. When I got home, I'd get a beer, put my feet up and wait for dinner to be served. I'd figure, "I've done my eight, so just leave me alone." Now, I'm part of a team at work, and I take that attitude home with me, rather than dump my work frustrations all over my family. I'm much more of a partner around the house. I help wash the dishes and do the shopping and stuff. My job here is to care, and I spend eight hours a day doing that job, so it's kind of natural that I take it home with me.'

Counter-posed to these features of work organisation at NUMMI was an array of forces reflecting valorisation pressures that limited socialisation. Under profitability performance pressure, management has sometimes sacrificed worker health and safety for profits. Management has never whole-heartedly accepted the union as a legitimate expression of workers' voice (Adler *et al.* 1997, 1998). Competitive relations within the organisation and between it and other parts of its institutional field have often undermined collaboration. However, analysis of work organisation must register too the profoundly positive effects for workers that flow from the socialisation wrought by lean production at NUMMI.

Case 3: Software development

As software has grown more complex over the past few decades, the software development process has slid into chaos. One 1994 survey of 8330 projects in 365 firms in banking, manufacturing, retail, wholesale, health-care, insurance, and government (Standish Group 1994) found that:

- only 16 per cent of projects were on time, within budget and met originally specified requirements – only nine per cent in large companies;
- 31 per cent of projects were 'impaired' and eventually cancelled;
- 53 per cent of projects were 'challenged' and the average challenged project met only 61 per cent of its requirements; and
- the average impaired or challenged project was 189 per cent over budget and 222 per cent over schedule.

It is therefore not surprising that over this same period, the software field has been the object of numerous 'rationalisation' efforts. Examples include structured programming, project planning models, information engineering, and object-oriented programming. Currently, one of the most influential efforts is based on the 'Capability Maturity Model' (CMM) (see Software Engineering Institute 2002).

The CMM owes its birth to the US Department of Defense's increasing frustration with the chaos in software development. The Department of Defense (DoD) funded the Software Engineering Institute (SEI), based at Carnegie-Mellon University, to develop a model of a more reliable development process. With the assistance of the MITRE Corporation and input from nearly 1000 industry people, SEI released the CMM in 1991. The model distinguishes five successively more 'mature' levels of process capability, each characterised by mastery of a number of Key Process Areas (KPAs). Level 1 represents an entirely ad hoc approach. Level 2 represents the rationalisation of the management of individual projects. Level 3 characterises the systematic management of its portfolio of projects. Level 4 addresses the quantification of the development process. Level 5 addresses the continuous improvement of that process. The underlying philosophy of this hierarchy was inspired by Crosby's (1979) TQM approach to quality in manufacturing (Humphrey 2002).

The CMM has become the basis for numerous software service organisations' improvement efforts in both the government and commercial sectors. Its diffusion has been driven in considerable measure by its use in sourcing decisions by the DoD and other government and commercial-sector organisations. The first sourcing evaluations pressed suppliers to reach Level 2, but by the late 1990s the bar had been raised to Level 3.

Accumulating evidence suggests that moving up the CMM hierarchy leads to improvements in product cost, quality and timeliness (Herbsleb *et al.* 1997; Clark 1999; Harter *et al.* 2000; Krishnan *et al.* 2000). But many sceptics remain unconvinced. These gains may be specific to the sampled organisations. They may be earned at the expense of developer morale and commitment, and given the importance of developers' attitudes to performance, any performance gains may therefore be ephemeral. Typical of opposition to standardised and formalised methodologies is this assessment by two well-respected software management experts:

> Of course, if your people aren't smart enough to think their way through their work, the work will fail. No methodology will help. Worse still, methodologies can do grievous damage to efforts in which people are fully competent. They do this by trying to force the work into a fixed mold that guarantees a morass of paperwork, a paucity of methods, an absence of responsibility, and a general loss of motivation. (DeMarco and Lister 1987: 116)

One software development manager, interviewed in my research, expressed the concern this way: 'Programming has always been seen as more of an art form than a factory process. Programmers are supposed to be creative, free spirits, able to figure things out themselves. So the software factory idea was very alien to the culture of programmers.'

Most LPT research on these kinds of efforts to rationalise software development has reflected a similarly deep scepticism (Kraft 1977; Greenbaum 1979; Friedman and Cornford 1989). Kraft (1977: 61) summarises the analysis this way: 'canned programs, structured programming, and modularization are designed to make the supervision of software workers by managers easier and more like the supervision of other workers... Such managerial techniques have made possible the use of relatively less skilled programmer, for what were formerly the most complex software tasks.' More recent LPT research has nuanced this analysis, more consistent with a contingency version of LPT (Beirne *et al*. 1998; Greenbaum 1998).

To explore the impact of rationalised systems such as the CMM on developers, I studied a large software consulting firm, conducting interviews with developers and managers in four units (see Adler 2003). These units all developed and maintained relatively large-scale systems for government clients. Two were at CMM Level 5, and two sister units were at Level 3. Interviews revealed several indices of socialisation:

- *Expanding the object of work*: 'At Level 5, you understand what other people are doing and why. Everyone can discuss and are involved in improvement efforts, not only technical but also process, organisational problems – versus at Level 1, where the only improvements people that can talk about are local and technical. And at Level 5, measurement is a part of life. At worst, people tolerate it. The majority see it as an integral part of their work – versus at Level 1, where measurement is not part of the culture, where it's not seen as having value, and where it's seen as waste, bureaucratic overhead, and people feel "Just leave me alone".'

- *Broadening the collective worker*: 'Before, I used to just go do the job. Here it's more of a team effort. There are more people working on development, so we need to coordinate with each other more closely. And we need to coordinate more closely with other groups, like QA.'

- *Deepening collaborative interdependence*: 'In a small organisation doing small projects, you have a lot of flexibility, but there's not much sharing. You're kind of on your own. Here, I'm just a small part of a bigger project team. So you don't do anything on your own. It's a collaborative effort.'

- *Socialising the tools used in work*: 'Developers want above all to deliver a great product, and the process helps us do that. What I've learned coming here is the value of a well thought-out process, rigorously implemented, and continuously improved. It will really improve the quality of the product. In this business, you've got to be exact, and the process ensures that we are. You have to get out of hacker mode!'

- *Socialising the development of rules and tools*: 'People have to be a part of defining the process. We always say that "People support what they help create." That's why the Tailoring Cycle [for defining the procedures to be used in the management of each specific project] is so important. As a project manager, you're too far away from the technical work to define the [procedures] yourself, so you have to involve the experts. You don't need everyone involved, but you do need your key people. It's only by involving them that you can be confident you have good [procedures] that have credibility in the eyes of their peers.'

- *Socialising skill formation processes*: 'We had an informal training and entoring program, and when we got serious about the CMM, we wrote it down. Writing the process down has had some great benefits. It's made us think about how we work, and that's led to improvements. For example, formalising the training program has helped bring some outliers into conformance.'

There were also counter-tendencies. The socialisation of the software development process under CMM was simultaneously stimulated, retarded and distorted by the valourisation process. On the one hand, valourisation pressures were expressed in the pressure from large customers for product quality, cost, and timeliness and in customer pressure too to adopt the CMM as a gauge of the organisation's commitment to those goals. On the other hand, valourisation pressures also had negative effects, creating:

- *Narrow, short-term profit goals that impeded investment in automation, simplification and support that would have had beneficial long-term effects*:

  One key challenge [in maintaining the use of CMM as a tool for process improvement] is maintaining buy-in at the top. Our top corporate management is under constant pressure from the stock market. The market is constantly looking at margins [...] That doesn't leave much room for expenditures associated with process improvement – especially when these take two or three years to show any pay-off.

- *Centrifugal effects of distinct performance pressures on customers and suppliers*: While process maturity encouraged more collaborative relations with clients for requirements definition and progress review, performance pressures often pulled the parties apart and limited this collaboration.

- *Tension between corporate interests and the collective interests of its employees*: While rules defining the development process often appeared to workers as enabling rather than coercive, some managers used these formal procedures as weapon against employees.

- *Tension between the collective nature of work and the individualising effects of the wage relation*: As vulnerable employees dependent on wage income, and reflecting their prior socialisation, developers sometimes resisted the new forms of interdependence associated with CMM Levels. While many developers appeared to embrace the interdependence demanded by high CMM levels, some were concerned that CMM-style rationalisation made the development process less 'people-dependent' and that their job security might suffer.

In aggregate, the effects of valourisation were weaker than those of socialisation, but the former were strong enough to make progress halting and uneven. In the words of one interviewee:

We still have to deal with the 'free spirits' who don't believe in process. These are typically people who have worked mainly in small teams. It's true that a small group working by itself doesn't need all this process. But we rarely work in truly independent small teams: almost all our work has to be integrated into larger systems, and will have to be maintained by people who didn't write the code themselves. These free spirits, though, are probably only between two per cent and four per cent of our staff. We find some of them in our advanced technology groups. We have some in the core of our business too, because they are real gurus in some complex technical area and we can't afford to lose them. And there are some among the new kids coming in too: many of them need convincing on this score. Most of them adapt, although some don't and they leave.

Socialisation and Skill

These sketches of the socialisation of the labour process under Taylorism, lean production and the CMM suggest a need to broaden the conceptual horizon in understanding skill. Skill matters not only in relation to its *level* but also in its *form*. Relative to complexity, training requirements often increased but also, and perhaps more fundamentally, this training has changed in form from apprenticeship to formal technical and scientific education. Similarly, work relations have changed not only requiring more interactive, social skills, but also broadening their scope. Braverman was correct to highlight the fundamental difference between the autonomous collaboration of peers in a craft workshop and the formalised coordination work in modern bureaucracies. But Marx's notion of socialisation signals the enormous *positive* significance of this shift in the form of training, knowledge, and coordination – a shift towards forms that embody 'universal inter-dependence' rather than rural and craft 'idiocy'.

Whereas neo-Marxist LPT focuses exclusively on the noxious effects of capitalist relations of production, the palaeo view advanced here sees skill as being at the intersection of the forces and the relations of production, and influenced by both. Using this palaeo framing, the broader research findings on the long-term, aggregate evolution can be synthesised under two headings:

1. *The impact of the progressive development of the forces of production*: The impact on task complexity is seen in tendencies to upgrading discussed in the opening pages of this chapter. The impact on work relations is seen in a progressive differentiation of roles and increasing collaborative inter-dependence at various levels: between workers (teamwork), work teams (process management), hierarchical levels (employee involvement), special-ised functions (cross-functional teams), and firms (supplier partnerships). Whence the growing importance of interactive, social and emotional skills

discussed in other chapters of this volume. It is true that the autonomy and nobility of traditional crafts are trampled underfoot in this process, but the larger mass of workers often find the complexity of their tasks increased and their work relations broadened. Increasing proportions of men and women are drawn into mixed-gender, interdependent work relations. Workers are also drawn from local isolation into the web of globalisation, which also tends to increase complexity and broaden relations in developing countries (Warren 1980).

2. *The impact of the maintenance of capitalist relations of production*: The impact of the relations of production too can be seen in both the task complexity and work relations dimensions of skill. Competitive pressures force firms sometimes to sacrifice long-term for short-term gains, and always to privilege firm over social benefits. Tentative moves towards inter-firm collaboration are constantly undermined by competitive rivalry. The wage relation privileges owners' interests over those of workers'. As owners' agents, managers sometimes find it profitable, if only in the short term, to deskill work, manipulate teamwork to create peer pressure, let horizontal specialisation degenerate into adversarial rivalry, and use hierarchy for 'command and control'. These effects should not be ignored as mere 'noise' in the data: they reflect the deep structure of property relations under capitalism. It is therefore appropriate that critical scholars should highlight and denounce them as reflecting an important, imminent tendency of capitalism.

What can be said about the relationship between these two sets of forces in the overall evolution of skill and capitalism? The neo-Marxist interpretation that has been dominant in LPT gives little causal efficacy to the forces of production and argues that capitalist development, shaped primary by the class struggle inherent in capitalist relations of production, leads tendentially to increasing misery, including the deskilling and degradation of work. On the palaeo view, the development of capitalism is profoundly shaped by the progressive socialisation of the forces of production. Over the long run, the overall effect is to create a working class that is increasingly educated, sophisticated, accustomed to the discipline of large-scale collective endeavour – and thus increasingly capable of successfully taking on the task of radically transforming society. (This thesis, please note, concerns *capability*: whether workers are *motivated* to undertake this historic, revolutionary mission depends on distinct, sociopolitical, superstructural factors.)

Marx's writings themselves are ambiguous on the relationship of the two sets of forces. Elsewhere (Adler 1990), I have argued that this ambiguity arises because these writings, even *Capital*, mixed the analysis of longer-term and shorter-term trends, and combined objective analysis with polemical advocacy. Since around the time of the First World War, the more radical parts of the left have argued that the palaeo view concedes too much continuing legitimacy to capitalism. The objection would appear to be that if capitalism continued to foster the development of the forces of production and the working-class's capabilities, it would be difficult to justify radical hostility to it. But in the palaeo view, there are plenty of fundamental, and increasingly compelling, reasons for our hostility. Even if the aggregate, long-term trend is towards skill upgrading, the unevenness of this process is a scandal that is increasingly resented. More generally, the left's hostility is motivated by capitalism's 'savage inequalities' (in Kozol's [1991] phrase), its persistent un- and under-employment, its recurrent economic crises and wars, and its ecological irresponsibility. The palaeo view allows the Left to advance this critique while acknowledging the progressive aspects of capitalist development. The neo view makes the critique sound like shrill polemic.

A good theory of skill is needed. A palaeo-Marxist version of labour process theory is a promising starting point. It allows us to characterise both the fundamental limitations of capitalism and how these limitations conflict with the long-term upgrading trend of skills. In the short term, prospects for radical change due to this escalating conflict may seem dim but the socialisation thesis puts history on the side of radical social change.

References

Abramowitz, M. and David, P. A. (1996) 'Technological Change and the Rise of Intangible Investments: The US Economy's Growth Part in the Twentieth Century', in OECD (ed.), *Employment and Growth in the Knowledge-Based Economy*, Paris: OECD.

Adler, P. S. (1990) 'Marx, Machines and Skill', *Technology and Culture*, 31:4, 780–812.

Adler, P. S. (1993) 'The Learning Bureaucracy: New United Motors Manufacturing, Inc.', in B. M. Staw and L. L. Cummings (eds), *Research in Organizational Behavior*, vol. 15, Greenwich, CT: JAI Press.

Adler, P. S. (2003) 'Practice and Process: The Socialisation of Software Development', unpublished manuscript, University of Southern California.

Adler, P. S., Goldoftas, B. and Levine, D. (1997) 'Ergonomics, Employee Involvement, and the Toyota Production System: A Case Study of NUMMI's 1993 Model Introduction', *Industrial and Labor Relations Review*, 50:3, 416–437.

Adler, P. S., Goldoftas, B. and Levine, D. (1998) 'Stability and Change at NUMMI', in R. Boyer, E. Charron, U. Jürgens and S. Tolliday (eds), *Between Imitation and Innovation: The Transfer and Hybridisation of Productive Models in the International Automobile Industry*, New York: Oxford University Press.

Babson, S. (ed.) (1995) *Lean Work: Empowerment and Exploitation in the Global Auto Industry*, Detroit: Wayne State University Press.

Beirne, M., Ramsay, H. and Panteli, A. (1998) 'Developments in Computing Work: Control and Contradiction in the Software Labour Process', in P. Thompson and C. Warhurst (eds), *Workplaces of the Future*, Houndmills: Macmillan.

Bell, D. (1973) *The Coming of Post-Industrial Society*, New York: Basic Books.

Braverman, H. (1974) *Labor and Monopoly Capital*, New York: Monthly Review Press.

Clark, B. (1999) 'Effects of Process Maturity on Development Effort', unpublished paper, http://sunset.usc.edu/~bkclark/Research.

Cohen, G. A. (1978) *Karl Marx's Theory of History: A Defense*, Princeton: Princeton University Press.

Crosby, P. B. (1979) *Quality is Free*, New York: McGraw-Hill.

De Geer, H. (1982) *Job Studies and Industrial Relations: Ideas about efficiency and relations between the parties of the labour market in Sweden, 1920–1950*, Stockholm: Almqvist & Wiksell International.

DeMarco, T. and Lister, T. (1987) *Peopleware: Productive Projects and Teams*, New York: Dorset.

Engels, F. (1959) 'Socialism: Utopian and Scientific', in L. S. Feuer (ed.), *Basic Writings on Politics and Philosophy, Karl Marx and Friedrich Engels*, Garden City, NY: Anchor Books.

Engeström, Y. (1987) *Learning by Expanding: An Activity-theoretical Approach to Developmental Research*, Helsinki: Orienta-Konsultit.

Engeström, Y. (1990) *Learning, Working and Imagining: Twelve Studies in Activity Theory*, Helsinki: Orienta-Konsultit.

Fraser, S. (1991) *Labor Will Rule: Sidney Hillman and the Rise of American Labor*, New York: Free Press.

Friedman, A. L., and Cornford, D. S. (1989) *Computer Systems Development: History, Organisation and Implementation*, Chichester: John Wiley & Sons.

Goldin, C. and Katz, L. F. (1999) 'The returns to skill in the United States across the Twentieth century', *National Bureau of Economic Research Working Paper 7126*, Cambridge, Mass.

Greenbaum, J. M. (1979) *In the Name of Efficiency*, Philadelphia: Temple University Press.

Greenbaum, J. M. (1998) 'The times they are a'changing: Dividing and recombining labour through computer systems', in P. Thompson and C. Warhurst (eds), *Workplaces of the Future*, Houndmills: Macmillan.

Grugulis, I., Willmott, H. and Knights, D. (2001) *International Studies of Management and Organization*, Special issue on the Labour Process Debate, 30:4.

Harter, D. E., Krishnan, M. S. and Slaughter, S. A. (2000) 'Effects of process maturity on quality, cycle time, and effort in software development', *Management Science*, 46:4, 451–466.

Herbsleb, J., Zubrow, D., Goldenson, D., Hayes, W. and Paulk, M. (1997) 'Software quality and the Capability Maturity Model', *Communication of the ACM*, 40:6, 30–40.

Hirschhorn, L. (1984) *Beyond Mechanisation*, Cambridge, MA: MIT Press.

Humphrey, W. S. (2002) 'Three Process Perspectives: Organizations, Teams, and People', *Annals of Software Engineering*, 14, 39–72.

Kenney, M. and Florida, R. (1993) *Beyond Mass Production: The Japanese System and its Transfer to the U.S.*, New York: Oxford University Press.

Kern, M. and Schumann, M. (1984) *Das Ende der Arbeitesteilung?*, Munich: C.H. Beck.

Kozol, J. (1991) *Savage Inequalities: Children in America's Schools*, New York: Crown.

Kraft, P. (1977) *Programmers and Managers: The Routinisation of Computer Programming in the United States*, New York: Springer-Verlag.

Krishnan, M. S., Kriebel, C. H., Kekre, S. and Mukhopadhyay, T. (2000) 'Productivity and Quality in Software Products', *Management Science*, 46:6, 745–759.

Littler, C. (1982) *The Development of the Labour Process in Capitalist Societies*, London: Heinemann.

Marx, K. (1884) *The Poverty of Philosophy*, Chicago: Charles Kerr & Company.

Marx, K. (1973) *Grundrisse*, Harmondsworth: Penguin Books.

Marx, K. (1977) *Capital*, Vol.1, New York: Vintage.

Marx, K. and Engels, F. (1959) 'The Communist Manifesto', in L. S. Feuer (ed.), *Marx and Engels: Basic Writings on Politics and Philosophy*, New York: Anchor.

Mathews, J. A. (1994) *Catching the Wave: Workplace Reform in Australia*, Ithaca, NY: ILR Press.

Nyland, C. (1998) 'Taylorism and the Mutual Gains Strategy', *Industrial Relation*, 37:4, 519–542.

Piore, M. J. and Sabel, C. J. (1984) *The Second Industrial Divide*, New York: Basic Books.

Reich, R. (1993) *The Work of Nations*, London: Simon & Shuster.

Schachter, H. L. (1989) *Frederick Taylor and the Public Administration Community*, Albany NY: State University of New York Press.

Smith, C. and Thompson, P. (1999) 'Reevaluating the Labor Process Debate', in M. Wardell, T. L. Steiger, P. Meiskins (eds), *Rethinking the Labor Process*, Albany: State University of New York Press.

Software Engineering Institute (2002) 'Process Maturity Profile of the Software Community, 2002 Mid-year Update', http://www.sei.cmu.edu.

Sohn-Rethel, A. (1978) *Intellectual and Manual Labor*, Atlantic Highlands, NJ: Humanities Press.

Spenner, K. I. (1988) 'Technological change, skill requirements, and Education: The case for uncertainty', in R. M. Cyert and D. C. Mowery (eds), *The Impact of Technological Change on Employment and Economic Growth*, Cambridge MA: Ballinger.

Standish Group (1994) 'Chaos study report', www.standishgroup.com.

Thompson, P. (1989) *The Nature of Work*, London: Macmillan.

Turner, H. A. (1962) *Trade Union Growth, Structure and Policy*, London: George Allen and Unwin.

US Bureau of the Census (1975) *Historical Statistics of the United States*, Washington, DC: US Government Printing Office.

US Bureau of the Census (2000) *Statistical Abstract of the United States*, Texas: Hoover's Business Press.

van der Pijl, K. (1998) *Transnational Classes and International Relations*, London: Routledge.

Wardell, M., Steiger, T. L. and Meiskins, P. (eds) (1999) *Rethinking the Labor Process*, Albany: State University of New York Press.

Warhurst, C. and Nickson, D. (2001) *Looking Good, Sounding Right*, London: Industrial Society.

Warren, B. (1980) *Imperialism: Pioneer of Capitalism*, London: Verso.

Author Index

Subject Index